THE POPE'S DIVISIONS

THE POPE'S DIVISIONS

The Roman Catholic Church
Today

PETER NICHOLS

HOLT, RINEHART AND WINSTON
New York

Library of Congress Cataloging in Publication Data
Nichols, Peter, 1928–
The Pope's divisions.
Includes index.
1. Catholic Church—History—20th century. 2. Catho-
lic Church—Doctrinal and controversial works. I. Title.
BX1389.N525   1981   282'.09'04   81-4501
ISBN 0-03-047576-7   AACR2

First American Edition
Printed in the United States of America

1 3 5 7 9 10 8 6 4 2

This book is dedicated to the memory
of my mother who did not quite
manage to see it finished

Give us gods. Oh give them us!
Give us gods.
We are so tired of men
and motor-power.

D. H. Lawrence

We're all ready to go. If you
tell us we have to give our lives
now, we're ready
(Crowd shouts approval)

Unidentified Jonestown suicide

We must not forget that the human soul
however independently created
our philosophy represents it as being
is inseparable
in its birth and in its growth
from the universe into which it is born.

Teilhard de Chardin

ACKNOWLEDGEMENTS

I do not intend expressing gratitude to all those inside and outside the Vatican who have helped me to write this book. Some of them would not thank me for it, and if I were to mention individuals I would not want to leave anyone out. The original idea was mine. It might have stayed just an idea had it not been for the encouragement both warm and practical of my editor William Rees-Mogg. And this was followed at Times Newspapers by another real sign of confidence from Sir Denis Hamilton, the editor-in-chief.

I have purposely avoided a bibliography because the aim of the book is the ambitious one of trying to deal as a single individual with a vast subject which fascinates. There has of course been some reading, but it is supposed not to show. Periodicals have helped keep me up to date, particularly *Concilium*, the invaluable *Tablet*, *Civiltà Cattolica*, *Il Regno* and that unfailingly relevant publication *America* of the Jesuits in New York. I mention these rather than others because they have a life around them beyond the printed pages.

I would frequently have been lost, like any foreign correspondent, if it had not been for innumerable kindnesses from colleagues in every part of the world I visited as well as in Rome.

My wife showed endless tolerance in two ways: as a wife and as a Catholic.

The extract from the libretto of *Billy Budd* by E. M. Forster and Eric Crozier is reprinted by permission of Boosey & Hawkes Music Publishers Ltd, London, and Boosey & Hawkes, Inc., New York.

The extract from the libretto of *Bluebeard's Castle* is reprinted by permission of Universal Edition Ltd, London, and Boosey & Hawkes, Inc., New York.

Murder in the Cathedral by T. S. Eliot is published by Faber and Faber.

Thanks are due to the BBC for allowing quotation from a radio programme written and narrated by the author.

CONTENTS

INTRODUCTION

Like its subject, this book is presumptuous. More than its subject, in a way, because I am presuming to look at an institution that claims to possess the full truth about man's relationship with the divine, and, at the same time, I am allowing myself the luxury of commenting on it. I ought to be daunted but, except for inevitable moments of doubt, I found the subject less awesome than I might have expected. When the inevitable moments of doubt came, they were usually made much easier to bear by some unexpected coincidence. For instance, I was worried about a first draft and despondently thinking that the subject could be of little interest to anyone, when an ex-Jesuit friend suddenly asked me, in a rather intense way over lunch, what I, as an outsider, thought about the whole phenomenon of Catholicism. I forget now what I said but I know that I felt a strange pull of gratitude for the fact that, quite unintentionally, he had said what I wanted to hear most of all at that moment; he had expressed genuine curiosity about this pretentious thing that I was doing.

From the beginning, my own curiosity had been profound because until almost the last words of this book had been written I did not know what my own feelings would be. But I knew they would certainly not include the scorn expressed in Stalin's famous question: 'How many divisions has the pope?' To write a book about something one does not care about is, for me, a waste of time. Life is not long enough to dedicate it to the half-convincing. I am not now talking of questions of belief. What I find convincing is the fascination of the subject, not necessarily the teachings of Catholicism, which are a quite different consideration. Even that, though, can be overwhelming at times. Once, when it was getting so, I happened to be talking with a highly placed, highly intelligent prelate at the Vatican. He suddenly said in a very relaxed way, which had nothing to do with what we were just talking about: 'Whatever you do, don't forget to laugh at us; make some fun of Mother Church!' I probably should have followed that advice much more than I have.

I am not a Catholic, clearly, and that is one of the several negative reasons why I could write this book. I do not belong to the organization I am writing about. I am not among the divisions. I am in no institutional sense a religious person. I am not a priest-journalist with open-necked grey shirt and tense smile, or a member of a religious order looking for a more emancipated form of service, or a lapsed Catholic, or even a former priest, or a devout churchgoer who writes an occasional column of a devotional kind. In this sense, I do not belong to the large part of that numerous tribe which seems fatally attracted to write about the Vatican and so becomes the principal but frequently distorted diaphragm between the Vatican and the world at large. Like no other body I know, the Vatican collects around its offices writers who can see it only in a special light—of childhood memories, adolescent pain, resentment, even tranquillity of mind—and as a consequence of their own convictions, or needs, or grudges, or mistakes, or disappointments. All the observers who regularly follow the Vatican's affairs are not, of course, in this category and there are some who are highly professional indeed. But this strongly subjective element is one reason why the Vatican gives the impression of not expecting people to look at it straight in the eyes, and not knowing how to react if they do. So many of those with whom it deals directly do not do so; 'Mine eyes dazzle!' they seem to be saying.

I was baptized an Anglican at the age of fourteen, rather to the bewilderment of my school friends. A cynic would say that a decision that cost me a lot in emotional exposure provided a full vaccination against any need for a strong religious belief in the future. Such strong feelings that I have now about institutionalized religion come mainly from the fascination of watching the interplay between the structure, the formalities, the ceremonies and the human element that may sometimes be hidden, sometimes burst out temporarily, to triumph over the rest.

I can well believe that convinced Catholics see the pope as Peter's successor; that the huge Masses celebrated by the pontiff in

16

a football stadium, or for that matter in St Peter's itself, are regarded as solemn re-enactments of the last supper that Jesus ate before his crucifixion. I understand why Catholics think as they do on these matters and on many others. I have spent the greater part of my life in the company of Catholics. My wife is a Catholic. I can now, without difficulty, see the Catholic faith not only as massive in its weight, but as something perfectly natural. I certainly do not see it any more as an Anglican. I have long grown out of the view, implicit in my early education, that the real triumph of Britain's modern history was to defeat a series of Catholic conspiracies.

I have lived in Rome throughout the whole period of what can be called the modern papacy: from the final hermit years of Pius XII, through the brief cyclone of the reign of John XXIII, the painful complexities of Paul VI, to the pair of clumsily named John Pauls. I have been lucky. Whatever one may think of popes, these were all men of stature. Living in Rome does not mean looking just at popes. Much of the world still passes through the old sacred city. The ecclesiastical world does so, of course, and much more in recent years as the Vatican has become increasingly important to the rest of the Christian world and of steadily growing interest to the whole world. But ecclesiastics are not the only type of person who make Rome, and Italy as a whole, an excellent viewing point for following what is happening in the modern world. Italy's part in creating Western civilization was unrivalled; it has a litmus quality indicating the good and the bad to come. Italy is as lucid as ever about the extent and the nature of the crisis enveloping Western civilization. More than any other Western country, it is living that crisis, in the sense that while the problems are much the same elsewhere, they are, for a variety of reasons, more acute and more dramatic in Italy. And since it also has the papacy grafted on to its own capital, the country is in a unique position to measure the relevance of religion, as an institution, to the problems of modern society.

When I went to the Escorial, the palace of Philip II, who sent the Armada against England, I felt a sense of past power but of simplicity as well. Journeys to Latin America and to the Philippines gave me a curious respect for this huge Iberian power, which had not managed to invade England—a matter I realize now of almost marginal importance—but which had implanted on huge regions, sometimes with force and cruelty and the full power of the state, a religion which remains, despite the fact that the colonial powers are no longer there. Spain and Portugal are relatively tiny now, in terms of influence: latecomers even to the European Community. What they have left behind is something incomparably greater for mankind's future than their present political weight. The old Spanish and Portuguese territories across the Atlantic and in Asia are the vanguard of a new Catholicism. Soon Latin America will have half of the world's Catholics. And that is saying a lot. The 700 million Roman Catholics are the biggest religious community in the world and undoubtedly the strongest. This is the real fascination. Catholicism is a big force. It did not need the election of the Polish pope, John Paul II, with all his glamour, to make this clear. He is a natural protagonist, and frequently I have had to make an effort to prevent an appraisal of him dominating the book. The real point is a purely utilitarian one. These Catholics are numerous and growing, particularly in the parts of the world where humanity's future rests—meaning largely what we stupidly call the Third World, which soon will have to be admitted to be the First World. So what they have to offer, and what they intend to do, is of the greatest interest to all of us as the second Christian millennium approaches, with all the psychological difficulties this will bring. Indeed, is bringing.

I remember, as part of my childhood reading, a passage from a great music critic who thought that Wagner would always need apologists. I have always regarded the Catholic Church as Wagnerian in the sense that it is richly varied and flows in a controlled, but seemingly endless, stream through history, making St Cecilia a rather inadequate musical patron. But in this other sense it is still more Wagnerian; despite its mighty flow and equally majestic claims, Catholicism produces more apologists than do other great religions. Mozart has no apologists, Schubert only for his length, Beethoven an occasional excuse on the grounds of his deafness. And if all things were the equal of their claims, the Catholic Church would also be above the work of those who are constantly trying to explain it and, where certain of its elements are concerned, to explain them away. In part, this is because it is more than a faith. It has a great weight of doctrine accumulated over the centuries which extends into practically every field of human activity. It has a controversial history as a temporal power behind it and a huge and elaborate structure over it. The Mayas and the Egyptians used the pyramid as the shape for their religious architecture: and the Catholic Church for its hierarchical structure, with the pope at the top.

INTRODUCTION

The Catholic Church has frequently needed its apologists. But surely the time has come for it to do without them; to stand up and say, in particular to non-Catholics, what its approach will be to the principal issues facing mankind as the psychologically weighty date of the second Christian millennium approaches. Some of the faithful would argue that John Paul II has tried to do exactly that. He has been warm and human and communicative in his dealings with the masses, a kind of firm hand of the law as he rides into the crowds in St Peter's Square on his white jeep or soars down out of the clouds in a white jet. But discipline is first and foremost with him, despite his human qualities.

Ecclesiastical institutions tend to use a measure of time that is all their own. The cliché about the Vatican is that 'it thinks in centuries.' If that is the case, then the Vatican is making the opposite mistake from the early Christians who thought the world was coming to an end any minute; a view that probably distorted a number of decisions in the first years of the Church. Without this perspective, St Paul would be even more difficult to accept on some of his teachings, especially his moral instructions, such as his advice not to marry unless absolutely necessary. Even Jesus himself was difficult to follow on the question of when the Kingdom would come. The Vatican takes the view that it is going to be there for a very long time. With so long a history behind it and its long experience of dangers regularly survived, it probably feels there is no good reason to change outlook now. By any standard, however, 2,000 years is a long period and quite sufficient to allow a few conclusions to be drawn about the performance of humanity's most influential religion.

The approach of the year 2000 may well coincide with the greatest threat so far to human ingenuity in facing the problems of the planet. The challenge is dramatic; not because there will be a direct confrontation between crisis and responsibility, recognizable as a turning-point in history—history manages to avoid such banalities—but with the Western world so clearly sick, an accounting of some kind will have to be made. Europe and Europe's main religion have been too closely intertwined to be treated separately. This is all the more true now that Catholicism's future is seen to be outside Europe, and not necessarily in areas which look on European ways as at all worthy of being copied. 'Virulent' was the word that came to my mind when I listened to an African priest talking to me on the subject of the need to remove the European element from Catholicism's character:

'. . . we have to go deep into it and give our people their faith. They are not giving our people the white man's culture, the white man's mentality, the white man's ways, the white man's traditions . . . . This is taking Christianity as it is, *en bloc*, without discerning what is really Christian, and will give us the danger of not ever having really become Christian . . . .' That type of feeling, an urgent need for an intimate, recognizable Christianity, expressed by the use of local traditions, can only grow stronger as the West visibly weakens.

Essentially, the West's problem is a moral one, as is normally the case in a period of economic and political decline. The first Christian Emperor, Constantine, recognized this when he called on a comparatively young and sturdy creed to provide a spiritual bulwark for the declining Roman Empire. The bulwark could not save the Empire but Christianity was well able to survive the Empire's fall and was set to play its part at the centre of European history, complete with its hierarchy and its sense of the state. What began as an expedient turned into a new phase in human history. Is there any point in looking to Christianity now, especially to Catholicism, to perform another such miracle? Or is it now the turn of the once sturdy bulwark to collapse under the weight of the new decline? Or even to help that decline?

1

THE CATHOLIC PLACES

AN ELDERLY SICILIAN turned round during a Mass at the principal Jesuit church in Rome and, pointing to the African and Asian and Latin American priests concelebrating at the altar, said with some emotion that what now gave him the greatest satisfaction about his faith was the involvement of all races: the world suddenly became one to him. He was not quite right, just as the choice of priests from each continent was a little misleading, in the sense that Catholicism is not represented equally throughout the world. But all the main areas of the world have some sort of tie with Rome and so, for him, a real relationship with the very bricks, mortar, the baroque angels, the silver-cased arm of the saint, which formed the more familiar background to the service he was attending. Roman Catholics form 18 per cent of the planet's population. It would be difficult, I think impossible, to find another 18 per cent of the world's population with the same sort of strong loyalty in common and with equal influence. With every allowance made for indifferent and non-practising Catholics, they count for more than their actual literal numbers and, if allowed to do so, or if they allow themselves to do so, will have an influence in the future far beyond the share due to them at the last official count as 739,126,000 out of the world's total of 4,094,110,000 human beings.

There are a few countries without Catholics but, with the quite fortuitous exceptions of Afghanistan and the two Yemens, they are not very prominent in the world's affairs. The others are Bahrain, Greenland, Oman, the Faroes and the Maldives. There are great differences from country to country, and from continent

21

to continent, in the ratio between Catholics and the whole of the local population.

The highest proportion is in the Americas with 62.3 Catholics for every 100 inhabitants, a decisive predominance which is at its most overwhelming in Latin America. Europe lies second with 40.2, then Oceania which has about a quarter of its population Catholic. Asia has the lowest proportion with 2.5 per cent and this figure would be much lower still if it were not for the presence in Asia of one large country, the Philippines, with a huge Catholic population. It is, in fact, the country with the sixth largest Catholic population in the world—thirty-six million—and if its somewhat anomalous contribution were withdrawn, the Asian percentage would drop to just under 1 per cent. Africa is second to last with 12.5 Catholics to every 100 inhabitants but with a rate of increase in its Catholic population which will assure the continent a leading place in the future in Catholic affairs. In numbers, Latin America will comfortably remain ahead and account for more than one half of the total Catholic population in the world by the year 2000. Africa, because of its present lack of great religions and its freedom from the cultural confusion in Latin America, is the continent most likely to give Catholicism a new stamp.

Belloc had a way of identifying the Catholic world which he summed up in the lines:

> Where'er the Catholic sun does shine
> There's music and laughter and good red wine
> At least I've always found it so
> Benedicamus Domino.

I have not. One reason for this is that the world, and Catholics more than others (I think), is nowadays taken up with problems of social justice and development and the application of religion to the problems of individuals in a way quite unprecedented unless one goes back to Christianity's early years when pagans, such as the Emperor Julian, were angry at the way the troublesome Christian sect dealt so effectively and lovingly with the practical problems of both its own members and, sometimes, others. Belloc's agreeable, but naive, optimism now sounds centuries old, a form of religious maypole-dancing by comparison with the increasing activism of the Catholic faith as it begins to look with a realistic eye at the problems around it and to sense, to put the sensation no higher, the social shocks to come. There can have been no time like the present in which the qualities Julian grumbled about will be crucial to religion's sense of relevance.

Europe was a comfortable base for centuries, and remained so in statistical terms until about two decades ago. At that time, around 1960, the Catholics of Europe and North America, counted together, still outdistanced those of the Third World by 267 million to 251 million or, in percentage terms, 51.5 to 48.5. Today, Latin America, Africa, Asia and Oceania together are ahead of the Europeans and North Americans, and it is estimated that by the year 2000 about 70 per cent of baptized Catholics will be in the Third World. Europe now boasts the country—West Germany—with the lowest birthrate in the world. Some twenty-six of the world's thirty-three industrialized nations have birth-rates at, near, or below what is considered the replacement level.

The facts are easier to find than to interpret. That 70 per cent of Catholics which will be in the Third World will in fact be living in areas which in the year 2000 will be inhabited by 90 per cent of the world's population. This, however, will not be a return to the rural life, from where Christianity first came and where Catholic-ism thrived in the past, because the estimates are that the huge move in many of the Third World countries away from the land will continue on such a scale that room will have to be found for 1,000 million more people in the cities. Urban unemployment is already a serious problem in many cities of the less developed countries, as are such other basic requirements as food, safe drinking water and adequate medical care. There can be no need to look far to see why the social conscience is becoming so sharp a part of modern Catholic thinking. This conscience will have to be remarkably effective if it is to help the situation in what are becoming the base-lands of Catholicism in the world.

Brazil and Mexico lead the world in the size of their Catholic populations and they are followed by Italy. But Brazil with over 100 million Catholics and a high birthrate has double the Catholic population of Italy and, of course, Italy, the nerve-centre of the Church's European base, is now among the industrialized nations with a falling birthrate whereas Brazil and Mexico are not. The rest of the list of countries with more than ten million Catholics each continues with four other Latin American countries, namely Argentina, Colombia, Peru and Venezuela; then come five European countries, beginning with France and working down-wards to Spain, Poland, the Federal Republic of Germany,

Czechoslovakia. There are two North American countries, the United States and Canada; one in Africa, Zaire; and one in Asia, the Philippines. Apart from the United States, Canada, Zaire and West Germany, all these countries have a very high percentage of Catholics varying from 98 per cent in Spain to about 70 per cent in Czechoslovakia.

There is an obvious enough pattern of where Catholic predominance is to be found at present. First, Latin America is uniformly and almost totally Catholic, a remarkable situation when one recalls that Catholicism was largely imposed by the Spanish and Portuguese occupiers. Despite their methods, they have left behind them Catholicism's continent of the future. Even now, Latin American Catholicism is exerting an influence which a matter of a few years ago would have been regarded as unthinkable. Its contribution is understandably in the direction of Catholicism's relationship with social problems. It is a weighty contribution. It could not be made if something had not changed in the wider field of Latin American culture, a kind of synthesis, a self-awareness, and a self-evaluation. It is a curious fact that in political terms Latin America remains the example to avoid at all costs, while in ecclesiastical and more broadly religious matters it is a highly respected generator of attitudes. One of the clearest ideas I took away from the Puebla Conference of the Latin American hierarchy in January and February 1979 was the impression made on non-Latin American prelates of a very clear sense of the maturing of a recognizably regional outlook. There were differences of course, often very sharp, but there was also something substantially inter-continental in approach. And yet, the situation is more fragile than it seems. The warning of how wrong things can go and how quickly this can happen is provided by Cuba.

The island used to be just like the rest of the continent, over 90 per cent of its population following the Catholicism which the Spaniards had brought with them and which continued to rely heavily on priests from abroad. That was the situation when Castro took over the island in 1958 and which was maintained more or less intact until the Bay of Pigs disaster in 1961 brought in its wake a serious clash between the Church and the regime. As a result, non-Cuban priests were expelled, some 598 priests and more than 2,000 nuns were forced to go. Today there are about 200 priests in Cuba, the schools have been nationalized, Catholics meet obstacles in trying to enter public life. The population has increased rapidly in the last fifteen years. Now there are no more than 40 per cent of Catholics among nine million Cubans, a percentage drop of more than a half. Before the revolution, Cuba, in ecclesiastical terms, was just like anywhere else. The lesson is that massive figures suggesting widespread belief can very soon be shown to be vulnerable when facing a difficult reality. There is no likelihood that the situation will improve in Cuba from the Church's point of view.

The spinal cord of European Catholicism—what was once the backbone of the whole faith—is that group of countries which could be defined as Latin Europe with a few rather less typical promontories which nevertheless belong to it. The old heartlands are Italy, Spain, France, Portugal, Austria and Belgium, with the peripheral but powerful Catholic communities in Ireland and the three Communist countries of Poland, Hungary and Czechoslovakia. These are the lands which gave Belloc his roseate view—before the arrival of the Communists of course—of Catholicism's character. The Communist regimes have had no effect in Europe similar to the success of Castro in reducing the number of believers, and for the most part no longer try to. Poland remains well over 90 per cent Catholic and if Hungary has only about 60 per cent this is because of a large Protestant presence. The Church in Hungary does not represent the national spirit in the way that it does in Poland because in some part it owes its following to the reimposition of Catholicism by the Hapsburgs after they drove the Turks from Hungary in the eighteenth century. There are other distinctions between the position of the Church in the three Communist countries. In Czechoslovakia there is real repression and the Vatican makes little or no headway in seeking more freedom of action from the government. Hungary is developing a kind of wary form of coexistence with the authorities, and Poland, of course, as everyone now knows, could be the personal kingdom, the temporal domain, of history's first Polish pope if ever the Communists should decide to go away.

West Germany is the one example of a clear gain by the Catholic Church as a result of the Communist advance into Europe. Some say, of course, that the Communist incursion may in the end be all gain, that Eastern Europe is refurbishing its Catholicism under its Communist masters and will return to stiffen the flabby moral sinews of the West. But that is a totally different set of considerations from the statistical truth that West Germany has proved in every sense a very profitable place for Catholicism. The effect of the division of Germany was to cut away a substantial part of the country which was almost entirely Evangelical. Eastern Germany has about 7 per cent of Catholics at the moment, while the West has more than half its population Catholic. Catholic preponderance over the Protestants was reached at the beginning of 1977 when the Catholics were able to announce with unecumenical but understandable pride that they were ahead of the Evangelicals in numbers 'for the first time since Luther'. It was true enough but the Catholics had some help from many of the 1,200,000 immigrant workers, of whom 55 per cent are Catholic and only 10 per cent Protestant. Catholic loyalty is also involved. Figures show that far fewer Catholics leave the Church by comparison with other denominations—and in a very basic sense. Only in West Germany does taxpayers' money go direct to the churches unless the citizen expressly refuses to contribute. This act of refusing to be taxed for the benefit of one's church has grown sharply among Evangelicals, less so among Catholics. Taxation is one explanation for the wealth of the West German Church. Some of that wealth goes to Latin America, and the West German bishops, who undoubtedly are a highly conservative group, are frequently accused of backing traditionalist causes in the emerging continent. It is a rich Church, and one which is devotedly anti-Communist.

Yet it is France (with a population 85 per cent Catholic), the home of the greatest revolutionary threat to Catholicism before the present challenges of Communism and the consumer society, which has produced the spearhead of the traditionalist revolt. The shock of the French Revolution must have left behind it an element of total conservatism. This archaic element could have been seen, almost intact, outside France a generation ago in Quebec, because traditional Canadian Catholicism was reinforced in the later eighteenth century by immigrant French priests anxious to reconstruct the *ancien régime* that had been overturned in France. But that is very logical. It is less logical on the surface that modern France, which produced some of the earliest experiments in facing social realities, such as the movement for worker-priests, should also have given to the Church its sternest and most effective critic from the far-Right, the arch-traditionalist, and former missionary, Archbishop Marcel Lefebvre. He is only understandable in the historical context of a type of Catholicism with a part, however small, that still clings to tradition because it is traditionally still in a state of shock from the effects of 1789.

Certainly Archbishop Lefebvre does not make a very notable personal impression, and this is surprising when one reads his solemn strictures accusing the Vatican of having turned Catholicism Protestant and making it an instrument of the Communist conspiracy. I found him unexpectedly mild in manner: ineffectual. There he would stand with all the accoutrements of drama: a message to make the faithful tremble, a devoted circle of helpers, the splendid sitting-room of a right-wing Roman princess, an audience eager to cheer some good religious nostalgia in the midst of doctrinal and social confusion. He said what they wanted to hear. He was against the Vatican Council and all it stood for. He was against change. He represented the true church. He appealed to all that sentimentality which Pinter expressed in *No Man's Land* with the lines: 'In my day nobody changed. A man was. Only religion could change him and that at least was a glorious misery.' Lefebvre had not changed but the religion in which he believed had, and he would not accept this. But it was petulance more than passion. It had nothing of the great conservatism of the late Cardinal Ottaviani, for instance, the self-styled policeman of the Church and last of the real Inquisitors; or of Ottaviani's friend Cardinal Ruffini, who was said to close the windows of Palermo's arch-episcopal palace as he prepared to address the Sicilian bishops, so as not to allow irrelevant interruptions from the Holy Spirit. Lefebvre was not in that class. He founded his 'Priestly Confraternity of St Pius X' and his traditionalist seminary at Écone near Geneva. He gained a following in France, in the United States, in Argentina, some in Britain. He was strong enough to be a painful nuisance to Paul VI, whom he mimicked badly, but less in face of the stronger manner (and more conservative outlook) of John Paul II.

It would be unfair to make Lefebvre the standard-bearer of modern French Catholicism, even if surveys (conducted by the Progrès de Lyon) estimated that a quarter of French Catholics supported his challenge. One of the best pieces written about his sentimental attraction and the subsequent tedious disappointment came from the American Catholic novelist (what is a Catholic writer, really?) Mary Gordon, writing in *Harper's* magazine:

> And so *l'incident Lefebvre* engages my imagination. It inspires in me an embarrassing richness of nostalgic fantasy; sung Gregorian Masses, priests in gold, the silence of Benediction, my own sense of sanctity as an eight-year-old carrying a lily among a hundred other

eight-year-olds on Holy Thursday. The society sparks the romance of a lost cause, perhaps the least dangerous romance of all. I imagine Lefebvre a gallant, clerical Charles Boyer, bathed in a clarifying bitterness. When I learn that he has dedicated a chapel in Oyster Bay, Long Island, I am interested. I imagine a new brand of American conservative priest. God knows there has been no dearth of conservative Catholic priests, but they have all been of the beefy John Wayne or the florid Bob Hope variety, hysterical about sex and Communism with a lousy sense of pulpit oratory.

She is talking here as much about the American Church as the French, and in fairness one must add that the French bishops played a splendid part in the Vatican Council and did so on the basis of a revitalization of French Catholicism in the forty years up to the opening of the Council. Mary Gordon remembers priests in gold: I can remember Edwige Feuillère and Jean-Louis Barrault in Claudel's *Partage du Midi*; Poulenc's music is still a delight, and not only for *The Carmelites*; Bernanos, Roualt, Mauriac, Teilhard de Chardin, Congar, de Lubac. No one need be a Catholic to agree that reaction and a dry inflexibility are not the hallmark of French Catholicism. Like the other countries whose hierarchies led the liberal cause at the Vatican Council—the Germans, the Dutch, the Belgians—the French are now more somnolent these days, as if they had all learnt the lesson that their countries can no longer be the Church's pacemakers.

Enquiries show a certain optimism in France about the future. Some 80 per cent are convinced that the faith will still be strong in fifty years' time. But, like English Catholics, the average French Catholic is much less convinced that the Church has a right to talk about sexual morality than it has on issues more specifically recognizable as religious.

I do not know, if the choice were forced on me, whether I would want to be an English or a Dutch Catholic. Both saw the hierarchy restored at much the same time: 1850 in England and 1853 in Holland. It is odd that two countries with similar histories should have developed such opposing forms of Catholicism. Both countries are sea powers, ex-colonial powers, both countries fought for their existence against the Catholic powers of the Counter-Reformation, to the point that one gave the other a Protestant king lest dynastic (and Catholic) intrigue should threaten to return a Catholic monarch to London. The great traditional historians of both were anti-Catholic and, while iden-tifying constitutional propriety with a Protestant monarch, saw the Catholic powers as prone to intrigue and conspiracy against the sturdy independence of the Protestant world. So much so, that the one piece of the British Constitution which is written refers to the ban on Catholic monarchs or consorts. Civil liberties are still seen to be tied up with anti-Catholicism. And the old ghosts prove oddly difficult to lay, even in a country where religious life has a strong element of ecumenical hope.

The ban on a Catholic monarch or consort is not only constitutional in origin. It derives in part from the Catholic insistence that in a marriage between a Catholic and a non-Catholic the parents must undertake to bring up the children as Catholics. The issue arises in Britain in all its constitutional splendour, but obviously it is one that is widespread throughout the Catholic world, or, better, the Catholic *demi-monde*. And that is exactly why the British Constitutional situation is of great importance. If there were sufficient goodwill, it could be settled between the Vatican and the British government so that this rather ridiculous ban on Catholics at the apex of the system could be resolved in a way that was applicable to all couples suffering from this problem of religious distinction in married life. These 'mixed marriages', as they are tastelessly called, are certain to increase. This is because of the growing concentration of the world's population in cities, which means that the traditional, smaller communities where individual religion was of greater significance will have less weight in the scale of the world's population.

Already a constructive set of new possibilities is becoming attached to mixed marriages: in the United States for instance, and in Asia where there are comparatively frequent marriages between Catholics and members of other religions, there is a growing idea that these meetings at the individual level of different faiths can help, each in a small way, to improve relations between followers of different beliefs. During the 1980 International Synod at the Vatican, devoted to family problems, the bishops heard testimony from married couples. Almost all of them were Catholic, but one couple consisted of a Catholic and an Anglican and they aroused a certain interest by recounting their experience of being able to pray together as Christians but not go to Communion together because they belonged to different denominations. So far, the only official move made at the Vatican, despite all the ecumenical activity, was to agree to replace written promises about the education of children by verbal ones.

There would be an attractive sense of historical justice if the

British monarchy should become the means for settling the problem everywhere in the world of those couples which include one Catholic partner. Certainly Britain's recent monarchs show no prejudice towards their predecessors exiled because of their Catholic faith. The Queen looked through some of the Stuart papers when visiting the Vatican and the Queen Mother actually paid for the restoration of the tomb in St Peter's of Cardinal Henry, Duke of York, the brother of the Young Pretender. The fact that the Prince of Wales is seen publicly escorting a wide variety of young women, including Catholics, has revived the royal marriage issue as a popular question. All it needs now is settlement, whether or not a personal case is involved, and a settlement wider in its application than the curiosities of British views of royal religion.

Catholicism is growing steadily in England: from 0.3 per cent in 1851 to about 10 per cent today. A Catholic has not yet been prime minister, which is curious when one considers that a Catholic has been President of the United States and that Italy, of all places, has had an Anglican as prime minister in the person of Sidney Sonnino.

English Catholicism looks half-serene. The fundamental doctrines of religious faith are accepted without apparent strain, rather as the British Constitution is accepted. A greater confidence and a will to assert a distinctly English outlook were stimulated by the outstanding success of Cardinal Hume at Westminster. Teaching on morals is more widely challenged, particularly on such matters as divorce, extra-marital sex and birth-control, though not yet in the deeply disturbed and almost indignant way in which these matters are faced in the United States. These problems will become increasingly important however. Rome's attitude of giving way on none of them could have been calculated to increase their importance, especially as English Catholics put their views forward in a balanced but unmistakable way at their first National Pastoral Council, held in Liverpool in 1980.

I have an impression that English Catholics insist on the need to be ecumenical because, consciously or unconsciously, the idea of Anglicanism as the established, accepted, respectable, official and very English church makes them unhappy; they can see insufficient reason for this position of privilege, and would like it for themselves. The Dutch Catholics, at the other end of the Catholic spectrum, have challenged much more in the field of religious belief and in matters of morals. In some places they have practically done away with the concept of the institutional Church and, despite that element in Dutch history of Protestantism triumphant over the nation's enemies, have taken on themselves the task of reviewing society and religion in an attempt to bring together advanced and modern models of both. That was the case, at any rate, in a part of the Dutch Church until the Vatican intervened. I am convinced that the Vatican's conduct in opposing the Dutch experiments was tragically wrong, but that is something best dealt with elsewhere.

In fact, the Dutch, if one must find a numerical category, belong less closely in their Catholicism with Britain than with Switzerland and West Germany. All three are more or less equally divided between Catholics and Protestants. In the Scandinavian countries, Finland and Iceland, the Catholic proportion of the population remains stubbornly below 1 per cent. These five countries have between them fewer than 120,000 Catholics. It is worth recalling that the European Community, to which only one of them belongs, is predominantly Catholic. The nine have a proportion of more than 58 per cent Catholics, and with the addition of Greece, Portugal and Spain this figure will go beyond 62 per cent. John Paul II's election changed the position in Europe more immediately than in any other area. He has a Gaullist view of Europe, which he sees as beginning at the Urals. His position was very clear even before his election, and he has shown no sign of changing his mind. He has grasped the point that many supporters of the European Community prefer not to accept; that Europe may be split both politically and in religious terms between East and West but both owe their inspiration to southern European cities—Rome and Constantinople. In the past, however, the Vatican has seen the growth of the essentially Western European Community as favourable. John Paul II much less so, and he has expressed serious misgivings about the Western European outlook which he sees, with that of the United States, as a contorted acceptance of the consumer society he constantly criticizes. One of his closest friends in the Sacred College of Cardinals, who had an important part in his election, said to me that he himself believed there was a genuine religious revival in Eastern Europe and that missionaries would come from there to re-evangelize the West. The first, he added, had already arrived at the See of Rome. I was glad he told me this: at the same time, I hoped he did not say it too often in John Paul II's hearing.

I was struck by the reactions of a group of young Romans, all of them seriously practising Catholics, who went to find out for themselves the form that revival is taking. They were members of a community intent on living their faith in terms of modern urban life, and they hired a bus to tour Poland and look at the religious background from which the pope had come. The first shock —there were others—was that Jesus had a subordinate role. The Virgin Mary came first and the Polish pope second, with Jesus, as these young people put it, a bad third.

The cardinal who spoke of the pope as the first missionary in reverse, had some intriguing accounts of why he felt there is a rise in religious feeling in the East. He noticed one such sign when visiting the western Polish city of Liegnitz, which is a Russian military centre. Many Russians lived there and brought their families with them. He told me that their wives, in particular, made a rule of buying religious objects before going home on leave: crosses, images, all manner of religious souvenirs. They sewed them into their clothes, even their husbands' uniforms, and took them back to Russia. The late Orthodox Patriarch of Bucharest told two similar stories. Once, when he was visiting Moscow, he showed the girl who cleaned his hotel room some small crucifixes and asked her if she knew what they were. She replied, of course, they were crosses. Asked if young people had crosses, she replied, of course they did, that many of her friends hid them or had them in their pockets. His second story concerned the visit of a Russian dance-company which visited Bucharest. A young man, very good-looking the Patriarch said, made an athletic leap towards the centre of the stage, his shirt split and there on his chest, for the whole official audience to see, hung a large cross.

This is heart-warming, if you like, to the devout. But there is not a lot to be complacent about in the knowledge that religion of a kind survives persecution. The real question raised, the deeper question, is whether the form of religion which emerges from the crucible is really so pure. Could it not also be distorted?

The election of a Pole to the papacy in October 1978 brought a lot of interest to bear on religion under Communism. Too much, probably, because a lot of the interest was inspired by the wrong reasons, including an undignified and totally unjustified Western chauvinism, as if a religious revival in the East were somehow a victory for the West.

The Balkans, like Russia, belong more to the Eastern Orthodox than to the Catholic tradition. The one country among them with a strong Catholic presence is Yugoslavia. Practically a third of the population is Catholic, some 40 per cent Orthodox and 11 per cent Muslim. It is the only Communist country which has normal diplomatic relations with the Vatican, and normality is also the impression of church-going there: guitars when they were fashionable and modern versions of old Croat hymns. Albania may still have some Catholics—there are estimates of up to 10 per cent—but there is no news of them and they could only be existing in circumstances of extreme repression, worse, in European terms, than the Czechoslovak experience. Romania has about 6 per cent Catholics and Bulgaria a tenth of that. And, finally, Russia has an estimated 1.2 per cent.

The Russian case is of particular interest; apart from anything else because of the influence the Soviet authorities could have on Eastern European governments. It was no coincidence that John XXIII concentrated his efforts on Russia to ensure the presence of an observer from the Russian Orthodox Church at the Vatican Council. He achieved his aim and also the release from a labour camp of the leader of the Ukrainian Church in communion with Rome, Joseph Slipyi, whom Paul VI later created a cardinal.

It was said that John XXIII clung to an old dream for the conversion of Russia. For centuries, the rivalry has been great between Rome and Moscow and the advent of Communism made the dream still more real. The Catholic basis within the country not only is small but is present in rather exposed, and thus sensitive, parts of the Soviet Union. This is because the bulk of the Russian Catholics became a part of the Soviet Union as a result of conquest during the Second World War. The two Baltic republics of Lithuania and Latvia have the majority of the Soviet Union's Catholics. These are also the only places in the Soviet Union where the Catholic hierarchy is recognized. There are an estimated two million Catholics in Lithuania and a quarter of a million in Latvia. Slipyi's church was practically destroyed in its homeland when the Soviet authorities in 1946 ordered its forcible absorption by the Orthodox Church, and now it is officially under the Patriarch of Moscow: its numbers are estimated at 3,500,000.

Asia, too, has its own huge magnetic void: the unknown potential but powerful attraction represented by China. In 1949 when Mao Tse-tung took China from Chiang Kai-shek there were an estimated three million Catholics in the country. Then all official ties were broken. The Communist authorities established a Patriotic Catholic Church which the Vatican has never recognized. For some three decades indications about the real state of Catholic survival in China were slight and unreliable. Then, with the change in China's outlook towards the rest of the world, the Vatican was quick to send its emissaries: first, a Chinese-born Jesuit, and, later, members of the Sacred College itself. The first impressions were favourable in the sense that the survivals of Catholic life were more substantial than had been feared. More people had managed to retain their faith than had been expected. More priests, even if forced to earn a modest living in lay life and forbidden to practise their priestly duties, had succeeded in keeping their integrity, as had some who were in labour camps. Letters began arriving at Vatican Radio from Chinese listeners to the broadcast Mass in Chinese. All this stimulated what I am sure is a special attraction, almost a temptation, of the Catholic Church towards China. The first time this attraction was brought home to me was when a young American priest told me that he thought Christianity was moving towards temporary extinction in Europe and would be reborn, in full simplicity, elsewhere, in some other civilization. And the first likelihood he mentioned was China. I remember a French missionary telling me in Bangkok that the Chinese population was easier to convert than the Buddhist Thais. The Archbishop of Bangkok has a face which shows his Chinese origin. The same can be said for the Cardinal-Archbishop of Manila. And there, in the Philippines, Jesuits expelled from China wait for the chance to return. How tedious the Philippines must seem to them! A beautiful country but almost entirely Catholic and now, for the first time, sending its own missionaries out to other Asian countries. Here the Filipinos can feel that, in one field at least, they are superior to the massive Chinese presence.

Asian Catholicism is numerically a minute force, but it is attractive and looks set for an original future. India is the most religious country on earth (ahead of the United States), according to George Gallup's findings, and is looked on by the Jesuits as the most promising country of all for future members of the order. The physical proximity with Hinduism has inspired fascinating liturgical experiments, which Buddhism and Islam have failed to stimulate. The Philippines is deeply involved in integrating its own complex cultural past with its Catholicism, as well as in building up a monopoly voice in opposition to the country's ruling dictatorship and the excesses of the military. In Indonesia, Islam claims nine out of ten people and, while it is not so insistent as in Iran, it plays the part that the Catholics have in the

Philippines of a brake on an authoritarian regime. There are three million Catholics in Indonesia and their most impressive achievement is their school system. There is a heavy preponderance in the schools of ethnic Chinese, so much so that the Catholic schools there are sometimes referred to as Chinese schools.

Ironically, the Near East, which saw the historical origins of Christianity, has very few Catholics indeed, with the exception of Lebanon. And that Crusader country with its bitter civil war, which sees Christians fighting Arabs, continues to give a sad example. There are about a million Maronite Christians in Lebanon, representing rather more than a third of the population, and they are among the group of churches, known as Uniate churches, which follow the Eastern liturgy but owe allegiance to Rome. These groups are usually a small following within a larger Eastern church: there is, for example, an Armenian Catholic Church as well as an Armenian Orthodox Church, just as there is a Coptic Catholic Church. (I made one of the grossest acts of unintentional rudeness when I was taken to meet the head of the Armenian Orthodox Church. He asked what sort of coffee I liked—I could take no more acid lemonade. I said, 'Turkish, Your Holiness.' He replied very kindly: 'Do you mind if we call it Oriental coffee?')

These are the Catholic places. Division by country or by continent is necessarily rough. But it provides some indication. So too does the distribution of the 1,556,754 persons regularly at work in the apostolate. According to the Vatican's statisticians, this total is lower than the real one because they obtain their figures from the bishops throughout the world and so miss people working outside the local diocese, in, for instance, the administration of religious institutes or charitable and welfare bodies. This, nevertheless, is the official figure, and it is made up of 403,801 priests, 4,456 permanent deacons, 68,426 laymen religious, 946,398 professed women religious and 133,673 catechists in the missions. This is a colossal force, especially when one considers that they are almost all dedicated to celibacy and so can devote their whole lives to their work and be far more at the disposal of their superiors than could people with families.

They are unevenly distributed. Central America has a proportion of 1.4 priests to every 10,000 baptized Catholics, Africa 3, Europe 9.1, Oceania 9.8 and North America 11.6, bringing an average for the whole world of 5.5 priests for every 10,000 Catholics, and, in terms of the total population of the world, 1.4 Catholic priests for every 10,000 of us.

To these can be added the candidates to the priesthood, who numbered in December 1977, the last available figures, 200,406 in the two stages of secondary and theological studies in the world's seminaries. These figures include men training to be secular priests and those studying for the priesthood with religious orders. There is a certain wastage, particularly in countries where the state-school system is poor and youths go to the seminary for an education rather than because of a vocation. The official wastage figures apply only to the diocesan seminaries: in 1977, out of the 127,168 seminarists enrolled, 13,468 left.

The most striking statistics show the relationship between the number of advanced candidates to the priesthood and the number of priests. Take the seminarists who are at the theology and philosophy level: on a world-wide reckoning there are just over 15 of them for every 100 priests. In Asia, that relationship changes to 44 seminarists to every 100 priests, in Africa to 32, in Latin America 22, in Oceania about 18, in North America 15 and in Europe 9.4, the lowest proportion of any of the continents.

One of the traditional strengths of Catholicism is its system of schools. The schools and universities in the United States are the showpieces, and it it true that the hierarchy there has created an impressive alternative to state education, though at a surprising moral cost. It is evident that these schools were established with the excellent aim of providing a good education which would, at the same time, be a Catholic education. In that they succeeded, but the effort itself is seen to have brought about the excessively organizational element in American Catholicism: the reverence for the dollar; the selection of bishops who would be successful at fund-raising; and the habit which grew on some bishops (and is still present in a few today) of concentrating on diocesan finances but keeping the details a closely guarded secret. I happened to be in Chicago when the conflict between the archbishop, Cardinal Cody, and his own priests was passing through one of its tenser moments: among the stories they told of that unpopular archbishop was that every cheque over ten dollars had to be signed by him. This attitude almost surely had its origins in the financing of the schools, and there is now a new awareness of the dangers attached to expressing religion in terms of schools, hospitals and other public works. 'We are having to think', an Indian bishop said, 'whether we can continue to spend large sums of money on schools, which also absorb the energies of our priests, when so many people are poor, and many have not heard the Gospel.' The question could perhaps be particularly pertinent in a country such as India, which presents the Catholic hierarchy with two huge problems: how to make the Gospel a real message to a seemingly unlimited number of hopelessly poor people, and, secondly, how to take that message among Hindus who already have a religion which they find, on the whole, satisfactory, with its own scriptures, saints and moral teaching. 'What do I tell a priest to say to the Hindus when I send him alone, the one Catholic priest, to work in Benares?' was the worried but half-humorous comment of the bishop who happens to have the city holy to Hinduism in his own diocese.

Whatever the rights and wrongs of building or not building schools, the system as it stands is formidable. At the end of 1977 in all the countries of the world where the Catholic Church is present, there were 79,207 elementary schools with a total of 20,800,000 pupils; on the same date, the number of students in the Church's 28,000 secondary schools was over 10,270,000 while 986,000 people studied at Catholic universities. This massive system is altruistic: indeed the Vatican puts first things first. These schools 'receive those who wish not only to learn the truth of the faith but also to gain a general education'. In some countries, in unexpected ways, the Catholic schools act as a useful pillar of the faith in broader ways. In Hungary, for instance, members of religious orders must teach if they wish to have legal recognition of their status as nuns, friars or monks. There are eight Catholic schools in Hungary because each of the four accepted religious orders is allowed two. Sometimes a Catholic school will provide an extremely useful service in educating future leaders: in Tanzania, for instance, President Nyerere is the product of a Catholic mission school and the White Father who was once his headmaster remains close to him and presumably still has some influence. But the balance is not all positive. The virulently Marxist ruler of Mozambique was brought up by Jesuits. So was Fidel Castro, at a school now moved to Miami. Not everything that seemed so heart-warming about the variously coloured faces concelebrating at the altar of the Jesuit church in Rome survives analysis.

The Catholic world is divided into 2,372 ecclesiastical territories. Ecclesiastical territories, broadly speaking, mean dioceses or other territories governed with ordinary jurisdiction which nevertheless are not dioceses but have other names, such as prelatures, abbacies *nullius*, apostolic administrations, vicariates apostolic, prefectures apostolic, and so on. The genuine dioceses are, for the main, episcopal sees and these account for 1,640 of the total number of ecclesiastical territories. The metropolitan sees follow with a total of 402, then the 54 archbishoprics, and last but grandest of all the 12 patriarchal sees. As an indication of the relative weight of the Latin rite and the Uniate branch of Catholicism, only 139 of these 2,372 territories belong to the Uniates. Europe has a large share of the world's bishoprics—514, nearly a third of the total—and is only overshadowed by the 583 comprising the combined number of bishoprics in the Americas. More than half (eight) of the patriarchates are in Asia, which is an indication that historical more than actual importance maintains these august titles. The European share of two tells the same tale: one is Venice and the other Lisbon. The two in Africa are a reminder that the northern shores of that continent were once great Christian areas.

Ecclesiastical territories are broken down into what are officially called 'pastoral centres', which usually means a parish but which is defined as a certain part of an ecclesiastical territory with its own church, people, and pastor for the care of souls. There are 331,960 throughout the Catholic world, an average of 140 to every diocese with an average number of 2,228 Catholics to each one. Again, the relationships vary in different parts of the world: in South America there are 71 centres to every diocese, each with an average of 5,857 Catholics, whereas in Europe the respective figures are 211 and 1,823. Most are elements in the parish system, though about a fifth are mission stations.

This panorama provides little more than the bare bones of the way Catholicism is distributed and organized throughout the world. It is enough to show that it is a formidable network with an ability to shape opinion which, though it cannot be finely calculated, is quite clearly immense. The base is broad, if much more solid and effective in some parts of the world than in others. It is a centralized body, almost an empire, given its traditional monarchical structure with the pope at the apex of the pyramid in Rome, and, at the moment, a pope, in John Paul II, who comes so completely from the central European tradition of prince-bishops. His methods are imperial, too: the harangues to the crowds; the insistence on keeping the centralized government in his own hands; the constant travelling to show himself to those vast throngs unable to make the journey to Rome (still the great majority despite every development in travel). This prince-bishop, or, for that matter, anyone else who is pope, faces two sets of problems. One is abroad in the world at large and by no means confined to the Catholic world, because it affects the whole population of the planet. The second faces the pope in Rome, because it is more strictly a matter of how the Catholic Church's forces can best be organized to carry out its task of influencing its members for their own good and, given a highly speculative future for the whole race, the good of us all.

2

GALILEE AND BABEL

I HAPPEN TO LIVE on a lake in the Mediterranean part of the world, and ought therefore to have been able to foresee pretty accurately the behaviour of Galilee. I was still surprised by the energy, the symbolic richness and the sheer variety of mood with which it responded to its visitor's subconscious appeal to it to evoke once again that brief but unique moment in its own history that was so vital to the whole world. Its reply was to pass from light rain to brilliant sunshine to a sudden, violent, drenching storm ended by one, single, huge thunder-clap, and then back to sun and to light rain—all within the time it took to order, eat and pay for a fish called a St Peter and take a walk along the shore. It was as if the lake was determined to show all its attributes and feelings and reactions, as well as all the moods that accompanied the preaching, the walking on the water, the fear at the storm, the dangers and the triumphs and the disappointments.

I think more than anything the lake's caprices and gestures were a warning. There is an infinite variety in the interpretation of the central figure of Christianity. The good shepherd came early. But look at the Byzantine mosaics at Ravenna—that odd last limb of the imperial vision in the West—and their grandeur comes from the serenity of a Christ in his heavenly glory, at home and at peace in majesty. The most famous Christ of all, in what might be called Catholic terms, is Michelangelo's vindictive judge in the Sistine Chapel, the very place where the popes are elected, a painting which in my experience grows less convincing and less appropriate the more one sees it.

My impression of Jesus in the Catholic world of the second

millennium is that he has returned to be very human. In the most familiar interpretations for this generation, Jesus is far less a king in majesty or a judge or, for that matter, much of a saint in the conventional idea of sanctity. So much so (or, better, so little so), that a learned periodical, *Concilium*, could raise the issue as to whether Jesus would nowadays be seen to have the qualities of official sainthood. Would the Catholic Church now canonize Jesus of Nazareth, looked at in his purely human attributes and actions?

A much greater question, the answer to which will never be revealed, is exactly what Jesus himself had in mind in the way of an institution for carrying on his work after his death; or whether he envisaged anything specific on the issue at all. Did he really foresee a church, with a priestly caste; with a teaching authority of its own; with the power to condemn and confirm, to sort through ancient manuscripts and decide which were divinely inspired, to devise classifications of good and evil, to organize missions to Africa and Asia; with ranks and functions, and strict orders of precedence among its officials, nationalist affiliations and religious orders; and with a complete, professional vocabulary? 'Bless my soul!' as the youthful Mozart wrote to his cousin:

> a thousand curses, Croatians, damnations, devils, witches, sorcerers, hell's battalions to all eternity, by all the elements, air, water, earth and fire, Europe, Asia, Africa and America, Jesuits, Augustinians, Benedictines, Capuchins, Minorites, Franciscans, Dominicans, Carthusians and brothers of the Holy Cross, Canons regular and irregular, all slackers . . .

Or was Nietzsche right in supposing that Jesus uttered a 'No to all that was priest or theologian . . .'? Did Jesus foresee what we now mean by the Catholic Church? He was at home in the synagogues and knew the Scriptures, but he displayed nothing of the religious professionalism of Paul, for whom the ordering of religion was so much a part of his life and character, first as a Pharisee and then as a Christian. Paul was an organizer and a born berater of the less energetic, the less convinced, less dedicated members of the communities he established. 'I would be miserable,' he says, 'if I could not preach.' Having to preach at all, one feels, must at times have made Jesus miserable, as if it meant that his example and presence were not enough, even for his chosen disciples.

Anyone who has been to Central America must regard that area as one of the test-retorts of contemporary Christianity. Even its shape is right, that narrow, concentrated strip of land between the bulks of North and South America, a kind of waist swelling against a tight bodice. Jesus the man, Jesus the rebel against social injustice, Jesus the liberator are an inspiration there. Yet in El Salvador, the most sensitive and tragic part of this vital area, there is also a lot to be heard about a totally different aspect of Jesus: the 'Salvador' from whom that unhappy republic takes its name is the Jesus of the Transfiguration, the most magical and other worldly incident in his life.

The difference between two versions of Jesus, or a version and a vision of Jesus, is not of course a problem limited to Catholics. The time for the apologists for Catholicism to change their outlook has surely come: more, the time has also surely come to end the whole idea that there are two distinct sets of problems in the world, one a set of Catholic problems and another a group of problems concerning non-Catholics. It has been rather easy in the past for Catholics to hold that no one outside the Catholic Church can ever really grasp what it means. Similarly, many non-Catholics have tended to shrug their shoulders at a certain stage and cease to pry further into Catholic attitudes because they were convinced that Catholicism could not properly be grasped from outside. The truth as I see it is now more complicated and more interesting. Very few 'Catholic' problems exist today that are not shared by believers in other faiths or by non-believers. Moreover, the problems which face the whole of mankind are now so vast that they make no distinction of faith.

The Church is moving the way of the world, but rather faster than the rest of us, and equally reluctantly, towards the turmoil of the Third World. If it can be argued that the Second World is now ready, having had its faith sharpened under Communism, to supply missionaries to the West, the Third World cardinals are quick to tell the West that life cannot go on being lived here at so high and wasteful a rate, and that Europe, because of economic changes and the geographical location of the world's increasing population, has lost its primacy. In ecclesiastical terms, this shift can be seen in papal elections. When Pius XII died in 1958, Europe was still the continent with the largest number of baptized Catholics and this was reflected in the membership of the Sacred College of Cardinals. Of the fifty-five cardinals whose task it was to elect his successor, thirty-six were Europeans—of whom eighteen were Italians—and of the nineteen non-Europeans, five were North Americans and one was from Australia. Hence, only thirteen were from what we now call the Third World and recognize as the world of the future. By the time Karol Wojtyla was elected pope, in October 1978, exactly twenty years later, Latin America had become the continent with the greatest number of baptized Catholics, with Europe lying four percentage points behind. The Sacred College was totally changed. There were fifty-six non-Europeans and for the first time they outnumbered the Europeans, who were fifty-five. And forty-four of the non-Europeans came from the developing world.

Yet Catholicism remains anchored to Europe. Rome is in Europe, and the Church's centre could never move. Moreover, Europe and Christianity, more specifically Europe and Catholicism, are so closely intertwined historically and culturally, that only the severest wrench could part the two, and then not cleanly, into separate functions. I remember being in the great Benedictine, imperial monastery at Ottobeuren in Bavaria at a meeting intended to offer a spiritual backing for European unification. The main speaker was Cardinal Benelli, already Archbishop of Florence but still looked on as the closest adviser of Pope Paul VI. His conviction was simple. Europe would not be united (and he was speaking here more of Western Europe in pre-Wojtyla days) until its spiritual basis in Christianity was accepted. The clear implication was that the wedding, practically the condition of one flesh between Europe and Christianity, had to be nurtured and given back its former strength. A strong Europe would mean a strong Christianity and a strong Catholicism, and this was the fundamental way of looking at all these problems.

This outlook enhances the question of authority, another of those 'Catholic' problems felt by nearly everyone. Could a European revival ever be effective enough to maintain the European stamp on Catholicism? I do not believe so: I do not believe the continent can find that sort of moral authority again; I do not think the Catholic Church could find that degree of disciplinary authority again, and I believe that it would be regrettable if it could. The Wojtyla phenomenon may have given the impression that Catholicism has done just that. The reason I do not think so is because I think that, for the first time in its history, the issue of authority in the Catholic Church has taken a new form. Arguments about authority in the past have been about who rightfully possessed it; the issue now is what the nature of authority should be, and how it should be applied. This subject runs through many different facets of Catholic life, from the disciplining of theologians to the insistence on birth-control, to the idea of what a pope should do and how he should act.

The Catholic Church accepted the need for change when John XXIII called the Second Vatican Council. This meeting of the whole Roman Catholic hierarchy lasted from October 1962 to December 1965, and consisted of four sessions. It was the twenty-first General Council, or Ecumenical Council, in the Church's whole history, according to Roman calculations. It produced sixteen documents of varying interest (the worst on public relations), some 27,000 pages of records, and its deliberations filled about 138 miles of recording tape. Like many other people, I mistook it for the greatest religious event of the century. Something worthy of that name has yet to come. The Council was important in changing much of the style of Roman Catholicism as an institution: it became more open and more flexible. But at this distance in time, it looks like another piece of evidence for the innate conservatism of deep-rooted institutions. When institutions are weak, they cannot change themselves. Reform is too much. When they are strong, they no longer want to—and that applies too to a show of strength.

The years of the Council saw the Church apprehensive about its future and therefore seeking relations with other Christian churches. Yet it was not confident enough to attempt those fundamental changes which would have placed it on a genuinely new course. Now it no longer has to: the crowds literally stampede to be there in the stadium, even die in the attempt. That is not a prelude to change: the swallows are swans and they are a prelude to *Lohengrin*, not a new spring. The institution remains dominated by the interrelation of three elements: the personality of the reigning pontiff, the imposition of rules from on high, and the constant source of mass loyalty—the overwhelming strength and the principal temptation of Catholicism—a loyalty just waiting to be tapped.

The result of the Council's work was to alter internal balances. The Council taught that the pope was not alone in governing the Church but that all the bishops had their responsibility, acting as a college with the pope at their head, ostensibly like the apostles around Jesus. This is the teaching known as collegiality. It did not please the conservatives at all: they liked a strong papacy, which means strong authority at the centre and a strong Curia in Rome. The late Cardinal Ottaviani said that he could find only one scriptural reference to collegial action by the apostles, and he quoted it with attractive malice: 'And they all fled.' Yet the publicity given to, and obviously enjoyed by, John Paul II had even some of the Vatican's arch-conservatives complaining that nowadays they no longer had an inch for themselves on the television screens. Lay people were made to feel important by the Council's definition of the Church as 'the People of God'. The status of the ordinary priest remained least changed, which is one of the reasons why so many of them left the Church in the immediate post-Conciliar years and why many of those that remain are the most confused category in the Church.

I remember an English priest, working in southern Italy, saying to me after the Council that a good result of all the confusion caused by open debate was the dramatic fall in the number of priests. His argument was that only if the institutional Church looked like it was failing completely would there be a chance of real reform. At the moment there is a slight improvement in recruiting for the priesthood.

The presupposition of the Council was the prospect of less religion in the future. That was why the need seemed urgent and comparatively easy to foster relations with other Christians, as well as with the other great religions. Instead, interest in the various religious faiths is growing, with a special increase in popular beliefs, the occult and the sensational. The professionals must have mixed feelings. If they are honest with themselves, they will admit that they have no certainty of controlling these new leanings towards religion. And if they succeed in doing so, the result could be no more than the apt way in which the Chinese describe a pyrrhic victory: generals only win because there are generals on the other side.

I think it was Sir Thomas Beecham who said that the world would be a better place if its inhabitants were forced to listen to a quarter of an hour of Mozart every day. I can see his object in trying to coax mankind from its darker side into the light of sublime beauty. The movement is not that way. There is now a widespread conviction that the world, instead of becoming more human, is becoming less so. It has lost, or is losing, humanity itself. The more hardened we become, the weaker and the less sensitive become the curbs which public opinion should apply. The more that is known about the sufferings of hundreds and millions of fellow-inhabitants of the planet, the less concern there is about their fate. I would not like to try and define evil, or wish to trace its origins to the beginning of the world or beyond. I can only say that there is much more of it about now than there used to be. In Melville's terms: the Claggarts are far outpacing the Billy Budds. I make no claim to any special sensitivity, but I am increasingly aware of a strong reaction inside me towards people whom I feel, on first meeting, to be in some way negatively directed: to have too large a proportion of malice, or envy, or some other defect that disables their personalities. I keep having to remind myself of the dictum of the Christian historian Herbert Butterfield that belief in the fundamental goodness of the human mind is a dangerous and recent heresy. What is happening upholds, sadly, Butterfield's view. Perhaps people are right in looking for protection in religion.

There is a darker side to religion, just as there is a darker side to the human temperament. I do not mean the massacres carried out in the name of religion, the persecution of one religion by another, or wars declared for the sake of religion, though threats of this kind seem to be returning. But in these examples, other factors are strong, such as nationalism, dynastic ambition, aggrandisement, personal sadism. I mean the dark forces that religious feelings —distorted perhaps, but religious feelings none the less—can release in the human mind. It is better not to forget Jonestown. One of the great questions is whether institutional religion is in a sufficiently strong position to face not only a greater amount of evil in the world, but also the unknown factors that religion can release. This is an age that wants gods. It wants reassurance. The Catholic experience of the last few years is a dramatic example of this quest for protection. The phenomenon of the newly powerful papacy is less a question of the personalities of the modern popes and much more the reaction of millions who act as if they had been starved of such protection, and need it.

The shift of weight from the centre to the periphery, the problem of how true authority should be used, the bid to bring ancient institutions up to date to face such surprises as a new type of religious experience rather than an end of religion: these are some of the challenges which Catholicism is facing. And they are perfectly clearly not just 'Catholic' problems.

There is one problem totally Catholic. It is the problem of Rome. This is where Galilee cannot help at all. Nothing can help except an honest confrontation of the real difficulties which Rome continues to bring with it. I spend a lot of time among the baroque splendours of papal Rome. I believe I know its humours. It is one of Christianity's sacred cities; the other is Jerusalem, and between them they crushed Jesus.

I suppose that fate was fitting for a teacher who came, to use the ludicrous phrase of Marx, from 'the idiocy of rural life'. Of course Jesus was fatally drawn by the magnetic pull of Jerusalem. That is understandable. No other city in the world can have been written about with such love and longing and emotional involvement as Jerusalem. Dreamers throughout the centuries have dreamt of taking it for their own, or of building it anew elsewhere, along with a new heaven and earth. Jesus could go nowhere else to die. Luke felt drawn to set the post-Resurrection appearances in Jerusalem rather than in Galilee because he felt it to be a more holy setting.

The magic is fast going. Perhaps it was never really there in Christian terms. One feels in Jerusalem that so much was in vain. Jesus went there. He himself was overwhelmed by the city which, as a consequence, saw the most important events in human history. But there was no mutual impact. So now the Christian keepers of the Holy Sepulchre look as arrogant and mercenary and generally as unpleasant as the temple-people whom Jesus condemned. Nothing remains, of course, of the temple itself (except a piece of wall), which must have been the centre of Jesus's thoughts whenever he went to the city. The Israeli official presence is efficient, severe, not very congenial and much less so after the Israelis built ugly rings of buildings to increase the Jewish proportion of the population, and set up the government's offices in the Arab quarter. The vigorous young Israeli soldiers must be very like the Romans were to the Jews 2,000 years ago.

The Vatican's policy towards Jerusalem has been little heard. They tried and failed to give the city a special status guaranteed internationally. The only body through which the kind of special status the Vatican had in mind for Jerusalem could have been negotiated was the United Nations. But there is now neither interest nor a majority. As a result, the Vatican fell back on a proposal for a form of international supervision of the holy places themselves, whether Christian, Jewish or Muslim. With this went an appeal directed at the Israelis to treat Jerusalem as a city sacred not only to them, and to show special sensitivity in making changes. The appeal was disregarded.

Rome is a different story. It had no direct part in the ministry of Jesus except to supply the form of death which has made the cross the most potent symbol in human affairs. Rome was the historical, not religious, choice as Christianity's future centre. Christianity arrived there when the weight of empire was already heavy on the city. Its habit of mind was authoritarian. It was the capital of a polyglot empire. The Christians increased and gradually became its predominant religious force. It was as far away as one could be from Galilee.

And so the legend has grown that Jesus would have hated it. I cannot say that he would, and I believe a great deal too much has been written of what havoc Jesus would wreak inside the Vatican's offices, if he ever managed to get past the Swiss Guard at the gates. Certainly he was an un-Roman personality, inclined to hint as much as to rant, enigmatic not legalistic. Had he stood trial in Rome instead of simply going through a series of interrogations in Jerusalem, he would have puzzled the Romans. He attempted no passionate defence of his actions. Unlike St Stephen, the first of the martyrs, and so many since, he delivered no final address before his execution. This is the element which surely should be considered more than an outburst of physical violence from him if he saw the souvenir-sellers in the square in front of St Peter's. No one can properly say how Jesus would behave. Without doubt, however, the air of authority, the imperial inheritance, the atmosphere of a pretentious bureaucracy, are an increasing embarrassment. Morally they weigh down the Church's centre with the wrong symbols, when the real strength is now elsewhere. I was in Bangkok when a priest became very excited about his few visits to Rome. He went there occasionally to do business, he said; his business was the promotion of social justice. 'But I cannot stand, I cannot look at', he said, 'those monuments to imperialism. They anger me. Just to think that the obelisk in St Peter's Square was stolen from the Egyptian people. Why not give it back? What point does it have . . .?' He was as angry as the African priest who said that his people, by being converted from Europe, were risking not ever becoming properly Christian in African terms at all. This is no time to alienate the leaders of Catholicism's future masses. Already there are troubles enough.

3

THIS CROOKED AGE

I T IS QUITE absurd to look at the greatest of the world's
institutions that deal with man's spiritual wellbeing and
survival without looking at the same set of problems in an
earthly context. The two levels are too closely related to leave
either one aside. The argument might once have been convincing
that Christianity is so other-worldly a faith that this world,
because of so small account, can be ignored. That is not possible
now, because Christianity itself, certainly a great part of Roman
Catholicism, is seeing more confidently than ever that a vital and
possibly crucial element in religious belief is that it has relevance to
the difficulties of life on earth, especially the problems involving
the suffering poor and those starved of their humanity because
denied justice. This awareness explains why the Vatican established a special commission after the Council, called 'Justice and
Peace', expressly to deal with these aspects of human life in the
light of the Catholic practical conscience. Equally indicative of the
thinking of today is that this commission has found some of its
time taken up with the very real problem, not of peace but of the
danger of an outbreak of nuclear war.

The re-emergence of a strong papacy for the first time in the
modern age—and the first time on this scale of popular following
in any age—brings responsibilities of its own. No pope can
actually be blamed for becoming popular when two factors, over
which no pope has any control, heavily influence the scene. The
first is the greyness of most of the world's leaders. This is not a
time like John XXIII's reign, which looked all the better for being
flanked on one side by Kennedy and on the other by Krushchev.
As an English-speaking cardinal (not, to be frank, very taken by

49

the papacy's present vast popularity) put it: the world's stage was so empty that 'any pope elected was going to fill it.' And John Paul II was not 'any pope': he was a master at leading the crowds where they thought they wanted to go. He was able, as the same cardinal said, to bring out 'the kind of deep longing in many people for reassurance and for conviction and, indeed, for the simple truths of the faith'. It is fascinating to follow how anxiety advances side by side with efforts at finding security: for instance, the revival of popular religion apparently to offset fears of what the inventions of advanced science might do to us. Another well-known cardinal, who may best also remain anonymous to concentrate attention on his words rather than on his identity, made this remark: 'Well, I think something new is happening in the world. I should say the pope appears not so much as the head of the Catholic Church today but as the voice of human conscience. Speaking in the United Nations, speaking everywhere, it seems that there is a sort of attraction to him as being the voice of voiceless people. So that's a sort of new image of the papacy.'

It would be a mistake though to regard John Paul II as simply a figure of bouncing enthusiasm, a papal Pangloss. John Paul II surprised an audience in the early stages of the Afghan crisis by announcing that a group of scientists had reported to him on the effects of nuclear war and had come to the conclusion that a mere 200 of the estimated 50,000 nuclear bombs in existence in the huge arsenals of the Great Powers would be sufficient to destroy most of the planet's biggest cities. In what appeared to be his contribution to the *Apocalypse Now* style of thinking, he devoted much of his homily for New Year's Day to this scientific evaluation of the immediate consequences of a nuclear conflict. The principal findings were that between 50 and 200 million people would die from immediate or indirect consequences of nuclear explosions; resources of food would be drastically reduced because of the radioactive residue in agricultural land; there would be dangerous genetic changes in human beings, flora and fauna; while changes in the ozone belt of the atmosphere would leave men exposed to unknown factors prejudicial to life. Finally, in a city devastated by a nuclear explosion, the destruction of all urban services and the terror provoked by the disaster would impede all help to the inhabitants, creating a terrible nightmare. It was urgent, the scientists had told him, that people should not close their eyes to what an atomic war would mean to humanity. The pope added that such reflections brought the question: can we continue along this road? He was even more cryptic in sketching the world's dangers in his message for Easter 1980: 'You who are building the world of peace . . . or of war? You who are building the world of order . . . or of terror?' He has not let his popularity as a leading figure on the world's stage prevent him from revealing the bad news.

His facts are not particularly surprising in themselves. People cannot help but be aware of the fact that a nuclear war would cause huge destruction and that life would be a miserable business if ever the human race should unleash its mightiest weapons. But John Paul II is usually regarded as a man who communicates confidence: it was poor Paul VI who was inclined to moan and wring his hands in public. His most striking note of warning, far too dignified to be called a moan, was contained in his important Christmas address in 1977 to the Sacred College of Cardinals:

> Dark shadows are pressing down on mankind's destiny: blind violence; threats to human life, even in the mother's womb; cruel terrorism which is heaping hatred on ruin with the utopian aim of rebuilding anew on the ashes of a total destruction; fresh outbreaks of delinquency; discriminations and injustices on an international scale; the deprivation of religious liberty; the ideology of hatred; the frenzied apology of the lowest instincts for the pornography of the mass media which, beneath false cultural aims, are concealing a degrading thirst for money and a shameless exploitation of the human person; the constant seductions and threats to children and the young, which are undermining and sterilizing the fresh creative energies of their minds and hearts: all these things indicate that there has been a fearful drop in the appreciation of moral values, now the victim of the hidden and organized action of vice and hatred.

To return to John Paul II and the threat of war: he was known to be a man who was shrewd in interpreting the feelings of the masses. And so it was a surprise that he should be so gloomy. His mood was confirmed, however, by the Justice and Peace Commission's decision to spend its next assembly looking at the threat of war. There could be no doubt that the Iran and Afghanistan crises had made the Vatican worry about the peace of the world in a way it had not done since the Second World War, with the possible exception of the Cuban missile crisis.

Voices from the past return with a new significance of warning, at least this is so in the case of the Jesuit Father Daniel Berrigan, who served nearly two years in prison for opposing the Vietnam war. He still feels (writing in June 1979 in *America*) that:

> We have found to our dismay that the teaching of our church on nuclear war leaves most American Catholics untouched. That teaching is unequivocal and clear. But somewhere between Rome and the Atlantic coast, the voice of Peter is deflected. On abortion, by way of contrast, the voice is heard. What are we to do with those who are born, if in ten or twenty years the world is reduced to ash?

He says that he turns frequently to the Book of Revelation. He calls it 'the Nightmare of God'; he goes on:

> The nightmare is ourselves. In the eighteenth chapter I read that an angel shouts: 'in a mighty voice, Babylon the Great is fallen'. This must be thought cold comfort. I am not afflicted by a death wish. But if the words are taken seriously, they seem to imply a mighty crisis in history. More, they announce that the utter ruin of the imperial venture is at hand. . . .

Berrigan is lofty, poetic, and heroic, right or wrong, but a convinced and intellectual prophet. He and his brother Philip were among the first of the opponents of the Vietnam war. Both were Catholic priests at the time. Philip left the priesthood and married a former nun. Daniel remains a regular member of the order. But not only the intellectuals have their dreams of disaster: so, too, do the simple. This is the account a young priest working in a dormitory for down and outs in Syracuse, New York, gives in *America* of one of the poor, defeated inmate's dreams:

> Frank says he's got one thousand guardian angels to protect him. His theology has to do with Hell's Angels. Says his sister is married to their president and one call to California and Frank fancies that some one thousand bikes will purr across the continent like swastika'd killer-bees to avenge his wrongs in a flourish of chains and shot-guns. Dream on, Frank.

Another set of problems is certainly connected with the tensions in international affairs that returned so sharply in 1979 and 1980. Premonitions, fears for the future, a sense of impending catastrophe are common in various fields of human activity, from the anxieties of the dying Einstein to horror-comics and the whole corpus of novel-writing about the disasters of the future—and not so remote a future at that. The current interpretations of the classics are a useful indicator. By the early eighties, critics had begun to take notice of the fact that a series of striking productions of *Othello* by London's leading companies all disconcertingly concentrated interest on Iago, not the hero; when Joseph Losey filmed *Don Giovanni* he prefaced it with Antonio Gramsci's remark about the difficulties of living between two eras, as a means of giving the old opera contemporary significance. His point was that we too belong to a troubled era, about to face something that will shatter society, in the way that the French Revolution, which broke out two years after the opera was first performed, shattered the polite but doomed society of the Don. One is left to look for comfort to the dictum of Marcus Aurelius, an emperor who lived in an intellectual atmosphere not unlike our own for certain of its fears and for its sense of suspension between two eras. Aurelius noted down the thought: 'To be in the process of a transformation is not an evil, just as it is not necessarily good to be the product of transformation.'

Clerical commentators have not failed to notice this feeling that man believes he is approaching the end of his tether. This premonition of catastrophe is the principal observation which the Scaloppian writer and publicist Father Ernesto Balducci put to a conference, organized in Florence in May 1979 by the Stensen Institute, on the rebirth of the religious element in contemporary life. He raised the question of whether Europe is facing 'a true and proper cultural apocalypse'. He drew attention to the vital question of whether Christianity is another of those historic forces destined to collapse with the apocalypse or whether it has the capacity to overtake the danger and provide the beginning for a new future. He added the unpalatable consideration (to those inclined to judge a revival of religiosity indiscriminately) that certain leaders of powerful religious movements, such as Sun Myung Moon, inspirer of the 'Moonies', David Berg, founder of the 'Children of God', and Jim Jones, of 'Jonestown' infamy, showed no signs in their earlier lives of moral worth. Rather they showed forms of sexual aberration and sadistic despotism. Their fascination, Balducci said, was not the result of a religious message but of their ability to arouse obscure forces of confusion by expressing them in religious symbols and phraseology. Thinking of them brings back the great phrase of Goya: 'When reason sleeps, the monsters wake.'

The *fuga mundi* had struck Western civilization, Balducci said, as a result of the flight into the irrational, following the failure of technological rationalism to bring or give confidence. There was the return to what was thought to be Mother Nature, the search for surviving symbols of a pre-industrial age, the adoption of contemplative practices from Oriental religions. Some people saw all this as meaning a genuine revival of religion but he, in fact, believes it is not this but something which I personally see as deeply disturbing: the phenomenon he describes is that of the collapse of the anthropological fold on which the foundation of our rational humanism was based. What emerged from the crack was not the need for God as much as a sense of nausea with this world, the resentment of man against the models of life which had let him down. What Father Balducci calls this 'syndrome of historical desperation' is behind the millennial movements, those groups largely of Protestant origin who are daily awaiting the end of the world; the transplantation into Europe of Oriental monastic practices; and the agricultural communities inspired by anti-technological considerations: everywhere, he says, there is refusal of this world and its end is expected.

Strangely, a part of the Catholic Church is going in the opposite direction. The movement is strong for a more practical Christianity: religious are leaving their communities to try and deal with life among the poor and underprivileged. Father Balducci's plea is for an approach by the Church of 'militant hope'.

This idea of a bitterly disappointed humanity is common; so, too, is the conviction that the world is passing through a period of history which marks the end of an epoch and a civilization. Father Bartolomeo Sorge, a leading Jesuit with close connections at the Vatican, maintains that we are living through a cultural transition of hitherto unknown proportions. He edits the Jesuit periodical *Civiltà Cattolica* and in his editorial articles he expresses his opinion that the choices taken today will decide the future course of society for a long time to come. He adds that there is a widely held view that it is no longer possible to run the risk of once again nurturing false hopes. He lists some of the idols which man has constructed in recent centuries only to see them shattered: the myth of the period of the Enlightenment that the god of reason was capable of solving everything; the mirage of unlimited human progress, first fed and then contradicted by the industrial revolution; the self-sufficiency of early twentieth-century nationalism and of the regimes born of the October Revolution; up until the most recent myth of all, that of development, which has ended by generating new forms of colonialism and of oppression while putting humanity on the road to ecological disaster.

This series of shattered hopes might yet, Father Sorge thinks, bring men back to the Church and to Christianity. This Christian hope has its own specific character differentiating it from other human hopes. It is not based on a philosophy or an ideology, nor on human forces alone nor on one social class. Its religious and transcendent dimension cannot be overlooked—in order to make it largely a promise of social and political liberation—without, in St Paul's words, 'diluting the word of God as innkeepers water their wine'. In reality, Sorge argues, we are not Christians because we hope for the end of the capitalist system of production or for the collapse of totalitarian regimes in the East and in Latin America, but we hope for the end of all forms of injustice because we are Christians.

He is strongly against the temptation to do very little and simply trust in God. The gospel of hope is not, he says, an invitation to stay doing nothing while waiting for the end of time but, instead, a creative task of renewal of a world which, because of the injustice and the atheist hopes which traverse it, runs the danger not of truly liberating man but of leaving him to perish miserably in the quicksands of the status quo, against God's design.

Father Sorge believes it extremely important to have and to demonstrate Marxism's measure because that too is a god that has failed. By adopting the complementary role of Christian hope with its critical nature, it is essential, on the one hand, to recognize honestly the real expectations aroused by Marxism and, on the other, to point out the intrinsic incapacity of a materialist and atheist approach to fulfil them. He accepts that the hope of liberation, which Marxism has helped to develop in the world, is in itself true and good, and should not be allowed to end in disappointment. Its deadly error, he says, is in its methods and the solutions which it puts forward. Lacking an integral and transcendent vision of man and history, Marxism gives absolute importance to realities which, in fact, are partial and which, as a result, prove inadequate for a more just and fraternal world. Above all, the inadequacy of the Marxist hope, which pretends to be global, is shown by its tragic silence when faced with the most dramatic human questions including suffering and death.

Fathers Balducci and Sorge seem to me to have a good focus. They have caught the confusions, fears and frustrations, and the conviction that history may well be about to play some giant trick. They both see the danger of spurious religion: it can look like the real thing but is in fact an expression of disgust or despair; it can raise hopes yet again and then dash them, with the likelihood of dramatic consequences. They both see that the Church has a special responsibility to give a lead, and to be clear that its lead is in the right direction. One of the Catholic Church's most authoritative voices saw this state of the world, this 'crooked age' as Peter called it, as one of the principal practical reasons in favour of ecumenism. This is Cardinal Suenens in his book on ecumenism and charismatic renewal:

> This same imperative duty to unite forces itself upon us as we approach the end of the twentieth century, precisely because of the state of our world which, in so many respects, is drifting along aimlessly, despite some undeniable advances. How many injustices and inhuman acts surround us, and what apocalyptic threats are weighing on the future and survival of the world!

A millennium is a menacing thing, with apocalyptic premonitions. Many Christians thought that the end of the first millennium would bring with it the end of the world, and many good people have the same forebodings now, with more rational motives, about what the second one will mean to the human race. The fact that Jesus is now not thought to have been born exactly at the beginning of the Christian era does not detract from the portentous magic of the numbers, just as reasonably clear hints in the Gospels that Jesus was born in Nazareth, not Bethlehem, have not succeeded in making the traditional star of Christmas wane, or the three wise men any less real to the vast majority of the faithful. Few want correction along the road: myths must go untouched.

The New Testament is much less helpful than the Old in suggesting the right mental focus for looking at a change in historical epochs, because of the atmosphere of urgent foreboding it creates. The coming of Jesus is presented as the greatest event in human affairs since the creation of Adam. It must, logically, have shattering consequences. If God became man and redeemed the world, life cannot just go on as before. Jesus himself is partly to blame because he sometimes gave an impression that the effects of his teachings might well be immediate. 'I tell you this: the present generation shall live to see it all. Heaven and earth will pass away: my words will never pass away.'

The much more emotional, drastic, Paul also elaborated a theory of tension, aimed presumably at keeping his followers within the discipline he laid down. The second coming might happen at any time: 'The time we live in will not last long.' He was also plagued by the idea of evil in the world from its very beginning, and the inevitability of evil-doing by everyone, including himself:

> I do not even acknowledge my own actions as mine, for what I do is not what I want to do, but what I detest. . . . For I know that nothing good lodges in me—in my unspiritual nature I mean—for though the will to do good is there, the deed is not. The good which I want to do I fail to do; but what I do is the wrong which is against my will, and if what I do is against my will, it is clearly no longer I who am the agent, but sin that has its lodging in me.

This attitude of seeing evil everywhere has misled people into supposing that Paul has a new and deeper significance for the present crooked age than for any other. It has been said that another Paul is needed to inspire a renewal of the Christian faith amidst this recognition of evil circumstances. With all due respect to the saint, the idea of generalizing sin and evil instead of seeking to identify what is wrong and putting it right, would surely invite disaster.

The difference in Paul's approach raises the intriguing question of whether he and Jesus ever met. It would not be unlikely. They were about the same age and the young Pharisee may have studied in Jerusalem. He hardly ever quotes Jesus directly. He does not talk about events in the life of Jesus, though Paul was very near those events and interested enough in Christianity to persecute its early communities. He met Peter, and James, the 'brother' of Jesus, and the fact that he quarrelled with them should not have so dampened his curiosity that he would have failed to glean everything possible about the earthly contacts of the Saviour he met in the famous vision on the road to Damascus. It has been said that Paul avoided mention of the human Jesus out of respect for the apostles who had actually known him. Intellectually, it could be argued that Paul was not interested in Jesus the man because the whole weight of his teaching is on the consequences of the Resurrection. How much more would be known, surely, if Jesus had written an epistle to the Romans, let alone two to Corinth.

Essentially, the threat which many people see to the future of Western civilization is violence. This violence takes material and moral forms: there is violence to the planet by over-population and by irresponsible exploitation of its resources; violence in the form of the threat of nuclear warfare; and violence as an increasingly normal element in the behaviour of people towards each other, the proliferation of what Conrad, a great if early exponent of the threat from terrorism, called 'the apes of a sinister jungle'.

No pope has far to look for dramatic evidence of these apes and of the sinister jungle from which they come. Few cities have grown so fast and so chaotically as Rome, and this swift untutored urban growth is one of the causes of violence. When it became Italy's capital in 1870, Rome had 200,000 inhabitants. It now has over three million. Between 1951 and 1971, the population almost doubled. Much of the increase was caused by immigration from the countryside around the city and from the poor south.

The cities are blamed, and rightly, for much of the dehumanization that has sent the human race back in the opposite direction from the path of development of the human personality. At their worst, the cities are symbols of the harshness of cement, of loneliness, and of the failure of the system to maintain the promises of a more comfortable life, a more secure future, and recognition for individuals as citizens who matter. Life in an industrial democracy now often means living in an urban anthill. Corpses spread on asphalt somehow reach the peak of human alienation: the murderer who departs—he scarcely escapes because the risk of apprehension is slight—with the roar of an over-exploited engine; the elderly woman pulled down to the ground as she tries to rescue her handbag from a snatcher. The drugged screams from the brothel windows; the constant screeching of the burglar alarms that grow suddenly and stridently, like aural poppies throughout the city at night; the street-cleaner at dawn sweeping cigarette-ends and syringes into his bin; the insistent promise of pornography on the cinema hoardings; the wail of the ambulance siren; the howl of abandoned dogs—these are some of the signs of the city. It is now beyond all comprehension that 'civilization' once actually meant living in cities. The civilized man once found his place in an urban community: an elder of Antioch where Christians were first given that name, a lucky man born amidst the magnificence of Neapolis with the entrance to the underworld a comfortable day's walk away, a boy from Syracuse and lyrically proud of it or, greatest privilege of all, citizenship of Rome, the centre of the world.

The problem is not simply European. The towns of Africa are swelling in the same way. It is true of Latin America too. As the factories settle to work and the traffic regularly blocks the roads, pollution rises like a huge thunder-cloud full of noxious chemicals instead of rain: not the cloud from which the voice of God would ever be heard calling for recognition of his transfigured son. No prophetic voice could emerge from this atmospheric desert. The spirits of the once-revered ancestors cannot talk to the urban poor in the African shanty-towns. The immigrants have cut themselves off from their roots, and their new perplexity turns easily to the knife or the club to give them some sense of still counting as a real person: action itself, even when cowardly and ugly, is a proof of human existence. I can hurt: therefore I am.

This urban future was inexorably traced at one of the most harrowing, disquieting, international conferences that I remember attending. Appropriately, and with a little malice aforethought as well as a sense of the rightness of things, it was held in Rome. The organizer was the United Nations Fund for Population Activities, which has as its Executive Director Mr Rafael Salas who is Filipino and Catholic. His own report put the picture squarely: especially the point that the massive cities in which the human race will be increasingly enclosed (unless the nuclear holocaust comes first) are comparatively new to the human experience.

Around the year 1800, less than 3 per cent of the population of the world lived in urban areas. By 1920 this figure rose to 14 per cent. The proportion of urban populations still formed only 25 per cent of the world's total in 1950. In that period, urbanization was closely related to industrialization, and hence it occurred mainly in the more developed industrial countries. Cities became the centres of economic activity and transport networks. United Nations projections show that urban population of the world has been growing at nearly 3 per cent a year, about one and a half times the current rate of growth of the world's population. But there is a crucial difference between the developed and developing worlds: the estimated annual growth rate of the urban population in developed countries is about 1.7 per cent a year, while in the developing countries it is over 4 per cent. World urban population has doubled since 1950 and seems likely to double again before the end of the century. About 50 per cent of the world's population will live in cities in the year 2000.

In 1950, there were only six cities in the whole world with populations of five million or more, and their combined population was only forty-four million. By 1980, this had risen to twenty-six such cities, with a combined population of 252 million. By the year 2000, indications are that this number will rise to approximately sixty cities, with an estimated population of nearly 650 million. Just thirty years ago, there was in the less developed countries only one city, Shanghai, with a population of five million or more. By the year 2000, there will be forty-five and most of them will be in Asia.

The biggest city of all will be Mexico City. With an estimated twelve million at the moment, it gives an impression of suffocation by people and pollution. There is only a narrow gap between sun-rise and smog-rise. By 2000, it will probably have thirty-one million people. The second largest city will be Sâo Paulo with an estimated 25,800,000, followed by the Tokyo–Yokohama complex with 24,200,000. Shanghai with 22,700,000 will be lying fifth, and Calcutta with 16,700,000 inhabitants eighth, closely followed by Jakarta and Seoul. Even Manila, already something of a nightmare, without even having reached the list of the twenty-three largest cities in 1975, will have 12,300,000 inhabitants by the end of the century. Manila is of course, nominally, an almost entirely Catholic city and already, in the dreadful slums of Tondo, the priests are forced out of the insufficient number of churches to say Mass in the squares because of the press of the people. And by 2000? It does not bear thinking about, any more than does the growing and already very real threat of violence on the streets. I was advised there not to go out after nightfall and after two groups of friends were each robbed at knife-point on two successive evenings, I could understand the warning.

These are aspects of urban life that make the concept of the sacred city seem a contradiction in terms. The problem has already reached one complete stage of development in Western Europe's cities: the first generation is now fully grown of persons born in the slums and shanty-towns which economic expansion brought with it, and which hopes for a better future made more bearable at the start. Those hopes are now past and more illusory than ever because even industrial expansion has gone. Just one example from the United States: statistics giving a rise in unemployment of black teenagers from 16.5 per cent in 1954 to 36.3 per cent by 1978 were generally dismissed as seriously underestimating the real situation, and so the real size of the threat.

Rome itself inspired the most disturbing voice against the effects of unplanned industrial expansion. The tragic poet and film-maker Pier Paolo Pasolini was born in Friuli, in the far north-east of the country, but he moved to Rome and wrote much of his work in the Rome dialect, taking as his own world the slums of the city's periphery. He made it easy for those who wished to disregard him to do so. His scandalous life, his homosexual masochism, his sordid end at the hands of a male prostitute on a piece of waste land at Ostia on the coast near Rome, kept his name preserved in its malodorous reputation. Yet, with sensitivity, he touched the nerve-centres of present and future danger inherent in the condition of abandoned youth. He condemned the levelling process by which even Italians were forced to become products of the same uniform mould, as a result of both the industrialization which had replaced agriculture as the country's economic basis, and the standards of the consumer society that replaced the old peasant values with nothing more than the empty drive for acquisition. He looked back not to a rural age of gold, but to what he called the age of bread, when people had to work hard just to obtain what was necessary for life, whereas now they work to acquire more and more of what is totally unnecessary, and destroy their own humanity in the process.

Pasolini was both catholic and marxist—without capital letters, because the terms were understood by him in the broadest sense—and it was rationally as well as emotionally correct that he should have been a passionate admirer of John XXIII, the pope who came from the peasant world. Pasolini's setting of Matthew's Gospel was his best film and probably the best of any film setting, so far, of the life of Jesus. More gaudy versions have since supplanted it but his film, which he dedicated to the memory of John XXIII, is the best study of the combination of strength and mysteriousness so characteristic of Jesus. Sometime his version will be superseded because interest in Jesus, or the quest for what he was really like, is one of the signs of the new fascination which religion is providing. However, Pasolini's work, of which this film is a part, will blossom with study as an unpleasant, unwelcome and instinctively correct reaction to what has happened in the world as Western civilization firmly places itself on a road leading away from the advance which many people had believed to be inevitable. Technology and the feeling that war had been left safely behind can reasonably be said to have clouded minds to the full force of extreme pessimism that would have been realistic.

If Dostoevsky is to be believed, the very absence of war may have contributed to the dehumanizing process. 'And in what manner', he asks in his diary:

> is present peace, prevailing among the civilized nations, better than war? The contrary is true: peace, lasting peace, rather than war tends to harden and bestialize man. Lasting peace always generates

cruelty, cowardice and coarse, fat egoism and, chiefly, —intellectual stagnation. It is only the exploiters of the peoples who grow fat in times of long peace. It is being repeated over and over again that peace generates wealth, but only for one-tenth of the people, and this one-tenth, having contracted the diseases of wealth, transmits the contagion to the other nine-tenths who have no wealth. And that one-tenth is contaminated by debauch and cynicism.

That too could be applicable to contemporary Western society, with a change in the proportions he gives, after three and a half decades of peace. But, like most prisoners of an uncertain malaise, the West reads its complaints into every diagnosis. Too great a threat of war? Of course. Too much peace? Certainly. And amidst uncertainties of this kind, the real absurdities of what war and preparation for war can mean pass without any particular notice, because they are part of a general ill-being and so escape vigorous condemnation. They are just more growth in the jungle of uncertainties. The Stockholm International Peace Research Institute sought to bring the facts of the cost of armaments more clearly to the public eye by inventing a unit of currency based on the cost of a single nuclear submarine. Slightly more than one is equivalent to all the aid sent to Latin America in 1977; one and a half would cover all the World Bank loans to agriculture in 1978, more than cover all the Third World imports of meat.

'I feel a horrible sense—I wouldn't say of superiority—but of feeling that they're like children playing with matches on top of a keg of gunpowder.' The comment covers the submarine example well enough but it was made in a much wider context: as part of an effort by a leading Catholic demographer to estimate humanity's chances of survival. Father Arthur McCormack believes there could be catastrophe if people show the same sort of indifference to the situation over the next twenty years as they have done, with a few exceptions, in the course of the last twenty. He brings population in early as a dramatic part of the problem. It took the human race from the beginning of time to 1930 to reach a total of two billion people: on present estimates, a further two billion will be added to the population by the year 2000. The difficulty is that the rate of increase is happening in the countries least able to cope with it, in the developing countries, and there the rate of increase is twice or even more what it was in the last century when the developed countries were increasing their population.

He believes catastrophe could be avoided, but in order to do so humanity must concentrate on survival. Where the catastrophic element comes in, he says, is that the nations are not geared to do this. They are engaged in wars and disputes that are not about such matters as the survival of the human race. In concentrating on survival, the human race will have to do many of the things which would be suggested by the sort of humanism, the Christian humanism, which has developed in the Catholic Church since the Vatican Council.

The Council solemnly stated that the joys and the hopes of the human race were the joys and hopes of the Church. Father McCormack feels that John Paul II has seen the broad canvas even if he does not know the details of some of the problems, he has seen that the Church has a motive power to offer the world. Having said all that, he admits that his real worries are whether the Church as a whole will gear itself for this terrific contribution to humanity. And whether mankind will receive it. The pope can speak and there can be very good principles enunciated but the human race must be prepared to listen; not only to the pope, because there are other voices of wisdom as well as voices of warning. Humanity must forget its comparatively petty pre-occupations in front of this huge concern.

Father McCormack is specific on the element of time. He feels that if we manage to get through the next twenty years we may well be out of danger. In the meantime, there is not the leisure to plan great changes in the international order. The instruments must largely be those we have. All you can do is modify: for instance, modify present patterns of trade and then perhaps we shall find in about 1995 that we have a new and better economic order.

The presence of the conference on population and the urban future in Rome in September 1980 was seen by at least some of the delegates as a reminder that a contribution is still awaited from the Church on this whole range of problems. As an institution, it gives far too little importance to population problems because of its teaching on birth-control. Despite the controversial nature of the application of this teaching in modern circumstances, there appears to be little sense in the Vatican itself that change should come, even if the only change were in the way traditional doctrine was enforced. The 1980 Synod, for instance, was remarkable for some courageous speeches on the need to face the pastoral if not the world-wide aspects of the problem. But they went unheard. And the ridiculous, as well as tragic, side of this failure to respond is that the Catholic Church will become increasingly a part of that world which it is unable to help. Essentially, it is at its weakest once the masses which can be called Catholic become part of the cities, just as its sexual teachings provide its heel of Achilles towards modern problems.

There are other contributions, or at least potential contributions. There is the example of an awareness of the problem and a response of providing a pattern of behaviour for others.

> And yet, our world is threatened by two ghosts: poverty and war. There is no way to abolish war unless we first do away with hunger, malnutrition, and the lack of human dignity which proceed at least in part, from intolerable injustice and oppression. In the next thirty years, when the number of human beings will have reached six billion, how will five billion of them put up with being deprived of their natural rights, especially when the number of nuclear powers will have increased beyond control? In the year 2000, if there is no change in present trends, the situation will be much worse. The rich will have grown richer; the poor poorer. The numerical difference between rich and poor and the qualitative difference between their standards of living will have become gigantic. How long can this go on?

The words are those of Father Pedro Arrupe, the Jesuit General, who was addressing the Third InterAmerican Congress of Religious held in Montreal in November 1977. He spoke in his capacity as President of the Union of Superiors General. Calling for a 'conversion to frugality', he said:

> How will they receive our harangues about justice if they see us enjoying a standard of living superior to many of our fellow citizens, if all we do smacks of privilege, if our connections tie us in with the rich, the oppressors, the ruling classes? On the other hand, how will anybody recognize the evangelical character of our message about justice if we set in play guerrilla tactics or violence, urging rebellious radicalism, or corrupting our work of conscientization with atheistic methodologies or ideologies? How will people be convinced that we believe what we preach if they see that we are too cowardly to denounce injustices in the spirit of the Gospel out of fear of reprisals on our persons or our works?

The importance of such statements as these is not confined to the requirements or satisfactions of those who have chosen the life of the religious orders as their vocations. The behaviour of both the clergy and the faithful lay people will have its effect on the whole process of how our world approaches the next one: and the next one does not in this case mean the everafter but the new world on earth which is about to face us all.

Rome has an institution, quite unclerical or ecclesiastical, indeed the opposite, which for more than a decade has sought to make the world aware of the dangers that face it. This is the 'Club of Rome', a group founded in 1968, limited to 100 members and still led by Aurelio Peccei. It acts as a kind of advanced watchdog on the human and ecological condition of the planet. Its tenth anniversary was marked by a fresh declaration to the effect that mankind is striding towards a momentous crossroads where there is no longer room for mistakes, yet with a system so fundamentally wrong that it is unable to provide mankind with its simplest requirements: the minimum necessary for life to all its members, the chance to be at peace with itself and to be at peace with nature.

These are mighty issues and it is only fair to say that the catastrophic, apocalyptic view of man's immediate future does not go without challenge. As far as the papacy is concerned, the attitude has been mixed and has depended very much on the personalities of the individual pontiffs. Paul VI was a pessimist by nature and was capable, especially during the middle years of his reign, of public expressions of fearfulness which contrasted unsympathetically with John XXIII's rejection of the prophets of gloom. John Paul II practically opened his first encyclical with a reference to the coming second millennium, but went little further than to comment that 'it is difficult to say what mark that year will leave on the face of human history, or what it will bring to each people, nation, country and continent, in spite of the efforts already being made to foresee some events.' The papacy is understandably reticent about taking a firm position on some of the questions involved in the Club of Rome estimates because of the controversial nature of its teachings on birth-control and its vital interest in the affairs of the developing world. Europe may still have the central position but it is a centrality of honour, not of fact. That said, the position of the Club of Rome is a notable contribution to thinking about mankind's future, the subject that must also be the Vatican's prime consideration.

The main single problem that the Club identifies is that of over-population, due to modern man's inability or unwillingness to control his own runaway numbers. According to the Environmental Fund of Washington, the world's inhabitants reached 4.4

billion at 3:42 p.m. on 9 July 1978 and every year sees 73 million more people, concentrated in poor countries. By the end of the second millennium, the increase alone in population from now will equal the total population at the time of the First World War.

This pressure is seen to be subjecting the human system to new, unbearable burdens when its condition is already critical. More than a third of the population is living beneath the poverty line and there can be no doubt that a no smaller proportion of its future children will be condemned to share the same fate. Much charitable talk exists about basic human needs, but no earnest drive at the very root of this knot of problems: to eradicate hunger, deprivation and ignorance from the world, once and for all. What an aim! The end of man's material problems, once and for all! The heart grows large and the mind has difficulty in comprehending such a concept. Especially when a more detailed look is taken at the estimate of what is required in purely material terms. Merely to build the physical basis of the human habitat needed before the year 2000 —houses, schools, hospitals, whole new cities, roads, harbours, factories—will require a task of construction similar to the one mankind has so far taken from the Middle Ages to complete. This colossal enterprise is tantamount to founding 'a second world' in two decades; yet lack of foresight will make it impossible while untold new problems and sufferings emerge.

Neither are there seen to be reliable plans or even ideas about how to find work for the 300 million able-bodied men and women currently unemployed; or how to create the 1,000 million more jobs that will be indispensable during the next two decades. Unemployment, always a human tragedy, the report states, particularly for young people, and a shameful blot on society at this macroscopic scale, evidences the shaky foundation of the world order and will eventually bring it to its knees.

The proud industrial nations of the West have failed to discover how to absorb their sixteen million jobless and at the same time check inflation. The usual recipe is given: expand productive investment and raise annual growth to 5 per cent. It should, nevertheless, be clear by now that most nations are up against so many constraints that they find it impossible to apply such simplistic prescriptions. The obstinacy with which the old, ineffectual if not counter-productive schemes are upheld confirms that the entire thought-process needs a good overhaul, even in developed countries, rather than the economic system alone.

The report's broader look at the international arena underlines the reign of that 'great disorder under heaven' that Chairman Mao used to denounce, though this is little cause for wonder. Still rampant is the principle of territorial sovereignty affirmed in the Peace of Westphalia, which, in 1648, brought to an end the Thirty Years War and feudalism. Most things have changed in the intervening three and a half centuries, except man's basic political philosophy. The functional unit of the world polity remains the sovereign national state. Nationalism, dictatorships, militarism and racism thrive in the name of this sovereignty, while the aspirations of minorities are trampled underfoot. This partitioning of the world among introvert, self-righteous sovereign entities, now numbering more than 150, is seen to contrast sharply with the reality of inter-dependence, thus causing the entire system to be ungovernable, and killing the spirit of world solidarity without which there can really be no future. Such a divided humanity can never be at peace with itself.

The syndromes of profound global malaise are described as quite evident. First, the North–South cleavage is widening. It divides the world even more drastically than the ideological and political walls which separate East and West, and, short of radical measures, it will prove unbridgeable. Commanding 80 per cent of the world's wealth and trade, over 90 per cent of industry and services, and nearly 100 per cent of the institutions of research, the North can dominate the world by sheer weight. The South, atomized into more than a hundred economically uncompetitive countries, unable to coalesce stably, is no match for it.

There is not even a real North–South dialogue aimed at doing away with these crippling inequalities. Only the South has defined its position, and that somewhat rhetorically, focusing on the imperative of a more equitable and sustainable international order. The northern democracies instead seem committed to a policy of status quo-ism aimed at averting change by rearguard or delaying action, which, in the long run, is no policy at all. The socialist countries try to keep aloof from any negotiations, as if the reordering of the world system were none of their business. The result is a situation of stalemate which paralyses the human system precisely when concerted action and direction are necessary.

Another pathological symptom is the fact that peoples and nations seeking security are, instead, being lured on by a mirage. The world is transformed into an armed camp and a frantic arms race is spreading from the Great Powers to scores of other countries, including the poorest. The cost of armaments is once again shown in its dreadful bulk: more than 1,000 million dollars a day or, as President Carter more dramatically expressed the painful reality: 'The world spent last year sixty times as much equipping each soldier as we spent educating each child.'

The first chapter of Genesis describes how, after creating man, the Creator immediately gave him his central place on earth, instructing him to replenish it and subdue it, and have dominion over the fish of the sea, and over the fowl of the air, and over every living thing that moved on the earth. Once the earth had been finally put in order, God asked Adam's co-operation in giving names to the various species of animals. The impression is clearly one of human dominance of the planet but it has taken from the Creation to our own day to see just to what extent man can really dominate his planet, and at what cost to his surroundings when he shows insufficient intelligence to protect them.

The Club of Rome has some catastrophic comments on this subject as well. Since *Homo sapiens* emerged, it is pointed out, upwards of 10,000 centuries ago, down to the hundred or so centuries of his recorded history, time and again he has had to face supreme tests and trials. Scores of empires, civilizations, lineages and even races have disappeared from one part of the earth or another. But man, as a species, continued his ascent. Now that he has risen to absolute stardom in the planet, the dangers too are global and can result in the total eclipse of his kind. On the other hand, though, and for the first time, man has the means of becoming almost absolute master of his own destiny.

He is not, however, seen to be behaving as if in any way aware of the huge responsibilities that this privileged position entails. Whether moved by greed or caprice, negligence or ignorance, modern man employs his science and might to kill and corrupt everything that life took billions of years to create and perfect. Even if this wanton and stupid behaviour had no consequences on his own existence, it would remain an insult to his vaunted humanity and will to inflict an irreparable cultural loss on the generations to come.

The West is given the greatest burden of the need to respond to this situation of global emergency. It is felt to have a greater moral duty and a greater direct interest. The West opened the path that held the promise of stupendous developments, and the West now stands out with its unparalleled capacity for mustering up in freedom a formidable wealth of information, knowledge and experience, plus extraordinary intellectual, material and organizational resources. So it has the overriding historical obligation of conceiving and proposing to the other groups a grand design for the future of humanity; it is the West that has more to lose by inaction.

Peccei himself is not totally without hope that the challenge will be met. In terms of optimism and pessimism he is in a similar position to that of McCormack. While talking to me about his report and the whole question of whether it was a case of survival for the human race or not, he said: 'The dangers are extremely high. But the possibility for avoiding disaster is there . . . . We have that possibility. But I think many deep changes must be introduced into human society and its behaviour.' The first and fundamental question was, he said, to understand the present and where the continuation of current trends might lead us. 'If we understand the plight we are in, I am sure that the human mind will find ways out. We have been prevented from understanding the situation because we were intoxicated by cheap petroleum. We believed in the words of economists who were preaching continuous growth. So we were detached from the real world into a make-believe world. I think that today people are wiser. They feel there is some unhealthy void in human society. They don't know what actually has to be changed, in what way and by whom. And so I think there is a general expectation of leadership, of an indication by some body, or some party, or community, or leaders, indicating a way out of the pit we are in at present.'

He sees religious faith as a contribution to solving the world's problems, though he keeps to a distinction between faith and ecclesiastical structures. Many of the churches, he says, like other bureaucracies, are too much rooted in the past. They have not been able to evolve in order to follow changes in the human condition which we humans have caused. But a belief in, and a communion with, the transcendent, he sees as having an enormous part to play. His final comment is on the shift in the basis of Catholicism towards the Third World: 'I cannot say whether this will offer the Church the possibility of no longer considering wealth, pomp, status more important than the true aspects of believing. I don't know, but probably it is better that Catholicism is moving from the rich North into the poorer, more genuine, South.'

A summary of the principal causes of the decline in the human condition, according to the Club of Rome's estimates, was given by Peccei at their Berlin meeting in the autumn of 1979. There are ten, and they serve as a useful indication of what the pessimists feel is going wrong:

1. The steady swelling of the world's population, which, by the year 2000, will be five times as big, and consume fifty times as much, as at the beginning of the century.

2. The practical impossibility of settling decently, employing usefully, and taking care of efficiently, this enormous mass of people. Today almost a quarter of the world's inhabitants live in absolute poverty and distress.

3. The impairment of the biosphere. The four main biological systems sustaining human life (oceanic fisheries, forests, grass-lands and croplands) are all under stress. Desertification threatens one-tenth of South America, one-fifth of Asia and Africa, one-quarter of Australia. Devastation and pollution are widespread.

4. The stagnation and the inflation eroding the world economy. The monetary system is in confusion and industrial civilization itself in question. The shadow of a vicious, unfathomable energy crisis is lengthening over most countries, both developed and developing.

5. That military spending is approaching the appalling record of 450 billion dollars every year.

6. The rampant social ills of injustice and intolerance. Their bitter fruits are growing alienation, social turmoil, civil violence and such degradation as terrorism, torture and genocide.

7. Anarchical techno-scientific progress. It rushes forward ignoring society's prior needs and capacity for absorption, distributing costs and benefits inequitably.

8. That the international polity is based on largely anachronistic, ill-functioning institutions at the national and international level.

9. The absence of real dialogue between North and South, or between East and West.

10. The world-wide lack of moral and political leadership.

On every one of these points, the Catholic Church has a perfect right to formulate views and let them be known, as part of putting forward its claim to moral leadership.

The general outlook contained in the ten points, that the situation is extremely serious yet could be met by some supreme effort, is gaining support. For instance, in February 1980, the international commission presided over by Willy Brandt published its plan of action to avert global disaster; it was on similar lines:

Current trends point to a sombre future for the world economy and international relations: a painful outlook for the poorer countries with no end to poverty and hunger: continuing world stagnation combined with inflation: international monetary disorder: mounting debts and deficits: protectionism: major tensions between countries competing for energy, food and raw materials: growing world population and more unemployment in north and south: increasing threats to the environment and the international commons through deforestation and desertification, overfishing and overgrazing: the problem of pollution of air and water, and overshadowing everything else the menacing arms race.

The report stated that such trends could not only continue but even worsen, though they were not inevitable.

The fact that the Catholic Church is moving (involuntarily but moving none the less) into the Third World gives it an extraordinary advantage. It is becoming less associated with the West while other churches are suffering the effects of the growing split between the developing and the developed parts of the world. Mentally, however, it is still dominated by the Western outlook. It looks at the world through Western eyes as if totally unaware of what has been described as the West's moral poverty.

Alexander Solzhenitsyn has stated that such poverty disqualifies the West from consideration as an acceptable alternative to Soviet tyranny. He sees the West as incapable of attempting anything more ambitious than defending the present situation but, because of its moral weakness, it can do so only by concessions and betrayal. In his Harvard speech, he said:

Western thinking has become conservative: the world situation should stay as it is at any cost: there should be no changes.

This debilitating dream of a status quo is the symptom of a society which has come to the end of its development.

But one must be blind in order not to see that oceans no longer belong to the West, while land under its domination is shrinking.

The two so-called world wars (they were by far not on a world scale, not yet) have meant internal self-destruction of the small, progressive West which has thus prepared its own end. The next war (which does not have to be an atomic one and I do not believe it will) may well bury Western civilization for ever.

Facing such a danger, with such historical values in your past, at such a high level of realization of freedom and apparently of devotion to freedom, how is it possible to lose to such an extent the will to defend oneself?

71

Like John Paul II, Solzhenitsyn is a man plucked from the East to live in the West. This transplantation has a great value. In the case of Solzhenitsyn it allows him to judge both societies by the same criteria and come to what is probably his most valuable conclusion: that the similarity of the problems facing the world is more powerful than the division between East and West: 'This is the real crisis. The split in the world is less terrible than the similarity of the disease plaguing its main sections.' It would be pleasant to suppose that the double focus is simply doubly wrong; that the clash of Soviet labour camps and Harvard must produce an unbalanced picture of the world. Or that the Club of Rome is simply suffering from an excess of post-capitalist conscience about what the West's basic economic system has done in the past. 'Stop these mournful noises!' is a possible answer, and a basic Beethovian belief in the fundamental sublimity of man is a comfort never so needed by the thinking elements of mankind as now.

The question whether there is now any point in being Christian has to be left to the individual to decide. Whether religion as such, and Christian religion in particular, has any relevance to the search aimed at bringing some light to a black prospect, is a less personal consideration, and can be faced with less sense of trespass. It has to be, for two reasons: the first is that the most melancholy of the analysts of our dilemma see a spiritual revival of some kind as essential to the world's salvation and, secondly, there are undoubtedly signs of a revival of religion itself, even if at times it presents itself in disconcerting forms. Religion for most people is not a rational matter. At its highest level, this irrationality is summed up in such concepts as: 'Thinking as God thinks', or the reassurance Jesus gave to the apostles: 'But when you are arrested, do not worry about what you are to say: when the time comes, the words you need will be given you . . . .' Of recent popes, John XXIII came nearest to this style of instinctive wisdom. Perhaps it is the best contribution in intellectual terms that the Church could make, if one could really believe that the Church as a whole is genuinely capable of thinking as God thinks. If not—and this would seem the more prudent course—the Church has to be persuaded rationally to make its own rational contribution to solving mankind's problems.

David had an eloquent experience of the need to reject the statisticians whose work is the basis for any rational approach to those problems. The twenty-first chapter of the Book of Chronicles opens with the words: 'And Satan stood up against Israel and provoked David to number Israel.' God apparently showed such repugnance towards the idea of calculating the number of his chosen people that he ascribed the thought to Satan; but one of the consequences in the Bible story is the building of the temple in Jerusalem. David carried through his idea of the census and God, who had sent him clear enough warnings to do no such thing, at least showed him the degree of clemency of leaving him to choose between three forms of punishment. David settled for pestilence and the punishing sword of the angel. As that is the background to the establishment of Judaism's sacred city, one could hardly find a more eloquent expression of how the sacred emerges from the irrational and the violent.

But the present age can only, in rational terms at least, envisage Satan as saying the exact opposite of what he said to David: something to the effect of eschewing statistics so that the gravity of the situation would be kept away from human calculation. A charming, if bizarre, example of this modern temptation came during the 1980 International Synod on the family, which ought, but failed, to have taken a clear line on the problems of population and sexuality. Monsignor Quinn, Archbishop of San Francisco, summoned up the courage (which later failed him) to rise on behalf of all the American bishops and announce that 80 per cent of American Catholic women used contraceptives, most of them of a type banned by the Church's teachings, and what was to be done about that. He was answered suavely by Cardinal Felici, the ultra-conservative expert on canon law, who said that statistics did not bother him.

Of all the modern popes, Paul VI was the most inclined to feel the presence of Satan in affairs, frequently referring to him as a distinct personage, active among us; apparently quite oblivious of the fact that John Milton used the façade of St Peter's in *Paradise Lost* to describe Satan's domain. Paul's was not a very modern approach to the problem of evil and was condemned in some intellectual quarters as archaic and so meaningless to the contemporary world. But it would be ridiculous if, because old-fashioned names for evil seem unsophisticated, the concept of consciously evil behaviour should be left out of estimates of the human predicament. More so than ever now, because the presence of evil has dominated the twentieth century more than any other, especially in terms of violence. The mindless slaughter of the First World War was followed by the calculated slaughter of the Second, so much so that protests against evil have become numbed just because it is so familiar a part of daily life. The battlefields of Flanders, the German concentration camps and the Soviet prisons have shifted the moral stance of humanity, even if evil is as old as mankind.

Countries less prone to a reversion to cruelty, meaning that they live under more restraints upon base instincts ('It is essential'—to have recourse again to the words of Herbert Butterfield—'not to have faith in human nature'), no longer react to cruelties committed in their name. Ireland is an example—both sides in the conflict. So too is the frequently empty, however high-sounding, reaction to the shocking deeds of the political terrorists. To give a single example: Italy was, to some extent, shocked by the savage kidnapping and murder of Moro, but, apart from expressions of indignation and pointless demonstrations, there was no real reaction equivalent to the horror of what had happened. A matter of weeks later the Italian national football team won a game and the whole of Rome was mobilized to celebrate this victory. Streets were packed with processions of beflagged cars, participation was colossal and knew no laws except to use every lung of the city to worship a distant and insignificant victory. A group of terrorists would have had little chance of remaining undiscovered had a mass mobilization of this kind taken place against them.

Instead, the country that lost one of its two or three most eminent politicians did so in an atmosphere of 'moral amnesia' —this is the phrase of Monsignor Ferreira Gomes, Bishop of Oporto, the only Portuguese bishop to speak out against Salazar's dictatorship. As a result, he spent nearly ten years in exile, much of it in Rome. The more pusillanimous of his colleagues, who failed to support him against the dictator, are now more uncritically happy with the democratic regime than he. Misleadingly gentle and scholarly in manner, he is frank in answering what bothers him most about his country's situation: 'Almost everything gives me the feeling of a signal of alarm.' He adds: 'The real danger that I see for Portugal is that we shall follow the Italian example, and I say this with full respect for Italy.' Without doubt, the strongest moral force among the Portuguese bishops (including the cardinal-patriarch), his outlook is anguished.

The force of genuine moral indignation and the potentially still stronger emotion of real compassion are lost reactions, and so the negative forces increase when they find that the positive elements in human life have no proper protection:

. . . For I could have saved him,
I could have saved him.
He knew it,
even his shipmates knew it,
though earthly laws silenced them.

It is a comment added in Britten's setting of Melville's story of Billy Budd, the good sailor destroyed by a combination of irrational evil on the part of his persecutor and too much rational caution on the part of the officer who, indeed, could have saved him.

When the irrational stirs, the outcome cannot be foreseen. The darkest as well as the lightest sides of the human temperament can be expressed through religion, particularly through religious innovation. The near-collapse of organized religion in this century, under the pressures first of agnosticism then of the consumer society, left the field open for renewal, revival and fresh invention within the half-deserted structures of the old faiths. Already the horrors have shown signs of how religious feelings can quickly go wrong: the excesses in the re-emergence of political Islam, the cruel cults which are not confined to California—these are forces that are perilous to release but impossible to keep fastened below the hatches of human behaviour. And the success and effects of *Mein Kampf* showed that centuries of Christian teaching can be very easily overturned.

The stakes are very high. Few eras can have offered choices of such great magnitude. Some see the present as the first time that the great religions of the world are sufficiently on speaking terms to permit the hope that there might be some degree of co-operation among them in seeing humanity through a critical two decades. Some believe in the prospect of at last reconciling two elements in man's nature that have seemed not only apart but in conflict: the scientific mind and the religious spirit. One is rational, the other only in part under control of the conscious mind. This is a time of religious experimentation and, as far as the Roman Catholic Church is concerned, the experiment has begun at the top, with a totally unexpected and new type of papacy.

The Vatican has what might be described as intimate interests involved in the usual analyses made about man's predicament, apart from the accepted responsibilities of the world's largest religious community. Leaving religion aside for the moment, the Vatican is unique in crossing the line between East and West —meaning the worlds of Communism and Capitalism—and between North and South, or the northern industrial democracies and the ostensibly developing world. In both these areas, the Catholic Church is deeply engrossed in concerns of great significance not only to itself: the effort at seeking working arrangements with the Communist world, the determination to be present with all the old Roman strength in the Third World. However, the pope is in Rome and that is what now matters in so surprising a way. To the average observer of affairs, the likelihood or not of a religious revival, particularly the threats as well as the promises it may bring, is probably not much of a concern. Nobody, whatever their belief, fears or prejudices, can overlook the new phenomenon of a papacy attracting the masses.

Publicity in itself does not necessarily mean power but it offers the opportunity for exercising power. The papacy has always had this opportunity in varying degrees. At its height it was the greatest power in medieval Europe. It has now found a new vitality at a time when fears are widespread for humanity's future and the level of leadership in the purely political world is unusually low. To say the least, it will be intriguing to see what the Vatican has in store for an age newly tempted by, newly attracted by, religion; for an age that may prove as crucial to mankind's development as the time when, five centuries before Jesus preached, the Greeks evolved a rational form of intellectual thought; or the confused period just before Jesus began his ministry; or the birth of Islam; or the Renaissance that saw man's new pride in himself soaring inestimably higher because of the advance of technological achievement.

It is an age where Satan himself still manages to appear on the covers of the news magazines; strange people roam the suburbs and the country railway tracks to chalk on blackened openings of little-used tunnels such phrases as 'God exists'. One feels a sort of pathetic gratitude but also a slight chill along the spine at the thought that there are still those anxious to take such trouble to tell us this. It is an age when an élite feels man to be no longer dependent on belief in either God or Satan—particularly not in Satan, and this brings one back again to the Polish pope:

> When the Devil says in the third chapter of Genesis: 'Your eyes would open and you would become like God,' these words express the full range of temptation of mankind, from the intention to set man against God, to the extreme form it takes today.
> We could even say that in the first stage of human history, this

temptation not only was not accepted but had not been fully formulated.

But the time has now come: this aspect of the Devil's temptation has found the historical context that suits it . . . .

These words were part of one of the Lenten addresses given to Paul VI and his closest advisers by the then Cardinal Wojtyla, Archbishop of Cracow. They make clear that he, too, sees this as a very special era in human history, almost the culminating era. He went on to suggest that we are experiencing 'the highest level of tension between the Word and the anti-Word in the whole of human history'. His election showed another side of how that era is approaching its difficulties; through what might be called the Wojtyla phenomenon. That phenomenon is complex. It includes not only a tremendous gift for dominating crowds but also an unexpected inner awareness, at times a highly sensitive pessimism, about the dangers facing mankind. John Paul II expressed this is his second encyclical which deals (I think for the first time in a solemn papal document) with the subject of God's love. He published it on the first Sunday in Advent of 1980. 'In fact all of us living now on earth', he says, 'are the generation that is aware of the approach of the third millennium and that profoundly *seals the change* that is occurring in history.' He closes with an appeal to those who believe differently from him in matters of faith 'at least to understand the reason for my concern. It is dictated by love for man, for all that is human and which, according to the intuitions of many of our contemporaries, is threatened by an immense danger.'

I never feel like applauding him when thousands of people are doing so around me. I did when I closed his *Dives in Misericordia*.

4

THE TWO DYNASTIES

IT IS A surprisingly short leap from fears of the end of the world to the book-filled study of a grey-haired priest in Amsterdam, who was sitting behind a large teapot amidst his scholarly confusion and saying: 'Believe me, the whole Vatican means less to me than the individual soul of one of my parishioners.' He confessed to having forgotten the name of the nuncio, the pope's official representative at The Hague. Clearly, this priest's world had come to an end. And it was the Vatican that had done it to him. This man had a high reputation as a pastor, especially among young people. It was about ten years since I had last seen him and I was saddened to see a good man so embittered, so changed from the thoughtful optimist of a decade ago who deeply believed in the efforts of Dutch Catholics to rethink their religion in terms of modern behaviour. Rome had put a stop to those experiments. This is not the place to decide whether Rome was right or wrong. It is the place to point out that Rome is unexpectedly powerful still; and that travelling in the Catholic world gives a fresh burnish to Rome's rod of authority.

The temptation if you live in Rome is to underestimate the importance of the capital of Catholicism for that 18 per cent of the world's population that theoretically owes its allegiance to the papacy. As far as the Vatican is concerned, familiarity does not breed contempt, but it gradually whittles away at any belief that such a strange little organization—and it is amazingly small —with its peculiar ways and massive pretensions can really exert so much influence. In canon law, the writ of the pope as Bishop of Rome is 'supreme and full, immediate and sovereign' over the whole Church. There are efforts aimed at making this legal definition even wider. For years now, a group of jurists in the Vatican have been working on the text of a kind of written constitution for the Church, known as the *Lex Ecclesiae Fundamentalis*, and that has a phrase which would specify that the pope's power extends 'to all the particular churches and their associations'. But even this is not convincing: not if you are in Rome. The *Lex* is the brain-child, surely, of Cardinal Felici, who is considered a shrewd if rather excessively cynical conservative, witty and amiable but a little ridiculous because of his passion for electronics and high-fidelity, even recording ceremonies in which he takes part so that he can see himself, so they say, played through on his own television set.

This is the way in which Rome cuts people and itself down to size. Like any other institution, the Catholic Church's headquarters claims increasing respect the farther away one is from it. The Vatican, moreover, has the defects as well as the advantages of a unique electoral system which suddenly places a single individual at the head of what is both an organization and a huge community. In Rome he is not only bishop but technically at the head of a staff administering the whole Catholic Church—the Roman Curia is supposed to be there simply to assist the pope—of which he is also head. There is no other post in the world that calls, ideally, for so great a variety of talents including, if possible, a genuine holiness. He will know too that the scepticism of the Romans will not be shared by much of the Church throughout the world. Most of the comments one hears about Rome from outside it are enthusiastic and sometimes very revealing.

I was in an elderly, converted fishing-boat called *Seaquest*, which was as Conradian as its name suggests. So were the surroundings on a torrid day of early summer, anchored off one of the islands of the Palawan peninsula. This was typhoon country, shark territory, still patrolled by pirates and, for a time, by 'boat-people' seeking sanctuary. One of their boats stood rotting on the beach of a neighbouring island. The inhabitants of this marvellous meeting place of the tough Chinese and the generous Malay temperament are kind and hospitable and, being Filipinos, almost entirely Catholic. They spoke no English. I asked a friend to ask them for me if they were in fact Catholic. There are still tribes in these islands who follow the old animist ways. There was no reply, just a puzzled failure of comprehension. I told him to put the question in another way. If they do not understand what a Catholic is, ask them what religion they are. The reply was prompt and proud and even I could understand it: 'Romanos!'

A priest in the southern United States saw John Paul II's authoritative presence as the answer to the confusion of ideas and beliefs among American Catholics. He was deeply worried about the effect the Church's hesitations and confusions were having, especially on the youth. With a dramatic gesture he said: 'Do you know what we look like here to young people? A bunch of fakes . . . .' And then he provided his own proposal to sort out American Catholicism. 'Buy John Paul II enough prime television time to explain to American Catholics what we are supposed to believe. He will convince us all.' The proposal was prophetic. John Paul II went to the United States in the following year and the television time was his. But prophecy does not necessarily mean effect. What the pope largely succeeded in doing in America was to reiterate doctrine, without touching the real problem of how to adapt doctrine to the realities of the American scene.

An African bishop made what sounded like a conventional remark: 'We knew how much we loved Paul VI when he was dead.' That sounds like, and was delivered like, the typical judgement of a Roman prelate, whose black face in no way detracted from his Curial manner, right down to the smile and the fussy way of arranging his white cassock as he took his place at his desk in the hot atmosphere of his study. He had religious objects on his desk like those on sale in shops around St Peter's, and was disturbed only by the onslaught of tiny mosquitoes. But his remark was a reminder that universality can have its superficiality. What he said placed his respect for Paul VI in the context of the cult of the dead which is so strong a part of the African temperament. In fact, he went straight on to talk about his ideas for seeking some way of incorporating into African Christianity the traditional habit of making sacrifices to dead relatives, who, most probably, were all the more loved once they too were that slight remove away, which is how many of his faithful visualize death.

The connection with Rome has strengthened since Paul VI made travelling an essential part of the papal office. The idea of travel was attractive. More people would see the pope but, much more important, the pope would know more about his followers, their problems and their achievements. In practice, these journeys have been one-way affairs. People have seen the pope, cheered the pope, joined the crowds to be present at a Mass celebrated by the pope: Paul VI was nearly assassinated in the Philippines, and this too, if paradoxically, made the excitement even greater, presumably because of the subconscious enjoyment of a martyrdom before one's very eyes. Only when John Paul II went to Turkey was there no sign of public enthusiasm. Islam is still the predominant religion in Turkey, even if the country is officially a lay state. To judge from the coldness of the reception at the airport, the government itself did not want a papal visit at the time. John Paul II accepted this situation because of his anxiety to meet the Ecumenical Patriarch of the Orthodox Church, who can claim a loose degree of loyalty from the family of Eastern Orthodox Churches, and who has his modest seat in one of the poorer areas of Istanbul.

In terms of power and authority, Rome has been the gainer from the papal habit of travelling, rather than the Churches in the countries which the two travelling popes have visited. Indications come from the strangest places. I saw a letter from a small community of nuns in Manila replying with a polite but proud refusal to the official request from the organizing committee for the projected papal visit to the Philippines for a financial contribution. Not a few deeply devout Catholics had come to the conclusion—which the nuns shared—that they would be better off without a papal visit. They gave two reasons. The first was that the country was ruled by an authoritarian regime—the famous 'conjugal dictatorship' of President and Mrs Marcos—and the papal presence could only strengthen a ruler intent on and shrewd enough to exploit fully such a visit. Secondly, the Catholic Church in the Philippines is at a delicate moment in its history. A part of it is determined to shake off the old image of an acquiescent prop to the rulers, whether Filipinos or, as in the past, Spaniards or Americans. Their fear was that the pope would have his preordained public success but that his known social outlook might well put out some of the lights so recently and painfully lit.

Elsewhere in Asia his presence would have a different effect. I happened to be in Bangkok in May 1980 when the Thai bishops were meeting in their National Conference. Thailand is of course an essentially Buddhist country: the king and queen are devout Buddhists and carry out religious duties expected of a head of state. Relations between the authorities of the Catholic Church in Bangkok and the royal house are good. But the fact remains that Catholics make up less than 0.5 per cent of the population. They do not have the almost total predominance of Catholics in the Philippines. They suffer from the problem that a real Thai feels Buddhism to be an intrinsic part of being Thai; just as the tiny Muslim minority in the Philippines is doubly difficult to deal with because its members cannot feel that they really belong to a country which is Catholic. In terms of relations with Rome, this means that the Filipinos can allow themselves the luxury of doubting whether it would be advisable to have the pope come there; for the Thai Catholics a visit, even a brief stop, helps them immensely in terms of local prestige. And for the same reason, the regular visit to Rome every five years—the *'visitatio ad limina apostolorum'*—is something very important to them. Yet the Vatican administration can at times seem to be dominated by the need to organize the pope's journeys.

The Thai conference took place while John Paul II was winging his way through black Africa, and one of the items on the agenda was what action the bishops should take, having received no answer from the Vatican to three letters sent about arrangements for the *'ad limina'* visits due to take place that very month. These visits are obligatory but mean a great deal because it is a chance for a small episcopate of ten bishops to feel part of a huge whole. The visits involve calling on some of the Congregations to make their reports and, usually, an audience with the pope. It is a symbol of the Roman Church's world-wide unity. They decided not to write again until the Vatican had answered their other letters. They felt neglected but not alone: one of the bishops said that the Indian and Indonesian bishops were meeting the same problems. The pronuncio in Bangkok could provide no better explanation than that the papal Household department worked under great pressure these days. This neglect of distant pastors who work in frustrating conditions also reduces the credibility of a pope's declared belief in the theory of collegiality. If they cannot manage to penetrate the Curia with their letters about visiting arrangements, they can hardly be expected to feel co-responsible for the Church's government. The Thais finally arrived in November 1980.

And the Thai bishops would of course like to see him in their country to feel support for the new tasks they are attempting: agricultural co-operatives, leadership courses in rural life, collaboration with Buddhists—all this marks a notable evolution in Catholic affairs which is not without its dangers given the nature of the regime. Sometimes the choice of where a pope goes can be as difficult as the choice of the places he must avoid. The small communities gain the most, not least because the visit can be kept reasonably intimate. For instance, apart from the men carrying machine-guns, the atmosphere in the Catholic church in Istanbul was very stirring when the pope visited there.

Popular enthusiasm for the papacy is now part of modern life. Symbolically, St Peter's, for all its bulk, is for the first time in its history too small for what used to be one of its principal purposes. Twenty years ago, the usual way to see a pope was to attend an audience in St Peter's. Then Paul VI commissioned a special hall for audiences from the Italian architect Nervi, giving at one and the same time the Vatican's first modern building of real interest (whatever happened to the idea of the popes as patrons of the arts?) and a warning that the spectacular side of papal behaviour was to be enhanced. Despite his own failure to establish a relationship with the masses, Paul VI had a remarkable flair for sensing developments in the mass-consciousness of his followers.

The pope was to become increasingly a showpiece, and so the world's biggest Christian church (anyone with doubts on the matter need only look at the lines across the huge nave which show to what point other famous churches would reach if placed inside the pope's basilica) would be too small. John Paul II had to abandon the basilica altogether for several months in the year because the crowds at his weekly audiences grew to the extent that scenes of violence broke out among ticket-holders expecting to find a place. And so he took to using not only the audience-hall but, on the same day, the vast square in front of St Peter's, and transferred the summer audiences to the evenings in order to try and avoid regular dislocation of the city's traffic.

This popularity is not just fortuitous, not just part of a far-flung tendency to form a crowd, applaud a well-known personality, wave and cheer, seek spectacle anywhere that it can be found, grasp at branches of blessed palm in St Peter's Square like the tense, old woman who, suddenly aghast at seeing her own hand empty, reached out desperately to snatch the nearest she could find in the packed crowd around her. This element is there; the square on Palm Sunday now looks like Birnam wood come to Dunsinane as thousands perform this ritual beneath the murmurings of spring. Hysteria alone explains little, however; it must be said that the modern papacy has produced a series of remarkable men.

The popes since the last world war fall naturally into two dynasties. Three consecutive popes were elected from the ranks of papal diplomacy, the élite among the Vatican's civil servants. This is not to say they were alike. It is like saying that they all went to the same public school. As individuals, they were very varied. Pius XII, who was elected just before the outbreak of the war, moved upward from the post of Cardinal-Secretary of State, or head of the whole organizational machinery of the Vatican, after earlier having been nuncio in Germany. He was quintessentially Roman in the sense that he typified the Catholic, titled upper-middle class of the city that had tied its fortunes to those of the Vatican and not to Italy. He was small and thin, with an intense smile and the perfect features and movements of an experienced high priest. If anyone talks of the priestly caste, Pius XII was the exact example. He looked the embodiment of regal formality, especially when taking part (and this is the test of the true high priest) in private ceremonies with only his cardinals present; the movements rather stiff and the smile seraphic, like some priest-king about to ascend with delicate tread the steps of one of those Mayan sacred pyramids, towards some intimate, lofty altar invisible to all but him. He personified hierarchical religion as much as Catholicism itself. He could have been the Dalai Lama just as well as the pope—or a Sarastro in *The Magic Flute* with the bass notes transposed for a counter-tenor—and one had the faint suspicion that he knew this. He loved crowds and took some sort of electric charge from the cheering and the shouts which at that time were enthusiastic enough but also compact enough to be accommodated with reasonable comfort inside St Peter's. History has already given him a label: that he was too reluctant to condemn Nazi atrocities against the Jews and too ready to draw up the forces of the Roman Catholic Church against Communism. This anti-Communist passion won from Stalin the famous deprecation: 'How many divisions has the pope?' A leading Italian diplomat recalls how he was received, as a young officer, by Pius XII as the war was drawing to a close. The pope asked him whether he was a Catholic and, hearing that he was indeed, asked him what he thought about the condition of the Church. The young man replied that he felt his own Catholicism to be so much superior to Communism that he could see no point in making public condemnations. The pope was angry. As he aged, this perfect model of the institutional holy man grew increasingly remote from his court and his advisers. When he died, a large German nun who had looked after him was unceremoniously sent away from the papal apartment with the cage of canaries the pope loved so much.

Pius XII was succeeded by John XXIII who was one of the most popular men of the twentieth century—perhaps the most popular of all, not in the sense of mass emotion but of love mixed with a feeling of gratitude. He was a diplomat too, of sorts. At the time of his election in 1958 he was Patriarch of Venice but he had spent all his life in the papal service abroad if not with great distinction. He in fact ended his diplomatic career as nuncio in Paris, an important post which he handled skilfully, but which he had not expected to be offered. When he told Cardinal Tardini, then Secretary of State, that he was surprised at his appointment, he received the frank answer back: 'And so was I.' He was then sent off quickly to Paris to claim the deanship of the diplomatic corps as an urgent matter, because the honour of conveying New Year wishes to the French government would otherwise have fallen to the Soviet ambassador.

His diplomatic experience had shown him something of the world. Equally, if not more important were his origins, which were deep in peasant Europe. That civilization is now nearly dead. Industrialization and the flight from the land by young people, strongly encouraged by the policies of the European Community, and the failure of the Church itself to protect its own values, have ended a way of life which lasted centuries. It was often harsh, frustrating, with ugly aspects of subjection; and human existence had to be lived too close to unsympathetic nature. At its best, however, it produced virtues which will now be lost with it. They included dour insistence on what had to be done, daily satisfaction with a day's work, trust in the supernatural to balance the vagaries of the natural, and an awareness of the supra-national, because this way of life did not stop at national boundaries. These were not only the origins of John XXIII, but also the areas of Europe where religion maintained its strongest hold. Cities are not made for religion; not even sacred cities: the Catholic Church quite incredibly ignored this truth while the post-war flight from the land was taking place and has since found no sure way of dealing with urban realities. Blake sang of a Jerusalem built among dark, Satanic mills; the prospect is more probable than the discovery in good time of a means for bringing a close religious feeling to the thoughts of an ordinary city-dweller whose human sensitivity has become as distorted, hardened, darkened as bodily organs by pollution. Suddenly, as the city grows, the cement enters the soul and any concept of such a scene as the Transfiguration departs not to the realms of unlikelihood but to a place light-years away.

John XXIII was an optimist. He lived in a temporary moment

of hope. His other great contemporaries were Kennedy and Krushchev, both, in their own ways, full of promise. His robust frame and quick step invited confidence. He was not a modernizer. He was not an innovator. His style was old-fashioned, out of date and exactly right. He had an extraordinary sureness of touch. His great concern was that the Catholic Church should throw off the state of torpor in which Pius had left it, be in a condition to rise to the great opportunities before it, discard the crabbed and cobwebbed character as well as the one-sided slant in international affairs. He was loved but did not seek popularity. Applause during his speeches made him irritable. He never tried to arouse crowds by oratorical prowess. He used no actor's skills. He wanted to say what he had to say without interruption. He was convinced that the Church urgently needed renewal but he sought to avoid any impression of presumptuousness.

He gave two reasons for not accepting an invitation to attend the Eucharistic Congress held in Munich in 1960. One was that Christ, not the pope, should be the centre of a Eucharistic Congress. The second was still more personal: West Germany was divided equally, in terms of population, between Catholics and Protestants but real power in what were still the times of Konrad Adenauer was largely in Catholic hands; so, John said: '*Non dobbiamo trionfare troppo*', a warning against too triumphant an attitude. His presence there would have brought him an easy victory but he did not see the need for it.

Demagogy is now so much a part of life that within a few short years John's approach has become a thing of the past. It has already been made to look old-fashioned. That does not mean that he was wrong. It would be difficult to find a statesman whose judgement was as sound; he was remarkably instinctive in the way his mind worked.

What can be described as peculiarly evangelical about John's approach was his habit of deciding by intuition, which only a man very confident of a degree of divine guidance can afford to do. He was not a step-by-step man. He saw unity with another church when he was talking satisfactorily with its leader. This is in the 'I am the light' tradition rather than that of institutional construction. At that moment, when the two men talked, unity was achieved. It might be, it would be, lost again later, but it had happened and might be recuperable.

John took the greatest decision of any pope this century by calling a General Council. The reason was because he knew that the Church urgently needed renewal and that he would not have the time to lead and complete the process. So he felt that the Church should be made to put its own self in order. There had not been a Council for over a century. He said that the idea to call one suddenly came to him and he, just as suddenly, accepted it. Similarly, when Tardini, his Cardinal-Secretary, died, John chose his successor from among the faces of the cardinals gathered for the funeral. Not before. He also expected from others the same readiness to respond. John was free of obsessions: the nearest he came to this was the severity with which he insisted on discipline from his priests. There is no indication that Jesus shared this view, or indeed that he regarded his disciples as priests in the sense of a separated caste. In general, nevertheless, the training John had given his mental faculties came unusually close to the methods of the teacher whose vicar on earth he claimed to be. This explained a part of John's appeal: he was convincing, not just professionally impressive. So did the confirmation he gave that there is no need to be either modern or traditionalist, advanced or reactionary to be loved and respected.

Nor indeed to be a foreigner. John was an Italian, like every pope from the early sixteenth century until the election of Karol Wojtyla in October 1978. He was more the product of the sub-Alpine peasant civilization than specifically Italian but, to be fair to the nation that claims him, he showed that an Italian was perfectly capable of doing everything that people for years had said would have to await the advent of a non-Italian to the papacy. Much too much can be made of the nationality of a pope. Arguably, the first Italian pope of modern times was John's successor, Paul VI, who came from the same latitudes of northern Italy but in practically every other way was different from John. His accent was notice-ably northern but he was not constricted by his native background in the way that the quintessentially Roman Pius XII was; nor did Paul's mind have the broadening experience of emerging, as John had done, from a type of life that was common to a large part of Europe, from Italy across to France, or as far as Poland for that matter. His outlook was only permitted to broaden as a result of a somewhat academic if encyclopaedic knowledge gained during a lifetime of working inside the Vatican's Secretariat of State. Except for a few brief years of exile as Archbishop of Milan, Paul spent his entire life within the sacred corridors.

Yet it was he who had to face the greatest challenges of all. First, he steered the Council to its end and then devoted the greater part of his efforts in the course of a long reign to maintaining the unity of the Church, which might well have suffered schism had he driven it too hard in one direction. This inevitably reduced the impression of determined leadership and gave unfair prominence to cases on which he made up his mind and was wrong. The classic case was his reiteration of the ban on artificial methods of birth-control, a decision which a wiser man would have left open, as a matter in doubt, rather than risking the obvious criticisms of having shown too little humanity and awareness of the pain he would cause.

This was not yet the greatest challenge: that was to come at the end of his reign. Paul VI became the first pope to face the full horror, in a personal way, of modern violence. Aldo Moro, the Christian Democrat leader, was kidnapped by terrorists in Rome in March 1978, held captive, and then murdered with a circle of bullets around his heart that left him twenty minutes to drown in his own blood. Moro had been a close friend of the pope before his election and afterwards consulted him frequently on what he was doing. He needed to: Moro's life's work was political conciliation and the day he was kidnapped he had reached the historic step of bringing the Communists into the parliamentary alliance supporting a Christian Democrat government.

No pope has brought more dignity and grief to a problem emblematic of modern life than Paul with his appeals to Moro's captors to free him. He wrote his final appeal in his own, neat hand; just a few brief lines in which he implored the 'men of the Red Brigades' on his knees to release his friend. *L'Osservatore Romano* published a photocopy with, evidently, an instinctive feeling that the single page would eventually be seen to be one of the most important documents of the reign. Then, having called for help in vain, he went to his cathedral of St John Lateran and publicly upbraided his God for having failed to hear his prayers. A vicar can occasionally talk back to his master and, on this occasion, Paul did so to great effect. It was the one act of rebellion of his reign—and the best. The crowds acknowledged this and suddenly and belatedly the dying pontiff understood what it was to be moderately popular.

He may have had another consideration in mind in appealing so strenuously to the terrorists. There was a strong Catholic element in the original leadership of the 'Red Brigades'. Renato Curcio, usually regarded as the most important of the founders of the far-left wing of the terrorist movement, was given a Catholic education, as was his wife, who was killed in a gunfight with the police. They are not the only ones, and the first few months of 1980 saw two conferences in Italy on the connection between the Catholic outlook and terrorism.

The lives of these three popes in the dynasty of diplomatists are recounted fully enough elsewhere. The object here is simply to draw attention to the vital aspects of their reigns and personalities, to suggest which way the papacy was going in the period before the arrival of the second dynasty—that of the John Pauls.

That the three were remarkable men in their varied ways is clear enough: sufficiently so to give them credit for a contribution to the great expansion in the power and potential of the modern papacy. Pius XII suffers from being the last pope before the great renewal inaugurated by John: the man on the wrong side of the era of change. He is certainly more difficult to accept than his successors because he was a more remote, obscure figure. He had brought the papacy to a dead end; a monarchy marked by immobility, not very relevant to the violent times of war and its aftermath. His doubts were better than his decisions.

John has the place of honour because his judgement was so impressive. Oddly, the efforts at having him declared a saint seem ill-suited. The process of canonization, with its inevitable professionalism (counting the miracles, hearing the witnesses, considering the case against), is wrong for him. Not because he fails to be as saintly as others who have been canonized, it is just that his saintliness needed something more in keeping with his own character than a long, bureaucratic enquiry by the Vatican. Something which lacks the immediate and the spontaneous looks inappropriate for John. Pius XII is also a candidate for official sainthood. It will sit him well. He helped prepare the way, with his claim to have actually seen Jesus in a vision.

Having said that the papacy gained in strength under these three men, a near contradiction must be added: under them the office headed in the clear direction of relatively less prominence within a reawakened Church. That may seem like casuistry: to speak first of the qualities of these popes and then write off their work as a downgrading of the office. That is not so. Pius XII was a high priest and actually the only pope to use the prerogative of infallibility since its definition as a dogma in 1870. He declared the bodily assumption of the Virgin an official teaching to be believed by all Catholics. But he was also cut off from the world. In his last years he had withdrawn from dealings with a large part of the

Curia and could not be said to have been administering the Church in any modern sense of the term. His remoteness had taken him beyond such matters. John was too old and too ill to do so, but he took the imposing step of calling a Council. Paul carried out the Council's teaching on the co-responsibility of the bishops, as a college gathered around the pope, in governing the Church. The papacy was still what it was, according to this teaching, but changed relatively by having this frame of bishops built around it. John was widely loved; Paul was not, until the end and then there was a release of feeling about him from the Moro affair to the day when his coffin lay, pitifully alone, on the steps of St Peter's beneath that massive façade, awaiting its simple burial. Yet the move with all of them, for different reasons, was towards a less prominent place for the papacy within the Church's own structure. Then came the two John Pauls and a sudden collapse of what looked like the road to the future.

Charity must have its place, even in papal elections, and charitably it could be argued that the election of Albino Luciani as Paul's successor fitted in an inspired way the pattern of a less prominent papacy and a more pastoral pope. 'The choice', Cardinal Hume said after the election, 'was the choice of the Holy Spirit.' There is a faint touch of truth to this assertion, in the sense that Luciani might have been history's man of destiny instead of being forced to hand over that title to his more colourful successor. He was almost what the moment required. He had been only a priest and a bishop throughout his whole career which ended, like John's, in Venice as patriarch, before his election. Apart from that similarity, he had had a totally different experience from the three diplomatists who preceded him. He had never been an administrator. He was not a thrusting person: he was inclined to hide rather than reveal his qualities. 'There was more in his shop', as one of the late John XXIII's friends summed up Luciani, 'than he put in his window.' This was Monsignor Loris Capovilla, the former private secretary to John XXIII, and he added: 'Luciani for instance could converse perfectly well in English, you know, but he was too timid to do so.' Moreover Luciani was supposed to have been open-minded on the question of birth-control. 'We would', in the words of a Catholic demographer, 'have been home and dry if he had lived.'

Others felt from the moment of his election that a mistake had been made, because whatever his qualities, revealed or concealed, they were insufficient for the huge responsibilities that faced him after Paul's difficult and crucial reign. He scarcely survived a month, yet in that short time something momentous began to be felt; something that could only have been guessed at during the final few months of rising popularity enjoyed by Paul VI at the close of his pontificate. Proof of the revival of popular feeling for the papacy was dramatic.

True, Luciani smiled a great deal and this seemed like a relief after the stern and anguished look of his predecessor. He had taken the clumsy double name to show his attachment to the policies of his two predecessors, but he immediately showed himself to be different from either. He had none of John's sturdy self-confidence, or Paul's intellectual style. The smile was not one of joy, but of nervous tension. He is said to have been appalled when he found the papal table piled high with papers requiring decisions from him, and it was also said that members of the Curia increased his sense of isolation by constantly insisting on the amount to be done and the urgency of it all. Luciani lacked not only the competence for such things but also the barrier which an effective secretary can provide. One of the strengths of John XXIII was the capacity and the dedication of Loris Capovilla, who has also seen to it that John's memory is kept fresh.

From the second speech Luciani made from the balcony of St Peter's, he became a favourite with the crowds. His apparently spontaneous remarks, which were of no great substance (with the exception of his remark about God as mother rather than father), were eagerly awaited. His style of the simple country clergyman had enthusiastic receptions. It was much less spontaneous than it looked, to judge by the rather contemptuous attitude of some of the Curia prelates. I was told he spent an increasing, almost obsessive, amount of his time preparing his 'spontaneous' sayings for the people, almost as a refuge from the weighty affairs to which he should have been attending, but for which he did not feel equipped. His public confession about knowing nothing about the administration of the Church was well received. With ordinary people he could do no wrong. This attachment to one seen as the odd man out instead of incumbent of the palace helps account for the rumours that he did not die naturally but was poisoned.

The Vatican itself contributed to this suspicion of something sinister by its blundering versions of the circumstances of his death. The finding of the corpse was ascribed to two different people. There were various versions as to what he was reading in bed when he died. One statement was to the effect that he died turning the pages of Thomas à Kempis's *Imitation of Christ*; another that he was looking at notes of a speech he was preparing, or perhaps even one of his 'spontaneous' remarks for the next audience. And then there was the peculiar prelude to the poor pope's death. Shortly before, he had received in his private library the Metropolitan Nikodim, Archbishop of Leningrad and Novgorod, who was in charge of the Russian Orthodox Church's external relations and who had stayed in Rome after Paul VI's death to meet the new pope. He did, and fell dead in front of him. And so, the satirists were able to pretend that, *Hamlet*-like, there had been a confusion of poisons and the Metropolitan had taken the poisoned coffee prepared for the pope, so giving him a few more days of life. In fact it was known that Nikodim had suffered from heart attacks. And then a disturbing medical history emerged about Luciani to accompany the decision of the Sacred College not to perform an autopsy. All this is worth recounting only because it recalls the uncertain atmosphere surrounding the papacy just before John Paul II triumphantly took up the reins. There was something in the air that spawned strange stories, but it in no way detracted from Luciani's popularity.

Long after his death, people kept pictures of him. Sometimes they were apologetic: 'Oh, yes,' a White Father in Africa said, rather diffidently, about the little photograph of the late pope on his desk, 'someone gave me that . . . .' No doubt someone had also given him a photograph of John Paul II in the meantime, but it was not in evidence. Even so, the full awareness of what was rumbling beneath the surface at the time of the first John Paul's death was still unclear. The diminished papacy was about to become a thing of the past, swept away by a galloping arrival from the East.

The winged hussars of Poland were an élite corps of noblemen, romantically active in their country's tormented affairs from the sixteenth to the eighteenth century; a life-sized effigy of one, proudly sitting on his horse, dominates a room in New York's Metropolitan Museum. They regarded themselves as direct descendants of the much more ancient Sarmatians. These nomadic tribesmen, to quote John Paul II's own description of himself on the day he became the first Pole to be elected pope, came from 'a distant country'. In fact, their geographical origins were the steppes between the Black Sea and the Caspian. Much more important was that the Sarmatians, with their scale armour and long lances, introduced to Europe the concept of the heavily armoured horseman who, in time, became the knight of medieval chivalry, a race that may be said to have finally become extinct when German tanks in the Second World War effortlessly swept aside the Polish cavalry. The Polish pope has been compared with King Arthur. His manly assurance, his disregard of caution, his archaic view of woman as a mixture between the Devil and the deep blue Marian perfection, give him something of the spirit of medieval knighthood. One of the most able prelates in the Curia, who was promptly given a high position by John Paul II, saw his new master in a medieval setting. He described him as sharing many of the characteristics of Thomas Becket, particularly as portrayed by T. S. Eliot in his dramatization of the saint's life.

Much has been said and written about Karol Wojtyla that is superfluous or misleading. He was first, or extremely unusual, in so many things, that the tendency is to look on him as a totally original phenomenon. Not only the first Pole to become pope, but the first pope from a Communist country, the first non-Italian for so long, the first modern pope from a residential archbishopric with no experience of work in the Curia (if one excepts the short-lived John Paul I), the first comparatively young pope in modern times, the first to arrive late to the priesthood, instead of being destined to it from childhood, and the first with genuine literary gifts that regrettably have too often failed to survive the efforts of his translators. All this is undoubtedly remarkable and so is a good deal more about him. More pregnant than all these distinctions was the reaction of the crowds from the very beginning of his reign. Any blame attaching to the Wojtyla phenomenon must be shared.

As I have said, he was not working from a totally stationary position before beginning his sprint; an urge to make the papacy popular was there before his candidature was thought of. The first John Paul was also the first to reveal the depths of the need felt by Catholics, and non-Catholics as well, to have a pope whom they could applaud and cheer, and who they could feel would some-how give them new confidence. American understanding of this need was extremely impressive. After the death of Paul VI, a group of American Catholics, for the first time, exercised the right to claim a hearing about the sort of pope they felt the Catholic Church needed. It was not surprising that the first such move should have come from the United States. The country is by far the most religious-minded of all the great industrial nations, and of other large countries only India is ahead in the importance placed on religion. American Catholicism has also seen a massive increase in the demands from lay people for a say in the affairs of the Church. Yet no one could have supposed that the Americans would have foreseen, with such accuracy, the sort of pope who would indeed be the first to satisfy popular demand (and there is no evidence at all that the conclave that elected John Paul I actually took popular American requirements into consideration). The American demand was for 'a hopeful, holy man, who can smile', and that is exactly what they got with the first John Paul.

This demand was put forward at a press conference held a matter of yards from St Peter's by Father Andrew M. Greeley on behalf of a committee 'for the responsible election of the pope'. The mood at times was light-hearted, as in the job description that Father Greeley outlined: 'Interesting work, guaranteed income, residence comes with position. Protection from proven security organization. Apply College of Cardinals, Vatican City.' He went on to explain, more seriously, that a careful sociological study of the 'top leadership position in the Roman Catholic Church' suggests that the qualities to be sought in a new pope are not so much characteristics of training or background as characteristics of personality and style: 'The job description for the papacy is a job description for the man who not only leads the world's largest religious denomination but who is far and away the most important leader on earth.'

No pope smiled more in so brief a time than John Paul I and whatever he said, the crowds applauded. Certainly he had some attractive qualities and the most outstanding one was a kind of bewildered innocence, as if he still could not quite understand what had happened to him. He gave a sense of security, not because he himself gave any impression of feeling secure, but because people could feel that he was one of them, not a distant hieratic figure like Paul VI or Pius XII, nor even a man of such unapproachably shrewd goodness as John XXIII. The applause came easily, too easily. There is an ancient recording still in existence of the great Italian comedian Petrolini, who delivers a speech as the Emperor Nero to the Roman crowds. As he speaks, they interrupt him more and more frequently with applause and, at each fresh outburst, he thanks them. As he goes on, he finds that he does not really have to say anything in order to have their applause and so he says less and less except to thank them as they applaud more and more, until there is nothing but applause punctuated with a frequent, staccato 'thank you' from Nero.

One had the impression with John Paul I that he need do very little indeed to win the enthusiasm of his audiences. His bright-eyed smile and the curl inevitably falling from beneath his skull-cap, directly tapped the stored energies of enthusiasm waiting to be released. When he died, overwhelmed by what had been thrust upon him, his face was set and serious. The saddest thing of all about the corpse was the pair of red, papal slippers, still showing almost no signs of wear. His reign of thirty-three days was profoundly instructive. First it showed the public mood. Secondly, it buried the notion of a small-scale papacy.

It is hateful to talk about gullibility, the urgent need to demand too little, the passionate desire to feel minimally safe, as the outcome of what, for many, modern living has come to mean. However, it is hard to see what else there is if we refuse the total condemnation of Solzhenitsyn: 'After the suffering of decades of human violence and oppression, the human soul longs for things higher, warmer and purer than those offered by today's mass living habits, introduced by the revolting invasion of publicity, by television stupor, and by intolerable music.' One would like to think so but is there more than a small minority that would give up its disgusting music or alienating television to find things really higher and warmer and purer than these instruments can offer? The over-estimation of the potential of human nature is not necessarily a mistake but the inflated vision of what the average person, at this stage in human history, will happily settle for is, alas, mistaken. There are now very, very few lofty aspirations. This soliloquy is not intended to suggest that the election of the Catholic Church's first Polish pope was a gesture of despair. It was an act of courage.

Knowledgeable commentators have attempted to convince us of how the little-known Cardinal Wojtyla suddenly emerged as the principal figure in Christendom. For all rational purposes, it is sufficient to say that he was elected pope after the failure of the Italians to agree upon a candidate among themselves. If the Italians had been in a position to put forward a strong contender, they could once again have carried the day. They were split and the likelihood of their being so had been foreseen by those cardinals in favour of an end to the long unbroken series of forty-four Italian popes. The brief reign of John Paul I had shown that the need was for a popular man without ties in the Roman Curia, and in obvious good health, so that the papacy's standing would not again be diminished by a sudden death. The courageous element was that the cardinals were willing to overlook what many people thought was an essential preliminary stage in the shift away from an Italian pope. This first step would be some uncontroversial candidate from a politically neutral country. Despite all the political dangers, a cardinal from Eastern Europe was chosen to break the Italian line.

The choice was immediately endorsed by public opinion. Too soon. Few people had supposed that the pope from the East would spring fully-armed with all the attributes of a powerful pontiff, filling—or rather, in the manner of Becket after he had been made Archbishop of Canterbury, over-filling—the post as if in an effort to allow no iota of its weight to be lost. Whereas Paul VI had made a sometimes anguished defence of papal prerogatives, John Paul II brandished them with assurance and vigour.

From the moment he began his reign he was self-assurance personified. Some people like to write books about the secret agreements made during papal elections, how one candidate is chosen in preference to another and what the effect will be on the Church. That is not a field I would want to enter. There must surely have been, however, widespread agreement at the conclave which chose John Paul II that, above all, the Catholic Church needed taking in hand, and that its long period of unease, confusion, experiments, of doubts and discussions, to say nothing of defections, which began with the later years of Pius XII and culminated in the Vatican Council, had now to be brought to an end. There is a hard side to Wojtyla's character that the cheering crowds cannot notice because he is himself at his most human when he is in the midst of cheering humanity. The blue eyes can turn very icy, however.

The first time I noticed this sudden freezing of the pope's features was during one of the journeys. As the aircraft was returning to Rome, the suggestion was made that the pontiff might like to talk about his impressions of the visit just concluded. He stepped into the main cabin accompanied by his press secretary, without any general warning and without any attempt at imposing some rules of behaviour on the journalists, who were fairly naturally excited to see him. The only ones prepared were the Italian radio and television operators who blocked the aisle and also the view for most of the rest of the cabin. The pope said a few words but could not continue because of the shouts of protest from farther down the cabin from people who could neither hear nor see him. A woman journalist shouted, 'This is not democratic!' The pope stopped; the eyes froze and he said, in a by no means pleasant tone: 'People who cry for democracy in this way do not know what democracy is!' And then he went back to his own cabin. This rather heavy-handed idea of discipline was well evoked by a monsignor of the Curia when I asked him what sort of a reign he thought this would be: 'Short back and sides,' was the reply.

That is more accurate than the constant harping on his Polishness. I never heard anyone blame Paul VI's mistakes on the fact that he was Italian, yet he was very Italian indeed. Most people who insist on how Polish John Paul II is usually mean that they do not agree with what he is saying or doing and find that it is easier to blame him for being Polish than, for instance, talking an unconscionable amount about the Virgin Mary, insisting on the old disciplines of Catholic marriage, of a celibate priesthood, and of the proper place for women in the life of the Church. Awkwardness is not necessarily Polish: Chopin is music's least awkward composer. Nor for that matter is the element of virile self-discipline which John Paul personifies. A Catholic diplomatist summed this up with the comment that John Paul II was the first pope whom he had seen who did not give the impression of being made of plastic.

The Polish influence which was strongest on him was probably his conviction that the Church could only perform its task when united. He was a model of loyalty to his own primate, Cardinal Wyszinski, when he was a fellow-cardinal widely supposed to have different views from those of the older man. He deferred to him in public. He was the embodiment of the unity of the Polish bishops on all public issues, a unity which assured them a position of real strength towards the Communist authorities. It is known that Cardinal Wyszinski convinced him to accept the papacy and it appears that Wojtyla's fear was that his origins in a Communist-ruled country might bring political difficulties and divisions to the Church. He was not the type to take such matters lightly. It is also a known fact that as his votes were rising, his friend Cardinal König, the Archbishop of Vienna, was sitting opposite him at table and raised his glass of white Frascati wine as a symbol of good wishes for his election. Wojtyla replied with a black look.

He is a closer of the ranks. No Italian likely to have got himself elected (the only rational Italian choice was in fact Benelli) would have pursued this course so relentlessly. Both his harsher side and his disciplining of what he felt to be divisive elements in the Church appeared in his celebrated suspension of the right to teach of Father Hans Küng, the Swiss theologian who taught at Tübingen. I remember Küng during the Vatican Council, when he was one of the most famous of the advisers present who helped shape the thinking of that group of liberal European bishops —French, German, Dutch, Belgian, Austrian—who dominated the Council and brought to it a vision of a genuinely new style of Church. They achieved something, but far from all of what they wanted.

After the Council, Küng remarked to me at his home in Tübingen that he thought Paul VI made a good pope because the need was to de-mythologize the papacy and, just by being there, Paul VI did so. It was not a kind thing to say about a painfully tormented pope but the meaning was clear. A pope shot through with doubts, a personality unable to make an effect on the masses, an insecure pope, would help the process of reducing the papacy to a post of no more than first among equals. It should be less evident and less surrounded by a purely historical (and not scriptural) mystique. I was having supper with Küng in Rome after John Paul II's visit to Mexico. On 20 February 1979 the pope had told the Latin American bishops at the Puebla conference how he saw the papacy. Speaking about Catholic unity, he said: 'It is unity around the Gospel, the Body and the Blood of the Lamb, and Peter living in his successors, all of which are different signs, but all of them highly important signs, of the presence of Jesus among us.' I asked Küng what he thought of that. His reply was: 'near blasphemy'. These two encounters summed up for me all that I had been thinking over the years of what was happening to the papacy, and, at the same time, what was happening to the Council and the aims which I attached to it.

I would add something else about that Rome meeting with Hans Küng. At this stage I do not think it is a betrayal of confidence. He was obviously deeply disturbed about the new course in Rome. He had given a press conference earlier that day in which he had made some criticisms but in general had been very loyal and, above all, had sought to explain the importance to him of being a Catholic. He was his usual able self but subdued. I found out why during supper.

He felt that he must speak out publicly about what he disagreed with in Rome. He said quite simply that he had no wish to be the constant critic. He did not want to be back in conflict. And he asked what consequences he could expect if he publicly attacked this hyper-popular pope. He was immediately told (not by me) that he should not do such a thing because he would be running dangerously against the current of popular opinion and would thus be very vulnerable. I confess to having said little because I could see no other path for him but to say what he felt he should, but I did not wish to be so craven as to stimulate a dangerous course of action in someone who was far from spoiling for a conflict. He did what I hoped he would do. As the first anniversary of John Paul II's reign arrived, Küng published a heavy attack on the new directions. It was widely publicized: I saw it in the *New York Times*, the *Frankfurter Allgemeine Zeitung, Le Monde* and in the widely read Italian weekly *Panorama*. The attack was harsh but not unanswerable. In fact, a sincere reply to Küng at that point would, I am sure, have been of the utmost usefulness, revealing the Vatican's position on the fundamental issues which were worrying Küng, and showing at the same time that a diversity of opinion expressed in the framework of a loyal discussion was still possible. The reaction of many Catholics though, lay people as well as prelates, to some of Küng's more challenging notions on the Church was that 'nothing was sacred', forgetting as the narrowly devout or the professionally committed tend to do, that everything is sacred.

New Year 1980 brought the Vatican's ban on Professor Küng's teaching, declaring him to be no longer a Catholic theologian. He had not been given a hearing in Rome. He had on several occasions been instructed to come to Rome and defend his ideas, but had refused. On the grounds of the methods of anonymous examination and the refusal to inform him fully either on the charges against him or the identity of his accusers, he preferred not to accept the invitation. His reply to the ban was bitter: he compared his situation with that of the Soviet dissident Andrei Sakharov, who had been exiled to Gorki shortly before the Vatican published its ban on Küng. The clash between pope and theologian was sharp indeed, fed probably by the fact that they have similarities of character in certain sensitive fields. They are both physically impressive, easily able to command popularity, histrionic in manner, self-assured, astonishingly good linguists and happy to give an impression of modern combativeness on the part of the Church. Küng was condemned because of his teachings, especially on infallibility. The timing, nevertheless, must stimulate the suspicion that the attack on John Paul II delivered in October 1979 was influential in bringing about the ban.

Before leaving this encounter between two of Catholicism's most heavily armoured knights, it is fair to give two of the main points Küng made in his own defence after the ban had been issued. On the position of the pope, he said:

> I have continually spoken out for a genuine pastoral primacy in the sense of spiritual responsibility, internal leadership and active concern for the welfare of the Church as a whole. It would of course be a primacy, not of dominion, but of unselfish service, exercised in responsibility before the Lord of the Church and lived in unpretentious brotherliness.
>
> It would be a primacy, not in the spirit of a Roman imperialism with religious trimmings, such as I came to know quite closely under Pius XII during my seven years of study in Rome: but a primacy in the spirit of Jesus Christ, as it was illustrated for me in the figures of Gregory the Great and Pope John.
>
> They were popes who expected, not servile submissiveness, uncritical devotion, sentimental idolization but loyal collaboration, constructive criticism and constant prayer on their behalf: collaborators of our joy, not masters of our faith, to adopt a saying of the apostle.

The second principal point is a reminder that the Church has made many mistakes in the past and could quite well be making another one now. He rejected a 'totalitarian conception of the truth' and listed some of the 'momentous' errors for which the institutional Church has been responsible.

> This list is immense and includes the excommunication of the Ecumenical Patriarch of Constantinople and of the Greek Church, prohibition of a vernacular liturgy, condemnation of Galileo and the modern scientific world-picture, condemnation of Chinese and Indian forms of divine worship and names of God, the maintenance of the medieval secular power of the pope up to the First Vatican Council, condemnation of human rights and particularly freedom of conscience and religion.
>
> Finally in the twentieth century the numerous condemnations of modern historical-critical exegesis (with reference to the authenticity of the books of the Bible, source criticism, historicity and literary genres) and condemnations in the dogma field, especially in connection with 'modernism' (theory of evolution, understanding of development of dogma) and in very recent times Pius XII's cleaning up measures (likewise dogmatically justified) leading to the dismissal of the most outstanding theologians of the pre-

conciliar period, such as Chenu, Congar, de Lubac, Teilhard de Chardin who almost all became council theologians under Pope John . . . .

The controversy summed up in this clash of two impressive men is disturbing. Either one takes sides, passionately (which is neither my business nor inclination), or one is tempted to see in it, given the massive problems facing humanity as a whole, another case of playing with matches on top of a keg of gunpowder: and that is said not only with full respect but perhaps with too much respect, because this temptation comes from a feeling that Catholicism could play a great part in the planet's affairs if it could make use of its very real strength. And to that strength, the strength must be added of a papal style which is different in more important ways than nationality or conservatism or popularity.

Like Becket, the first Polish pope gave the impression from the beginning not only of being intent on stretching the role to the point of straining its every seam, but also of being perfectly able himself to do other jobs with every success, and this was another of the crucial differences between him and the other popes of this century. He could quite easily be imagined as a great business manager, for instance, or a successful politician in the American tradition of serious and extrovert vigour. With all the other popes, the only question was what sort of pope they would make: it never entered one's calculations to think of them as trying their hand at something else. The difference in Wojtyla's case was due, in part, to his totally different background.

He was born in May 1920 at Wadowice in southern Poland at a time when his country's newly won independence (which it was to lose again while he was still a young man) was marked by revival in religious as well as political enthusiasm. His father was a non-commissioned officer in the Polish army and the family belonged to the modest middle class of state servants in rural Silesia. The mother was a pious woman and gave Wojtyla his first religious instruction, including an altar at which he prayed as a child in a white tunic that she made for him.

He was only nine when she died, and his father was frequently away on military duties, leaving Karol and his elder brother alone to look after themselves with help from neighbours. He was clever at school, and popular none the less. He showed literary talent and an ease in learning languages. In this, too, he was unlike other modern popes who were in the habit of giving the impression of being much more polyglot than in fact was the case. Wojtyla from the beginning was an excellent linguist. He expressed his flair for writing in poetry and in scripts for underground theatre companies, but his world was in the widest sense dramatic as well as sad.

He began university studies at Cracow in 1938 and had completed only a year and a half when the Germans invaded Poland and closed all academic life. He took work as a miner at Zakozowek and, later, in a chemicals factory at Solvey in order to escape deportation. This experience allowed him, later in life, to tell audiences of workers that he knew at first hand about their needs.

In 1941 both his elder brother and his father died. This must have been the gloomiest, as well as the most obscure period in his life. He emerged from it determined to forget his abilities as an actor, which would have promised him professional success, and ready to ask his bishop to allow him to study theology for the priesthood in the clandestine courses organized under the Nazi occupation.

This background suggests that there was a more lonely, probably darker side to his character and his faith than would be imagined from his spectacular handling of the crowds that regularly block Rome's traffic around the Vatican when he gives his audiences. One of the great examples he held up to his priests was the Polish Franciscan Maximilian Kolbe, who died in Auschwitz after volunteering to take the place of a fellow-prisoner—a married man with a family—who had been included by the Nazis in a group to be killed as a reprisal. Kolbe was beatified and Wojtyla spoke frequently about him, invariably with deep feeling. In 1971, the year of Kolbe's beatification, Wojtyla recounted, as a reply to priests in doubt about their vocations, what Kolbe told the camp-commandant of Auschwitz. Fritsch was astonished that a man should wish to take the place of another sentenced to death, and asked Kolbe who he was. The reply was simply: 'I am a Catholic priest.' Wojtyla went on to say, after the beatification in St Peter's: 'It is not enough to admire him amidst the glory of Bernini. We must ask him in the secret of our hearts, what he has to say to each one of us personally.' These words explain why one of his most characteristic beliefs is in a highly disciplined priesthood. It also shows a side of him that balances his performances with the crowds, because it is more intimate and personal and has nothing to do with a trained actor's technique.

That technique brought him much obvious satisfaction. During his first Roman summer the city had to contend with 800 motor coaches bringing fervent tourists every week to his Wednesday audiences. He could handle them with a conscious skill unknown in the papacy and unreachable by any politician of his day. He gave the feeling of confidence from his first public appearance as pope. This was the opposite impression to that which had proved so popular in John Paul I, and was one of his strengths with the crowds from the moment of his investiture. The very first words in Eliot's play about Becket are these:

> Here let us stand, close by the cathedral.
> Here let us wait.
> Are we drawn by danger?
> Is it the knowledge of safety,
> That draws our feet
> Towards the cathedral?

The answer to the question is perfectly obvious: Yes. Those busloads seek a sense of security; a person strong enough in his own beliefs to lend his strength to others. A little later another question is posed, and answered, about the impending arrival of Becket that raises some other issues of relevance to what has been happening these days at the Vatican:

FIRST PRIEST:
> Does he come
> In full assurance, or only secure
> In the power of Rome, the spiritual rule,
> The assurance of right, and the love of the people?

MESSENGER:
> You are right to express a certain incredulity.
> He comes in pride and sorrow, affirming all his claims,
> Assured, beyond doubt, of the devotion of the people,
> Who receive him with scenes of frenzied enthusiasm . . . .

The power of Rome would, in any case, mean something rather different for a non-Italian pope. Italian popes would know the city's faults and qualities more intimately; would have already adjusted to its failings and impositions; would not expect miracles of it; would have accepted that, as a diocese, it is probably the most complicated in the world because it actually includes the seat of the Church's central government.

A Pole would naturally feel closer to the power of Rome and its glory, for Poland is a fervently Catholic country, with a history of invasions and division, as well as a tradition that the archbishop-primate held the political power during the periods of inter-regnum, which were frequent because Poland used to be, like the papacy, an elective monarchy. The relationship throughout the millennium of Christianity in Poland was an intimate one between the nation, its religion, and the visible centre of that religion which is Rome. The motto of the winged hussars was '*Pro Fide Rege et Lege*'. The city can be no more sacred to anyone than to a fervent Pole, but it can bring its problems, too.

I began this chapter with the comment of a grey-haired priest in Amsterdam whom I had met after an interval of ten years. After I had drunk a cup of his strong and stimulating tea, I asked him what he felt about the situation in Holland, and I shall not forget his reply nor the cold despair to which this very thoughtful man had been reduced. At that time, the pope had not yet summoned the Dutch bishops to Rome in an unprecedented special Synod which ended predictably with their reduction to discipline. They accepted the Vatican's objections to what still remained of their experiments after the Vatican had broken the unity of the Dutch Bishops' Conference by appointing two traditionalists as bishops, one was Adriaan Simonis to Rotterdam in 1971 and, a year later, Joannes Gijsen to Roermond. Of the two, the first is certainly conservative and unchangeably so, but a pleasant man. His appointment brought at the time some applause from the strong body of Dutch Catholics—the experimentalists were always a minority—who saw in him a bishop who would now and again say no. Gijsen is not only extremely conservative, way out in Lefebvre territory, but also very difficult temperamentally. Until December 1975 the Dutch bishops had at their head the highly intelligent Cardinal Alfrink. He retired and was replaced by Cardinal Willebrands. The situation was now totally different. The bishops were divided four against two with an unpredictable primate. Willebrands retained his post as head of the Vatican's Secretariat for Christian Unity. With a foot in both camps, he had insufficient time to deal with either his work at the Curia or the Archbishopric of Utrecht. In addition to which, his long years in Rome had, in the eloquent words of an English prelate, 'rotted his foundations'.

The grey-haired Amsterdam priest said: 'We had the illusion twenty years ago that the Catholic Church in the Netherlands

—the Christian Church in general but more the Catholic Church —was able to make a profound contact with the new culture. Catholic people in Holland are people of emancipation and twenty years ago we had a very creative minority, in the social sciences, psychology, history, sociology, in journalism and also in theology, much more so than in England. We had a much higher level of theology than Catholics in England. And we thought we could reform the Church to a very profound Christianity, a reformation of all the people, including simple people. It was the genius of our bishops, and first of Alfrink, that we had a college of bishops favouring change. But ten years ago this evolution was broken, vehemently, from above and for ten years Dutch Catholicism has been a tragedy. There is despair. There is a flight of intellectuals and of simple people. There are public conflicts between the bishops. It is an immense, immense tragedy. Everybody has his personal reaction to this tragedy. I know the 30,000 people of my parish: many I know personally. They know me. They spread out before me the history of their souls, of their despair and of their hope.'

He poured more tea from the large teapot and went on: 'It is an immense tragedy and, in its way, I suppose, a comedy. No man has any more confidence in the bishops. Simonis and Gijsen are objects of emotion for many young people, objects, I would say, of hate. The other bishops have to remain, for necessity, closed. To be only diplomatic. No longer spontaneous. Alfrink was not spontaneous but he was super-intelligent. One of the most intelligent men I have ever met.

'The Vatican's theology is very closed. The supreme norm is obedience. It is not freedom in revelation. I think the pope is very good for Poland but I think he is not a realistic leader for Western culture. He is psychologically more open than Paul VI and attractive but it is an illusion to expect from this pope an intelligence able to grasp Western culture. People may have their illusions and are free to do so. I do not agree.

'We have much suffering in our Western culture. Britain, Holland, other countries, are full of people who cannot accept life or death, cannot realize love and cannot transcend their daily affairs. In this our world the priests are free to work but for me the institutional side of the Church has little importance. Yes, it is a tragedy. But the way of finding God for many people is independent of the Church's political evolution. My attitude is that God is present with the suffering, with the poor (not only the economically poor), and for the rest I am rather agnostic. Each year I have to accompany to the grave ten or twelve people who have ended their lives by suicide. I celebrate a requiem. I offer prayers, comfort friends and help the parents. All this is difficult to understand. I have just preached a sermon of forty minutes at the Eucharist on the subject, yet to me the final reason remains inexplicable. For me it is a normal experience to talk to young people about how to continue their lives or to accompany them to the grave. Some thirty years ago the number of young suicides was much higher among non-Catholics. Now both in Germany and in Holland there is no difference.

'Because I am an old man, and old in the priestly task, I have a personal parish, people who come to find me, who are marginal people. Some may have become physicians, captains of industry, but in their private lives many of them are marginal men. Many of them between the ages of thirty and thirty-five have broken marriages. Men of thirty-five who are unfaithful or homosexual have the same problem of solitude. Much solitude. And so they too are marginal. A man who wants to make an end to his life is marginal. My work is filled, filled with these people. A young man may finish his studies well. Yet, after five years I find him in a psychiatric hospital. He, too, for the rest of his life will be marginal. They do not want to be priests these young people. They will not give their confidence to a church in a state of moral tragedy. Each year about ten young men out of between four and five million Catholics decide to become priests. And even these ten are not of the old quality. Perhaps one or two, no more. All this is an immense tragedy. I feel that in the list of the priorities of God, the Church has the last place. And yet I am convinced that at no time was there a real danger to Catholic doctrine because we had a very calm episcopate. It used to represent all but the extremes of left and right but even the left had a devotion towards the bishops.'

His last words were for the Virgin Mary. 'It is not simple to define fundamental values. The significance of Mary is an example. After a period of extreme devotion to the Mother of Christ too little place was given her in the Dutch liturgy. But even a sentimental regard has to be examined in the light of the biblical basis. And now Mary is coming back in the wake of the tragedy.'

This confession must go without comment. It speaks for itself. But no doubt it says different things to different people. Better to be back for a moment to the certainties of Rome.

5

BLUEBEARD'S CASTLE

STALIN WAS QUITE right, of course, to laugh at the pope's military establishment, as such; and he could laugh more now, from whatever infernal Gulag he finds himself in, because Paul VI reduced the Vatican's armed forces still further so that today it consists of just a few hundred Swiss Guards. Paul also disposed of the Noble Guard and of the Papal Gendarmes while re-recruiting some of the more experienced members of this latter body into the special security service that he established for handling security within the Vatican, principally to protect the pope himself. The demise of the stately Noble Guard, with their breast-plates, plumed helmets and swords, as well as the uniformed gendarmes, was part of Paul VI's attempts at making his little state less archaically colourful, more at one with the contemporary world, like his decision to strip the red damask from the walls of the papal palace and replace this dusty ecclesiastical symbol of priestly self-satisfaction with walls dominated by neat beige colours and unobtrusive modern paintings.

He left matters a long way from solution of the essential problem of what, in a modern age, the headquarters of the visible Church should amount to. Robert Bellarmine, the Jesuit theologian who was a leading exponent of the Counter-Reformation, wrote in the seventeenth century that the Church should be 'as visible and palpable as the community of the Roman people, or the Kingdom of France or the Republic of Venice'. His dictum showed that saints can be as far off the mark as any of us in seeking apt comparisons, given that two of his three examples no longer exist and, in addition, modern Romans live in a conglomeration of a city with few elements left of a community. Something remains of Bellarmine's idea, however; or rather is coming back into prominence with the renewed popularity of the idea of the monarchical papacy, palpable, political and something to shout about.

Physically, the actual Vatican State is not much. Its 108.5 acres make it the smallest sovereign state in the world. Rainier's principality, that does little more than add to the gossip columns, is three and a half times as big, while Liechtenstein is 300 times bigger. The world's largest religious community and, from the West's point of view, the most imposing, is ruled from the smallest of states, which also includes within its tiny boundaries Christendom's biggest church. That is enough to explain that the Vatican is an unusual place. This minute state has been described as a pedestal that supports the Catholic world's huge community. Better, the tiny sovereign area is the point of a stylus that touches the whole world which revolves around it, extracting melodies, dissonance, strange noises, hope and disillusion. Since the closing years of Paul VI, this variety of sounds has been increasing, which is another way of saying that the Vatican is a concept with a variety of meanings. It is as well to get them all clear because talk of the Vatican is often loose, especially among people seeking to attack the idea of the papacy. 'Vatican elects Communist Pope', which was how the Reverend Ian Paisley's extreme Northern Irish Protestants saw the election of Wojtyla, is a fair example of glaring inexactness with one aim in mind: to strike at 'Rome' and all it is supposed to stand for. Even John Paul II, who was from the beginning of his reign an intellectually omnivorous pope, took several months to realize that his domains included a railway station.

Officially, the Vatican itself is dishonest about some of the elements of its own identity, as if happy to help confusion. The daily newspaper *L'Osservatore Romano* is closely watched over by the Secretariat of State, on a daily basis. It cannot be called a newspaper belonging to the species of the popular press; some of its front page articles are in Latin; even Ukrainian has come to be used now that they have a genuinely multilingual pope. Yet the Vatican, as such, will not allow it to be called an official newspaper. Vatican Radio is not official either but, in this case, perhaps with more reason. Not every script can be read beforehand. The radio has traditionally been in the hands of the Jesuits. Though many of them are bound by a special oath to the pope, they cannot be expected to interpret with complete accuracy the views of a changing establishment, however great the efforts they make. This was especially true after the election of John Paul II who at the beginning of his reign suffered from a certain lack of sympathy towards the religious orders, an outlook which he was later at pains to correct with such appointments as that of the Jesuit Father Martini to the Archbishopric of Milan.

The term Vatican is used loosely, not only of the pope's state but, even more freely, to symbolize the Roman Church as a whole, or the papacy. The words of some incautious priest who happens to work in the Vatican offices are often reported as 'Vatican says . . .' and sometimes what the Italian bishops have to say becomes a Vatican utterance because they are presumed to be reflecting the views of the pope as he is also Primate of Italy. In a sense the usages are all correct but, again, mainly from the point of view of people who see the lack of discrimination between one Vatican and another as damaging to the whole concept. In this the Vatican (in all its varieties) is guilty of being an accessory because it still insists on a ludicrous degree of secrecy that both confuses the issue and, inevitably, invites suspicion of its motives. A reluctance to be frank, which has nothing to do with the enigmatic behaviour of Jesus, should not be taken as a good enough reason to misjudge the institution, even if it, at times, seems set on being misunderstood. 'Kiss me, trust me, ask me nothing.' The words come from the libretto of Béla Bartók's only opera, *Bluebeard's Castle*, which might well be a parable about the Vatican. Bartók transformed a murderous, crude old legend into a touching parable of real understanding in the face of a pathological reluctance to reveal quite ordinary facts.

Mention of the papal palace and the whole unique, ill-understood, badly expressed, jealously protected, deeply disturbing little world behind its high walls—its striped guardsmen, its misbegotten denials, its bland smiles—evokes a special plea. The theatre—and the Vatican is essentially theatrical—requires the suspension of disbelief, whereas the Vatican urgently pleads that many beliefs and ingrained habits of mind be suspended in order to see what it is really like. So many certainties need looking at again if this complete embodiment of the institutional nature of religion is to reach the second millennium as protagonist of the self-completion of mankind, and not a confusing element in the choice of right and wrong. To what extent is it all that it seems?

> Lo!
> Bluebeard's Castle! Soon you'll see . . . but you know
> The story, know the moral. *Are you certain*,
> Ladies and gentlemen?

Bartók took the Bluebeard legend, threw aside the simple story of an innocent girl saved providentially by her brothers from the clutches of a murderous bridegroom, and turned it into something totally different. In his hands it became the tragedy of an over-secretive nobleman, forced to reveal himself, his possessions, his power, his sufferings, as his new wife inexorably demands his keys from him. The keys, in this case, are not those of St Peter that open the gates of heaven but those that unlock the seven tantalizing doors that contain the secrets of his life and his possessions, his aspirations and the symbols of his development: 'Ask no more. Be loved and love me.' It is a vain plea.

The State itself is the simplest door to unlock. Of course, it has its secrets, just as any set of buildings must have; just as the smallest area containing human life, however simple and straight-forward, must have its secret cavities. A monk's cell is not a cypher, and a long-abandoned grotto can, after centuries, retain the smell of death from the time it was used, long before, as a tomb. Yet much of the Vatican State is open to investigation and, for instance, it can be seen that it is a state which, quite by chance, has almost exactly a third of its surface devoted to gardens, and very beautiful gardens, a third to buildings and a third to squares. Much of its history, too, is clear in its essentials.

In classical times, the area across the Tiber known as the Vatican, with its bad reputation, was bigger than the present Vatican, beginning at Monte Mario and following the Tiber down to the Janiculum Hill. In terms of modern Rome, that means practically from the Trastevere area, now favoured by foreign residents as an artificial form of Left Bank, to the mass of the Hilton Hotel that breaks the Monte Mario skyline. It consisted of low-lying land along the river, and hilly country as well, with some small villages dating from Etruscan times that were in-habited by farmers and potters. The zone was regarded as unhealthy because the Tiber frequently flooded. Tacitus says that the plague that struck the army of Vitellius, Vespasian's rival, was due to the fact that they camped 'in the infamous area of the Vatican' and Martial commented that the wine produced from grapes grown in the area tasted like vinegar. The ground is still marshy. When Nervi was building the new audience-hall in the

Vatican for Paul VI, which was completed in 1971, he had difficulty in finding sufficient support in the wet earth for the huge columns bearing his vast concrete construction.

In social terms, the level of the Vatican improved somewhat during the Empire. Caligula's mother, Agrippina, built a villa there and others followed her example. Her son built his circus there, in the centre of which stood the obelisk which he had brought from Egypt by a notable feat of marine engineering. That obelisk now stands in the middle of St Peter's Square, where it was placed in the sixteenth century after a short move that nevertheless evoked some of the difficulties that the Romans experienced in bringing the monument to their capital in the first place. Nero enlarged the circus and had Christians killed in it, sometimes with prolonged cruelty. According to tradition, Peter was among them and, after being crucified upside down, was supposed to have been buried close to the site of his death, just as Jesus is said to have been buried a matter of a few yards away from the place of his crucifixion. St Peter's itself is supposed to have been built over the tomb of St Peter. This assertion has not been finally proved but archaeological examination beneath the high altar leaves no doubt at all about the reverence felt for the site as early as the beginning of the fourth century.

Constantine built the first basilica dedicated to the saint and took immense pains to place it exactly in a certain position. This involved destroying tombs in a cemetery still in use, and filling them with earth, which went against Roman custom and would undoubtedly have been unpopular. He had to cut away a part of the hill and excavate large quantities of earth, another labour explicable only by the fact that the siting was dictated not by comfort or by a search for originality, but by an urgent need to mark an object of great sacredness. That object was found, in the course of excavations sanctioned by Pius XII, under the main altar and below the level of the floor of Constantine's church: a two-tiered, niched construction with columns, which Pius XII unwisely publicly stated was the burial place of St Peter. Structures around the construction have been dated and are said to have been built between AD 150 and 170. A large number of votive coins were found near the columned construction, most of them from the fourth century and later, but a few as early as the first century. All this is undoubtedly sufficient for the conclusion to be drawn that some monument to Peter, perhaps marking the place where he died, has stood there since the second half of the second

111

century and was so revered that the first Christian Emperor went to great lengths to place his basilica exactly above this sacred memorial. The descent to see it, under the high altar of St Peter's, is one of the most moving experiences in the realm of something different in quality from what is usually meant by sight-seeing.

The sacred must be defended and that is how the Vatican early became a walled area. The first protecting walls were built in 852 some six years after a raiding-party of Saracens sacked St Peter's. Popes throughout the centuries expanded the walled area to take in more than the sacred site because the Vatican gradually became the place where the popes lived and set up their offices of government. It was not always so. The first popes lived in the Lateran Palace, given them by Constantine, and only after 1377, when Gregory XI ended the seventy-two-year period in which the popes lived in Avignon in southern France, did the Vatican finally become the seat of the papacy. The line traced by the present walls was reached by the seventeenth century.

For most of the papacy's history, the popes ruled over more than the Church and the walled area of the Vatican because they had states that included much of central Italy. The Vatican was a part of those states but also apart from them, rather as Jerusalem was under David.

The pope finally lost all title to sovereignty over any territory in Italy in 1870, as a consequence of the completion of the unification of the country. He remained in the Vatican as a self-styled 'prisoner' until 1929 when Mussolini came to terms with the papacy. The terms were expressed in a series of agreements on which the modern Vatican is based: an international treaty establishing the state of Vatican City, a financial arrangement by which the Italians paid compensation, and a concordat setting out relations between Italy and the Vatican. All these agreements are still valid.

It is worth making two points about the papacy's possessions. The first is that the loss of the states can be regarded as having been only beneficial to the Church. An indication of this benefit is still visible on what might be called the ecclesiastical map of Italy. The Church is held in high esteem in the Veneto area and Piedmont, both of which historically had strong temporal governments that dealt firmly with ecclesiastical pretensions. The Venetian Republic hung up priests in cages on the bell-tower by St Mark's if they were thought to have abused their functions. The Church is held in less esteem in areas where the temporal power was weak, such as the old southern Kingdom of Naples, and its standing is lowest where it used to be the direct ruler. It is no coincidence that the greatest Communist stronghold in Italy is the Bologna area where the mayor now administers from the former palace of the pope's governor.

The second point is that popes now, as in the past, believe a state of their own to be essential to them in carrying out their task. Pius IX explained why to the French Ambassador in 1871, just after he had lost Rome to the Italians: 'All I want is a small corner of the earth where I am master. This is not to say that I would refuse my states if they were offered to me; but so long as I do not have this little corner of earth, I shall not be able to exercise in their fullness my spiritual functions.' This is the essence of the justification for the existence of Vatican City. It is different from the idea of the pope simply as a temporal ruler. He feels that he needs a temporality in order to project spirituality and, within that hundred or so acres, he is fully at home—the master, the monarch and owner of practically everything one sees. There is another reason: independence allowed the Vatican to transfer funds freely from one country to another, as had been possible before 1870 and was again after 1929.

How does he conduct himself within his own domain? Certainly not as a democrat. There is no reason why Vatican City should be a democratic state. It is worth saying that it is not, however, to correct any mistaken impression that the modern papacy adopts the modern political thinking of the Western world. The Vatican's constitutional structure is indicative of papal political thinking within the bounds of the home territory. The pope's powers are absolute; he has full legislative, judicial and executive authority, and there are no democratic processes to represent the 4,000 people who work at the Vatican. The idea of a trade union was discussed in 1979 but all that came out of it was permission to establish an association of lay employees, which did not have the right to negotiate contracts. There is almost no private enterprise. The State contains a chemist's shop, managed by a religious order; two duty-free shops, selling foodstuff and drink and, the second one, household articles and clothing. Petrol and tobacco are sold to those authorized to buy them (shopping at the duty-free shops also requires a permit and far more of these are issued than there are inhabitants of the Vatican) and these concessions are in part justified by the fact that salaries are lower than in Italy while many of the employees have to live outside the walls, in Italy. There is no income tax on Vatican earnings and almost nothing is privately owned. On a well-known occasion a Syrian diplomat was explaining to a prelate the virtues of public ownership, thinking presumably that the Vatican followed the free-market system of the Western world, only to be told, rather sharply, that the Vatican needed no lesson in the practice of state ownership, which was the system followed within the pope's own city.

The inhabitants of Vatican City number about 730, of whom a little more than half have Vatican citizenship. This citizenship normally goes with a particular job or rank. All cardinals for instance are automatically citizens even if they do not live in Rome. No one is born a Vatican citizen and even if they were, they would have no particular privileges, just as living within the sacred enclave may have its curiosity-value but must, at times, be tedious. The gates are shut at night and there is no form of entertainment within the precincts, while regulations are strict—drunkenness is frowned on as is hanging out washing.

As a fully-sovereign state it has its own flag, made up of two fields, divided vertically. The field near the staff is yellow and the other white. Superimposed on the white field are the crossed keys ('Come, unlock it, are you frightened . . .?') and the tiara, which remains in place despite the fact that the last two popes were not crowned, accepting instead a ceremony of investiture. Paul VI was the last to be crowned but gave away the tiara immediately after his coronation. John Paul I refused a coronation; John Paul II followed his example, though with some regret, one feels. Certainly his decision was not intended as a move towards more democratic behaviour.

I was talking to a cardinal with a certain sense of humour about the extremely traditionalist Archbishop of Genoa, Cardinal Siri, who was a possible candidate for the papacy. I asked if the conservative Siri would have waived a public coronation. The answer was: 'Yes, he would waive it. But at night, in some vault of the Vatican, he would have invited his friends to a private coronation of the utmost splendour.'

Modern popes have not shown much grasp of labour relations. Paul VI introduced administrative discipline of a reasonably modern kind, including regular rates of pay, a pension fund and facilities for granting loans as advances of salary. He also laid down levels of termination payments. Before his reforms, administrative methods were totally paternalistic; people were given jobs because their faces fitted, or they were backed by someone with the papal ear, and they were paid by just as approximate calculations of their worth and needs. However, Paul's reforms were not enough. That could be expected in an atmosphere of volatile wage-demands in Italy itself, and the subsequent difficulties, which are quite genuine, of Vatican employees having to live, partly at least, on the Italian market. The real issue is much deeper: can a pope who constantly talks about the rights and dignity of man, fair salaries, the shortcomings of both capitalism and collective economies, afford to be judged a bad employer? There is a wall in a small street near Rome's central post-office that is much written on; one of the slogans that somehow never becomes illegible reads: 'Do not work at the Vatican—It is a false and faithless place.'

In March 1979 a group of Vatican employees, claiming to be 'in very serious economic difficulties', wrote a letter to John Paul II that opened with the harsh reminder: 'The figure of the pope is the only example in the world by which the truth he preaches as head of the Church can be directly checked in his work as head of state.' This is putting the matter very frankly but surely not unreasonably. Pretensions require some sort of practical demonstration and, because of the way the Vatican is administered, injustice can be put right, as the pope's correspondents pointed out, only by 'an act of sovereign justice'. They also made clear that the pope alone could do something for them: 'The principal motive in writing is the urgent necessity of solving the problem of the extremely low salaries of Vatican employees who, as always, without any right to speak, are forced to ask softly in deaf ears that have no wish to hear them.' This group of 'devoted Vatican dependants' ended its sermon to the pope as employer with the reminder that the answer to their problems lay in 'a will to face them with—even before justice and honesty—a Christian conscience and, for this, it would be enough to recall what the Gospels say about "a just wage" which essentially is what we are asking for'. They might have added that people with a special knowledge on the Vatican staff, such as technicians of Vatican Radio, are regularly passed envelopes containing enough extra money to keep them satisfied.

This odd, one-way correspondence between disgruntled employees and the pope was still in progress in mid-1980. A letter dated 22 July contained the proposal: 'Holy Father, do you not believe that between one journey and another you might come to earth, materially and among us, to solve, among so many problems, the ones we have and which are of your exclusive competence as Head of State?' The letter itself, according to its anonymous authors, was proof enough of an absurd situation: 'in the second millennium, with so much "progress", social justice, workers' unions, and papal encyclicals, if we want our problems solved, we are forced to write to the pope because all other roads are barred to us.' I do not as a rule like dealing with anonymous letters, but this one sounded convincing. I took it for checking to a high official of the government of the pope's state who had no doubts at all about its authenticity: 'a group of our senior civil servants,' he said.

It must sometimes strike a pope who travels a great deal that the privilege of moving always as a head of state is not all gain. The cannon roaring salutes at airports, the formal visits and addresses to governments and local authorities, the military bands: they all add superfluously to the programme and detract from the idea of pilgrimage, which is how these journeys have always been described from the first which took Paul VI to the Holy Land. But that of course is a different question from how the Pope's domain is administered.

The pope delegates his powers for ruling Vatican City to a commission of seven cardinals who hold their posts for five years and administer in his name. This commission meets once a month under the chairmanship of its president, who follows the daily details of the life of the state from an office in the administrative building that was first designed as a seminary, with a section intended for visiting dignitaries. The cardinals pass down their decisions to a staff of laymen headed by a 'special delegate'. John Paul II, uncharacteristically, took hardly any immediate personal interest in the running of the little state. Despite the fact that he likes to be the prime mover and knew no more about it than he did of much of the Vatican, he left the commission of cardinals intact, and showed little more than a benevolent interest in his principality.

Given the background, there is little reason to suppose that the Vatican has strong feelings for democracy. The effort can be, and has been, made to show that the teachings of Jesus reveal a preference for democracy, on the grounds that the human values he insisted on are those that inspire democracies rather than tyrannies, but it is difficult to imagine that Jesus had political preferences. He talks about kingship. Heaven is a kingdom, not a parliamentary democracy; God is the absolute key to all, and Jesus himself is ultimately represented as the lone, relentless arbiter between the good and the bad in the human race as they come up in judgement before him. There is arguably a strong distinction to be made between the teachings of the historical Jesus, charged with compassion for the humble, and the Old Testament prophecies of how the Son of Man would come upon the clouds and have sovereignty bestowed upon him, with glory and king-ship: 'and all men of all peoples, nations and languages became his servants.' It is an imperious image; a king mounted on the elements, not dragging constituencies behind him. It is also an accepted image. Why should the Vicar's behaviour in his own domain be any more proletarian?

There are good reasons. One is that democracy has won a claim to being a moral force in the modern world because it has opposed the two great totalitarian creeds of Fascism and Communism. (It is of some relevance that the Vatican came to agreements with both the principal Fascist countries, Mussolini's Italy and Hitler's Germany, while remaining for a surprisingly long period uncertain as to what attitude to adopt towards Communism.) Another reason is that democracies are inclined, now that anti-clericalism has faded, to leave a large measure of freedom to the ecclesiastical authorities. The Vatican has returned the compliment by showing itself far less interested now in having a direct hand or a privileged position in the affairs of Catholic countries. The most striking example is Italy. The election of a non-Italian pope more or less sealed a process which had been advancing for years towards non-involve-ment. Even with a Pole on the papal throne, interest in the Italian scene did not completely stop. In early 1980, for instance, some recommendations about the secretaryship of the Christian Demo-crat Party emanated from the Vatican. But they were ignored by the Party and could be in no way comparable with the days when Pius XII personally studied the proofs of local election results to be published the next day or prescribed excommunication for a left-wing vote. The consistent aim of the Catholic Church has been, and is, to conduct its own activities as it thinks fit, for which it requires more than that 'little corner of earth' which is Vatican City. It needs space within the body politic of all those nations where it is present so that it can pursue its mission unhampered.

A third reason for democracy within the Church is that some leading prelates see the Church as a whole as fully and properly convinced now of the superiority of the democratic system. The Church in Spain is an excellent example of the long-planned backing of a return to democratic methods despite its long association with Franco's dictatorship. The strain came later in the form of impatience among younger priests for more resolute change within the Church. In the United States the Church officially claims to have accepted both democracy and capitalism. It is exactly in such terms that the situation is described at the Washington headquarters of the National Conference of Bishops. Yet this is surely an understandable exaggeration due more to American national sentiment than to Catholic teaching or practice. It would be fair to say that the Church as a whole has not reached the point of preaching democracy and probably never will, and it is an even longer way from practising it. Even when the effort is made in America itself, the result can be disappointing. The democratic idea is so strong in the United States that priests and laymen speak of having a share in choosing their own bishops instead of leaving the decision in theory to the pope and in practice to the secret recommendations of the apostolic delegate in Washington after he has listened to a wide range of opinions. The more progressive they claim to be, the more they are inclined to press for this. Yet, in this large diocese of the north-east, an undoubtedly progressive archbishop had to admit that a survey taken in his own diocese about the choice of an auxiliary bishop revealed so much confused thinking among priests and lay people alike that the idea of letting them make the decision and then send it on to the Vatican was out of the question. As it happened, the apostolic delegate in Washington had an excellent knowledge of the diocese in question and of what sort of bishop was required there. So the fact that the real choice remained in his hands and was not left to the faithful can only have been welcome, non-progressive though it was.

The more liberal the Church has become, the more open towards the modern world, the more expensive it has become to run. The little state can make only a modest contribution towards the Vatican's money troubles. It issues its own stamps which bring in an estimated million and a half pounds a year. The Vatican is reaping some of the wild winds of its own refusal in the past to talk about its wealth. It still publishes no budget although Paul VI tried to put more order in the various offices dealing with money, and quite probably would eventually have arrived at public accounting of the Vatican's finances. The tradition of silence brought with it the habit of suspicion; either the Vatican had so much money it preferred not to reveal the figure, or such money as it had was invested in embarrassing places: in arms or in speculative building, for example.

There is now a little less secrecy, though nothing about the Vatican's attitude to money could be mistaken for frankness. Probably financial troubles have helped stimulate more candour about the Church's financial empire. The first experience of a deficit does wonders to concentrate the mind, to the point of at last wanting some understanding instead of insisting on a super-cilious secretiveness. Almost surely the Vatican has wanted to give some indication of the size of the financial effort it has been making in recent years to pay for its post-Council attempts at meeting the world face to face.

One effect of the Council was the establishment of new and expensive (by Vatican standards) offices for dealing with ecumen-ism, contacts with non-Christian religions, with non-believers, with the laity, as well as a completely new and potentially extremely important organ, the International Synod of Bishops, that meets every three years in Rome and has a permanent steering committee based there. Other offices were expanded to deal with the unprecedented volume of work. The amount of travel and more frequent contact with the world at large helped raise expenditure. From 1961, the Vatican's staff increased from 1,322 to about 3,150 in 1977. Paul VI, of course, attempted a reform of the Vatican's handling of its finances; like so many of his reforms it was tentative and left the real decisions to a successor.

Paul created what was intended to be an embryonic central administration for financial matters by creating the Prefecture for Economic Affairs which replaced a number of smaller depart-ments. This is the body which since 1968 has been responsible for the harrowing task of drawing up what is generally known as the Vatican's budget. In fact, there are two budgets. The Prefecture is supposed to prepare in May a series of estimates of expenditure for the year and then at the end of the year an actual statement of what was gathered in and what was spent. Neither of these documents, prepared in an atmosphere of the greatest secrecy, includes anything like all the Vatican's financial matters.

The part of the field which the Prefecture's budget covers includes the Curia itself, the offices, commissions, secretariats, councils and ecclesiastical tribunals, the upkeep of the apostolic palaces, the newspaper *L'Osservatore Romano* and the pope's diocese of Rome. It does not cover the Vatican's bank, which is the most glaring omission, missionary expenditure, Vatican

Radio, the administration of Vatican City (which has a small surplus largely from the sale of stamps and the income from museums, but has to pay for the radio), the Sacred Congregation dealing with the Oriental Churches, and the upkeep of St Peter's, which has its own administration, though the other three great basilicas—St Mary Major, St John Lateran and St Paul's Without the Walls—are included in the official budget. A highly important source of income outside the official budget is Peter's Pence, a sum contributed by the whole Catholic world through the dioceses every 29 June, the feast day of St Peter and St Paul. Among other things, the upkeep of the pope himself comes from Peter's Pence. John XXIII paid for the Council from this source.

All that is known officially from the Vatican about its budget is that the deficit in 1979 was 20,240,000 dollars. This figure was given to the assembled Sacred College of Cardinals in November 1979 when the pope suddenly called together his electors to discuss three points, of which one, and clearly the most urgent, was the Church's financial difficulties. On this there need be no doubt. The Vatican's finances have for years been shaky, to say the least. It is generally taken for granted that the Vatican has had an operational deficit from around 1973. By 1975 the financial crisis had reached the point that Paul VI rejected the estimates put before him, and severe but amateurishly uncoordinated economies were ordered. They did nothing to put the situation right, and caused a good deal of ill-feeling among high officials who, while fully aware of the poor way in which the administration was handled, received instructions to cut down on their orders for ball-point pens. The actual size of the budget is open to enlightened guesswork. One of Rome's most tenacious and best-informed experts in the field, Lamberto Furno, estimates that the income side of the 1979 budget was probably over 30,000 million lire.

The income side of the official budget is handled by a second body known as the Administration of the Patrimony of the Holy See. The Administration has two main sections: one deals with what are called 'ordinary' affairs and the second with 'extraordinary ' matters. The first section handles largely the Vatican's real estate, while the second attends to the stock-market holdings which originally came to the Vatican in 1929 when the Italian government paid compensation for the loss of the papal states: a milliard in stocks and 750 million lire in cash from Mussolini. Manipulation of this original endowment is the source from which the main entry side of the ledger is filled, as far as the official budget is concerned.

Another shrewd follower of the Vatican's financial tribulations, Paul Horne, estimated that investments in 1979 were around 100 million pounds. Because of a combination of conservative thinking and an effort not to appear crassly commercial, these investments brought in interest of between five and six million pounds a year. If he is right, it is not a great deal of money. It probably does not even cover salaries, however inadequate Vatican employees feel their treatment to be. Inflation in Italy has not helped, especially as the Vatican adopted the Italian mechanism of index-linked automatic pay increases. This has had the effect of making the staff cost more but not satisfying demands, because the mechanism constantly diminishes differentials.

The bank—known officially and rather ludicrously as the 'Institute for Works of Religion'—is kept out of the budget for a plausible reason. It handles not only the Vatican's own funds but also those of national hierarchies, religious orders, clergy and a few privileged private clients. These accounts are not supposed to be mixed with the Vatican's own dealings. Its assets are kept a secret. Here the fluctuations in the guesswork are just too great to inspire a lot of confidence. The cardinals at the 1979 assembly were not apparently told the secrets of the bank. Some of them might have wanted to know more about the half-told tales of the bank's association with Michele Sindona, the criminal bankrupt who had acted as adviser to the Vatican when it was selling its shares in the international property group Società Generale Immobiliare and in other Italian companies. The Vatican has never admitted to the losses it suffered as a result of involvement in Sindona's collapse and disgrace, though it has suggested that his advice was lucrative in other ways.

Peter's Pence, on the other hand, was explained to the cardinals. If it does not figure in the official budget, it is used to help cover the deficit. It is the one large source of income with a certain colourful quality, or better a pleasantly colourful quality. It represents the feelings of ordinary Catholics to individual pontiffs and so is a good measure of their popularity. Predictably it soared under the much loved John XXIII, sank under Paul VI and soon rose high, some say higher than under John, as a result of the profitable charisma of John Paul II. This annual offering is paid directly into the Secretariat of State and as it is the result of contributions from Catholics, rich and poor, it is arguably the source which most of all should be explained to the public, in particular how much it brings in each year and what use is made of it.

The whole field of finances is a sorry story. So too is the choice of persons to whom the finances are entrusted. Cardinal Vagnozzi, the head of the Prefecture, made a reputation for himself when apostolic delegate in Washington for narrowness. He is said to have differences about spheres of responsibility with Cardinal Caprio, head of the Administration, which if true could weigh heavily on efficiency. The bank is in the hands of a large, golf-playing American, of Lithuanian origin, from Cicero, Monsignor Paul Marcinkus who doubles as the pope's tour-manager. In both tasks he has enjoyed the confidence of two popes. He is unpopular with the press, especially the Italian press, which need cause him no anxiety because attacks from outside usually bring, in the world of the Curia, a backlash of solidarity. The East European background used to be regarded as a difficulty because it was held to explain what one Catholic journalist called the bishop's 'us and them' attitude to Catholics and non-Catholics. With a Polish pope his origins must be nearly as useful as the responsibility Marcinkus used to have for collecting American money to help the Polish Church. One of his aphorisms gave an excellent indication of the Vatican's banker's view of publicity: there was nothing wrong with the reign of Paul VI, he said, except what the press said about it.

Secrecy and silliness aside, the finances are in more than one way the Vatican's weakness. The real situation, however, cannot be as bad as it looks. It is difficult to believe, for instance, that if the Vatican needed money urgently for some important project, it would not be able to raise the sum required from one of the richer hierarchies, the American or the West German. Then there is the papacy's heritage of art. What, say, is St Peter's worth—a church which has had upon it the hands of Bramante, Raphael, Michelangelo and Bernini to enhance its sacred associations? Or the Sistine Chapel? Or, for specialized tastes, St Veronica's handkerchief, which is one of the principal relics kept in St Peter's, together with the lance of Longinus and others. At times there is a call to the Church to divest itself of its wealth, sell its possessions and give the proceeds to the poor. Anti-clericals make use of the Church's possessions for their attacks. When John Paul II went to Naples in October 1979, the local radicals ironically underlined the sufferings of a poverty-stricken city with the slogan: 'Wealthy Naples salutes the poor pope.' The Church must be seen to be poor—on this the advocates of a church devoted to social justice insist. In fact, Paul VI had a plan to give away the Church's artistic wealth in an ingenious way. He considered proposing (but later thought better of it) the making over of the papacy's art collections to UNESCO so that the Church as such could no longer be accused of hoarding priceless possessions while every minute saw deaths from hunger in some part of the world.

But there is a side to the Vatican's use of its money which is totally unappealing. Money is used to impose discipline over less experienced hierarchies. To give one example, from an African country: I met a rather shocked member of a religious order who had been present at a meeting of the local bishops with the apostolic nuncio. The nuncio upbraided them because one of their number had sought financial help directly from an American charity without sending the request through the nuncio's office. A copy of the bishop's letter was read out to the meeting and the name of the offending bishop revealed, while the nuncio made clear to them that the financial strings must remain in the Vatican's hands, and bishops forgetting that might well suffer as a result. This bullying attitude is another sound reason why the Vatican's financial affairs should be conducted in the full light of day.

The incident also raises the whole question of the rights and duties and usefulness of a papal diplomatic corps. They do a great deal more than dispense funds. There are papal representatives, most of them with full diplomatic status, in more than 100 countries with another ten accredited to international organizations of a governmental nature. The Holy See was represented at the Helsinki Conference, marking its return as a member of a full-scale diplomatic meeting since the Congress of Vienna. The usefulness of the diplomatic corps was criticized during the Vatican Council and proposals were put forward for replacing its personnel with laymen. In the meantime it has expanded greatly and it is still almost entirely clerical. In times when priests are in short supply and the Church is seeking to give the impression of being spokesman of the poor, a large presence in the world's diplomatic corps, which to ordinary people sounds like belonging to a glittering life of luxury, may well look out of place. Yet its power is increasing and it is now very much an élite. John Paul II's first appointments brought three diplomatists to the most influential posts in the Curia; nuncios are normally made cardinals when they retire and with that goes the privilege of electing the next pope, so they have every opportunity to reinforce their own profession.

Not that they need worry. Their duties and the character of their work was newly defined by Paul VI in June 1969 with a document which makes quite clear that the diplomatic corps was regarded by him as very important. The opening words of the document state that:

> The care of all the Churches, to which We have been called by the hidden design of God and for which We must one day give an account, requires that, as Vicar of Christ, We should be adequately present in all parts of the world and be informed about the state and condition of each Church.

Apart from a pope's own journeys, the diplomatic corps is one of the main means he has at hand to maintain this contact. Other methods are the regular visits to Rome which all residential bishops are obliged to undertake, and the despatch by the pope of a representative to carry out some special mission.

The nuncios and delegates are there to provide Rome with a much more detailed and frequent accounting of what is happening in the countries to which they are accredited and, naturally, to explain Rome's outlook both to the local Church and to the government. Paul VI summed up their duties in this way:

> The primary and specific purpose of the mission of the Pontifical Representative is to render even closer and more operative the ties that bind the Apostolic See and the local Churches.
>
> He furthermore interprets the solicitude of the Roman Pontiff for the good of the country in which he exercises his mission. In particular, he must concern himself zealously with the problems of peace, of progress and of the collaboration of the peoples in view of the spiritual, moral and material good of the entire human family.
>
> Upon the Pontifical Representative also falls the duty of safe-guarding, in co-operation with the Bishops, among the civil authorities of the territory in which he exercises his office, the mission of the Church and the Holy See.
>
> This is also the task of those Pontifical Representatives who have no diplomatic character; they will take care, however, to entertain friendly relations with these same authorities.
>
> In his capacity as envoy of the Supreme Shepherd of Souls, the Pontifical Representative will promote, in accordance with the instructions he receives from the competent offices of the Holy See and in agreement with the local Bishops and particularly with the

Patriarchs in eastern territories, opportune contacts between the Catholic Church and the other Christian communities and will favour cordial relations with the non-Christian religions.

This last duty is a recent addition to the work of the diplomatic corps and was added quite evidently in the light of the strong ecumenical feelings which influenced the decisions of the Vatican Council. A traditional duty which is of great importance is that of forwarding the names of candidates for vacant bishoprics to Rome. The diplomatic corps has a strong influence in the choice of bishops and the representative is specifically invited when sending names to give 'his own opinion and preferential vote'. They themselves are almost always bishops, but not of a residential see because their lives are taken up with their diplomatic work. The Vatican has therefore resorted to the device of giving them titular sees, or bishoprics that once existed but no longer do so because they have passed out of the Catholic sphere.

These nuncios or papal ambassadors claim the deanship of any diplomatic corps to which they belong: if the country to which they are accredited refuses to concede this right, the Vatican sends a pro-nuncio, which is virtually the same thing but the holder of this title can make no claim to automatic seniority, in which case the normal rule is followed by which the dean of the diplomatic corps is the ambassador who has been there longest. There is another variation of more importance. Countries, such as the United States, which do not have diplomatic missions to the papacy have an apostolic delegate instead of a nuncio, and he has no diplomatic privileges. The point, however, about all these diplomatic ranks in the papal divisions is that they do not represent the Vatican but the Holy See, that is, the spiritual authority of the papacy. A curiosity among books emerging from the pope's foreign service was the slightly scandalous novel written by a former papal diplomat, accredited as observer to the United Nations. The main character is a Russian spy. He takes the place of the observer to the United Nations Organization, who has been kidnapped by the KGB, and quickly—and to comic effect—picks up the habit of correcting everyone who describes him as the Vatican's observer, insisting that he represents the Holy See.

It is Vatican City which is recognized as a state, neutral and inviolable, by the international community. In its turn it exists for, because it is subject to, the Holy See. This apparently complicated relationship between state, pontiff and his post's august title, all talked of commonly as 'the Vatican', is set out in international documents so that the community knows exactly with whom it is dealing. This example comes from the preamble to the agreement with the International Atomic Energy Agency, on the non-proliferation of nuclear weapons, which the Vatican signed: '. . . whereas, moreover, the Holy See enjoys exclusive sovereignty and jurisdiction over the Vatican City State, of which the Roman Pontiff is sovereign . . . now therefore the Holy See, acting in the name and on behalf of the Vatican City, and the Agency, have agreed as follows . . .'

The opposite end of this diplomatic status is that many countries have permanent diplomatic missions accredited to the Holy See. At the end of 1980 there were about a hundred such missions. Most of them—ninety—were fully fledged embassies led by an ambassador, though not all were resident in Rome. Some countries accredited an ambassador resident somewhere near—Switzerland in several cases—who could come down regularly to keep in contact with Vatican officials and his colleagues. There were five legations including Monte Carlo and that odd institution, the British Legation to the Holy See. It was odd because of its level, which remained lowly despite spasmodic public discussion on the utility of making it an embassy. The legation was set up during the First World War by Balfour (with probably some twinges of his Methodist conscience) as a listening-post and as a means of keeping the pope informed about Allied intentions. It flowered again during the Second World War when the minister at its head was D'Arcy Osborne, later Duke of Leeds, who spent the war inside the Vatican and was regarded as remarkably successful in fulfilling the two aims for which the legation was originally established.

The late duke was seldom adequately followed. The Foreign Office totally missed the point that a low-level mission can have its special potential, if, for instance, the minister is chosen for a particular flamboyance of character, which can make up for lack of status, or if, even better, it is used as a posting for a comparatively young man in the middle of a promising career. It was the obvious place to send a forty-five-year-old diplomat likely to end his days as ambassador to Washington or Moscow, and decidedly not the place to send a series of men whose last post it was before retirement. The Foreign Office managed once to find the first: Sir Marcus Cheke was exactly the sort of flamboyant, gifted, baroque sort of character who gave the post stature because he had plenty to spare. He was much respected at the Vatican and John XXIII came to comfort him at his death-bed in a Rome hospital.

The question of raising the status of the British Legation turned largely on politics; but not only on party politics. Certainly the Labour Party was more favourable to the move, because Labour reckons to take more of the vote of Britain's four million Catholics. The Conservative Party was divided, a strongly Catholic cabinet minister, Norman St John-Stevas, favoured the change strongly, but others were wary of arousing anti-Catholic feelings. And not all the Catholics themselves were thought to be in favour of the change. The temporal power has never been a favourite element of Catholicism in England and a change would simply have accentuated it. Some of them may have felt too that Pope John Paul II was already pressing hard enough on the temporal side of the papal power. There was also the fact that, however lowly the legation was in Rome, the pope's represen-tation in London had no diplomatic status at all. London had an apostolic delegate, not a nuncio or pro-nuncio. The government did in fact grant the popular Archbishop Bruno Heim personal diplomatic privileges but his title remained that of delegate and the discrepancy remained as well.

The Americans are in an even less formal situation. Again, for reasons of internal politics, they do not feel they can afford to establish an embassy accredited to the Holy See, nor even a legation. They have a special representative nominated by the president. These representatives have no diplomatic status, even if on one (ill-judged) occasion the Americans sent a personality who already had the personal rank of ambassador, Mr Henry Cabot Lodge, former head of the American Embassy in Saigon and distinctly an odd choice to send to the Vatican. The representative is not stationed in Rome but comes for visits. He has a permanent office which is left during his absences in the hands of a State Department official. At the other end of the exchange, the Holy See is represented in Washington by an apostolic delegate who does not have diplomatic status.

The Vatican is a complex creation. It is what it is because of a series of specific decisions, historical accidents and professional requirements. It was never devised according to an agreed plan. A lot of people are now involved in a variety of jobs in 'this little corner of earth'. Like all complicated organizations employing many human beings, its tendency is towards secretiveness. Unlike other large organizations, it not only fears enquiry but feels it has some natural right to avoid frank investigation. It is understandable that fear of scandal is more strongly felt at the Vatican than elsewhere, despite the comfortable knowledge of scandals overcome in the course of a long history. There is another inhibiting factor which is genuinely felt, though questionable in its real usefulness: that limits on information are necessary to protect the Church's activities which, by their nature, do not depend on the world's consent or on the verdicts of public opinion. Paul VI was a reasonably open-minded pope towards the press (his father had been a rather gentlemanly sort of journalist), but he spoke of 'limits demanded by discretion and the common good'. This, in itself, is not a bad concept; it only sounds bad when it is expressed by the head of an organization already under criticism for a lack of candour.

There are, moreover, perfectly well-tried devices by which journalists can be kept informed of developments without too much appearing in print. The Vatican never tries, for instance, any system of background briefing by which accredited correspondents could be kept informed of progress on issues most likely to interest them. One excuse for not doing so is that the Vatican has more business with Italian journalists than with those of any other nationality, and in Italy also there is no tradition of informing correspondents on a confidential basis. A relationship of mutual confidence of this kind simply does not exist and so the Vatican's fears of having confidential information immediately revealed can be said to have some basis in reality. Fears are strong at the Vatican. It is a very fearful place. Whether fear comes from the likelihood of damaging one's career, or of breaking ranks, of being regarded as unreliable—there is a lot of it. In biblical terms, the Vatican forgets the clear statement by Jesus, after a particularly unsatisfactory performance by the disciples in failing to grasp his parables, that there is nothing hidden but it must be disclosed. Judas would probably be seen at the Vatican as the sort of man who would add to his hideous betrayal by giving his story to the press.

It is not just that fear is embedded in the system; the structure is wrong for any useful official relationship with the press, and the strain on the incumbent is telling. It is indicative that the Commission for Social Communications, the title for the public relations structure at the Vatican, lost its first head, Archbishop Heston, as a result of a heart attack and the second, Bishop Deskur, suffered a stroke. The difficulties go beyond a general inability to understand modern press requirements combined with an innate defensive attitude. Communication between the public relations side of the Vatican's bureaucracy and the executive is insufficient. The point has not been grasped that only a person with the full confidence of the pope himself, and access to him, can be in a position to talk intelligently to the modern international press about the Church's activities. In this sense, blame does not attach to individuals if the system fails to bring results, and relations remain unsatisfactory. The appointment of a highly considered head of this side of the Vatican's affairs would also help to solve another problem: that of the interferences from other departments once the necessary formalities have been gone through with the press department and permits obtained. Security or some member of the Household Office may well decide that his responsibilities have been trespassed on. Again, a complex, authoritarian organization encourages within its ranks a sort of defensive system of jealousies. The system itself helps this sometimes urgent form of self-protection. For all the attempts at modernization, the older ways still predominate at the Vatican, where the importance of a patron remains great and who you know is of more account than who you are, or whether your capacities are right for the job you seek. Inevitably purely personal rivalries are encouraged. Hopes were raised of an improvement in press relations with the appointment in 1980 of a British prelate, Bishop Agnellus Andrew, to be executive vice-president of the Commission. Early in his tenure he made an encouraging statement to the effect that the world's press sought the truth and the Church had no reason to fear the truth.

Explanations are easy. They are of much less importance to the Vatican's wellbeing than a better awareness of what is being lost by this obtuse behaviour towards the whole field of public relations. The Vatican attracts a large number of journalists, of whom many are not professional, being there more for the joy they personally receive in being close to institutional religion than for genuinely representing the institution of the press. However, with some regularity, the Vatican suddenly finds itself unwilling host to some of the world's best writers and broadcasters. Then it is seen at its fractious, incompetent, narrow-minded worst. The death of a pope, and the ensuing weeks of growing tension as the election of his successor draws near, sees the arrival of the highest number and highest quality of journalists. There is a fairly regular stream now that the papacy has returned to so prominent a position among the world's news-makers. The Vatican would gain a great deal if these correspondents were shown the workings of the little state and the departments of the Church's central government. It is an act of self-damaging irresponsibility not to make use of the press when it is there on one's doorstep, full of curiosity and, for the most part, reasonably well-intentioned.

It is all the more so given the papacy's deliberate appeal to the masses, an appeal which the Vatican can be said not to have sought in the first place; but once it saw what chances were there it responded to the rise of popular sentiment. This response brought new obligations. Probably many of the people who take part in mass demonstrations around the pope are not particularly concerned to know anything specific about what they are actually cheering—but they should be, and those that are certainly have a right to know. What attracts the masses demands to be fully revealed. This is an unhappy and threatening period in history; one in which the rational has a declining place. Mass suicides or the violent rise of semi-theocracies are the malign indications of the depths of these irrational feelings when they are brought together with a form of religious fanaticism. One can only hope that the good equivalents of these deep feelings are at least as powerful as the distortions; and that, in terms of institutionalized Christianity, means doing much more than using the channels of the faith from pulpits to the ecclesiastical press, or even those endless emanations of Gospel sound from American television screens.

The Vatican has no business seeking the best of both worlds, arousing mass enthusiasm, yet remaining secretive:

> All your castle must be opened,
> Light must drive the dark before it . . . .

Bluebeard did not like the prospect. It was against his natural propensities, too, but the effort must be made. It is not often that common sense dictates what is so thoroughly right to all concerned. This time it does, and expediency is also a virtue. What is required of the Vatican is to be ready to accept the full meaning of the universality to which it lays claim.

6

ROMAN CHOICES

THE PAPACY DOES not evolve. It has, instead, its ups and downs. It also has periods in which one part of its character is uppermost and others when it changes into something rather different, for a while at any rate. In musical terms, the papacy is fugal, in the sense that the one great theme is always there but making itself heard in different ways and in different combinations. Its claims have remained the same for centuries but the method of choosing the monarch, which has similarly remained unchanged, means that a man who is usually rather elderly receives these immense powers in an atmosphere of high drama so that constant change in style and methods is built into this archaic constitution. The world at large never quite knows what to expect from the papacy, or whether it should expect anything at all that is likely to influence the evolution of events.

The broad sweep of the papacy's changes throughout its history can be identified quite easily. It began to emerge as an institution in the fourth century and, until the close of the supposedly fateful first millennium, saw its prestige grow and its primacy expand beyond spiritual leadership of the Church to become its disciplinary authority.

Towards the middle of the eleventh century, two developments brought fundamental change. The first was the split with the Eastern Church in 1054 that has never been healed. Secondly, Rome became the centre of the internal reform of the Western Church aimed at eliminating lay interference and, with it, lay habits in ecclesiastical life. This is the period that saw the introduction of the rule of celibacy. Rome lost its primacy of honour in the East but gained a more powerful primacy in the West. Popes looked on themselves as the arbiters of affairs, over and above the lay authorities, and they shared this exercise of power only with the cardinals, who met frequently to advise the pope and deliberate with him. This was the pattern that, in general, prevailed for another 500 years. The change in the sixteenth century was towards a more purely monarchical rule, a pope who was king over the Church, mediator between this world and the next and lone in his authority. It was natural that popes of that time felt the need not of an active College of Cardinals to advise them, but of an efficient executive to carry out their decisions. That is why the Curia, the central machinery of government, dates from the sixteenth century.

What looked like final confirmation of a totally monarchical papacy in all its aspects came little more than a century ago with the first Vatican Council's decision in 1870 to give formal expression to the pope's primacy and his infallibility. This 'total' papacy seemed solidly set for the future as late as the reign of Pius XII, which is a bare two decades ago, and any great upheaval could have been envisaged at that time only by the freak election of a revolutionary pope. Anyone wanting change was left with his dream of 'if I were pope' and of where he would walk if he were shod with the shoes of the fisherman. Did Wojtyla have such dreams? Certainly Morris L. West's book was there on the bookshelf of the modest bedroom in Cracow which he left when he went to the conclave and never saw again. Did John XXIII amuse himself with such thoughts during his long career of comparative obscurity? Probably. Certainly he was the classic modern case of an ideal working of the archaic mechanisms. He was old, mature and unknown when he was abruptly placed at the apex of the pyramid. His reign was brief and dramatic and suddenly sent the Church forward in a totally different direction by his decision to call a Council. As far as a transfiguration can be accomplished in institutional terms, he achieved it, reminding the world and the Church that the old ways, summed up in his person, of old-fashioned religion and personal goodness could still make a profound effect on a modern public. It could be that his reign was the last occasion when benevolent tradition spoke with meaning to a declining civilization.

Pius XII would never have called a Council, and in his time most people would have agreed that Councils were a thing of the past. Nor, probably, would Paul VI, though he steered to an end the Council which John had summoned. Because of the different impact that every new pope could theoretically make, as both the election and its effect on the individual can be unpredictable, the ecclesiastical machinery must see to it that any fresh ideas that emerge are normally represented as a return to some half-forgotten evangelical truth, or a refurbishing of something everyone believed in anyway. The collegial notion of the papacy which emerged from the Council was presented as a modern version of the group of apostles with Peter as the foremost of them, but nevertheless among and not above them. Read in terms of the modern papacy, this meant that everything was of course just as it had always been but that, instead of being alone and absolute, the papacy would be framed by the rest of the bishops who would have their part in formulating policy. The object was to bring the papacy more in line with the times, make it more acceptable to other Christians and provide the basis for that unity in diversity which was supposed to be the hallmark of modern Catholicism.

All the arguments have been heard in the last two decades for this relative diminution in the status of the papacy within the Church, at the same time making it more acceptable to serious people who are not Catholic or even particularly Christian. Yet, ironically, it suddenly changed its position to reach a pinnacle of popular favour in a way that it had not done for centuries. Anyone attempting to reduce papal pretensions now would not only be challenging the institution's own arguments about its prestige but also the popular will expressed in acts of mass homage.

The claims of the popes in all their grandeur do not need any detailed re-examination; they are well known and, in any case, no amount of reasoning would now do more than reopen the argument, there would be no new understanding. The claims are there. They are firmly held, and they will not be relinquished. Little more need be recalled (and that briefly) than what the central claim amounts to.

Peter was accorded by Jesus a sort of primacy among the apostles and this has been handed down to the popes as successors to Peter in the Rome bishopric. Undoubtedly Peter stood out among the other apostles, sometimes for his rather obtuse responses to Jesus's promptings, sometimes for the special regard Jesus showed him and, on one famous occasion at least, for his sudden insight into how Jesus himself saw his own role: 'You are the Messiah, the son of the living God.' According to Matthew, this insight brought the appreciative response from Jesus:

Simon, son of Jonah, you are favoured indeed!
You did not learn that from any mortal man;
it was revealed to you by my heavenly Father.
And I say this to you:
You are Peter the Rock, and on this rock I
will build my Church, and the powers of death
shall never conquer it.
I will give you the keys of the Kingdom of Heaven:
what you forbid on earth shall be forbidden in Heaven,
and what you allow on earth shall be allowed in Heaven.

The extent to which this gratified comment from Jesus can be seen as the basis for the papacy's claims to universal pastorship is something for prelates themselves to bother with, given that such claims will not be withdrawn. The most striking feature of this exchange is that the scarcely nimble-witted Peter suddenly revealed his ability to think in that split-second, yet accurate way that was so characteristic of Jesus himself. This was something at the heart of the whole ministry of Jesus. Ten lines later, Jesus confuses matters by upbraiding Peter with the severe: 'Away with you, Satan.'

To Peter's leading position among the apostles one must add another undoubted element in the papal claims: that popes take their right to rule the universal Church, not from the papal election as such, but from their appointment as Bishop of Rome. The idea is still maintained that a papal election is in fact the choice of the bishop for the sacred city. This anchorage of the papacy in the Rome bishopric (and not vice versa) depends on two fictions. The first is that the pope's actual electors, that is the cardinals, still represent the Rome clergy. In order to give a semblance of authenticity, every cardinal from every continent is given what is called a titular church, in Rome. His arms are above the door and he is supposed to take some interest in its affairs though such interest can only be slight. The second fiction is that bishops are chosen by the people and clergy. They may have been at one time but they are certainly not now. If they were, the work of the papal nuncios would be much lightened.

The Roman attachment explains why Paul VI's ideas for changing the rules of papal elections in order to allow some representatives of the world's bishops, or even of laymen, to take part proved impossible. His most promising proposal was to allow the fifteen members of the standing committee of the International Synod of Bishops to take part in elections. Some are in fact already cardinals. Those that were not would have been allowed in on the grounds that their committee has its offices in Rome and meets there. But even this was regarded as too little justification for a change. The election remains the monopoly of the cardinals.

Cardinals were originally Roman prelates and acted as advisers of the early popes. In 1150 they were formed into a Sacred College of Cardinals, a term which still exists, and in 1179 were accorded the exclusive right of electing the pope. The twelfth century saw the nomination of cardinals from outside the Rome clergy and that change continued to the point that every continent is now represented in the Sacred College. The one innovation since the Middle Ages was Paul VI's decision in November 1970 to exclude cardinals over the age of eighty from the conclave. This decision was an attempt at making the conclave more acceptable to modern thinking; more credible, because the sight of sick, old men on their way to carry out this highest function accorded to any prelate, was thought to add a ridiculous touch to the process of choosing Christ's Vicar.

The diocese of Rome had little difficulty in establishing its dominant position. It outstripped Jerusalem early in Christianity's history. The ancient mark of the sacred placed upon Jerusalem should have given it an early lead over the pretensions of the imperial capital but the leadership of the Jerusalem Christians after the death of Jesus could not compare with the energy and imagination of Paul, and it was his version of Christianity that prevailed. The 'elders', as the Jerusalem leaders were called, including James, the 'brother' of Jesus, suffered much the same fate as Paul VI's elderly cardinals, and the chance was lost, if ever it existed, of keeping Judaism and belief in Jesus together. Paul, to the point of his martyrdom, coupled Christianity inevitably with the Roman world of which he was a citizen, away from Judaism that he had also served fervently in his days as a Pharisee. The Christian bishopric in Jerusalem in the early centuries was weak, while fresh prestige was accorded to Rome by the quality of its bishops as well as the tradition that the see had been founded by the apostles (though Peter was not the founder of the Church in Rome, and earlier had probably been the leader of the Christians in Antioch). The city grew swiftly and naturally to become Christianity's centre and Christianity itself settled in the capital that had sent the unpleasant Pilate to Palestine, and spread through the extraordinary travels and labours of Paul.

The rooting of the papacy in Rome is, in a sense, a saving grace. It makes the papacy a much more flexible office than it might seem to be with so many accretions of history and tradition upon it. A double character permits a choice of emphasis and that is how, for years, what might be called the progressive elements in the Church saw the future of the papacy: either papal or pastoral, depending on how much a particular pope placed his weight on being pope or Bishop of Rome. The demand for a pastoral pope, who would concentrate on his bishopric and leave the rest of the world to take care of itself, was at its height in the last years of Paul VI, years that, on looking back, were in several ways crucial for Catholicism's chances of dealing with the West's crisis. One constantly heard that Paul was too much the diplomat; too much the administrator and too little the pastoral leader of his own particular flock. This may have been true and certainly Romans did not look to this undemonstrative Milanese as their bishop in the way they did to the Roman Pius XII. Nor did the whole world look to Paul for guidance in the way it had when affectionately following John XXIII.

Most of Paul's career had been spent in diplomacy and administration within the Roman Curia itself. Except for his comparatively brief period as Archbishop of Milan he was the recognizable case of a non-pastoral, non-episcopal pope. And so it was on this point that the critics aimed their attacks. What was wanted was a pastoral pope, a good keeper of his own diocese with a minimum of other pretensions. They failed to understand that they were drawing general conclusions from a personal case and John Paul II was soon to show how mistaken their thinking had been. The real choice was not between a papal pope and an episcopal pope.

From the beginning of his reign, John Paul II gave conscious priority to three forms of activity: his mass audiences, his travels and his care of the Rome diocese. He was superbly equipped to do so. As far as diocesan work is concerned, he arrived with a high reputation as an active and successful Archbishop of Cracow. This background gave him the assurance needed to tackle one of Catholicism's most difficult dioceses, partly so because it has the Vatican within it.

Statistics give a stark indication of the poor state of religion in Catholicism's centre. In 1978 the officially estimated Catholic population of 2,677,000 produced two new priests for Rome's 284 parishes and 623 churches. By comparison with Madrid, another southern capital in Catholicism's old heart, Rome's showing is even more lamentable. Madrid has a much·bigger population, certainly, but it produced nineteen priests for the diocese and seventy-six newly ordained members of religious orders. Washington, DC, with a Catholic population of only 397,000, produced eight diocesan priests and ordained twenty-three members of religious orders.

Rome, in particular, suffers from a phenomenon of a striking failure on the part of young, religious-minded men to think of entering the priesthood. This seems to be an increasing dilemma, and one that could bring about some fundamental rethinking about the priesthood as a caste. It is not confined to Rome. However, the challenge arises strongly there, in what is normally a somewhat indifferent city, because believers see so many of the priestly caste around them; not all of them by any means a credit but usually very conscious of this sense of caste.

The quest for new priests is not the only indication of the health of a diocese, at least not to the extent it once was. That said, it remains indicative to use the figures of vocations as a sign of the health of the institutional Church. Other indications, moreover, support the idea that the Rome diocese is in a specially low state. There is rather too much of Bellarmine's 'visible and palpable' church in Rome; at the same time there are too many social problems, like that of the perplexed immigrants who flocked to the city expecting a better standard of living and soon found themselves lost in an urban ocean of indifference; too much sheer surface of the sacred city's area given over to irresponsible construction of huge concrete blocks of apartments with no green left between them and no community life around them. Rome has a unique problem: it attracted hundreds of thousands of immigrants during the years of promise and prosperity because people felt that the capital must offer the chances of work. They came from the countryside around Rome and from the deep south, abandoning farmland in the hope of making a new life in the city. The flow has largely stopped now but its effects are being felt increasingly. What most of the immigrants did not know when they decided to try their fortune in the capital was that it had almost no industry. It lives from shopkeeping, bureaucracy both civil and ecclesiastical, and tourism. Industry used not to be encouraged. From the beginning of its century or so of history as Italy's capital, there was no wish to surround the ancient city with the menacing phalanxes of the working classes. One result is that

Rome now has something much worse: a non-working class which is responsible for much of the violence and crime which came in the aftermath of shattered hopes. It can be said that all big cities have these problems. Yet only two decades ago Rome was about the easiest-going city imaginable for its size, still markedly human. Not sacred, but pleasant to live in. One could more readily understand the article in the Concordat between the Vatican and the Italian government by which the civil authorities are obliged to protect its 'sacred character'.

In the years of the boom, the Church missed an open invitation to try and halt the dehumanizing process corroding the cities, starting with Rome. It might not have managed to solve the problem but it could at least have been on the right side in seeking to achieve something which could only have gone to reinforce the Church's credibility. While the uncontrolled expansion of the cities was at its height—in effect, a dress-rehearsal for the problems the West is now facing—the Church missed the chance of placing itself in the vanguard of the moral forces intent on assuring men the minimum of dignity due to them by the proper use of the knowledge, sensibility and technology that are part of modern civilization, the better part of it.

A stand of this kind would also have allowed the Church the chance to lead the movement for respect for nature and the cultural patrimony. The Church at an early date in its history chose Western civilization as its base, and went on to inspire and enrich that civilization in such a way as to be able to claim a unique responsibility towards it. This is not simply a Roman matter: it is a responsibility present wherever the Church is itself present in what remains of Western life. If as much energy had been spent in studying the Church's organizational structure and outlook on modern life as was devoted to condemnations of Communism, dismantling of the first worker-priests' movements in France, campaigning against divorce, the Church's weight of conviction would now be immeasurably higher than it is.

> . . . the Church considers an essential, unbreakably united element of her mission this solicitude for man, for his humanity, for the future of men on earth and therefore also for the course set for the whole of development and progress. She finds the principle of this solicitude in Jesus Christ himself, as the Gospels witness.

These admirable sentiments come from John Paul II's first encyclical letter, entitled *Redemptor Hominis*, Redeemer of Man.

That was in 1979. Seven years earlier, and that much nearer to the crucial experience of expansion, a group of thirteen priests, working in the shanty-towns of Rome, addressed an open letter to the practising Catholics of the city, in which they stated unequivocally that the massive speculation in building had been carried out with 'no respect for the dignity of man'. The letter contained passages similar to the condemnations of the poet Pasolini:

> Day after day they built a city of violence. For the speculators, it was not men they were dealing with but animals, to be packed into reserves and exploited. The alliance in speculation of the clerical, political and economic power has made of this city an anthill where misery and splendour, poverty and wealth live alongside each other.

Sometimes the Christian conscience can be tiresome, because it looks intent on searching for something to be guilty about; the post-war failures, however, should not pass unforgotten simply because a more intelligent outlook has now superseded—or rather, contradicted—what went before.

I do not know who St Egidio was, and his identity does not bother me very much. He could become the saint—and in this case he would be a very fortunate saint, blessed among saints if that is a possibility—who will give his name to the whole process of narrowing the abyss, because an abandoned convent, formerly of nuns who followed St Teresa, is named after him. It has become the headquarters of a group of young people in Rome who are attempting with success a Christian approach to Rome's problems. They meet in the convent Church each evening for prayer and every Saturday for Mass. They have their own music which they have devised for the psalms and the hymns and the prayers. There are seats but many prefer to sit on the floor. The music is chant-like more than melodic, very Eastern and contemplative in its atmosphere. It is not a joyful sound but it is not overbearing or militant either: it is thoughtful and relaxed and deeply devotional. If these sounds were made in the Sistine Chapel, Michelangelo's huge figures would turn away in impatience. Usually there is a homily. I heard a rather rhetorical Protestant. He talked for much too long about liberation and Moses and was very insistent and at times carried away by the truths he was trying to communicate.

He was markedly Low Church. A young man beside me explained the trouble: 'He's getting old and wants to tell us everything every time he speaks.'

St Egidio is in Trastevere, the traditional neighbourhood in classical Rome of the poet-workers and slaves. It retained this plebeian, frank, self-confident and human style until a decade or so ago when its charms attracted the foreign community. And so St Egidio stands out still more in the midst of this area, which remains beautiful but has acquired the air of pretentious futility and a reputation for petty crime. It is very close to the Vatican.

I spoke to two leaders of this Community of St Egidio. The first said: 'We have been in existence for more than twelve years. It began at the Virgilio High School in the wake of the student revolt of 1968. It did not grow from a parish: there was no priest involved. A few students had the idea of making the Gospel livable. They had already discovered the poor and the shanty-towns of the other Rome. I want to say again that the community was born at arm's length from the official Church, I mean the opposite of most communities of dissent which emerge within the Church and leave it or arise as a reaction to it. Unlike the extreme Left groups we have practical ties with the city. We did not discover the Gospel and the city's problems because we were Catholics. We had to have the poor, we needed them. We had learnt a taste for humanity from the Gospels. It all started with six people, of whom two are still here. Now the community has 2,500 members throughout the city. We attempt social service in the poor periphery of the city. We are working in twelve of these suburbs. We have organized groups of young workers. We have set up schools for training apprentices and nursery schools which are managed by the parents themselves because we see the object of our life as being solidarity. We are experimenting with help for old people. In Rome there is a break between people and the authorities. We are trying to close it. Today the basic course for Christianity is human rights. We try to do something for foreign workers here. They did not exist for the Church until five or six years ago. Remember we are lay. We do not have a priest-founder; our organizational structure is that of an assembly. Everyone can come and say what they want. We were born outside the structure of the Church. It was not until the Rome diocese organized the conference on 'The Evils of Rome' that we began to have some rapport with the official Church. You remember a group of young people threw petrol over a sleeping

Somali near Piazza Navona and set him alight. We went and made an all-night vigil at the place where he was killed. Then we wrote a letter to the ecclesiastical authorities reminding them of their responsibilities towards foreign visitors. We reminded them what St Gregory the Great said when he saw a man lying dead in the road as he was going to church to celebrate Mass. He refused to celebrate: "This is Good Friday," he said. We were the first group to be invited to Castelgandolfo to spend an evening with Pope John Paul II. We spent three hours with him, several hundred of us. The absentees were away working. We sang some songs. We showed him a twenty-minute film on the problems of Rome. Then for three-quarters of an hour we had an assembly on youth, on violence, on the poor, on the periphery and the type of projects we were proposing. The pope told us that he went visiting parishes as Bishop of Rome but this could not provide him with much of the truth and so these meetings like today were good. He spoke very seriously against the consumer society. Then when he had finished his talk, he changed. You know there was something that reminded me of the Transfiguration. He stopped being severe and became friendly and affectionate. He is coming to visit us soon, here at St Egidio. The next church to us along the road is Santa Maria in Trastevere. It is the titular church of Cardinal Wyszinski and so he can easily come to us when he goes there, which he is sure to do, and quite soon I think. What does what we are doing mean to us? Well, it means how to be Christian in a big city. To affront solitude. We try to be a community of lay persons, normal people, who live the life of the city like everyone else, including the traffic. But we try to show that it is not essential to live *per se*, just for one's self. It's a sort of urban monasticism if you like, but lived in the city like everyone else lives and our own utopia of family and fraternity. We are not different from the others. Some of us are married. Some couples just live together. Celibacy is not the choice of something different but a different type of service. It is not that being celibate gives a special stamp that others have not got. Our financing is done by self-taxation. Everyone decides how much to give. We get small contributions from the local authorities towards the costs of our social projects. Some charitable organizations give us some money. We sometimes have a collection for special projects like summer trips for the old.'

The other young man picked up the argument by saying that they had started the community in 1968 in a particular climate for

141

Europe, for France and for Italy too. Young people were in revolt in Italy against the institutions of society. It was the time of the students' revolt. The community's roots were in the students' movement, in the Vatican Council and in the renewal that the Council has brought about inside the Church. The original aims were first to live radically the Gospel in their own lives; secondly to be aware of the reality around them and to have a sort of critical attitude towards this reality. From the beginning the idea of a community was important.

He saw two sides to Rome: a nice centre with its ancient monuments where the well-to-do families live; but around the centre there was this poor periphery which looked like part of a Third World city. And that was where the families of the immigrants lived, coming from the south to find a job. But they could not find a job, sometimes not a house either and so they lived in shanty-towns. That was where the community began to work, teaching the children to talk Italian because some could only speak Sicilian or another dialect. ('And it is much easier to understand English than Sicilian.')

The community was divided into four groups. There was a central 'mother' community formed by young adults, mostly people who were finishing university or already working. There were about 400 in this community including the founders. They had founded local communities in the poor quarters of Rome who gathered together in the same sense of spirituality as this central group and tried to embody the ideas of the community in their own lives. The other three main groups were of high school students, young workers, an adult group and a group of old people. The heart of the community was the prayer meeting every night and the Saturday Eucharist.

When you think of Rome, he said, you think of the pope, but there is a religious life at the base, made up of people who, alone, started to live the Gospel in practice and it is strongly alive today in Rome. There was a gap between the young people and the Church, which was growing. A quiet revolution was going on, and young people had more and more been leaving the Church. There were a lot of myths of the consumer society, a lot of drug addiction, especially in Rome. And what really hurt was that there was a big emptiness, because the Church was not much present and nor were the politicians. Nobody seemed to answer this emptiness. The community's effort had been to propose a form of religiosity that was full and started from the human questions of young people.

This community is profoundly Catholic, there can be no doubt of that. They are rational and able people. They are extremist only in their determination. There is no open challenge to the official Church, but they point out frequently that their origins were not within the official system and if their relations with officialdom exist now and are satisfactory, there is still a fact which should be taken into consideration by the official Church. In twelve years of devoted Christian work, of prayer and sacrifice, no one at St Egidio has thought fit to become a priest.

The decision of John Paul II to give his diocese high priority in his strategy very early in his reign must be accorded its due import-ance. He was doing something practical to follow the great gesture of Paul VI's plea to the terrorists. One way to meet rising violence is to try to reach the springs of it, and attempt to turn these acrid discharges into the clear waters of reason. John Paul II made clear this was his intention in an address to the newly appointed Italian Ambassador, Bruno Bottai, on 25 June 1979, when he specifically rejected the notion of opposing violence with violence but sought the enlargement of outlooks to give space for such ideals as love, justice, liberty and disinterested service to society.

His method of dealing with the diocese was to make highly publicized visits to individual parishes. He escaped the merely superficial effect of a spectacular but brief descent one Sunday that would leave untouched the real difficulties facing each congrega-tion. He first sent an auxiliary bishop to devote a week or more to a parish about to be visited, living its difficulties and preparing a dossier so that the pope would have at hand a detailed account of parochial life before making his dramatic appearance. The pope would talk to the faithful and then go off with the local clergy, inviting them to a meal with him. Subsequently the parish would be expected to follow the course agreed in meeting the problems indicated in the auxiliary's file. The Bishop of Rome was no longer a remote figure in his own diocese but a very real bishop with an organization able to provide him with detailed parochial briefings. The reformers had got their way and pastoral considera-tions were now high on the papal agenda. Instead of sitting at his

143

desk with a pile of diplomatic telegrams in front of him, he was out among the people, being their pastor.

Had they really got their way, however? The answer is that they misjudged the degree of choice between being an active pope and being an active bishop. John Paul II showed that by being more episcopal he still further strengthened the papal office. This was what the reformers had not foreseen. The pope was no longer open to the criticism made about Paul VI—that he was too distant a figure, out of touch with ordinary people because he was absorbed in the government of the Church throughout the world. That weakness had gone, and at the same time John Paul II acquired a new strength in his dealings with the bishops of the world. They could no longer regard the pope as unable to grasp their local problems because he was raised so high above them. Suddenly, the pope had become a leader in pastoral matters as well, with facts and figures, issues, problems and solutions at his papal finger-tips. The idea of the co-responsibility of the bishops in the government of the Church with the pope in the chair, but essentially one of them, was still further damaged. The irresistible rise went on: even a pope was seen to be able to enjoy the best of the two worlds of the diocese and the palace. Bluebeard and the spouse calling for the keys and for the light were not, as we thought, two people, but one. The sombre nobleman had in fact been struggling with himself to reveal two apparently contradictory sides of his troubled mind.

The heart of the palace is less the pope's private apartment than the Sistine Chapel where he is elected. A papal election remains a powerful mystery: dangerous and fascinating at once, with a stong touch of magic. It is carried out by a hundred or so members of the most exclusive caste to gather anywhere in the world to elect an international personality. They still perform the traditional procedure of voting in front of the high altar. For them, the Sistine Chapel shakes off that strident atmosphere that thousands of tourists bring to it during the day.

For the papal election it becomes once again a quietly famous place that has taken to itself that special attraction which fame gives, whether to persons or to buildings, poems or famous compositions, and of course, to popes. The chapel is not striking in itself. It is plainly rectangular, not large, and devoid of architectural features that engage one. It is now too small for the

old tradition accompanying papal elections, by which every
cardinal had his own canopied stall to sit in while pondering his
vote. The cardinals sit at tables now and one of the election's most
moving moments has gone: Paul VI was the last pope to see the
sight of all the canopies above the stalls slowly descending, as the
individual cardinals pulled the cords which lowered them, in
honour of the new pontiff who sat there alone with his canopy
raised.

The chapel is, of course, dominated by the Roman genius of
Michelangelo. Other great painters have painted frescos there,
including Botticelli, but the world queues to see the Sistine Chapel
because Michelangelo worked there, on both the huge ceiling and
the fresco of the *Last Judgement* over the altar where the cardinals
cast their votes. Michelangelo was Tuscan but his vision was
Roman: monumental, authoritarian, weighty, full of assurance,
strength and certainty, accustomed to decide and to give the law.
In the huge fresco above the altar, Jesus appears as judge and king,
bereft now of all enigma, ambiguity, mystery. The body is
clumsy, the face bullying and stern. He divides men into two
categories of good and bad, but the impression evoked is not one
of a being whose judgement would evoke much rational confidence. Only the horrors of the Apocalypse are there. He is so
obviously in possession of all power that transfiguration would
simply be an irrelevancy. He is a man's view of himself as God,
which is likely to be less endearing than a man's day-dreams about
what he would do if suddenly he became pope. The Sistine Christ
is either vengeful or rewarding. He has nothing of the subtlety and
ambivalence of the Gospel Christ, qualities also useful to a pope.
He is immediately recognizable as a stern ruler, majestic, no
longer likely to be mistaken for a gardener, or seen as a shadowy
fellow-traveller on the road to Emmaus. Suddenly in the Sistine
Chapel one doubts the efficacy, the utility, or the capacity of even
the greatest of artists to represent the divinity. Beethoven thought
he was reasonably near and was able to say of God: 'I have always
recognized and understood him.' Creativity is evidently a great
bond. But more so in music. Perhaps the Muslims are wise in
forbidding images or representations of the divine. Perhaps the
Catholic Church was wiser when, in the past, it insisted on
keeping its own music to a simple chant, and thus the minor
servant of the Word, for fear that the Word itself might be
overshadowed or that new, unwarranted emotions be stimulated.

Whatever the answer, the question is raised there in the Sistine

Chapel as to whether this is the proper atmosphere in which a man is chosen to become the Vicar of Christ. This is where he takes on those huge prerogatives, with every emotional pull added to what is basically a simple act of election, before the successful candidate is brought out on to the central balcony of St Peter's to be presented to the world as its new universal pastor, and to the people of Rome as their new bishop.

Yet the old method of electing popes goes on as it has done for centuries with almost no change. Paul VI, like both his predecessors, altered a few details, but essentially the election consists of voting by all the eligible cardinals, who are locked inside the Vatican for the purpose, cut off very effectively from all contact with the outside world until they have managed to produce a pope. In his Apostolic Constitution called *Romano Pontifici Eligendo*, Paul VI goes over the details of the three methods by which the cardinals could choose his successor. The first method is called 'by acclamation' or 'by inspiration' and occurs when, in Paul's words, 'the Cardinal electors, as it were through the inspiration of the Holy Spirit, freely and spontaneously, unanimously and aloud, proclaim one individual as Supreme Pontiff.' They are all to use the word '*eligo*' pronounced in an intelligible manner, or expressed in writing if a person is unable to utter it, and the election must be accepted unanimously by every cardinal in the conclave. The second method is called 'by delegation' and means that the cardinals may entrust a group of their members to elect the new pope on behalf of them all. The third and normal method is 'by scrutiny'. The speed with which the first John Paul was elected pope and the rather pious statements by a number of cardinals about divine intervention in their work led to some speculation as to whether he had been elected by acclamation. But it was not so. The scrutiny method remains the one by which modern popes are elected.

Paul VI wrote:

In this regard, we fully confirm the law sanctioned in ancient times and faithfully observed ever since, which establishes that for the valid election of the Supreme Pontiff two-thirds of the votes are necessary. In the same way, we will to maintain in force the norm laid down by our Predecessor Pius XII which prescribes that in addition to two-thirds of the votes there must always be one additional vote.

The aim of Pius's innovation, dropped by John XXIII, was to avoid allowing the crucial vote to be cast by the successful candidate himself. His own vote could no longer give him the two-thirds.

Paul then went on to describe the four phases of what he called the 'pre-scrutiny'. The first was the preparation and distribution of the voting cards by the Masters of Ceremonies, who give two or three to each cardinal elector. The second was the drawing of lots for three Scrutineers from among the cardinals, for three persons, known as 'Infirmarii', charged with collecting the votes of the sick, and for three Revisors. The drawing of lots is carried out publicly by the junior Cardinal Deacon. The next phase is the completion of the cards which must be carried out secretly by every cardinal elector who will write down, as far as possible in writing that cannot be identified as his, the name of the person he chooses, taking care not to write other names as well, since this would make the vote null. The card is then folded down the centre in such a way that its width is reduced to about one inch.

The cards have to be rectangular in shape and must bear in the centre of the upper half, in print if possible, the words '*Eligo in Summum Pontificem*'; on the lower half there must be a space left for writing the name of the person chosen and the card must be made in such a way that it can be folded in two. During the voting, the cardinals must remain alone in the Chapel, so immediately after the distribution of the cards and before the electors begin to write, the Secretary of the Conclave, the Papal Master of Ceremonies and the assistant Masters of Ceremonies must leave. After their exit, the junior Cardinal Deacon closes the door, opening and closing it each time this is necessary, as for example when the 'Infirmarii' go to collect the votes of the sick and when they return to the Chapel.

The actual voting is in its way elaborate. Each cardinal, in order of precedence, having written on his card and folded it, holds it up so that it can be seen and carries it to the altar, at which the Scrutineers stand and upon which there is placed a receptacle, covered by a plate, for receiving the cards. Having reached the altar, the cardinal elector kneels, prays for a short time, and then rises and pronounces aloud the following form of oath: 'I call to witness Christ the Lord who will be my judge, that my vote is given to the one who before God I consider should be elected.' He then places the card on the plate, with which he drops it into the receptacle. Having done this, he bows to the altar and returns to his place.

After all the cardinals have placed their cards in the receptacle, the first Scrutineer shakes it several times in order to mix them, and immediately afterwards the last Scrutineer proceeds to count them, picking them out of the receptacle in full view and depositing them in another empty receptacle. If the number of cards does not respond to the number of electors the cards must all be burnt and a second vote taken at once; if the number of cards does correspond, there follows the scrutiny of the cards.

The Scrutineers sit at a table placed in front of the altar. The first of them takes a card, unfolds it, notes the name of the person chosen and passes the card to the second Scrutineer, who in turn notes the name and passes the card to the third, who reads it aloud and in an intelligible manner, so that all the electors present can make a note of the vote on a sheet of paper prepared for the purpose. He himself writes down the name read from the card. If during the scrutiny of the votes the Scrutineers should discover two cards folded in such a way as to appear to have been filled in by one elector, and if these cards bear the same name, they are counted as one vote; if however they bear different names, neither of the votes will be valid.

When all the votes have been scrutinized, the Scrutineers add up the sum of votes obtained by the different names, and write them down on a separate sheet of paper. As he reads out the individual cards, the last Scrutineer pierces each one with a threaded needle through the word '*Eligo*' and places it on the thread, so that the cards may be more carefully preserved. After the names have been read out, the ends of the thread are tied in a knot, and the cards thus joined together are placed in an empty receptacle or on one side of the table.

There then follows the post-scrutiny stage. The Scrutineers add up all the votes that each individual has received. Whether someone has reached the majority of two-thirds plus one or not, the Revisors must proceed to the checking both of the cards and of the notes of the votes made by the Scrutineers, in order to make sure that these latter have performed their task exactly and faithfully.

Immediately after the checking and before the cardinal electors leave the Chapel, all the cards are to be burnt by the Scrutineers, with the assistance of the Secretary of the Conclave and the Masters of Ceremonies, who have meanwhile been summoned by the junior Cardinal Deacon. If, however, a second vote is to be taken immediately, the cards from the first voting will be burnt only at the end, together with the cards from the second voting.

Paul VI then went on to insist, with his passion for increased secrecy during a papal election, that every cardinal had to surrender to the Cardinal Camerlengo or to one of the three Cardinal Assistants any notes he might have in his possession concerning the result of each scrutiny. These notes were to be burnt together with the cards.

> We further lay down that at the end of the conclave the Cardinal Camerlengo of the Holy Roman Church shall draw up a document, to be approved also by the three Cardinal Assistants, stating the voting of each session. This statement, which is to be kept in the archives, shall be placed in a sealed envelope, which may be opened by no one unless the Supreme Pontiff gives explicit permission.

If after three days the cardinals have not found a pope, the sessions are suspended

> to allow a pause for prayer, free discussions among the voters and a brief spiritual exhortation given by the senior cardinal in the order of Deacons. The voting sessions are then resumed according to the same format. After seven sessions, if the election has not taken place, there is another pause for prayer, discussion and an exhortation given by the senior cardinal of the order of Priests. Another series of seven sessions is then proceeded with, and, if a result has not been reached, is followed by a fresh pause for prayer, discussion and an exhortation given by the senior cardinal in the order of Bishops. At this point the Cardinal Camerlengo of the Holy Roman Church will consult the electors concerning the manner of proceeding. The criterion of requiring, for an effective vote, two-thirds of the votes plus one must not be abandoned, unless all the cardinal electors unanimously, that is with no exception, express themselves in favour of a different criterion, which may consist of the delegation or of the absolute majority of votes plus one, or of ballotting between the two who in the session immediately preceding have gained the greatest number of votes.

There are surprising elements in this form of election. Despite the fact that much of the regulation depends on a kind of ritual suspicion among the contenders, there is a touching attempt at appealing to better instincts and at involving the whole Church in this solemn secret. Paul called on the cardinals not to be guided by friendship or aversion, or influenced by favour or respect towards anyone, or forced by the intervention of persons in authority or by pressure groups, by the suggestion of the mass media, or by force, fear or the seeking of popularity. 'But having before their eyes solely the glory of God and the good of the Church and after imploring God's help, they shall give their vote to the person whom they judge to be more suited than the others to govern the universal Church fruitfully and usefully.' He points out that during the celebration of the conclave the Church is united in a very special manner with the pastors and especially with the cardinal electors:

> and implores from God a new Head as a gift of his goodness and providence. In fact, according to the example of the first Christian community spoken of in the Acts of the Apostles, the Universal Church, spiritually united with Mary the Mother of Jesus, must 'persevere in one mind in prayer'; thus the election of the new Pontiff will not be something unconnected with the People of God and reserved only to the college of electors but will be in a certain sense an act of the whole Church.

When a candidate has reached the required number of votes, he is asked the question: 'Do you accept your canonical election as Supreme Pontiff?' Once he has accepted, he is asked what name he chooses. These questions are put by the Cardinal Dean or the cardinal first in order of seniority in the name of the whole College. The Papal Master of Ceremonies acting as notary with two assistant Masters of Ceremonies acting as witnesses draws up a document of acceptance.

After the acceptance: 'the person elected, if he has already received episcopal ordination, is immediately Bishop of the Church of Rome, true Pope and Head of the College of Bishops; and *ipso facto* he acquires and can exercise full and absolute jurisdiction over the whole Church.' And so it is done.

A conclave is a highly solemn affair and one can readily understand the wrath of some of the older cardinals when told that they would be denied the right to enter once over the age of eighty. Some of them actually denied the pope's right to take away this highest of honours, though in effect the decision was not challenged. Oddly enough, these elderly cardinals excluded from the conclave became an unexpected source of information for public opinion. Their colleagues who went in could hardly deny them the pleasure of a report on the proceedings, and the secrecy which binds a participant at a conclave does not apply to those who were left outside by the new law.

A lot of praying is done inside, and there is a daily Mass throughout the duration of the conclave. The sleeping accommodation, much of it improvised from office space (visiting a Vatican prelate during a conclave may well mean a walk round the gardens if his office is included in the sealed-off area), has all the essentials but is spartan. The food, cooked by nuns from the Vatican's guest house, is adequate but plain, the wine an inexpensive white, and served in the splendours of the Borgia apartment. More secrecy than ever was imposed by Paul VI for the election of his successor, not only by his order that the whole conclave area be tested for hidden electronic devices, but also by his instruction that all notes and documents brought into the Sistine Chapel be burnt after every round of voting. The other slight changes made to the arrangements are largely due to the need to deal with a much enlarged Sacred College, after John XXIII broke the maximum of sixty laid down in the sixteenth century.

Originally the dual aim of the temporary imprisonment of the cardinals was to prevent interference from outside powers, and to place pressure on the cardinals, by physical discomfort, to come to a prompt decision, given that the Church is literally without a head during an interregnum. Once a pope dies, the everyday affairs of the Church, as well as the preparation for the election, are in the hands of the cardinals. However, they cannot take decisions of real import and, once they have been closed inside the Vatican, can no longer deal with even the ordinary business of the Church. Both reasons remain valid. The increased importance of the papacy in international affairs means that the secular powers are more interested now than at any other time in the history of the modern papacy in who should emerge from these curious deliberations.

A superficial but illuminating example of how outside influence can have its effect, is provided by the affair of the interview given by a leading Italian cardinal immediately before the conclave that elected Karol Wojtyla. Cardinal Siri, the highly conservative Archbishop of Genoa, gave a characteristically free-ranging interview to an Italian newspaper, in which he spoke badly of the barely buried John Paul I, as well as of the idea of collegiality. He asked the editor of the newspaper to hold the interview for publication until the morning after the conclave began, so that the cardinals would be safely locked away from the influences of the world and there could be no question of its having an effect on proceedings (the cardinals are not permitted newspapers, television or radio). Despite Cardinal Siri's request, the interview was published on the morning of the opening of the conclave; more, it was circulated to all cardinals, at the instigation, so it was said, of another Italian cardinal who saw himself and Siri as rival candidates. This rather unhappy little intrigue was certainly not decisive in ending the series of forty-four consecutive Italian popes, but it was an added indication that a change would do no harm. The change came.

But not in the process of election. Efforts quite apart from that of Paul VI have been made to broaden the conclave, with the aim of giving the bishops of the world a genuinely decisive role as part of their projected closer collaboration in the work of the Church's central administration. A plan was put forward on these lines in 1969 by Cardinal Suenens, then the Belgian primate and one of the most successful performers at the Council. His frankness in calling for change cost him much disfavour in Rome: some say it cost him the papacy. His plan came to nothing and nothing more has been heard of such ideas since the failure of Paul VI's own draft. It may seem strange that a pope cannot have his own way. That was at a point in Paul VI's reign when he was still vigorous and had as his principal adviser the formidable Giovanni Benelli, then Substitute at the Secretariat of State and later Cardinal-Archbishop of Florence. Benelli was not the man to fail to get his own way easily. I remember plainly his frame of mind when he explained to me that the reforms had had to be abandoned. He was genuinely saddened and irritated. Yet the popes themselves cannot escape from an image of the Church which history has imposed on them.

In fact, it is all there, expressed symbolically, in the Sistine Chapel itself. Even the greatest admirers of the art of Michelangelo must agree that the place represents a summit of art and of power, a concept of Christianity long left behind as an ideal. The world is not like that any more. Nor is its view of religion, and nor is the religion it needs.

7

CURIA AND SYNOD

SINGLE-MINDED MEN ARE frequent among the personalities that history has decided are worth remembering. A much smaller group, and in many ways a more interesting set of people, are those who leave options open to others. John XXIII decided that it was up to the Church to settle its problems because there were too many of them for him to try to face in the brief time left to him, and so he called a Council. Paul VI was the quintessence of one who purposely unlocks doors but does not go through them himself. He was the opposite of Bluebeard.

An example, and one that is filled with fascinating chances for the future, is the choice Paul left concerning his own administrative staff and the bishops. This issue is much like the dilemma between a papal pope and an episcopal one. It turns on the question of whether the traditional civil service of the Church, the Roman Curia, should have the pope's ear, or the comparatively new International Synod of Bishops, which was set up in 1965 by Paul VI as a means of expressing the Vatican Council's requirements on the responsibility of the bishops in taking their part in the central government of the Church. This might sound a tedious and bleakly constitutional matter concerning only the popes themselves, a few priestly civil servants and some bishops. But it is not. It may not have the immediate attractiveness of Mother Church's public travails with birth-control, pre-marital sex and the threat of women priests, but its implications are deep indeed. Characteristically, Paul VI half succeeded in his handling of the Roman Curia. He introduced a reform which brought a few immediate changes but left open to his successors the chance of profoundly changing the way in which the Catholic Church is governed. He could have been more resolute, but that was not his way.

The Roman Curia is a rambling structure which has not been remodelled since Sixtus V took it in hand and gave it its modern—well, fairly modern—form in 1588, the year of the Armada. There have been reforms in the meantime but the principal innovations have brought a change in the relationships of power within the traditional structure rather than fundamental differences, of which the most important is the way in which the Secretariat of State has gradually become predominant. At the same time, a whole new, and what still remains a subordinate, section has been added to the Curia since the Council, including a set of offices dealing with such subjects as Christian unity, relations with non-Christians, relations with non-believers, the family, lay people, justice and peace and, of the greatest potential importance, the International Synod of Bishops.

The Roman Curia remains the instrument through which the pope conducts the administration of the Church, at least in theory. In practice, the Curia can sometimes be shown to have had a mind of its own. At other times, especially after the election of John Paul II, it has been in part ignored while other parts have been used more extensively than before, depending as a rule on the personal relationship of the pope with the various heads of departments.

Its core is the Secretariat of State. The Secretariat is by no means the oldest Vatican department but its weight has grown consistently under the modern popes and its recognition as the Curia's main executive and co-ordinating body was completed in Paul VI's reform of August 1967. People spoke at the time of the humiliation of the older forms of Curia life, because the reform meant that the work of all the other departments had not only to be co-ordinated by the Secretariat but duplicated by this all-powerful department. Its original function was as the pope's personal secretariat. It had grown by 1968 into what in lay terms could be called the prime minister's office. It now has sections dealing with practically all matters which concern the Church's central government, from political questions and diplomacy to the liturgy, appointment of bishops, the problems of priests, the religious orders, and so on. The department which has its work revised by the Secretariat is not supposed to know (in the general line of the Vatican's fatal attraction to secrecy) the identity of the prelate who carries out the review. I remember one eminent prelate, then working in the Sacred Congregation dealing with doctrine, who told me that he had managed to identify some of the anonymous commentaries from the Secretariat of State by getting to know the print of individual typewriters. A cynic might suppose that one way by which administration could be simplified and money saved would be to abolish everything except the Secretariat of State. That, however, would be ingenuous, because the Curia as a whole is not a diminishing instrument but a rapidly proliferating one. The increase in size between 1961 and 1978, just the increase, amounted to more than the whole Curia in the time of John XXIII. And he was credited with the remark when asked how many people worked in the Curia: 'About half.'

The Secretariat, as might be expected, increased sharply. In ten years it went from a personnel of seventy-seven officials to 114. Though the main organ of the Church's central government, it shows less of the effects of internationalization of the Curia than other departments. Some ninety-one out of the 114 were Italians. But the blood was reasonably new. Two-thirds of the officials entered the Secretariat after the reform of 1967. The first round of recruiting was carried out by Monsignor (now Cardinal) Benelli, and he says that the appointments were carefully made with the intention of bringing more efficiency into the tired Roman air and more of a pastoral outlook instead of a strictly bureaucratic one. He has quite understandably noted a falling-off since he moved from Rome to Florence, but nevertheless the different spirit did to some extent come in with the reform and has survived where heads of departments favour this more contemporary outlook.

The head of them all, and head of the Secretariat, is the Cardinal-Secretary of State. Even if there were any doubt about this, Paul VI underlined it by placing the Cardinal-Secretary in the presidency of a newly devised committee of all the cardinals who are heads of Congregations. This committee does not meet often but it has a great potential importance in that it contains the seed of a form of cabinet responsibility. Its purpose is co-ordination. It was imposed on the traditional idea—which still operates but less than before—that the cardinals who head Congregations saw the pope privately and regularly to discuss the business of their offices. This method was not only wasteful in time but an open invitation to intrigue, which is one of the Curia's failings.

Not all Cardinal-Secretaries have made use of their position. Paul VI appointed the Frenchman Cardinal Villot, who briefly survived him. But he was not an effective administrator and no match at all for the stronger-minded Italian prelates around him, Benelli in particular. John Paul II asked Villot to stay on, which he did with reluctance, and he died in office on 9 March 1979 almost as an elegant final gesture to press the pope into making up his mind about the Curia and providing it with the necessary leadership. There was little excuse for the period of waiting, as John Paul went on to appoint the obvious and no doubt the best choice, that of Monsignor Agostino Casaroli, who was then created cardinal, a little belatedly, as his former colleague—and, in some senses, rival—Benelli had already been installed in 1977 as Cardinal-Archbishop of Florence. The wait must have been worth while for even Florence has nothing to compare with the infinite intricacies, challenges, illusions and realities of power which the head of the Roman Curia will grow accustomed to have around him.

Agostino Casaroli may well be the last of the great civil servants of the Church to have spent his life within the Curia and breathed its somewhat claustrophobic atmosphere from youth to the summit of administrative power. His appointment as Cardinal-Secretary of State restored the highest office of the Curia to a man of the Curia. (Paul VI's appointment of the French Cardinal Villot was a characteristic attempt to refurbish the Church's impression of internationality—a personal choice which ensured originality would not go beyond the incumbent's nationality because of Villot's ineffectual personality.) Casaroli is small, frail-looking, soft-spoken, extremely polite, and so precise that he chooses his words like a bird pecking the appropriately flavoured seed. He comes of modest family from northern Italy and, ceremony apart, lives simply. His only brother died during the war. In Russia. The impression of frailty is misleading.

Casaroli has managed to avoid much of the unreality of Curial life. As a young priest he became chaplain to the prison for minors that was then quite close to the Vatican, in a small square in Trastevere. He has never lost interest in this work. For years he was closely interested in an attempt to help prepare former young offenders for a constructive future. Pius XII made over a gift of money he had received from an American for the purchase of a villa at Porta San Pancrazio, on the advice of Monsignor Montini (later Paul VI). Villa Agnes became a centre for retraining young ex-prisoners. It has since closed but Casaroli maintained contact with some of the young people he had helped, watching them settle and start families; following what they made of their lives.

They were an excellent means whereby a Curial servant could keep in touch with the world beyond the walls. Because Casaroli was aware of human difficulties, frequently at a humble level, he was less inclined than some of his colleagues to see such issues as divorce and abortion and the Italian political scene in terms of battles and crusades. He had seen young families suffer. He likes to play music in his office: Mozart, Bach, Beethoven, polyphony —always, as one of his closest associates with an office near him put it, 'always very beautiful music'.

This is the man associated from 1963 with the Vatican's Eastern policy, that is, from its inception by John. Before becoming Cardinal-Secretary, Casaroli was Secretary of the Council for Public Affairs, dealing with what other powers would refer to as 'foreign' policy, but which the Vatican does not accept as such. This office has an appropriate history. It was successor to the Sacred Congregation for Extraordinary Ecclesiastical Affairs that, in turn, owed its existence to the decision of Pius VI in 1793 to have a special office monitoring events in France after the revolution—the original 'extraordinary ecclesiastical affairs'. The title was dropped only in 1967 when the present one was adopted.

This Council for Public Affairs is presided over by the Cardinal-Secretary, who is its Prefect. It is much smaller than the Secretariat of State but economizes in manpower by sharing some of its services, such as the interpreters' and personnel departments. Its work is left largely in the hands of its own Secretary—not the Cardinal-Secretary—the post Casaroli held before his promotion. He was succeeded by Monsignor Achille Silvestrini who had been working closely with him for years at the Council.

Silvestrini was an excellent choice because of his warmth and approachability, as well as his diplomatic skills. He was made an archbishop so that his rank would be of a level with his functions. Not a diocesan archbishop, of course, but a titular one, which meant that he had rank, but not the responsibilities, of a residential ordinary. He took the title of Archbishop of Novaliciana. There were two other prelates consecrated archbishop on the same day, both members of the diplomatic corps and so with titular sees, and then there were twenty-two residential bishops from all the continents. The ceremony took place in St Peter's. Each new bishop had his guests and there were several hundred people at the Mass. The pope was to preside. The ceremony began with one of those strange moments which remain obstinately in the mind, as if containing some special significance beyond the ceremony itself. The Mass was on a Sunday afternoon. Brilliant late-May sun attempted to make a bridgehead through the main doors from the square. A candle burnt each side of the bronze statue of St Peter. There was a moment of tension when it was thought that the pope was arriving. Then there were three minutes of quiet before he made his actual appearance. The lights came on and the basilica was brilliantly lit for his entrance. He walked sturdily down the aisle. All decorum vanished. A previously disciplined and apparently relaxed congregation suddenly changed to a stadium crowd. They shouted, cheered and applauded. The clerics giving out the orders of service booklets threw them up into the air so that the crowds could push and struggle for them. The charisma came and for a time the magic went, until the solemn act of consecration which can hardly fail to be a moment of moving dignity.

The appointments of Casaroli and Silvestrini implied some assurances on policy. Nothing more final can be stated, because John Paul II soon showed the habit of not meaning what appeared obvious from what he said or did. He was a different type of pope from any of his near predecessors, and not only because he was a Pole and younger than them. John had been essentially pastoral, Paul VI inclined more to be political while John Paul I was more 'religious' and so less predictable. Nevertheless, Casaroli stood for the change in the Vatican's policies not only towards the Communist world but throughout all the field of relations with governments, Catholic or otherwise. Silvestrini had taken a personal part in the difficult negotiations at Helsinki which included the safeguarding of religious liberty among the freedoms specified in the final agreement. Both men saw the Vatican aligned with the supporters of *détente*. Silvestrini's successor as Undersecretary at the Council for Public Affairs was Monsignor Audryss Backis, a prelate of Lithuanian origin and mixed French and American background. The result was a more political Curia in the sense that its leading personalities came from the world of international affairs. Villot, while certainly no politician, had seen his task as one of liaison between the Vatican and the world's bishops. His departure might have been expected to prompt John Paul II to reinforce the International Synod of Bishops. Its Secretary General at the time of John Paul II's election was a close friend and fellow-Pole, Monsignor Rubin. Rubin had in the past made no secret of the fact that he thought the Secretary General should be a cardinal in order to enhance the Synod's prestige, especially after the failure of Paul VI's plan to bring the steering committee of the Synod into papal elections. John Paul II made him a cardinal but took him away from the Secretary Generalship. In his place he appointed the more able Monsignor Jozef Tomko, a Czech with a long career in the Curia; but he did not make Tomko a cardinal.

To return to the Curia, the Secretariat of State has a second official of great influence under the Cardinal-Secretary—the Substitute. His full title is Substitute and Secretary of the Cypher. He deals with the detailed business of the Secretariat in a way the Cardinal-Secretary, with his other functions, would be unable to do. The Substitute is regarded as the second personality of the Curia after the Cardinal-Secretary. Traditionally, this was the office which included among its responsibilities the handling of Italy's internal affairs, including politics, a task said notoriously to over-influence papal decisions affecting the whole Church. Its first and by far its most distinguished incumbent after Paul VI's reform was Giovanni Benelli. For more than a decade, under the weak Secretaryship of Cardinal Villot, Benelli was the effective leader of the Curia. He had Paul VI's confidence and admiration for his ability in handling a massive volume of work. In a sense this ability was Benelli's weakness. It made him highly unpopular with other prelates (including Villot), who thought he was trespassing in their fields. It also, probably, left him with too little time to think. His energies made him a great executive, and he was a much pleasanter man than the impression he gave in public. His departure was missed more than was expected. He had been so long the pivot on which the whole government turned that anyone with urgent business to do—and access to him—went to Benelli. He personified the reform which had placed such centralizing powers in the hands of the Secretariat of State. Since his departure, there has been no one either of his calibre in the post or with his desire to impose efficiency on a machine in which he deeply believed.

His successor was Giuseppe Caprio. His way of following such a vigorous man was to claim that he was overwhelmed by the job and, of course, the old school of Vatican watchers took this to mean that he was really tremendously in command. In fact, the situation was as he described it: he *was* overwhelmed; and he was moved to one of the financial departments. John Paul II's choice for the post was a Spaniard, Monsignor Eduardo Martinez

Somolo, a conservative, but not a particularly energetic one, with a cheerful manner. The fact that he was Spanish and came from the nunciature in Bogotà was taken to mean that John Paul II wanted to destroy the idea that the Substitute, among other things, kept a close eye on Italian political affairs. In this he succeeded. Not even the most suspicious of anti-clericals could have supposed that Martinez intended to be the grey eminence of the Italian political scene.

The three men, then, who count for most in the Church's central administrative life are Cardinal-Secretary, Substitute and Secretary of the Council for Public Affairs. Below the somewhat forbidding level of these departments, the historic form of the Curia emerges, much as it ever was. The main departments of the traditional Curia are known as Sacred Congregations. Some hope was expressed during the Council that the epithet might have been dropped so that the presumption would not be seen to be too far outstripping reality. The body which came under particular attack was the Holy Office, then the most important of all the Congregations and still infamous as the Inquisition. This was the first of the Congregations to be established, and the first in the honour usually accorded it. When it was set up in July 1542 to defend the Church from heresy it was called the Sacred Congregation of the Universal Inquisition. Its name was officially changed in 1908 to Sacred Congregation of the Holy Office, a name by which it had been known informally for centuries. After the Council, its name was once again changed to Sacred Congregation of the Doctrine of the Faith and the pope was no longer to be its Prefect, an anomaly which had given it special prestige for centuries. It lost its pride of place but, as the Küng and Schillebeeckx cases showed, much of its traditional methods of secret inquisition remain.

The idea of Sixtus, in the sixteenth century, was that the departments of the Curia should consist of committees of cardinals who would jointly handle the field of business allotted them. As the foundation of the Inquisition showed, the idea was not new even in his time. But Sixtus brought method to the task of devising a modern administration just as he did to the replanning of the centre of Rome on a rational basis, an idea for which Via Sistina still does him credit. Some of the present Congregations go back to his time. Others have been added since or have had their names changed. Each has a cardinal as Prefect, and a committee of cardinals which meets at regular intervals to follow the Congregation's work. From the beginning there was an element of the 'brake' in Sixtus's view of the Congregation. In 1588 he set up the Sacred Congregation for Rites, which brought free development of the liturgy in local churches to a halt, and so the situation remained for centuries.

Paul VI added some bishops who were not cardinals to these committees as a sign of his acceptance of the episcopacy's part in the Church's government. But they arrived after the Secretariat of State had established its power, and bishops were allowed no presence in its affairs. A second innovation was to take most of the leading positions in the traditional Curia—not in the Secretariat of State or the Council for Public Affairs—out of the hands of Italians. John Paul II did not, in his early appointments, place much importance on this plan for internationalization. He replaced a French Cardinal-Secretary by an Italian, and confirmed the Council for Public Affairs in Italian hands. As his first appointment to a crucial post in the traditional Curia, he made the change from an American at the Sacred Congregation for the Clergy (where, admittedly, the late Cardinal Wright had made little positive mark), to a highly conservative Italian, Cardinal Oddi; an appointment which came as a shock to many priests, especially younger men who had hoped that they would find someone in that post with at least some comprehension of their problems. The attitude of the pope himself to the priesthood made a sympathetic figure at the Congregation for the Clergy all the more desirable. His position was clear from the beginning: the priesthood was for life, celibate and totally masculine. And so he showed little sympathy with priests who felt they could not continue in the traditional caste-system.

John Paul II's early appointments gave little indication of his future intentions. Casaroli, Silvestrini and Martinez belonged to the cheerful, more open face of the Church. Oddi did not. The pope appeared to be personally close to Cardinal Baggio, the conservative head of the Sacred Congregation for the Bishops, and to Cardinal Seper, the Yugoslav head of the Sacred Congregation for the Doctrine of the Faith. There was even some fear, before Casaroli's appointment, that Baggio would become Cardinal-Secretary, a post for which he was not equipped. Oddi's appointment looked strange alongside the incumbent of the Sacred Congregation for the Religious Orders, the open-minded Argentinian Cardinal Pironio, who had trouble early in the reign avoiding the use which the pope wanted to make of his

Congregation as a disciplinary organ for difficult members of religious orders. He was also known to object to the pope's extreme reluctance to allow priests, religious or otherwise, to give up the priesthood if they were so inclined.

There are nine of these Sacred Congregations. Apart from those already mentioned, the remainder deal with the Oriental Churches, the Sacraments, the Missions, Canonizations and Catholic Education. The functions of the heads of these Congregations immediately cease on the death of a pope. The new pope can, on paper, change his entire executive as soon as he is installed or, if he wants a complete change but is of a legal turn of mind, he could simply not reappoint heads of departments when they finish the term of five years, after which, in line with Paul VI's regulations, they must be reconfirmed in office. This rule applies to 1,500 officials. No pope has the excuse of being forced against his will to accept the Curia's ways; there is every weapon in his hand for forging his executive in just the way he wants it. It is equally logical not to be anti-Curial. If they are not operating properly, it is not altogether their fault. They should be changed. It is facile and pointless to suppose that if Jesus found his way into the Curial offices he would tip over their desks and fling their filing cabinets to the ground, tear up their salary cheques (and envelopes of cash payments above the agreed level), and remind the manager of the Vatican's bank that God wanted his house to be called a 'house of prayer for all the nations', and not largely an administrative machine for the Italians. What is much more relevant is that, thanks to Paul VI, a pope can change the Curia at will.

The Curia itself has never wanted for its own defenders. Like troopers responding to the trumpet, the older men replied with passion and a sort of manic charm to the attacks on the Curia during the Council years. Its greatest defender then was the formidable, nearly blind Inquisitor, Cardinal Ottaviani, who described the Curia as 'a great teacher of Christian life and Catholic action'. He went on (and this is his personal answer to the trite view that Jesus would not have approved of the Curia): 'It seems a contemporary of the apostles in its glory, so full of life that it seems to have been born yesterday, high and yet humble like a mother, and misunderstood only by those who do not know her.' Few would talk like that now, in public. Yet ten years after the reforms had gone into effect, the Secretariat of State had ready a set of notes, in four typewritten pages, to remind members of the virtues of the reform.

The effects were seen to be the introduction of modern methods of work, a more pastoral character within the Curia, changed relationships with the local churches and an advanced degree of internationalization, particularly in departmental heads and the higher grades of the bureaucracy. The non-Italians had brought with them experience unfamiliar to the old Curia, a mentality more capable of understanding the Church in the world, and a more comprehensible way of expressing themselves. All this is true as far as it goes. The total effect of change, viewed from outside, is nevertheless substantially less than this official verdict would suggest. More than anything else, the Curia mentality is long in dying. The fussiness of the cleric in his office, the lack of confidence in what is happening outside the walls, the weight that Rome itself imposes of instinctive centralization—this is the seemingly eternal Curial outlook that John Paul II cleverly hid when he appointed attractive personalities at the Curia's head with his first nominations. The older, primeval promptings of a holy bureaucracy have not gone away, and the non-Italian arrivals have not so far had so purgative and tonic an effect as has been claimed for them.

How precise it all is! I was sitting late one morning in one of the waiting-rooms of the Secretariat of State. I had an appointment with a great prelate of unusual openness of mind. These waiting-rooms serve a double purpose: you wait there until the person you have come to see arrives, and you talk there because it is not a habit at the Vatican to invite visitors into individual offices. The room is square and the walls covered with that beige damask so typical an innovation of Paul VI. A strip of wood painted gold separates the ceiling from the walls. There are two paintings, both framed in gold: one is quite a delicate flower-arrangement; the other shows Christ in Gethsemane, a rather weak-looking, defenceless individual in a salmon-coloured robe, appearing distinctly sorry for himself, as he kneels among the olives. There are a sofa and four wooden-armed chairs, all covered with a material practically the same colour as the walls. The ceiling is of stone with a chandelier of white glass at the centre. The floor is red and grey mottled marble. There is an ornate marble-topped table under the salmon Jesus with an internal telephone and a pen chained to the table. There is a notepad beside the telephone. The windows give on to an external loggia (magnificently frescoed) but you cannot see that because the windows are frosted as well as barred. Suddenly there is a double noise of jolting suddenness.

The midday cannon has been fired from the Janiculum Hill along the river towards Trastevere and the clocks of St Peter's have struck the hour. What precision indeed! My host arrived a little later, but it would have been too much, too dangerously much, if he had arrived at the very second that the cannon fired and the clocks chimed. I allowed myself one thought about Jesus and bureaucracy: it was that he performed some of his miracles simply to put right the logistical and administrative shortcomings of the disciples. That is very un-bureaucratic conduct: almost a show of contempt for the administrative processes.

Rome's influence is heavy, and is more noticeable outside Rome because in Rome itself so much is taken for granted. I was at the headquarters of a National Episcopal Conference in Africa, drinking coffee with a group of young African prelates, all with a clear future before them as leaders of the hierarchy in their country. One of their jokes was about the ones among them who had managed to stay intelligent by avoiding invitations to go to Rome to complete their studies. 'He's smart, because he stayed at home.' Joking it may be, but the undertow is serious. Rome prepares you for everything you understand about the Roman Catholic Church, whatever your colour, intelligence or—and this is the serious implication—your instinctive promptings. Avoid going there and you will stay smart, but you will not get on. Go there and you will lose your spontaneity and originality. You will no longer be smart. The Curia epitomizes this attitude, and some people react against it. 'I went to Rome to complete my studies,' said a tall, blond Dominican in Amsterdam, 'and luckily I have managed to forget everything they taught me.' He celebrates without vestments, prefers being called 'John' rather than 'Father', and has a large, regular congregation of mainly middle-class Catholics who would read about Rome in their own newspapers as the place which mindlessly bullies the Church in Holland.

It is better, in fairness, not to try and put the best face on things. The Curia's foundations were laid in the sixteenth century when the idea of an autocratic papacy was at its height. Much of that original system is still there. The new offices dealing with matters which the old papacy would have contemptuously dismissed as beneath consideration have made little mark, with the partial exception of the Secretariat for Christian Unity. In all, some sixteen new bodies have been created as a result of the Council. These bodies are sometimes referred to as the 'new Curia' and have marked differences from the older, but more powerful departments. The total of 144 officials in these offices show a more international character. There are almost as many non-Italians as there are Italians. The staffs are smaller compared with the twenty-five officials working at the Sacred Congregation for Bishops to the maximum of seventy dealing with the missions. The only one of these offices which preceded the Council is the Secretariat for Christian Unity established by John XXIII in 1960 as the result of a proposal from Monsignor Jaeger, the Archbishop of Paderborn, which was put into effect by the Jesuit Cardinal Bea as the Vatican's first institutional contact with the ecumenical movement. It is still a comparatively modest affair of nineteen officials, among whom only five are Italian. It cannot yet be said to have achieved one of its original purposes: to bring to the Curia a more open outlook on the world. It is the most successful of the new bodies and, undoubtedly, it has been useful in forging a series of contacts between Rome and other Christians, but there is always a danger that its work will prove misleading. Just because it has not become involved in the old Curia (to some extent to its credit), it is inclined to present an idea of the Vatican's attitudes to the rest of Christendom which is over-optimistic in terms of the Church's machinery as a whole.

These offices cost comparatively little. The Secretariat for Non-Christians manages with an expenditure of less than 10,000 pounds a year; the Secretariat for Non-Believers spends about 12,500 pounds a year. The Council for the Lay has eighteen officials, the Justice and Peace Commission fifteen, the Secretariat for Non-Believers eight. By comparison with the huge functions they are supposed to carry out, these staffs and financing are tiny. Even so, there have been moves in the midst of the Vatican's financial crisis to economize by amalgamating some of these new bodies or abolishing some if not all of them, ostensibly on the grounds of expense but, in fact, to remove a potentially disturbing element from within the body politic of the Curia. Arguably, they might be maintained and perhaps expanded while the old Curia, with the exception of the Secretariat of State, could be practically abolished. That would be one way of looking at a problem which, some time, a pope will have to approach with real decision.

The danger at the Vatican is that innovations arrive without the departure of older habits. As a result, popes have a constantly more complicated balancing act to perform if they wish to make use of the existing machinery without upsetting the equilibrium imposed in general by history and more particularly by their immediate predecessors. In this sense, it is fortunate that there have been so few changes in the workings of the Curia since the time of Sixtus V. The reforms of Paul VI were only the second since the 1588 constitution; the first were Pius X's changes in 1908 that left the original form untouched but attempted to lay down the individual responsibilities of each department with more precision, and to clarify the juridical as opposed to purely administrative powers of the various Congregations.

The growth is still much too luxuriant for one man to control. The spirit at work in the offices is out of date in a very specific meaning of the term. It is not old-fashioned; there need be nothing wrong with that. Its out-of-dateness began and stopped at a particular moment in time, in the sixteenth century, when a particular form of papacy existed that was a child of its time. The popes lost their states with regret but there can be no doubt at all, now, that the loss was salutary for them. What is also perfectly clear is that no pope has rigorously thought through all the advantages to be gained by the fact that he need bother now about only 'a small corner of earth' and not about a principality that is more than a pedestal for the exercise of his spiritual functions. Apart from trying to run it well, the pope is no longer under any obligation to interpret the system that surrounds him, and which he personifies according to any requisites of time and place. It does not have to be Italianate, nor marked by the tortuous ramification of the baroque. It does not have to respond to modern conditioning in the sense that the papacy must do what is popular. The whole theory of the 'small corner' is one of liberation. Just as the whole world can be seen in a grain of sand, so the whole world can be most effectively dealt with from a tiny area.

One pope, one day, is going to have to decide whether he is more a bishop among bishops or a monarch among functionaries —that is the choice seen by those who seek to place the Curia in contradiction to the International Synod of Bishops. That decision will be among the most crucial any pope could make. Some see it as the key to the Church's prospects for credibility in the future. Journeys, mass audiences, spectacular visits, only conceal the issue.

The idea of the Synod opens a whole new door, rather a new set of doors, in Bluebeard's castle. This body was established by Paul VI in September 1965 in response to a request from the Council for an organ devised especially with the purpose of expressing the Council's teaching on collegiality. The Council was then in its fourth and final session. Paul responded to the request, but he was careful to see that his new creation should in no way encroach on the papal prerogatives or unduly worry the Curia, which he was then planning to reform. It was not to be a part of the Curia, and came directly under the pope's authority. It was consultative and so could not force on the pontiff, even with a majority vote, any decisions to which he objected. The pope has the exclusive right to summon it, to decide on the place of the meeting, to confirm the election of its members, to fix the subjects for discussion and the agenda, to preside if he wishes or, if not, appoint a person to preside in his absence. He can suspend a Synod, move its meeting-place, or dissolve it. He nominates the Secretary General and decides himself what recommendations from the Synod he need take into consideration.

Any idea of the Synod as a democratic body is best promptly forgotten. It could develop in such a direction and the pope could, if he wished, allow it to deliberate as a legislative organ, but that is not very likely. Its composition varies according to whether the assembly is general, extraordinary or particular. A general assembly deals with arguments important for the whole Church, on which the pope wishes to hear the views of the world's bishops. Its membership consists of the patriarchs, archbishops and bishops elected by National Episcopal Conferences, varying in number from one to four depending on the size of the conferences. Then there are ten representatives of the male religious orders (there is no place for nuns), who are chosen by the Rome Union of Superior Generals, and the cardinals who head departments of the Curia. An extraordinary assembly deals with subjects of a similar weight but which require more urgent handling. The participants this time are the chairmen of National Episcopal Conferences and three instead of ten religious. A particular Synod is called together to deal with issues involving one region only. The participants are the bishops of the region and the cardinals who head departments in the Curia responsible for dealing with the subjects under discussion. The pope has the right to nominate personally other bishops, priests or religious whose presence he feels desirable to any of these types of Synod, up to a total of 15 per cent of the ordinary members.

The International Synod has not so far proved an inspiring body. It meets only every three years. Not only is the principal subject given it by the Vatican but so also is the basic working paper. In fairness it must be said that the working paper is circulated well in advance: for the 1980 Synod on the family the document was widely publicized months before the meeting was due to begin. The Synod does not debate. It listens to a series of statements from its members most of which have been prepared in advance and agreed by the body which the member represents, such as a bishop representing his National Conference. It meets in a smaller hall of the Nervi building where papal audiences are held. Geographically and symbolically the main Curia offices are between it and the papal apartments.

The Synods already have their formal pattern. Each opens with a solemn concelebration presided over by the pope, who delivers a homily. The first plenary session may also begin with a speech from the pope. The Secretary General gives a report on the work of the steering committee in the intervening three years and a report is read on the general state of the Church in the world. The plenary sessions take place in the mornings from nine to twelve and from five to seven with pauses for the Ora Terza prayer, the Angelus, the Adsumus and another Angelus at the end of the day. There is an average of twenty speakers in a morning and they speak in the order of the requests they have made to the Secretariat General so that there is no discussion at this stage, simply statements. This procedure lasts for three or four days when the Synod breaks up into eleven language-groups which prepare their own reports. These reports are read in the general assembly where comments can be made and, if necessary, the groups can meet again to amend them.

All this material is condensed into a series of draft propositions which are then put to two distinct votes. The first vote is on whether the individual propositions are acceptable as they stand or are to be rejected or require modification. After modifications have been made, the propositions are put to a straight vote of acceptance or rejection. So far no Synod has issued a complete document of its own. Rather, they have made over their debates and propositions to the pope who can then issue a document on the basis of this material. Advocates of the present type of Synod point out that what was probably the best document of Paul VI's reign was based on the discussions of the International Synod on the subject of evangelization.

All types of Synods have been tried, in the six sessions which have taken place since 1967. There is no point in recounting the histories of all or any Synod. It is worth recording that at every Synod the restrictions attached to this body were very evident, as were the efforts at making free with what were supposed to be papal wishes. This is an ancient trick of the Curia by which none-too-confident bishops are told that something they may be thinking of proposing would displease the pope. Of course, the benefits of a Synod cannot be judged just by what it does. It may accomplish nothing in the way of novel documents or important declarations while much can come from the mere fact that bishops from all over the world have met and grown to know each other better, and also have got to know the Curia together. There was a famous occasion during the 1974 Synod when the African bishops must have felt that they knew the Curia better. It is worth recounting.

The bishops of the whole African continent had helped prepare a panorama of the African Church to be read by one of their number at the Synod. Their document was in English. It contained a passage dealing with their relationship with the papal diplomatic corps. This passage went:

> Following the signs of our times and the thinking of most countries of Africa, we humbly ask the Holy See to see to it that the image of the Vatican Diplomatic Corps take a more universal (Catholic) character than the present one which is seen as 'mostly Italian'. It is painful to hear now and then accusations that the Vatican (the Holy See) is practising nationalism in the Catholic Church. We also feel it is necessary to revise the terms of competence of the Vatican Diplomatic Corps in relationship to the local Churches (Episcopal Conferences) and to the local governments in Africa. Since the establishment of the Episcopal Conferences, it is good (and necessary) to clarify the boundaries of duties and competence of the Episcopal Conference and those of the Vatican Diplomatic Corps in relation to ecclesiastical matters of the local Church and in relation to the Vatican and the Sacred Congregations.

This was a useful set of proposals and undoubtedly expressed a widespread belief among the African bishops that they were being hindered in their roles by the behaviour of the pope's representatives—who were indeed mainly Italian, while those that were not Italian were West European or North American—the obvious intention being to mark a distinction between themselves and the local hierarchy. The document, however, had to be delivered in Latin at the Synod and the Curia provided a translation which read:

> The legations which the Supreme Pastor sends to the nations of the world manifest the universal character of the Church and shows the care which the Church has for all the needs of man while it carries

out the task of evangelization. The better the legate accredited to the public authorities is linked with that of the local churches and Episcopal Conferences of Africa, the more the work of evangelization will be favoured in the immense space of this continent.

The Africans must by then have known what they were up against. But the issue was not limited to them. The question is whether there is a choice between two visions of how the Church should be administered and secondly which vision should be chosen. The choice is between, on the one hand, a papacy which works largely through the Curia, a Curia which is difficult for a pope to dominate because it has its own ways and habits ingrained by long practice, and the custom of handling power; and, on the other hand, a papacy referring regularly to the Synod and, through it, to the National Conferences. The International Synod has a permanent steering committee in Rome which could also fulfil an advisory function between sessions of the Synod. The Curia could become smaller and the diplomatic corps be made largely redundant, except for a few roving ambassadors whose base would be in Rome. The Church ought then to regain a more apostolic character and shake off the last of the temporal trappings which have effectively hidden that character in many ways. In this vision of Church government the bodies which would be accorded a new importance would be the Synod with its steering committee and the committee of cardinals which periodically brings together all the heads of departments of the Curia, both new and old.

And yet, despite its attractiveness, this vision has its drawbacks. The heavily centralized spirit of Rome is part of the spirit of the place in which the leadership of the Church settled. It may be in conflict with what is known of early Christianity, but it is in keeping with the mental habits of Rome. The need to refer to Rome, even in living memory, was insisted upon to such a degree that it looks more like a psychosis than a vision of Church government. Cardinal Suenens says: 'The list of things for which a bishop had to have recourse to Rome bordered on the unbelievable, extending even to having to ask permission to allow a nun in his diocese to change her will, or a sick priest to say Mass in his own room.' Already, it is greatly improved. After the Council, the Curia has had to consult the bishops far more frequently because of the teaching on collegiality. That meant a great deal more work in circularizing bishops with draft documents, proposals, requests for their views or information, and the handling of their replies. It is not just a one-way traffic. The Curia felt that the bishops were now obliged, on the same principle of their share in the responsibility of the Church's government, to keep Rome informed about what they themselves were doing. Collegiality can have two faces, and this one looks suspiciously like a modern development of centralization, not its opposite.

It has also meant that bishops have considerably less time to spend in their own dioceses, unless they are in a fairly remote part of the Catholic world. There have been improvements and most of the bishops have a broader view of the Church's problems as a whole. They know each other better. Pope John's former private secretary, Monsignor Louis Capovilla, maintains that they show a higher degree of intelligence in the statements they make. They not only have more correspondence with Rome, more calls on their time actually to go to Rome, but in their own countries they have more collegiate activities because of the development after the Council of the National Episcopal Conferences. These organizations existed in some places before the Council. Now they are the rule throughout the Catholic world and are much more highly developed meaning, for the individual bishop, another cost in time. They are extremely useful to a man with ambition, a man who feels that the price in time is worth the chance of preferment. That is the meaning of ambition. They are the place to make one's name as an ecclesiastical organizer or administrator, with the next step a place in the international Synod where, among others, Karol Wojtyla made a name for himself. The Polish horseman made a few preliminary sallies before arriving to take the papacy. He attended every Synod; he was elected and re-elected a member of every steering committee between Synods. No one knows more about its workings than him.

The Synod is one of two things: it is a Sleeping Beauty awaiting a papal kiss to arouse it to full dominance, or it is a rather modest chorus of worthy ecclesiastics whose sombre debates manage to avoid interesting the world at large with no difficulty at all. This character is typical of a creation of Paul VI, such an extraordinarily gifted creator of opportunities for others.

John Paul II, if anything, clouded an already confused issue. He called a special meeting not of the International Synod but of the Sacred College of Cardinals in November 1979 to discuss the Church's outstanding problems, including the problem of the budget, as if this were the natural organ of consultation. It was—in the Middle Ages. Some of them arrived in no happy humour. They had been called together at short notice and the busier of them had had to cancel a series of engagements in their own dioceses. They were given insufficient time to prepare for the meeting, which was devoted mainly to the Vatican's financial situation and the Roman Curia. The pope did not do the same, by way of cancelling previous engagements. He went off for most of one of the three working days to spend time with Rome railway workers. To quote one normally rather easy-going cardinal: 'I was frankly furious.'

And, finally, the machinery of the Synod has been tried with the particular Synod on the Dutch Church. It is still hard to know what to say of this event. In time and nature it was near to the suspension of Hans Küng and came shortly after Father Edward Schillebeeckx, the Belgian Dominican teaching at Nijmegen, had been called to Rome for interrogation. It was the time when John Paul II's popularity had taken a plunge downward, after a year in which he could do no wrong. It was the period in which the Vatican formally announced, in *L'Osservatore Romano*, suspicions of a conspiracy against the stumbling hero. The cartoons were no longer kindly. They showed him walking across the water of his swimming-pool (shades of *Jesus Christ Superstar*), announcing that he was tired of serving a master, with the Leporello-like state-ment: 'A few years of sacrifice and I'll set myself up on my own.' It was the time the joke was going the rounds of the apparition of Jesus who assures him in a vision in the Vatican gardens that there will be no more Polish popes, 'At least not in my lifetime.'

The Dutch bishops were quietly routed at the Synod. Their discomfiture was followed by at least fifty journalists from Holland, who saw the event as a surrender to the overwhelming forces of the Vatican and to the pope himself who, this time, spent practically every day at the exchanges. The Dutch were welcomed by the official spokesman at the opening press conference, with a pardonable slip of the tongue, as a group from Poland. I asked a good friend in a high position in the Curia if he saw much of the pope and he said yes, certainly. There was no difficulty in dealing personally with him. 'But once something is decided,' he added, 'it is quite likely that I shall have a telephone call in the afternoon, telling me to do something quite different, not from the pope but from some Polish nun.' Clearly the pope was surprisingly willing to make himself unpopular if he felt the circumstances demanded such a course. But nobody was any nearer to knowing how best the Roman Catholic Church should be governed, which, given its still centralized character, is not a matter of minor importance. Nobody, that is, except the pope himself. John Paul II's handling of the 1980 Synod on the family was distressing for those who supposed that the idea of a collaboration between Rome and the bishops of the world on the great issues facing the Church would be encouraged. The Synod sat for a month and produced a wide variety of views and outlooks. The pope's closing speech, with which he claimed to be summing up the views expressed by the 216 prelates who attended the Synod throughout the whole month of October, could well have been written before they arrived.

8

THE INSTITUTIONAL BARRIER

I N THE LITTLE Mexican town of Oaxaca, which John Paul II
visited as part of his Mexican tour in January 1979, there is
an experience to be had that is both frightening and
reassuring. The town has a famous Saturday market. The reality
of it is better than any description because most descriptions
simply seek to say what it is like and what is on sale there, when
really the creation of the world is there, every Saturday; for the
whole day this act of creation lasts, and is then dismantled and put
aside for a week.

Peasants arrive from the surrounding countryside with their
foodstuffs, their hand-woven clothes and blankets, their animals,
spices, cheeses, vegetables; everything imaginable and some
things which are not. Tables, with benches around them, grow
from the ground as if they too were used to the weekly transformation; and suddenly food is there, hot, so burning with chillies
that a man can get drunk simply dousing the heat of the spices and
pepper. The Madonna watches over them from a portrait
mounted on a pillar and lit with neon strips; so does Jesus,
generously displaying his bleeding heart—both of them emerging
from a forest of bright flowers with their intent expressions, as if
to say that Genesis is now over, a thing of the past, and that we are
the ones now, not the old legends of the Old Testament, or the old
gods of the Mexican Indians. Somewhere in the middle of the
market there is a church.

Mass goes on with six or seven people in the congregation.
There are thousands at the market. But, wait. At the end of the
nave farthest from the altar where Mass is being said stands a
Madonna dressed all in black. She has a stern face, but not

174

insensitively so. She is enclosed in glass and there is a wall behind the statue which isolates her from the liturgical rite going on behind her back, while allowing, at the two sides, entrance into the main nave for those who want to hear the priest. Few do. They come in, they kneel on the bare stone. They make that strange gesture of the Mexicans of a cross across the heart and then a kiss blown to the goddess. They stay ten minutes or a quarter of an hour, kneeling on the stone, just looking with adoration at the statue, occasionally moving the lips in some spontaneous prayer, or request, or confidence. As they rise at the end of their meeting, others from outside take their places on the stone floor. The masonry shines like the Madonna's crown. They come and go endlessly. With their market, they have created the world once again and have come to talk quite personally with the figure they can best accept as their interlocutor. The means of communication is very personal; it ignores the organized religious function and turns to the familiar image for reassurance, for help, for advice: a resort to the age-old practices of silent worship directed towards a benevolent figure which requires no liturgy, no organization, and makes no claims on them. Of course, these were the same people who cheered the pope, delighted that he should talk to them with a sombrero on his head, his face red with their sun, idolized, and a child under his arm.

Here we are on delicate ground indeed. This is a civilization that had Catholicism imposed on it in the sixteenth century by the Spaniards. It is still straining against a full acceptance. A whole shop-window in the southern town of Mérida is given over to dozens of coloured, plaster figures of the Trinity, in many sizes, as if three forms of God may be much less than they had before the Conquest but the multiple idea remains easier for them than one. Even the tradition behind Mexico's national Madonna in her shrine at Guadaloupe, in what is now a suburb of the capital, is anti-imperialist. Legend has it that one of the few Indians converted immediately to Catholicism after the Spanish Conquest saw a vision of a woman accompanied by blinding light and unearthly music. She said that she was Mary, and told the Indian to inform the bishop that she wanted a church built on top of the hill on which they met. Thus, the place which inevitably became the most sacred locality in the western hemisphere was sited outside the capital and away from the centres of the newly established colonial power. The location had another recommendation: the Aztecs had once had a temple there, dedicated to the mother of the gods. One must keep in mind something which is impalpable but important: the need to try and isolate what is effective religious feeling and what looks like it but is in fact anomalous.

The Mexicans of course, in 1979, gave the pope a triumph. A small town such as Puebla produced solid banks of people, a million of them, welcoming the first pope ever to come and see them. To complete their excitement, they found he was a showman of astonishing virtuosity with crowds. Quite erroneous ideas were circulating at the time that the welcome was so overwhelming because the pope had shown his displeasure at seeing the Catholic Church in Latin America used as a centre of political opposition. In fact the response was a perfectly natural expression of enthusiasm for a unique occasion. It had a totally different devotional aspect from the normal habit of going to church to hear Mass or talk to the saints in a personal exchange. These are elements found in different forms throughout the Catholic world. American Negro Catholics, for instance, with their jazz and blues adaptation of the Mass, seem to manage to combine the liturgical with the personal element more easily than the Latin Americans; while the Dutch see the liturgy as so flexible that it can be adapted to practically any personal requirement. An even more flexible attitude comes from a black hall-porter in a chaotic African hotel: suddenly he confides that for years he prayed in Catholic churches with no return at all and changed from Catholicism to attend simple prayer meetings—'Now Jesus listens, I know he does. And another thing, people don't speak badly behind each other's backs.'

The delicacy of the ground is not so much in the theorizing that can be done around the behaviour and remarks of religious people. It is in the practically unexplorable field of the real weight of religious thinking done by the normal human being, and the relationship of this thinking with the institutions of organized religion. Do the two frequently combine? Sometimes there is a strong feeling that it is happening. Then gradually the focus changes. For instance, the emotional power grows very strong indeed when naturally religious people, new to Christianity, meet for Mass in a simple church made of mud over a wooden frame.

Christmas morning in a remote area of Tanzania, towards the Zambian border, is cool with every now and again a downfall of sheets of rain beating on the iron roof. There are seats for less than half the people, who have walked, some of them for many miles, from their huts in the hills for the visit of the bearded, Spanish priest who makes the hazardous journey by Land Rover twice a month, with a battered suitcase containing the chalice and the host and an undecorated white vestment. The women are all in brightly coloured, traditional clothes: turbans and long dresses to the ground. The men are in well-worn shirts and light trousers. They listen hard to the priest. He is popular and backs his fluent Swahili with eloquent mime and gestures. He might be a conjuror in a village hall; the amateur magician that Jesus was accused of being. He baptizes two babies: 'Fiorenza! What a name!', and the choir with native drums and tins with stones inside, shaken to the strong rhythms of the Swahili hymns, gives a more natural sense of emotion to this meeting around a small doll dressed as a Christ-child and placed on a table in a red crib decorated with tinsel, with the head raised to look, still-eyed, at the congregation. The first lesson is read by a girl in a red turban with nervous but obviously well-practised intonation. The lectern is hand-made of rough wood. The wooden altar is painted green with a yellow painted cross standing at each end. In front of the Christ-child a white-painted collection plate stands on a native drum. The second lesson is read by a boy in a red check shirt who hesitates thoughtfully while reading as if the words are new and vaguely puzzling to him. The congregation follows intently and they take Communion with what looks like the urgency of spiritual hunger. They all behave naturally yet give the impression that this morning is a big event for them. The thunder and the rain; the drums and the shouting and the shaking; the vigorous encouragements from the priest; the silent, staring doll; and the wild flowers and palm leaves decorating the mud walls: the combination is really strong. These people are poor. They are by nature religious; a quality which they retain even when their whole background changes. It was a huge Negro carpenter sitting in his Pontiac in New Orleans who confirmed the point: 'We are people who need to worship.'

Yet, there is a feeling of delicacy, that these fervent, singing Christians are still very close to the spirits of other religious worlds. Their bishop has no difficulty in answering which of the commandments they find most difficult to follow: the first. The idea of one God, the bishop told me, jealous of his unique position and demanding exclusive worship, is hard for a people accustomed to think of a spirit world inhabited by countless powers for good, for evil, for helping them, for tormenting them; there to respond to the right appeals and the right spells and incantations, to bring rain, or a husband, or health. In the spirit world there are their ancestors who follow closely what the living do. Most, if not all, of their forebears are pagan and, who knows, they may be hurt or displeased that their descendants have accepted a foreign religion. The background to the lives of these Christians explains the impression that their worship is all the more moving because it is brittle as well as emotional. It might not stand up to a real challenge from the old ways.

Some are strong enough to meet the challenge. This same mud church saw a genuine drama of martyrdom when the most forceful lay member of the congregation died a painful death from poisoning. He knew that he was in danger and told the congregation from the pulpit that if anything should happen to him, they should not worry; someone else would take his place and preach and teach the same things to them as he had done. He went to bed with acute pains in the stomach which nothing could allay. He died. One minor mystery was solved. His wife had never understood what he did with his money, because they never had as much as he earned. It was found that he had opened a small bank account for every girl who became a nun, so that she need not go empty-handed to the convent. A young man called Simon took his place in the pulpit and told the congregation that he would be telling them, without fear for his personal safety, exactly the same truths as his dead predecessor.

Others must find the challenge too strong. Faced with the fear of angering the spirits, they probably make mental compromises. For most of them the fear is not that an angry pagan will order a poison potion from the local expert and kill them, but that a revered relative or a spirit, who had been helpful to the family in the past, should be angered. Not only old beliefs are condemned but familiar customs as well. The Catholic Church will not baptize children from families that do not follow Christian rules, meaning largely those which are not monogamous families or families that permit sexual relations before marriage. It is a harsh decision because it gives the fullest condemnation to a custom still regarded by many as normal, while other failings, not so much in evidence, provide no obstacle to baptism. Some say that the Catholic Church in Africa is young, because it has been there barely a century; others say that it is both old and young because 1,900 years of European experience were grafted on to the Church in Africa at the start, like a naive painting of an old man's face on a child-like body. Certainly, it came unprepared for what it would find. Now it knows a great deal more, thanks in part to the studies made by missionary priests into the traditional beliefs of their parishioners.

However, the African Church remains too much a white church, whatever the colour of the faces of the faithful or even of the majority of their bishops. It is astonishing how Roman a black bishop can be. From their studies in Rome they pick up not only the intellectual ballast of their faith but also the mannerisms of the typical monsignor of the Roman Curia. In many cases they are much less independently minded than the European missionary priests who work under them. They are by no means unaware of the problems; even Rome could not do that to them. They will talk of ideas with which they are experimenting. One is that the survival in the popular mind of the living world of the dead might somehow be attached to the Christian belief in the communion of saints who are there to help the living as much as live themselves in glory in the next world. No one can say how long it will take before the Africanization of the priesthood will be complete, including a transformation of the Africans themselves, many of whom have mainly absorbed only the European guise given the Christian religion.

A fine mission church stands up on a hill near one of the roads towards the African interior, along which the slavers marched the unfortunates whom they had rounded up in their villages and took in chains to the market in Zanzibar. Higher up the hill from the mission is a camp that the local people said was a training camp for guerrillas engaged in the struggle to bring black majority rule to the whole of southern Africa. It was the same Christmas Day as that of the Mass in the remote mud church. This much bigger church had a crib and some decorations. There was a kindergarten near and a clinic run by Italian nuns. The missionaries and their guests ate roast gazelle with the local red wine. I was among them. The nun who cooked was rightly famous throughout the area for her skill. Her personal mark was to combine the recipes of her native Campania with African ingredients and the effect was fully successful, a genuine process of cultural Africanization. There was a lot to eat. We interrupted eating between courses to hear the young man who had taken the place of the poisoned catechist and who was a poet. He had been brought from his village to the main mission-station as acknowledgement of his courage and to give him support. He recited one of his poems, or rather, half sang it to a guttural chant which was based, he said, on the old Arabic tunes his people had picked up from traders on the coast. After coffee, most people needed to go to sleep. I did not. I wanted to walk around the station in what was now the dusk of early evening. I went into the church which had a mock-Renaissance airiness: very Italian in style. It was empty. I looked at the crib, and the books and periodicals on sale. I went out, walking down the flight of stone steps. A little black boy in a red and black check shirt sat on the steps. He looked up at my white face and black beard, took my hand and fell on his knees with a cry of: 'Jesus Christ!'

Mistaken identity is not the full story. Nor is the conclusion that an innocent black boy in search of God thinks that the search is over because he sees a white man come out of a church on Christmas Day. The problem is of wider significance, just as was the scene in the church at Oaxaca. It raises the question of how Catholic individual Catholics are. Is it just a question, as Graham Greene says somewhere, that at a certain hour in the morning you feel very Catholic, at other times less so, and sometimes not at all? It is easy enough to say that 18 per cent of the world's population consists of Catholics. But it is very difficult to know what percentage of each of them is Catholic and what percentage is not. Almost everyone seems to have their reservations somewhere. The Dutch statistics showing that in the space of twelve months there are more suicides in one parish than new priests throughout the country are again as indicative as the higher total in Mexico of regular drunkards than regular churchgoers. That is one side of the problem; the other is to discern what Catholicism's fundamental character is, not just what being a Catholic means. Catholicism remains European, which was what confused the little black boy on the steps. Yet there is every reason to suppose this to be wrong: the religion did not rise in Europe and now, in particular, a strongly European character not only makes it less acceptable to non-Europeans but means, at a time of sickness in the West, that Europe's ills are taken to other people along with European Catholicism. Many parts of the Catholic world want to be able to adapt Catholicism more to their own way of thinking and behaving. The European end of the same problem is to try and see what remains at this present stage of the continent's history that can truthfully be said to spring from Christian, and particularly Catholic, inspiration. And in the broader field, though local churches will want to have more of their own ways in how they conduct their religion, Catholicism must presumably have some sort of recognizable character even if it is not European. Without this, it can hardly have a sense of direction. It is this sense of direction that Europe hitherto has provided.

The individual churches will have to provide this for themselves. One way in which they are doing so is to seek new ways of worship which bridge the gap between local customs and culture and the European ways of worship. This is the meaning of the saffron robes, suggesting Hinduism, in Indian Catholicism; the use of local music: 'an Indian Catholic', one bishop said to me, 'would expect when he goes to church to hear Indian music.' Shoes would not be worn in the sanctuary. The congregation would squat not kneel. 'With our people, sitting down is a mark of respect and so they sit during the reading of scripture. We shall need two or three generations to perfect our ideas on liturgy. Hinduism is 4,000 years old. It has its saints, its feasts, its fasts, its pilgrimages, its holy places, its ceremonies for every stage of human life. It has its mystical element. How can we go to them and preach a new religion? What new element can we give it? Why, indeed, do we preach to them? They do not become better people. We used to say "to save them" but that is something you can't say any more.' He raised another question. 'How do you preach in a country with great poverty? Do you build a church or a school? Do you set out to train a priest or a teacher? Should the Church do social work first? In the end, both must be done. But the problem in this world is the next world: humanization must be one with divinization.

'Our school system is working well. But we face the problem of whether the Church has invested too much in its schools. Are they serving the poor? The Church in India does not lack money. But we must make ourselves less dependent on money from outside. Then, our priests live at a higher standard than other people. And this raises the question: is this an Indian Church? Some say, stop getting money from abroad. Others say there is nothing wrong with this as we are a *Catholic* church and one day we shall be giving and not receiving. Non-Catholics know that our money comes from abroad—from Propaganda Fide and other sources—and say this is a new colonialism. Yet we have no problems of vocations. In my own diocese, I am the oldest priest. There is not one Indian seminary which is not over-full. Southern Indians find mission work in the north very attractive. We do not have serious problems with the government. We disagree over the untouchables. The government gives them help with housing and with jobs. But if they become Christians they are no longer allowed to apply for these privileges because they are no longer untouchable once they have joined the Christian community.'

I was in a packed suburb of Manila called Buting where I felt the same atmosphere of participation that I had experienced in that tin-hut church on Christmas Day in Africa. But the problem there was in a sense greater than that of the Africans. The Filipinos are consciously in search of their identity beneath the layers imposed on them of Spanish and American influences. They have always managed to retain something in their more informal religious practices. This is especially true in semi-dramatic representations of Gospel stories because they are a people given to drama. The moving processions at Easter, for instance, belong to this popular tradition: processions carry statues of the Madonna and of Jesus immediately before the Easter Mass and the meeting of the two images, known as the *Incuentro*, is witnessed with great enthusiasm. Or when the statues of Joseph and of Mary are carried to the doors of the village and refused hospitality, an idea particularly painful to the open-hearted Filipinos.

But until recent years the 'popular' and the official elements in worship were kept apart. Now the attempt has been made to rethink the liturgy in terms of Filipino culture. The Mass at Buting was led by a Belgian missionary but it followed the Filipino liturgy largely devised by a Benedictine, who is head of his order's Liturgical Institute in Rome, Father Anscar Chupungco. He is perfectly aware of the dangers. 'It will take a laborious effort to define what is indissolubly bound up with superstition and error, or to make an index of forbidden customs and traditions. What one sometimes dismisses as superstitious may be in fact a manifestation of faith, unsophisticated and unpolished perhaps, but basically genuine faith none the less. In the case of Filipino popular religiosity it is difficult to determine where faith ends and where superstition begins.'

Father Chupungco sees something in the power of images even more potent than the Oaxaca reverence for the Madonna. 'Quiapo's Black Nazarene, for example, is referred to not as a statue of Christ, but quite simply as Christ himself. Physical contact with sacred images amounts to a contact with the power of the person represented.' He does not see this need for examining the origins of the cultural consciousness to get over the accretions from outside as simply a problem of the Third World which had Christianity imposed on it by colonial powers. 'For indeed while Asia presents problems of evangelization because of its deep-rooted religious traditions, Christian Europe presents problems of re-evangelization because of its entanglement with secularization. Perhaps it is not blasphemous to say that Rome is in dire need of missionaries.' Wise popes in the past have been understanding about local differences in worship. Chupungco points out that the famous letter of Pope Gregory the Great to Augustine probably typified the attitude of the Church at that time. Augustine was quite resentful of the independence of the bishops of Gaul and complained to Gregory of the lack of uniformity with the liturgy of the Roman Church. The pope showed no apprehension at what was happening but directed the Apostle of England to adapt from any church, whether of Rome, Gaul or anywhere else, those usages that would be beneficial to the young Church.

Father Chupungco has a high-sounding phrase for the urgency of the problem. 'Indigenization is thus not an option, but a theological imperative arising from incarnational exigency.' He believes that the Church cannot remain a stranger to the people with whom it lives: it must be adopted by them. 'After the example of Christ who became a Jew, the Church must become Filipino. This pluralistic view will not hurt the universality of the Church: on the contrary it will foster it. For there can be no truly universal Church without truly local churches.'

The honest mind is hard put to it to arrive at any accurate estimate of Christianity's contribution to Western life, how far it belongs and how far it does not. Too much is too obvious: the Madonnas and the Last Judgements and the Crucifixions and the Resurrections and the Transfigurations of the great painters; the devotional music; the great Christian poets and writers. Too little is borne in mind of what must have been, and remains, of great importance to humbler people: the constant work of honest priests for nearly 2,000 years that cannot all have gone to waste, though at times it seems it has. (And now is one of those times.) There are the stimulus of the Christian message to the individual conscience, the practical advantages of personal piety, even—and one says it necessarily with a touch of scepticism—the behaviour of those few statesmen who have preferred to follow what they felt was right, according to the teachings of the organized church, rather than the pure dictates of political reason.

People can, and do, say with every conviction: 'I cannot imagine what I would have been like if it had not been for Christianity,' and they go on to talk about the painters and the poets and so on; but it is not possible to say that the world is safer because of Christianity, or that the individual is likely to do less wrong if left to his own devices because the civilization he lives in has felt the influence of Christianity for centuries. Would a Hindu, totally unaware of Christian teachings, be able to write an accurate list of Christian qualities by observing human conduct in the European base of Christianity? Gandhi's harsh verdict remains relevant: 'I love Christ, but I despise Christians because they do not live as Christ lived.'

Better still, what would be the view of one of the modern desert fathers? They found the spiritual strength to move their mental processes out of the frame of the physical into a familiarity with other worlds and other contexts, leading them, as Kipling could describe with such surprising persuasiveness, beyond the normal limits of the human mind. Efforts, too often quite inadequate, have lately been made to copy them. Fads apart, a genuinely contemplative view of the civilization of that large part of the world calling itself Christian would be of great value in detecting what went wrong.

The attraction of the Eastern contemplative spirit is beginning to be felt more now by Christian prelates; it is no longer the preserve of members of mock-Oriental cults, or searchers after the exotic in religious experience. One reason for its popularity is probably because the contemplative tradition helps to make up for the falling away of the traditional, Western belief that life is meant as a proud play of human personalities, drawn from the classical respect for man himself. Religion combined with this humanist approach as a result of Christianity's alliance with Greek and Roman thought. That looks to be the case no longer. The form taken by the popular revival of religion is not heroic; it is anti-élitist. Civilization itself, because of its chronic weaknesses, can no longer maintain this tradition on its own. Herbert Butterfield was right when nearly three decades ago he sensed the tragic reversal of this process.

In some of the aspects of it which the world most prizes today, our respect for personality has grown with the growth of civilization, even while the power of religion in society seems to be declining: though it is possible that the development of a more thorough-going paganism may turn all the tendencies of the twentieth century in the opposite direction.

Who can really tell where religion ends and other factors intervene to shape human behaviour? The danger is to ascribe wrongly to religious feeling what in fact belongs to something else; or to keep too strictly to the issues that the prelates, religion's professionals, argue about.

There is more than discouragement to be had in attempting to penetrate this delicate ground of religious feeling and action, the intimate acting within a person of some sort of religious consciousness. It is presumptuous to begin with and a trespass into the hidden workings of the human mind. It could be highly disagreeable; Lord Acton stated that practically all great men were bad men—so what hope is there for little, ordinary men? There is no good reason except inverted snobbery to suppose that such men have less reason and less opportunity to be bad than their more eminent betters. It is disturbing because it is mysterious, unforeseeable, yet not without menace; like sitting back in the coach to the airport, looking across the frozen white wastes of a Canadian winter, after hearing a bishop's views on why religion in Quebec, of all places, is in such dire straits, and feeling a gentle, regular motion against one's arm and slowly understanding that the attractive girl at one's side is looking at the same austere scene without seeing it, because she is concentrating on fingering her beads as she recites the rosary. Sibelius with the undertones of Puccini, both would be needed to reconjure the feelings that such a moment arouses.

9

THE ROAD TO FATIMA

THE DRIVE FROM Lisbon to Fatima is boring, dispiriting. Tattered advertisements for a bullfight, a deeply frustrating feeling that over to the left, just a few miles from this featureless atmosphere of colonial churches and unremarkable Latin living, lies the grey movement of the expanse of Atlantic breakers. There, the huge waves pummel the empty beaches, scouring clean and fresh every corner of the rocks and sweeping away the debris from the deep sands on a strong refreshing tide. But all that is a little way off from the road we have taken. The road to Fatima, close to the ocean but oblivious to it, ignoring that gigantic existence of the waves, is taken by more and more people nowadays. They are people who want to visit the place where the Virgin Mary is supposed to have appeared six times to three shepherd children after they had received three preliminary visits from an angel. The phenomenon of the renewed popularity of the sanctuaries is widespread throughout the Catholic world and already was before John Paul II began his tireless visits to so many of them. So is the revival of devotion to Mary; which at times is something more limpid than the march to the sanctuaries, at other times much the same thing, as it becomes involved with the whole phenomenon of a newly urgent interest in popular religious symbols.

It would be a brave man who was willing to say exactly what this interest means. Is it part, for instance, of a religious revival after the flight from religion in the sixties? Does it genuinely have anything to do with religion at all? Is it just another sign of the decadence of Western civilization, the final betrayal, before the catastrophe, of the West's great gift of rationality? Certainly it is something quite different from the half-and-half belief of the Catholic Indian in Oaxaca who is addressing his old gods by talking to the Madonna on his knees and ignoring the institutions which the European world tried to impose on him. It is different from the tide-like mental motions of the European Catholic who feels his faith increase and subside with the hours of the day, and different from the attempts at embedding the liturgy in popular culture. 'There will be a lot more religion in the future,' someone pointed out to me, ruefully, as I was setting out for Portugal, 'much of it of an unpleasant kind.'

Fatima is an unattractive place, but it would be foolishly romantic to suppose that reports of the supernatural require a natural atmosphere of evocation, or, for that matter, to suppose that a place officially declared to have been the scene of miraculous happenings would be allowed to preserve its decorum.

That is not necessarily a part of the experience at all. The ancient Coptic Church in Egypt, for instance, to use a non-Catholic example, has experienced this revival of popular enthusiasm as part of a broader renewal of enthusiasm among its followers, varying from a middle-class fascination with monasticism to a religious curiosity in the villages which sends representatives to the Coptic centre near Cairo every Friday, when the head of the church, the Coptic pope, answers questions put by the faithful who record what he says on tape and take the recording back to the villages. The Copts claim Mark as their founder and go back, as they proudly say, to 'the times of the Pharaohs', which gives them a sense of superiority over the far more numerous Muslim population, who have dominated the country after conquering it throughout most of the Christian era. They claim six million adherents, though the government is inclined to halve that figure. They are on quite good terms with Rome and delegations meet once a year to discuss theological differences, which the Copts believe are almost resolved. In June 1968, the Vatican made an ecumenical gesture towards them by giving back the skull of St Mark, which had been stolen in 1150 by Italian seamen and taken to Venice where it remained—in St Mark's of course—for the intervening centuries. Crowds broke the airport barriers when the relics arrived in Cairo. And just a few months earlier, the Coptic world was amazed by reports of the appearance of the Madonna in a Cairo suburb called Shubra. The Coptic authorities immediately declared the apparition genuine, asserting that miraculous cures took place at the same time. The point is that the location of what is taken to be a supernatural event need not be romantic: the Shubra appearances took place on the roof of the local church. And, secondly, the return of the remains of Mark to Cairo was a fascinating example of the popular religious element in ecumenism which, on the face of it, would need a somewhat rational approach.

From Shubra to New York is a long step, but even there you may feel not that far away from the road to Fatima. A sophisticated newspaper carries a large advertisement about the alleged appearances not only of the Virgin Mary but of Jesus himself, at Bayside. The advertisers explain how to reach Flushing Meadow, the new location of the apparitions which had been changed from Bayside 'at Heaven's request'. Propitious dates are suggested for fresh appearances and messages, to say nothing of the possible repetition of such miracles as cheap rosaries which turn to gold during the vigil. A woman in Phoenix, Arizona, had the odd experience in November 1977 of seeing what she said was the face of Jesus in a tortilla. She saw not only the face but also a message consisting of four letters: 'K.J.C.B.', which she interpreted as meaning 'King Jesus Coming Back'. She was reported in a local newspaper as saying: 'I don't know for certain why the Lord chose to relay the message in a tortilla, but I believe it is because he wants to get down to our level.'

What is known as the 'Holy House' at Loreto, near Ancona in central Italy, is thriving as never before. There, the attraction is a small stone building, now incorporated into a large basilica. The small building is supposed to be the house in which the Virgin Mary and her family lived in Nazareth. Tradition has it that on 10 May 1291 it was lifted off its foundations by divine forces and moved to Dalmatia, where it settled on the summit of a hill at Tersatto, a small town some sixty miles south of Trieste. The people of the place awoke one morning, according to the legend, to find the house standing there, of reddish stone, with a wooden roof painted blue and decorated with stars, and, inside, some earthenware vessels and a small altar with a wooden cross over it bearing the inscription: '*Jesus nazarenus rex judaeorum*'. On the right of the altar was a cedar statue representing the Virgin with a child in her arms who blesses the world. The local priest was as mystified as anyone, but took the course of praying for enlightenment, which he received in the form of a statement made in a vision to him by the Virgin:

Know that the house which has been brought of late to your land is the same in which I was born and brought up. Here, at the annunciation of the Archangel Gabriel, I conceived the Creator of all things. Here the word of the eternal Father became man. The altar which was brought with the house was consecrated by Peter, Prince of the Apostles.

Some three years and seven months after its arrival at Tersatto, the house set off again and reached its present site in the hills behind the Marche coast.

These are just a few random examples that show that Fatima, and its increasing number of pilgrims, is in no way unique. It is not just the sanctuaries—the places where the supernatural is supposed to have intervened in a direct way in the affairs of ordinary humans—either. Loreto may strain anyone's sense of credulity but its custodians maintain that there is a growing tendency among ordinary people to give immediate credence to claims of miracles or divine visitations. A woman living near Loreto spent her time writing down messages and warnings and instructions which came, she said, directly from Jesus. He had asked her to build him a church on a hill quite close to the massive shrine of Loreto but to make it even larger than St Peter's in Rome. She had a substantial following. Neighbours of mine tell me that they know a wandering holy man who visits them, and during the prayer-session makes blood drip from his crucifix.

Fatima gives the impression of being closed, despite the facts that the ocean is only thirty miles away and the huge square of the sanctuary has room for a million pilgrims. There they stand in reverence, carrying their sick, covering the vast expanse on their knees (some with pads tied round their knees, and others, who want to suffer even more, without any protection), and throwing candles on the fire burning near the place where the Madonna is supposed to have appeared. She was said to have been dressed in white of such brilliance that it shone more brightly than the sun, and was suffused and more intense than that emitted by clear water through crystal hit by the strongest rays of the sun. This somewhat forced description was given by one of the three children, Lucia, to whom the Madonna and the angel are said to have appeared. Lucia survived the other two and returned from the cloister, to which she had retired, to be present at Fatima for the highly controversial visit of Paul VI in May 1967.

The pope risked, and indeed incurred, criticisms that Fatima was no place for a pope who was supposed to be leading the renewal of Catholicism, directed in part at closing the gap between religion and the modern scientific mentality. At that time, too, Salazar was still alive, and the pope was felt to be enhancing indirectly the position of a dictator in the midst of a colonial war. Certainly, the story of Fatima has little to do with the scientific mentality. The account, officially declared 'worthy of belief' by the Catholic Church in 1930, is more notable for its colourfulness than for any scientific revelation that might help understanding of the supernatural world.

The three children concerned were a brother and sister and their cousin. Lucia was the cousin and the eldest of the three, having been born in March 1907. Her cousin Francesco was little less than a year younger, and his sister Giacinta was born in March 1910. They came from modest families and watched sheep. They were born at Aljustrel, a small collection of houses about three-quarters of a mile from Fatima; it was, and remains, an unprepossessing place, despite what has happened to it and its grandiose old Moorish name, presumably given it during Muslim domination of Portugal to honour the daughter of the prophet of Islam.

In spring 1916—the exact date is no longer recorded—the three children claimed to meet an angel at a rocky hill called Loca de Cabeço, near Aljustrel. It was raining, and the three sought shelter among the rocks. When the sky cleared, according to Lucia, a strange light appeared in the east and moved towards them. At its approach they saw that it had 'the form of a youth of fourteen or fifteen years of age, whiter than snow, and transparent as crystal struck by the rays of the sun, and of great beauty'. He approached them and said: 'Do not fear! I am the Angel of Peace. Pray with me.' He knelt, bowing his head to the ground, and made them recite, three times, the following prayer:

> My Lord, I believe, I adore, I hope and I love thee. I seek forgiveness for those who do not believe, who do not worship, who do not hope and who do not love thee.

Thereafter, having risen, he said: 'Pray thus. The hearts of Jesus and Mary receive the voice of your supplications.' He then disappeared. The shock was such that the three said nothing about it, not even to each other.

The angel made two more appearances of which the last was the most dramatic. He appeared with a chalice and a wafer that was shedding drops of blood. He gave Lucia the wafer and the other two the contents of the chalice saying: 'Take and drink the body and the blood of Jesus Christ, horribly outraged by ungrateful men. Make atonement of their crimes and comfort thy Lord God.'

Six months later, according to the children, the Madonna made the first of her six appearances to them. She asked them if they were ready to bear the pain God would send them in an act of redemption for all the sins which had outraged him and to implore the conversion of sinners. They accepted. She told them to recite the rosary every day and then, according to Lucia, she began 'to rise slowly towards the east, and finally disappeared into space, surrounded by a bright light that appeared to open a way for her among the stars'. There is little point in recalling what is supposed to have happened at the subsequent five appearances of the white lady, except for the last which has gone down as the one accompanied by a special miracle.

In the words of Giacinta's father: 'All had their eyes fixed towards the sky when, suddenly, the sun stood still, and then began to dance and to jump. It stood still once more, and once more it began to dance so that it appeared as if to break away from the sky and hurl itself upon us like a huge wheel of fire. It was a terrible moment. Then the sun stopped and returned to its normal position in the firmament.' A final miraculous claim was that the people in the crowd of about 70,000 who had gathered to see the miracle and had been soaked in the rain found they were dry—and that was the last of what was officially said to be the authentic and 'wholly credible' apparitions to the three shepherds.

There is still some curiosity about what is called the 'secret of Fatima'. An official publication about the shrine states:

> Much has been written upon the secret of Fatima, often exaggerating its importance through an urge of what is odd, occult and sensational.
>
> But the true secret of Fatima is already known to all: it is that of prayer and penance. And, if one can speak of dividing the secret into sections, the first two are also already revealed: the vision of Hell given to the three shepherds; the revelation concerning wars, the spreading of atheism and the persecutions of the Church. These revelations were made public by Lucia in 1941.
>
> The third part has not yet been made known. Upon Lucia's advice, this section was not to be published until 1960. If it is as yet unrevealed, this is only because there appeared to be no need for it to become widespread. Set out in writing by Lucia and delivered to

the bishop of Leiria, who never read it, it was later taken to Rome where it is preserved in the archives of the Sacred Congregation for the Doctrine of the Faith. As far as we know, this part of the secret has only been read by Pope John XXIII and by Pope Paul VI.

There is little or no point in arguing about whether the Holy House of Loreto really did what legend says it did, or whether Lucia and her cousins saw what they said they saw. What is important is that an increasing number of people seem anxious to think so. It is difficult to say what a man with so complicated a mentality as Paul VI intended by his gesture of going to Fatima (he had been to Loreto too but before his election to the papacy). He must have known that he would be attacked. Salazar could scarcely be regarded as good company in which to be photographed by the world's press. He must also have been aware that the temper of the Vatican Council, which he had closed two years earlier, was strongly inclined towards less uncritical manifestation of devotion to Mary. The object was to prune excess, given that the Catholic Church was seeking to appear more attractive to the contemporary mind, and to have better relations with other Christian churches, some of which find the Catholic insistence on prominence for Mary unacceptable.

The Council itself decided against approving a separate document on Mary, and placed its thinking on the subject within the context of its main document on the Church as a whole. This decision was thought at the time to be favourable to modern, progressive Catholicism. It can be fairly compared with the Vatican Council's views on the papacy: that, for good reasons, it should take a relatively less prominent place in the whole field of Catholicism. The pope and Mary had grown above themselves, disproportionately claiming the obedience and devotion of the faithful. Doubt and reality had gone out of the stained-glass window.

Paul saw differently. At the end of the Council's third session, he declared Mary the Mother of the Church and, with a gesture that aroused suspicions of a return to the most florid concepts of privileges claimed by the popes, sent a Golden Rose to the Fatima sanctuary. The title he gave to Mary—she, in fact, has plenty and needed no other, given that one of the pretexts for going to Fatima was to mark the twenty-fifth anniversary of the decision of Pius XII to consecrate the whole world (no less) to the Immaculate Heart of Mary—is seen by Marian enthusiasts as a sign of great courage. It is argued that the pope bestowed this title personally because the Council would not have agreed to do so.

That is probably correct, but Paul VI was more far-sighted than the Council, or more emotional about Mary than it was the fashion to be in his time. His insistence on flamboyant new titles for Mary no doubt followed his own private feelings about the Madonna. He may, too, have sensed that the direction the Church had taken at its Council was too sophisticated for the mass of ordinary Catholics. Whatever his reason, he judged the situation accurately. People, and in particular young people, felt the pull of the sanctuaries. And he prepared the way for John Paul II's apparently insatiable appetite for visiting sanctuaries, which soon became accepted as a commonplace of his reign. That change in itself marks the difference in the approach of the general public to the whole question of the acceptability of Marian sanctuaries.

Statistics back up one's own impressions. A study of young Catholic adults in the United States and Canada, published in 1980, revealed, in the words of Father Andrew Greeley who took part in the survey, that 'Mary, perhaps the most important cultural symbol in 2,000 years of Western history, is alive and well in North America, even among young people.' The study showed that 'the Mary image proved to be stronger than either the Jesus image or the God image.' Another of the authors of the report commented: 'Bernard of Clairvaux was right: "if you fear the father, go to the son. If you fear the son, go to the mother . . . ."' Greeley, in a few words of verse, summed up the condition of the 'broken Mary myth' of some years ago:

Rejected, Madonna, as obsolete,
Discarded in ecumenical distaste
A worn out image buried with all due haste
and quickly forgotten by a smug élite.

But he is able to report a transfigured image as the result of the survey. This is the summary of its outcome:

More than 75 per cent of the young adults said they were 'extremely likely' to think of Mary as 'warm' or as 'patient' or as 'comforting' or as 'gentle'; 65 per cent of the respondents checked all four words as 'extremely likely' while 50 per cent rated Jesus as high on all four images.

Nor were the Mary images irrelevant. Our 'madonna scale' (one point for each of the four words checked as 'extremely likely') correlated positively with social commitment, frequency of prayer, concern for racial justice and sexual fulfilment in marriage. Mary is not only still fashionable but it seems also still 'relevant'.

He even manages to argue from the good 'madonna ratings' of non-Catholics married to Catholics in the survey that 'Mary may actually be an asset to ecumenism instead of a liability.'

Paul VI may have felt that he was doing a service to religion in general, not only to the Catholic religion, by making a diplomatically hazardous visit to a shrine which reinforces the idea that religion still possesses supernatural elements that can enter everyday life. He may have instinctively grasped the point that many Catholics were out of step with the Council because they wanted the old popular beliefs. They wanted to touch the very tree in whose branches Mary is supposed to have appeared, to pray in the reddish-grey brick of the house where Mary is said to have lived before the building began its miraculous travels. 'We are seeing'— these are words of Fatima's rector, Father Luciano Guerra—'that man discovered that he cannot create love in this world. When he sees this he looks elsewhere. It is part of the understanding that love cannot exist without God. The Marxist experience seems to be finishing. The great Marxist theologians sought to create a society without God. Some young Catholics also took part in this experiment. Even within the Church something similar was attempted by young people who argued that the love of God was found in particular among the working classes and argued from this that the class-struggle was still necessary. But Russia can no longer be a model; nor China. Acts of terrorism are acts of final desperation. Communism moreover imposed an élite. Young people will no longer accept this. Not from the Church either. They want to breathe the air of heaven themselves. Jesus is much more an ordinary man to them. They look at that side of him which was that of a man like other men. The idea of the sanctuary is similarly direct. It is not enough to be told, as they used to be, that the real sanctuary is the body of man. They want something now with a presence that they can feel. And so the Madonna is returning, and with her the idea of mass gatherings. Our priests too are feeling a closer relationship with Mary. Even the charismatic movement is Marian, here. Remember, it is the concept of an élite that they do not accept, the young people.'

The Vatican Council—with its teachings on the responsibilities of the world's bishops in the government of the Church rather than a supreme, unquestioned pope; in its emphasis on the Church as the People of God—was of course élitist, as it was in its efforts at redefining the position of Mary and of the pontiff. Paul VI implied that he understood this problem in his speech during his audience in St Peter's on 3 May 1967 before leaving for Fatima:

> To her who, for the safety of this modern world of ours, has deigned to show her maternal countenance once more, all sweet and luminous, to the poor and little ones, and recommended prayer and penance as sovereign remedies, to her we raise our supplications. This is the reason for our pilgrimage.

He made clear that he attached no élitist significance to what he was doing. Rather the opposite.

The issue raised by this recourse to the sanctuaries—towards, one might say, a more tangible and immediate form of religious feeling—has far greater relevance than the superficially more absorbing question of whether the miraculous origins which are claimed for many of them are true or not. It is worth recalling that 1978 was one of the rare years in which the Holy Shroud, the piece of ancient linen kept in Turin and said to be Jesus's winding-sheet, was publicly exhibited, to crowds numbering hundreds of thousands. The utility of Fatima at this point in history is that it raises the question of whether the first appeal of Christianity should be directed towards an élite or to the masses. The second aspect is whether the shift in the second half of this century—against the expectations of many of those most concerned about the future of religion—towards a revival of popular ties, is a favourable development for humanity as a whole. Fatima has its secrets, but the answers to these two questions would more than satisfy my own curiosity.

A view which comes from far away from Fatima, but not so far in terms of religious history, is one put by a prelate whose faithful live as a small minority among Muslims. Catholicism in Pakistan was established mainly by the occupying powers, by the work of British military chaplains and by the Portuguese in Goa. The ancient strength of Christianity in the sub-continent is in the south; Cardinal Cordeiro, the Archbishop of Karachi, prefers not to see his comparatively tiny group of Catholics as an élite but comes near to the concept in defining the faith's importance as a minority belief: 'I think the importance of Christianity is really if it were to act as a kind of a sign of what is really good, humanly good, and accompanied by all sorts of emphasis on human rights. . . .'

The Gospels on this point are at their most enigmatic. Jesus is seldom classifiable. It is true that he preached very strongly in favour of the humble and the poor, though he was not, himself, necessarily a poor man. In itself, his is rather an élitist position. He did not identify himself with any social class, and his followers and friends were upper class as well as simple people. Joseph of Arimethea, who gave Jesus his tomb, was rich; Nicodemus was high in the social scale. There is little reason to suppose that Jesus preferred the company of one class to another. He talked of his followers as the salt of the earth which should not lose its savour, and if ever an image is élitist, it is this one, because salt is required in minute quantities to transform the flavour of a whole dish, and without it, the result is unacceptable. He was brutally tormented by the ordinary ranks of Roman soldiery, whereas centurions were inclined to recognize his extraordinary nature. It is conceivably true—and this is argued in Spain—that the sponge full of vinegar offered to him to drink while he was on the cross was not actually vinegar but *gazpacho*, a soup containing vinegar that the legionaries would have learnt to use to quench thirst while serving in Spain, but really the argument is about as convincing as a red carnation. The rank and file were largely recruited from the Hellenistic city states and so were basically anti-Jewish. Long after his death, Christianity was installed as the official religion of Rome by the Emperor, not as a result of popular demand.

The real extent and significance of the revival of popular religiosity, what can fairly be called un- or even anti-élite religiosity, is difficult to gauge. It is there in the statistics and clear to the naked eye. Academics in Italy have looked into such cases as the arrival of over a million people in the little town of Vallepietra in the Lazio for the celebrations of the feast day dedicated to the Trinity, or the growing numbers going to the semi-pagan snake festival at Cocullo in the Abruzzi. Anyone who has lived for any longish period in the Catholic south of Europe will know that feasts for local patron saints looked ten years ago as if they were due for extinction. Young people, especially, could see no more charm in the ingenuous music of the brass bands, the unsophisticated dancing, the fireworks, the processions with the statue of the local saint—a miracle-worker as often as not—and the bicycle race or some other attraction for the sporting-minded. These celebrations now have far more life. In no way do they look condemned to slow extinction. That the phenomenon exists is clear; what is less clear is whether it was always there or whether something new is happening. Or whether that élitist atmosphere left by the Council, which Fatima balanced in so striking a way (and may well defeat), was unfairly restrictive over the simpler forms of religious expression which are now returning to their former strength.

There is an element in the Catholic mind which likes to admit to nothing new. That is why the Council's more interesting developments in teaching were usually put forward as something that had been there all the time but required rediscovery or redefinition or re-expression. And so the fact that the Marian cult is now much stronger than it was a decade and a half ago and stronger than most people at that time thought it could become again, is explained as a reassessment of teachings which had never been in any way repudiated. I remember the words of a Benedictine prior who said, I am sure quite rightly, that veneration for Mary was an essential part of Catholic belief and its renewed strength should be no cause for surprise. Even when it appeared to be less prominent, it was there and powerfully there.

'After the Council, there was a sort of reaction against popular devotions and religiosity.' The words are those of a Mexican theologian, Father Carlos Soltero. He said that he saw the return of older ways as part of a spiritual revival in his country. 'In the last five to ten years,' he went on, 'the ancient religious traditions —what we call popular religiosity—have become better appreciated than immediately after the Council. I think that even the most serious theologians are learning to reappreciate them. I'm afraid it is not always easy to make the distinction between a genuine popular religiosity and superstition. So we cannot go back to the opposite extreme and say that everything within popular religiosity is good. No, there are many aspects that have to be purified. But some theologians, let's say fifteen years ago, had come very easily to the conclusion that popular religion had no value at all. But that is wrong. We have to try to discover what is valuable and what is good and try to point out to people the things which are not really Christian in their practice.'

The Jesuits are inclined to see another element in popular religious feeling, which goes back to their experiences in China. They talk still of a great 'what might have been' if the Vatican had shown sufficient intelligence to allow them to continue their work in China, which was aimed at involving popular religious beliefs and traditional behaviour in the new faith which they had brought with them. This integration of the Church into the local culture happened under the Jesuits led by Father Matteo Ricci who worked there in the late sixteenth and the seventeenth centuries. Their methods were condemned by Rome in 1704 in one of the historic errors committed by the Church. Chinese ideas, such as veneration of ancestors, were prohibited to Christians and the traditional Chinese names for God and Heaven were forbidden. The Chinese answer, after serious attempts at explaining the situation to Rome, was persecution. This does have something to do with popular religiosity. The logic of the ban would also have punished the devout little believers addressing Mary in the Oaxaca church or, for that matter, the rapt Greek woman, dressed in a shabby black dress, who knelt on the stone floor of the Orthodox church in Istanbul, almost motionless throughout the entire service when the pope went there to see the ecumenical patriarch. That was an unforgettable scene. The pope had come to the little church in a still predominantly Greek section of the city to take part with the Ecumenical Patriarch Dimitrios in a joint service. On each side of the pope sat a man in quite an elegant lounge suit, one of them with a small moustache, and each with a machine-gun in his lap. It is unusual to see guns in church and unusual, for that matter, to see a pope in an Orthodox church in Muslim Turkey. Close to this scene from Buñuel, but far, far away from it all, was this little dishevelled, dark-haired woman, ecstatically in contact with something quite personal which had little or nothing to do with the proceedings happening around her in the church, certainly not the machine-guns.

But examples of this kind do not quite reach down to what this fresh impulse to popular devotions really means. I asked a priest-psychologist, Don Tommaso Stenico, who has worked a lot with young people, whether he saw a revival in popular religiosity and what he thought about it. He said: 'I would say that, in a way, religiosity has always been there because it is essential in some form. Man naturally seeks a relationship with the infinite, with the omnipotent. There were some very useful innovations after the Council when the road was taken to elevate popular religiosity to a level of genuine religious belief and many young people took to it with enthusiasm. Not so much the older people. But the effect was like a fire that burnt brightly and then went out. They returned to what was almost a pre-Conciliar position. What is coming back now is a need felt by them to base themselves on some sort of religiosity and the Church must profit from this moment and give this religiosity a proper content. At these feasts of the patron saints, for instance, we should give ideas to back up what these people are unconsciously trying to remember: they are remembering the community, and we should see that the idea is formulated in Christian terms.

'The same for the autumn feast days for the dead or the Marian devotions in May. These occasions must not be neglected, because they represent a broad expanse of faith. And it can be very beautiful, this recuperation of the old ways of the faith. But popular religion has to be protected against an ingredient frequently found in it: barter. "You grant me a favour and I'll light a candle to you or make a pilgrimage or give you a present." A bargain can be struck with Heaven. "If you are up there, God, or Mary, or whoever, you have to help me because I need you. You have to listen." There is non-acceptance of the will of God. It does not accept the originality of Christian prayer which lies in its adoration of God, its gratitude to God, its admiration for God. It is almost always in relationship to something else—the harvest, the weather, love, specific things which have nothing to do with gratitude. Apart from the magic elements, there are dangers of opportunism and egoism. And, in young people, something much worse.

'I detect a kind of "last beach" approach by some young people whose behaviour is marked by a strong return to the need for a father-figure. The destructiveness of the late sixties and early seventies was due to the rejection of the idea of the father and of everything representing it. Now the need for a father is back and if they do not feel a response in terms of faith, what else can they look to? They probably do not even see things in this way. They have not yet understood that many of them are spiritually in the middle of a long adolescence. But if they do not find satisfaction, I cannot foresee what will happen. It could be very serious.'

I am fascinated by all this, but still astounded. This is a much less rational age than I, at least, expected it would be. By one of those strange coincidences that have marked the writing of this book, I was preparing this chapter when I went to lunch with a highly intelligent American lady banker who suddenly let drop the remark that Hitler's career was made possible because people could no longer stand the rationality of the Weimar Republic. That is the type of risk one can legitimately see behind a heavy emphasis on the attractions of the irrational, especially after a period in which, in the Catholic world at any rate, the rational was insisted on rather too much. Quite early in the career of Jim Jones, photographs were sold of the cult-leader to rub on afflicted parts of the body and to ward off burglars. Above the throne from which he presided over the suicides at Jonestown, the words were written: 'Those who do not remember the past are condemned to repeat it.' To suppose, however, that the irrational has to be bad would also be foolish. Paul VI was probably trying to make this very point when he went to Fatima: that the irrational in religion is not only not necessarily bad, but essential, even natural. Even Shaw admitted that history is not changed by rational men.

This of course is especially true of religious leaders. And in this sense a strong and personal papacy—what the Vatican Council was trying to avoid—may well have history on its side. Religious movements and institutions are usually founded, led, split, re-founded, revived, because of the activities of a strong personality. Religion is the terrain of the influential individual, the man who can impose himself, make people follow him. It is not just a Christian characteristic. It is the opposite tendency to that other fundamental idea of Western civilization, that democracy must distrust the overbearing individual as a matter of principle. Even this distinction is not quite correct. The Catholic Church in what might be called its rational days, by which is meant the period when the Council's approach was being formulated, was certainly not seeking to adapt itself to Western democracy. The Church's own style of democracy is now quite clear: it allows occasional outbursts of debate which nevertheless must in the end reach a broad degree of consensus, and this consensus is applied throughout the Church. What the Church was trying to avoid was one man's or one group's expression of all the Church's certainties.

The Marian revival which Paul VI foresaw, and the Council did not, became a hallmark of John Paul II's reign. It is still delicate ground. I have not hesitated to place it among aspects of popular religiosity. I do not however agree with the extreme Protestant view that devotion to the Madonna is not only wrong but an obstacle to ecumenism. I am inclined to agree with the results of Andrew Greeley's Marian survey that in this stage of religious development, the Marian approach has something to offer in the way of a bridge between institutions and the type of popular expressions of religion which are not by any means the prerogative of Catholicism. In Latin countries, for instance—Fatima's rector made this clear about Portugal and it is certainly so in Italy—the charismatic movement is distinctly Marian. This movement has grown faster than any within the post-Conciliar Catholic Church and is almost surely the most effective ecumenical phenomenon at the popular level.

Again, I am aware that the ground is delicate, but I still would not hesitate to place the charismatics on the road to Fatima. And this despite the fact that the movement arose from fundamentalist Protestantism in the United States and not on traditional Catholic territory at all. Catholicism may well have to depend on this extremely popular development to satisfy those of its followers who are not at the point of putting on the knee-pads of the square at Fatima but who need something more than what normal institutional worship can offer.

I went to a meeting of Catholic charismatics at the Gregorian University in Rome. I know I could have found something more dramatic, more emotional. But I felt that the atmosphere would probably be more acceptable in the precincts of the pope's university, which is administered by the Jesuits, and that the proceedings would not therefore get embarrassingly out of hand. The welcome was informal: I asked for the priest who had invited me and the youth at the door replied, 'You must mean Frank.' I did, but I did not know that was the name by which he went in the group. The group of thirty or so was international. The principal language was English; in fact it was the only language I heard though I had expected to hear the strange sounds of what charismatics call 'speaking with tongues', which they believe to be the Holy Spirit speaking through them as happened at Pentecost to the disciples. I would say that the dominant feeling was of extreme mutual respect. No one appeared to feel embarrassed about the presence of others. A Negro rose and, holding his arms above his head, recounted a dream about a person he saw amidst the dark waves at night. It was inconsequential and he admitted as much by saying, with a slightly apologetic tone: 'Well, that was the dream and I wanted to share it.' A middle-aged blonde lady stood up, placed her hands above her head and said: 'I read the newspapers before coming here. They were full of dreadful news. I said to myself why worry. We all of us love each other. We can live in peace with each other so we must shut out the bad news we read about and be happy in our love of Christ.' There were murmurs of approval. What struck me most was the thought that millions of Catholics throughout the world now hold these prayer-meetings regularly.

The charismatic movement arose from Pentecostalism, which was founded in 1900 by Charles F. Parham when he opened a Bible school with about thirty students in Topeka, Kansas. This is the account Father Francis Sullivan, of the Gregorian University, gives of the movement's birth.

> The only textbook in use in this school was the Bible. Parham's method of instruction was to propose a question, and then set the students to work searching the Bible for all the texts that might provide its answer. Towards the end of 1900 he proposed the question: 'What is the scriptural sign of a true baptism in the Holy Spirit?' From the accounts of Pentecost and the other 'descents of the Holy Spirit' described in the Acts of the Apostles Parham and his students concluded that the one sure scriptural sign of baptism in the Holy Spirit was the gift of 'speaking with other tongues'. A wave of enthusiastic fervour swept through the school: uninterrupted prayer for such a coming of the Holy Spirit was carried on for several days and nights. On January 1, 1901, a woman student, Agnes Ozman, asked Parham to lay his hands on her head while they prayed; when he did so she experienced her 'baptism in the Spirit' and began to 'speak in tongues'. Within a few days, all the students and Parham himself had a similar experience. The first 'Pentecostal group' had come into being . . . .

From Topeka, Pentecostalism spread to Texas, then to Los Angeles where its success was immense. In 1906 it arrived in Europe, first in Scandinavia and then in Great Britain and the Continent. It subsequently spread to all parts of the world and became the fastest growing movement in Christendom, especially in Africa and Latin America. A branch of it called neo-Pentecostalism formed the bridge with Catholicism, which must have seemed totally remote from this style of popular·religion. Neo-Pentecostalism means followers of the Pentecostal ideas who nevertheless have remained within their own older Protestant churches.

Four Catholic faculty members at Duquesne University in the academic year 1966–7 read two books by neo-Pentecostalists and sought out a group of these Protestants—Episcopalian and Presbyterian—in a Pittsburgh suburb, with the express intention of learning from them how to receive the baptism in the Spirit. After attending several prayer-meetings with this group, two of the Catholics asked that they might be prayed for and have hands laid on them by the members of the group: 'when this was done, they had the typical Pentecostal experience and began to speak in tongues.' These two went on to organize a Pentecostal group among the faculty and students at Duquesne University; from there the movement spread to Notre Dame and other universities, and to parishes, convents and monasteries in all parts of the United States.

The extraordinary quality of Catholic charismatic renewal is that it has remained disciplined within the control of the hierarchy. There appear to be no separatist tendencies, no feeling of the need to break away from the Church. Catholic charismatics do not regard the movement as a substitute for normal worship. They attend Mass in the normal way, sometimes as a group, sometimes as individuals in their own parish church. The prayer-meetings are not allowed to become a rival. Moreover, the bishops soon recognized that the movement could be a help but at the same time had to be closely controlled. The Bishops' Conference in the United States, for instance, produced a report on the movement in late 1969 which had its distinctly cautious passages:

> Proper supervision can be effectively exercised only if the bishops keep in mind their pastoral responsibility to oversee and guide this movement in the Church. We must be on guard that they avoid the mistakes of classic Pentecostalism. It must be recognized that in our culture there is a tendency to substitute religious experience for religious doctrine. In practice we recommend that bishops involve prudent priests to be associated with this movement.

But the acceptance was also there. That acceptance has grown, and much of the credit for it must go to Cardinal Suenens, the former Belgian primate, who has made the movement very much his own. He believes very strongly in its importance for Catholicism and for ecumenism. I asked him during the meeting of the Sacred College in Rome in November 1979 whether he felt there were signs inside the Catholic Church of a fresh religious spirit, a spiritual renewal. His reply was: 'Yes, I really believe that there is something like a sort of new Pentecost.' He added: 'Of course the word Pentecost is a very strong one, but a spirit blowing is surely there in a very striking way. The renewal of prayer: the renewal of—what should I say—of a living community of Christians coming together to live their Christian life in community. You have many new, charismatic communities, all over the world. I think these are a strong element for the future, because, if you can show what Christianity means—just saying to people, look, those little groups, they are living it seriously—it's very contagious in a good sense.' He sees the movement as a return to Christian origins: 'I think it is a sort of new experience of what the apostles had in the beginning of the Church. Pentecost meant the transformation of those poor disciples of Jesus. They were very weak people. They left Jesus when he was arrested. They were really transformed during those days spent in the upper room. . . .'

One of Rome's most influential prelates, Father Vincent O'Keefe, the leading Assistant-General of the Jesuits, has personal recollections of what Cardinal Suenens has done for the movement. He said this to me: 'I think he has done an awful lot, I don't want to say to justify the movement but to help a lot of people understand what it really means, and take the charismatics from what might be called the lunatic fringe that a number of people would associate with such a movement. During the meetings of the International Synods here in Rome, he used to arrange to have a group of charismatics here and what he would do was ask them to pray especially for Pope Paul VI and the bishops gathered at the Synod. And he would tell Pope Paul about it, and he got him interested in it. And he also arranged that they had a wonderful Mass in St Peter's. There they were in the basilica and they had to wait. Many of the old Vatican hands say it was one of the best waiting groups they had ever dealt with. While waiting they prayed and they also began to sing, making very clear that they felt at home in the house of God even if it was this huge and famous basilica. Pope Paul himself said he was struck by them, by the way they handled themselves. Then Cardinal Suenens made very clear that the charismatic movement was a very legitimate part of the Catholic religion. He traced the beginnings of this right back to the primitive Christian communities, when they met together, prayed together, praying out loud and helping each other to share the faith. Again, it is something that the more intellectual Catholic would not be at ease with. You sort of parade everything out in the open, things which some people might want to share only with our Maker himself. Yet I think that a man like Cardinal Suenens, who would be second to no one in an intellectual approach to things, and a consummate theologian, felt and made other people feel very comfortable within the movement.'

This incident told a lot about how Suenens handles the movement and his own outlook on its usefulness: 'One time during a Synod here in Rome, Cardinal Suenens had his charismatic group going. Anyone could speak. You could offer something for consideration or a prayer. As I looked around the room I noted other prominent clerics present including Cardinal Poletti, the pope's vicar for the Rome diocese. Something Suenens said affected Poletti very much. He said that as a bishop he did not have many chances to pray with his people. There was the Mass of course, but that is such a stylized form, and he did not, he said, get to meet people in their homes, to meet ordinary people in an ordinary place and pray with them, not just taking the lead but letting them take the lead. I remember Cardinal Suenens dealt very well with someone who was getting hysterical. This was not the place for that, he said very firmly . . . .'

There are dangers from that blacker side of religion that can never be forgotten, the Claggart side of exploitation of a too human belief. Anglicans in Britain have found that charismatic prayer-groups were producing patients at psychiatric hospitals who claimed possession by the devil or evil spirits The phenomenon was said to be associated with the mushrooming of 'house groups' or 'house churches', of which there are said to be several thousand in Britain and which consist of groups of people meeting regularly to engage in unstructured forms of prayer and spiritual experience. Like the Catholic groups, they base themselves on the teachings of St Paul, who speaks of ecstatic experiences, including that unfathomable quality of speaking in tongues, and esoteric philosophy. The experiences recorded among patients are taken from the Church Society's publications. The examples are Anglican but there is no reason to suppose that Catholics are a world or more away from such problems, even if, so far, the hierarchy seems to have kept these freer, individualistic movements in greater check.

The stress and insecurity of modern living can quite evidently carry susceptible persons towards belief in possession, especially if they are suffering sexual difficulties and traumas. But essentially the victims have a belief, if a morbid one, in the power of religion to settle their problems for them. This is a little publicized side of religion because the professionals clearly do not want such distortions placed alongside the beauty of the revealed truth. The devils of Loudun are not so far away and possession and exorcism have become increasingly a part of everyday life because of their appeal to popular novelists and the cinema.

I would nevertheless have no difficulty in placing this vastly influential movement of charismatics and private prayer-groups on the road to Fatima. There is a big difference between the movement and a pilgrimage. The main distinction is that the pilgrim seeks the exact place, the actual physical background where something miraculous is supposed to have happened, with the hope of being vouchsafed something similar, rather than specifically seeking the background of ordinariness so that the praying and the speaking in strange, incomprehensible sounds seems more natural and a part of everyday life. This is the great attraction of the charismatics. Whatever they do that is wonderful happens very near the kitchen sink. The highest form in art of this ordinariness reaching for the sublime is probably Rembrandt's *Holy Family* in the Amsterdam Museum: a solid, reasonably comfortable family which has somehow in the midst of it this unfathomable mystery. The sanctuary is different: it is the place where events are supposed to have happened which are apart from everyday life because they are miraculous or magic. Both bring the temptation of closing the individual in on him or herself, like the woman at the Gregorian meeting who wanted to stop thinking of events outside the loving circle of the group. An Indian scholar working for the Vatican's Commission for Justice and Peace, Anthony Chullikal, pointed out that the charismatic movement was quite strong in India but there was the danger that the Christian involvement with social problems would be lessened by this recourse to prayer and contemplation. 'You need not neglect prayer and contemplation,' he added, 'but you must be aware at the same time of the necessary structural changes that will contribute towards human dignity, equity and solidarity among people so that the distance between rich and poor, the powerful and the powerless would be mitigated.'

For the moment, I would place ecumenism on the road to Fatima, too, and not yet afloat on that limitless ocean which is tantalizingly near. Suenens sees the charismatic movement as vital to ecumenism and I think he is right. This spontaneous attitude is the one likely to press the case for ecumenism forward from below rather than leaving it to the endless series of talks between the various churches, which are in many cases negotiations as much as examples of common witness; and from most points of view, particularly the Catholic view, this is not a field where very much is in effect negotiable. For several years now, from the last years of Paul VI, moves towards greater unity between Catholics and other Christians seem to have been in abeyance. The Catholic Church came late to the ecumenical movement. John XXIII established a new climate. His method was both frank and intimate. He set the new tone in his address at the Vatican Council to the observers from other churches: 'We do not intend to conduct a trial of the past, we do not want to prove who was right and who was wrong. All we want to say is: "Let us come together. Let us make an end of our divisions." ' In his more intimate way, he replied to the representative of another Christian church who asked him in private audience when he thought unity would be achieved, to the effect: 'Don't you feel that we two have achieved it now?' He also set up the Vatican's special Secretariat for Christian Unity, the body which was to put into continuing effect the consequences of the reversal of the old fortress mentality.

The Secretariat has probably done as much as can be expected of it. It has opened and maintained relations with all the leading Christian churches. Progress has been varied. The new relationship with the Eastern Orthodox churches for instance has been based more on historic gestures than on theological discussion: Paul VI's meeting with the Ecumenical Patriarch Athenagoras in the garden of Gethsemane; the annulment of the anathemas pronounced at the time of the eleventh-century break between the two churches; the visits both of Paul VI and John Paul II to Athenagoras's successor, the Patriarch Dimitrios I at his little centre in the Fanar, one of Istanbul's less imposing areas. The question of theological discussion suffers from the immense obstacle that the Orthodox world is split into national churches which owe only a formal allegiance to the ecumenical patriarch, who, moreover, has a very modest number of followers and a government which does not like his presence in Turkey. This dislike is not a feeling against his religion but against what is seen to be a survival of the old Ottoman Empire which sought to appoint one and only one interlocutor with other religions, with the Patriarch of Constantinople as the proper channel for official dealings with the Empire's Orthodox subjects.

A rapprochement with the Orthodox would be the greatest ecumenical feat of them all. This, in the words of Monsignor Charles Moeller, the Secretariat's secretary, is 'the root of the matter'. It is argued at the Vatican that if there had been no division between Eastern and Western Christianity, there would have been no break away by the Protestants. And so a return to unity between East and West would influence more strongly than anything else the return to unity of other churches. John Paul II adds more personal considerations: his view of Europe as reaching the Urals rather than stopping at the borders with Communism requires this ecumenical as well as political approach, while at the same time he recalls that southern Poland, where he comes from, was first evangelized by missionaries from Constantinople even if, as it is said, they acted on the promptings of the Bishop of Rome.

There have been gestures between Catholics and Anglicans. In 1960 Dr Geoffrey Fisher became the first Archbishop of Canterbury to call on a pope since the Reformation. Ramsey, Coggan, Runcie, have all since met popes, and Ramsey was actually accorded the accolade of an embrace in the Sistine Chapel beneath Michelangelo's *Last Judgement*. Apart from the gestures, there has also been a long series of theological talks between the two churches. They dealt with the principal problems dividing them: how each saw the Eucharist, priestly orders and authority. Anglicanism after Orthodoxy is seen at the Vatican to be a vital partner, because it represents something which claims to be catholic yet at the same time reformed. Hence, unity would reflect well on both sides. The theological groundwork is already laid, and on a personal level it is no doubt useful that Archbishop Runcie is himself an expert on Orthodoxy and is against women priests, an issue totally unacceptable to Rome but one on which the Anglican Communion is divided.

Certainly the Secretariat has created a whole new set of contacts with leaders of other churches. The Catholic Church works much more closely with the World Council of Churches than before, though it is not a full member. The fact that Paul VI visited Geneva, the citadel of Calvinism, in order to show his respect for the World Council is probably the most forgotten of all his journeys; and, if by no means dramatic, because the public was understandably little interested in the pope's presence, the effort he made is still worth recognition. Strangely enough, the only visit undertaken by John Paul II comparable with this—in terms of a reception which lacked the cheering masses to which popes are accustomed—was the journey to Turkey. And this too, not coincidentally, was an ecumenical affair. The popularity of John Paul II was double-edged, as far as ecumenism was concerned. He made an impression on non-Catholics as well as Catholics but, as a leading theologian at the World Council of Churches said to me in Geneva: 'When their own affairs are going well, Catholics are less interested in the others.' Certainly their own affairs were going well. At the same time, John Paul II has seldom missed an opportunity to express his deep interest in the ecumenical movement. He even quoted Luther in Germany. One of the first acts of his reign was to declare the Catholic commitment 'irreversible'.

The urgency for re-establishing unity was probably best expressed by Suenens when he said: 'The Lord's spiritual testament tells us that unity among his followers is not only the proof that we are his, but also the proof that he is sent by the Father. It is the test of the credibility of Christians and of Christ himself.' The matter could hardly be put higher than that. And I think he may be right when he says that Providence seems to be assigning to the charismatic renewal a specific role full of promise for the future. The trouble with ecumenism, I suppose, is that too much of it is constantly relegated to the future, and so it has an air of unreality about it, like a dream shared earnestly by too few. It is said that if someone dreams it remains a dream but if everyone dreams it becomes a reality. Experts say that if more than one radio is tuned in to the same station, the reception is better. The ecumenists have not done their tuning. Perhaps the right approach is a combination of John XXIII and Suenens. The pope was for forgetting the past, but he did not have a step-by-step programme for the future: unity happened spontaneously as two leaders of different churches talked to each other. And Suenens adds the by no means negligible point that such a thing can happen among people who are not popes or archbishops or moderators but ordinary Christians. Paradoxically, ecumenism needs something of the road to Fatima.

Where the outlook can and must begin is in the Catholic Church's relations with the other great religions. These dialogues need the symbol of the ocean and not the pilgrimage. Certainly there are signs, small signs and not unmistakable ones as yet, that a closer understanding among the great religions of the world will mark the second Christian millennium more deeply than any great changes in Christian consciousness.

I was at Davau City, in the south of Mindanao, the southernmost island of the Philippines, where there is a strong Muslim minority. They are still known as 'Moros' and history presents a long and continuous struggle with the Catholic forces. For centuries the 'Moros' were in a condition of intermittent warfare with the Catholic authorities. Reaction to President Marcos's dictatorship and the cruelties of members of his armed forces under his martial-law regime helped bring Muslims and Catholics together. The church in Mindanao had had a Pastoral Congress shortly before I arrived. Muslim relations was on the agenda as were the cruelties of the soldiers and the need for social justice. I asked the young secretary of the Congress what he would have thought of Muslims before the Church, directly, and the regime, indirectly, brought Catholics and Muslims closer together. 'I would think like any other Catholic that the Muslims are dirty, dishonest, untrustworthy and violent,' was his reply. He added that Muslims suffered individually even greater cruelties than Catholics from Marcos's soldiers.

In Ankara on 29 November 1979 John Paul II made the most interesting speech of his Turkish visit: it was a reminder to the tiny Catholic community of the respect due to Islam and the need to develop spiritual bonds between them. Given the amount of scepticism at the Vatican about the chance of making progress with the Muslims (to say nothing of what was happening in Iran) the pope's speech was very remarkable. He made no mention of the basic difficulty in Vatican dealings with Islam: that Muslims accept Jesus as a great prophet even if they place Mahomet above him, while Christians can offer no more reverence towards Mahomet than to acknowledge that he was a powerful force in history. In his broad view of relationships, the pope said:

> The universe, for the Muslim, is destined to be subdued by man in his quality as representative of God: the Bible affirms that God has ordered man to subdue the earth and also to 'till and care for it'. As God's creation, man has rights which cannot be violated, but he is also bound by the law of good and evil which is based on the order founded by God. Thanks to this faith, man will never submit to any idol. The Christian obeys the solemn commandment: 'You shall have no other God to set against me.' The Muslim, for his part, will always say: 'God is greatest.'

Other signs: in Thailand, the Catholic Church's development office organizes courses in rural leadership and there are more Buddhists than Catholics attending them. A French missionary with many years of work among the Thais said that recently for the first time Buddhists were talking in their homilies on the radio of a Supreme Being. The idea is gaining ground that the other great religions are in some way related to God. Christians claim that there is one God and so these religions must also be related to that God. It is now difficult when travelling the Catholic world to find anyone who still believes in the need to go out and convert all the Buddhists, Muslims and Hindus possible to Christianity.

Now the Church is seen more as a community which must give an example, bearing in mind as it does so that the other great religions may have their own role, equally valid, in God's sweeping design. If so, then the object should not be conversion but a sincere dialogue, a mutual sharing of beliefs so that a fuller truth may be discerned and, to deal with these requirements, full freedom must be given to Asian theologians to respond to a reality totally different from the European mentality. It is unfortunate that the Islamic revival has been associated with the dark, sinister side such as the whippings and segregation of women, and the cutting off of a thief's hand. I remember when I was in a strictly Muslim country—Saudi Arabia—I was asked if I would like to prolong my stay by a few days in order to see a felon publicly beheaded.

This was the formula given by a group of four Little Sisters of Jesus, the community founded by Charles de Foucauld, to a member of the staff of the Asian Bishops' Conference Office for Human Development. They lived in a Muslim slum in Karachi and had broken down the religious barriers. Mr Denis Murphy asked them what the Church should do to be acceptable to the other religions. They said: 'First, Christians must be seen to pray. Muslims and Hindus appreciate a life of prayer. They don't see Christians as a prayerful community. Rather they see us running things, like schools. Second, we must be poor. For Asia, true spirituality is inseparable from poverty. Third, we must love the Muslims and be with them in their daily lives, not necessarily doing things for them but being there with them in good times and bad.' With this outlook, conversions are not important. Quality is. The Archbishop of Karachi, Cardinal Cordeiro, shares the view that his tiny community amidst so many Muslims should be distinctive for the value it places on such qualities as justice and honesty in government. These are views of thinking members of a church which has 1 per cent of the continent's population. There is a good deal to be said for these views even where the Church has, on paper, an overriding majority of the population.

Sometimes I think that the test-case among all the Catholic Church's attempts at opening dialogues with religious groups it once despised (and not so long ago) is its relationship with the Jews. It is the most difficult of them all, and not only because Jesus was a Jew. The early Christians, with a remarkably precocious political sense, very soon after the death of Jesus found it expedient to place the full blame on the Jews and exonerate the

Romans. That condemnation, which meant so many centuries of suffering and of ghetto life for the Jews, was only rescinded by the Vatican Council a decade and a half ago. And still there are formidable difficulties.

Some are quite reasonable. The two sides see the relationship in different ways. The Vatican sees it as a question of the ties of the Christian faith with Judaism, without which, of course, Christianity as we know it could not exist. The Jews are much more interested in more practical considerations such as the Catholic world's view of Israel which is seen by the Jews as a modern embodiment of Judaism, and the treatment of Jews in everyday life. The Vatican has no diplomatic relations with Israel and is suspected of favouring the cause of the Palestinians. And such suspicions are not unfounded. In 1974, the Israelis accused Bishop Hilarion Capucci, the Patriarchal Vicar of the Melchites (Eastern rite Christians in communion with Rome) in Jerusalem, of gun-running for the Palestinians, tried him and sentenced him to twelve years' imprisonment. He was freed on the request of Paul VI who undertook to send the bishop, who was an active organizer for Arafat's Palestinian Liberation Organization, to work in Latin America. He stayed there for a time, setting up a PLO headquarters, and was next heard of in Damascus and then practically superseded the apostolic nuncio in Teheran in a new role as intermediary between the pope and Khomeini. He kept his official place in the PLO, despite the fact that at much the same time the pope insisted that Father Robert Drinan, the highly respected Jesuit member of the US Congress, should give up his seat as priests should not be directly involved in the political process.

Not only have the Vatican's views on Jerusalem's status been totally disregarded by the Israelis, but even acts devised with the best intentions. When Paul VI began his series of journeys by visiting the Holy Land he wanted to leave as a permanent memorial a university at Bethlehem which would provide, in particular, poor Catholics with the chance of a good education without having to leave the country. The university quickly became, as the Israelis quite rightly say, 'a hot-bed of the Palestinian cause'.

I wish the dialogue could go better. So much of it is fascinating. For instance, the Jewish view of Jesus is a salutary one because it is professional and at the same time unhampered by the need for awe, and thus human qualities emerge more clearly. Dr Nicholas de Lange, Lecturer in Rabbinics at Cambridge, gave an excellent summary of how Jews see Jesus in a lecture named in memory of Cardinal Bea, first head of the Vatican's Secretariat for Christian Unity and architect of the Vatican Council's exoneration of the Jews for the death of Jesus:

> The Jewish followers of Jesus during his lifetime were involved in a real, fleshly encounter, and they responded to the undoubted power of his personality and his message. But they were surely mistaken if they believed he was the Messiah who would rescue Israel and inaugurate a new and happier age. The condition of the Jews actually deteriorated after his death. The early Church made brave efforts to explain the apparent failure of his mission and to convert it into a triumph, but these efforts, however successful they were among gentiles, never succeeded in convincing the vast mass of Jews.

There is a refreshing candour untouched by cant in these reflections and an attitude which the most certain Christian could do well to consider for a moment, if only to show strength enough to reject such ideas rationally:

> In the sense in which I understand these terms as a Jew, I cannot see Jesus as the Messiah, the son of David, or as the inaugurator of a Messianic age. I do not count him among the prophets, as our Muslim brothers do. I cannot think of him as Lord, or as *the* son of God, and I certainly do not believe that a man can *be* God. It is not the way of Judaism to engage in a 'cult of personality', to elevate any one human being above all the others. Abraham, Moses, Isaiah were great men, with a great and enduring message for mankind, but they were merely men and shared our human weaknesses. I cannot think that Jesus was greater than these. Nor can I accept that Jesus's purpose was to do away with Judaism as he found it. He had his criticisms, to be sure, but he wanted to perfect the law of Moses, not to annul it. The Christian hostility to this law strikes me as a betrayal of Jesus's teaching as well as a serious barrier to the recognition of the Christians as truly part of the people of Israel . . . .

The attraction of this attitude is in its implication for Christianity of a very Jewish characteristic, that of constant self-criticism. The Judaic tradition is of a halt in Jewish affairs when they acted in a way which displeased God. Christians have the advantage of believing that they possess the final revelation because of God's entry into human affairs. There is no reason why this should preclude a constant measuring of conduct against what has been revealed. And it is no bad thing to remember that, if Israel's

213

conduct in Jerusalem is criticized, and rightly, the Christian presence is nothing to boast about, in the past and now.

The Israelis deserve a great deal more sympathy than they are usually accorded for having to deal with a problem which, before they came to rule Jerusalem, caused trouble to the Turks and to the British: the state of chronic disagreement among the various Christian communities and particularly those with rights within the Christian holy places. In the whole of Palestine there are about thirty-five different Christian churches and communities. Of these, six different Christian churches claim rights and privileges within the church of the Holy Sepulchre—Christianity's most sacred place of all. The claimants, apart from the Catholics, are the Greek Orthodox, the Armenians, the Copts, the Syrians and the Ethiopians. Because of the constant quarrelling of the representatives of these historic Christian churches, the keys of the church of the Holy Sepulchre have been in the hands of a Muslim family for the last seven centuries.

The agreement which the Israelis inherited on how to deal with the Christian churches represented in the sacred city is called the *status quo* and lays down in detail the situation as it exactly existed in the year 1757 and was sanctioned by the Ottoman government of the time. This situation was confirmed by the sixty-second article of the Treaty of Berlin in 1878. The document on which the Israelis work is a definition of rights and privileges drawn up by a British official in 1929 which sets out to describe precisely what the *status quo* is. The introduction to this document opens with the words:

> It is probably true to say that no question more constantly exercised the Moslem rulers of Palestine and took up more of their time than the ever-recurring difficulties and disputes arising out of the circumstance that the Christian Holy Places in Jerusalem and Bethlehem were not in one ownership but were shared and served by several communities. In this respect, the experience of the British Mandatory Government has not differed greatly from that of their Ottoman predecessor . . . .

The comment is urbane but has strong undercurrents of real frustration at the antics of quarrelsome Christians. Much of the document on the *status quo* concerns rights and privileges, often minute, but it occasionally lays down some more general principles, such as these:

. . . authority to repair a roof or floor implies the right to an exclusive possession on the part of the restorers. Again, the right to hang a lamp or picture is a recognition of the exclusive possession of a pillar or a wall. The right of other communities to cense at a chapel implies that the proprietorship is not absolute . . . .

This is what the *status quo* lays down for the holiest part of all the church:

The Tomb Chamber itself is entered by a low doorway. The Tomb is covered by a marble slab and, over it, hang forty-three lamps that are always kept burning. Of these, the Orthodox, Latin, and Armenians have thirteen each, and the Copts four.

The ledge above the slab is divided between the three rites: the centre portion is Orthodox, the left angle is Latin and the right angle Armenian, while the two projecting ends are Orthodox. The votive candles of each Community are supposed to be kept on the portion of the ledge allotted to it. The pictures and candlesticks all belong to the three principal rites and they alone have the right to officiate regularly within the sanctuary.

A footnote gives an eloquent idea, however couched in official language, of the type of dispute which constantly arose (and still does)—in this case a quarrel for possession of the Chapel of St Nicodemus between the Armenians and the Syrian Jacobites:

As an instance, a fracas occurred between these Communities at the conclusion of the Holy Fire Ceremony, in 1927, when the Syrian-Jacobite Patriarch placed his chair in such a way as to prevent the exit of the Armenian procession: see Appendix C and Deputy District Commissioner's letter No. 1900 10/22, of 25 June, 1927, to the Chief Secretary.

This constant scandal has had its diplomatic repercussions, because several countries, France and Russia in particular, showed a propensity for exploiting a favourable shift in the balance of power to further the interests of the churches they favoured in the Holy Sepulchre. It is more than a scandal now, because an ecumenical movement is officially functioning and it is incapable of inspiring less Levantine conduct on the part of Jerusalem's official Christians. One horrified visitor on his first visit to Jerusalem rushed to the Holy Sepulchre to see it before the Muslim custodians closed it for the night and managed to enter the Tomb chamber, where the money collected from visitors during the day was being counted by an elderly, bearded priest. He had arranged it in bundles of various currencies on the slab itself and with an impatient movement of the finger showed the late-arriving pilgrim where to put his money: 'Sterling? Over there . . . .'

Would the Romans have managed to impose more dignity? Biblical evidence is that they could not. Had they possessed the secret of combining sacred places with seemly conduct, there would have been no need for Jesus to throw the merchants out of the temple.

10

WIVES AND SISTERS

THE GREAT SHRINES are dedicated to the feminine object of pious devotion: Lourdes, Fatima, Czechtokowa, even Knock must now be added to the list of first-line Marian places since John Paul II said there that the formerly modest place was the goal of his highly successful visit to Ireland. The implication of the weight of the feminine element in the Catholic approach is correct in a way. Wherever one goes in the Catholic world, women have some sort of prominence. Where they are made to suffer most, they are most praised. Where they are the most demanding category among Catholics they cause the sort of fear, perplexity and anger that mere men could never arouse. Where there is an attitude of tolerance towards feminist aspirations, it is a lofty one of self-convinced male certainty that the ladies will soon give up their unsettling activities. When I asked the view of the National Bishops' Conference in Washington on the women's movement for ordination within the Church, I was told—and this would never be said of the pilgrimages to the sanctuaries—'We are waiting for the steam to go out of it.'

The analogy says more than it appears to do. Steam is an old-fashioned driving force whereas the women's movement in the United States is modern and not at all the sort of machine that would be driven by steam. The fuelling is powerful and, if anything is certain about the future in religion, will not lose its driving force, and may quite soon be seen as the biggest instrument for radical change in the Church of all the new movements which have shaken Catholicism in the course of the last two decades. It could be blocked: not by men, or by the Vatican's expostulations against a leading role for women in the Church, but by other women, the pious women, usually lay, on whom the bishops can rely to oppose the claims of the pious feminists.

I do not say this because I wish to advocate the cause of religious feminism. I am indifferent to it as such, but deeply impressed by the inadequate responses to it which can only be explained by the whole atmosphere of muddle which surrounds the Catholic Church's attitude towards women as women. The one remark for which the unfortunate John Paul I will be remembered is his reference to God the Mother rather than God the Father. His death soon afterwards gave the cartoonists the chance to show him streaking happily heavenward shouting 'Mamma!' His own reply to the amused and confused reaction to his remark was the perfectly correct one that the concept was not his own but Isaiah's. He might have added that Hindu thinking includes the idea of a feminine supreme being: 'Her vision', Ramakrishna said of the Divine Mother, 'dries up all craving for the world and completely destroys all attachment to sexual passion and money . . . .' Some Christian thinkers have sought to transpose this idea to one of the members of the Trinity, though to which one is apparently still left as a matter of choice. Of course, the Church itself is always referred to as feminine, often irritatingly so (presumably) to the feminists, given that only men can conduct its mysteries.

The Catholic Church through the centuries has managed brilliantly to maintain a double image of the woman, which is varied and fascinating, with the added interest, from the point of view of authority, that it leaves very limited space for pretensions on the part of the women themselves. After all, the Devil spoke first to a woman and not to a man and, to some pious minds, that dialogue seems to be still going on. But against that dangerous image of the temptress is another type of woman, who strains credulity still more: of sinless origin, with an immaculate readiness to obey and to accept, always loyal despite some rather doubtful passages in the Gospels on the point, usually riding on clouds or moons, with stars for a halo. Yet even the good woman, this model of suffering sweetness and proud maternity, cannot lead worship; she can only worship.

This double view of Catholic womanhood has had a huge success throughout the centuries. It has somehow managed to preserve the strength of the Mediterranean cults of the mother-goddess, the idea of the woman as mediator with the divinities, whose very feminine comprehension of weakness will make her a winning advocate to explain away the faults of imperfect man, yet with the comfortable certainty that even so persuasive a creature cannot invade the male monopoly as keeper of the sanctuary. No human computation could ever assess the amount of comfort and ease of mind and discipline that the two concepts of woman have brought to generations of believers throughout the centuries. And, for that matter, the artistic inspiration that it has offered, particularly to painters. Beauty seems to come naturally to this concept. So much serenity is expressed in countless Madonnas, so much joy in motherhood and appreciation of purity that the image might have been expected to survive intact indefinitely. The attraction was not reserved by any means to men; the pious women who oppose feminist ambitions do so with in mind this other idea of womanhood, with which they are familiar and which they do not wish to lose.

Beauty is there even when the creative artist is criticizing the idea. There is a fascinating woman in Spenser's *Faerie Queene* who represents his idea of the Catholic Church. She is called Duessa, a word which does not exist in any known language but clearly suggests a duplicity of character. She is depicted as a woman inclined to wear gorgeous clothes, ride on animals with many heads, offer golden cups containing magic potions, now and again briefly losing her beauty and turning back into a witch. It is the opposite to Belloc's sun-soaked, wine-drenched image of joy. For all the aesthetic charms and powers for inspiration of this traditional Duessa, the double concept seems now to be facing its first serious challenge from within the Church. And not just from the feminists, though they are the best equipped as a task force.

The feminists themselves have something of a double image too. And this is also their strength. The right to be ordained, just like men, means two things. The first is the relatively simple demand summed up in the slogan 'equal rites', which is also comparatively simple to rebut from the official side. The Vatican's case was fully put in a document issued in 1976 by the Sacred Congregation for the Doctrine of the Faith. Its principal argument against ordination is that the priest when celebrating at the altar represents Jesus and Jesus was undoubtedly a man. One of the replies of the feminists to this argument is that the men he himself ordained did not fall into the mould of the priest at all and so no one should, logically, be ordained a priest who is not a married Jewish fisherman. But on the straightforward assertion and counter-assertion level, ignoring all implications, the Vatican looks to be on reasonably strong ground. The Vatican admits that the behaviour of Jesus towards women was remarkable, given the habits of his time: it was against the tide of current opinion. And yet, he did not place a woman among his disciples. He went so far as to insist on the equal rights and duties of men and women in marriage, but not in apostleship. As a result the tradition is lacking within the Church of calls for the ordination of women. Why start now, after all this time? The function is seen to remain necessarily a totally male preserve. They reject the argument that women may well genuinely feel they have a vocation; because even if women feel so, this cannot be accepted as a real vocation as membership of the priesthood is something under the control of the Church itself, and the Church must authenticate a vocation. Women are vouchsafed an important mission in the renewal and the humanization of society, but they cannot aspire to become priests, and if they do the Church will not place its seal of acceptability on their aspirations.

The second image involved in the case for women priests is much more formidable. There is a highly intelligent stream of thinking which sees the ultimate aim as the entry of women into the priesthood, but not the existing priesthood. The idea is that the Church, and in particular the caste-system on which the priesthood is based, should be so reformed and changed that the question of masculine and feminine in a new priesthood based on service not power would become irrelevant. This is why some feminists are against ordination altogether. And not only feminists: I heard a young man preach very forcefully in an Amsterdam church. I asked if he was a priest, as no vestments were worn in that particular church and so it was difficult to tell. I was informed that he was studying for the priesthood, lived with his girl without offending the community who wanted to hear him preach, but he would probably not be ordained because there was a growing feeling in the parish against any more ordinations.

The first time I spoke to Rosemary Radford Ruether, who might be called a high priestess of the cause of women's ordination, she talked about the 'gut-hatred' felt by priests for feminists, and the use of the Eucharist as a 'power-instrument' by them. She felt the opposition to women's ordination both overwhelming and inadequate. She herself does not accept the powerful–powerless relationship, but acknowledges its existence, while adding that the average priest is not intelligent enough to talk seriously about the women's movements. 'They are more at home with businessmen and at sports clubs . . . Many of them were trained in the old ways of traditionalist theology and institutional management and so ideas pass them by . . . .'

The replacement of the power-basis of Christian society with a model of service is the foundation of the most serious feminist thinking. They interpret one of the most famous sayings of Jesus as a deliberate statement reversing the traditional idea of the patriarchal community which placed and kept power in men's hands. The text is in Matthew:

> Do not call any man on earth 'Father'
> for you have one Father, and he is in heaven.
> Nor must you be called 'teacher':
> you have one Teacher, the Messiah.
> For whoever exalts himself will be humbled:
> and whoever humbles himself will be exalted.

Jesus is taken here to be addressing himself to men, calling on them to give up their power and to join the new community of service; men, because, in the existing community, they were the ones with power, not the women. The charge here is that a male-dominated Church has put aside the real significance of this call to service. Popes call themselves, as one of their titles, 'Servant of the Servants of God', which they may or may not be, however one cares to look at the matter; but they are certainly not servants in the concept of divesting themselves of patriarchal authority, which they do symbolically only once a year, on the Thursday of Holy Week, when the pope washes the feet of twelve men in his cathedral at the Lateran.

A further argument of the feminists, drawn from the background of the actual life of Jesus, is that on many occasions he went against Jewish customs and the law in his relationship with women; the point here is that he must have meant to exalt their position. The outstanding example is that in Jewish law women were not permitted to give evidence, yet Jesus gave to women the privilege of being able to declare before anyone else the incredible fact of his resurrection. This argument can be double-edged, because it annoys Jews, who have no wish to be blamed for the Christian treatment of women, and who maintain that the feminists are misinterpreting the relationship between Jesus and the law, relying on a new and questionable myth. The ancient Hebrews invented patriarchal society; before them, goddesses reigned unchallenged in matriarchal splendour, and so Jesus had to try to restore the balance, but failed because of the persistence of Jewish attitudes in the Christian tradition. This myth is felt to be based on a series of fallacies—an exaggeration of the plight of women in Jewish society so that the position adopted by Jesus would stand out by contrast. This effect was gained by quoting only the worst aspect of Jewish law, which, like the New Testament, is ambivalent about women. This could be compared with the conservative Christian position of quoting certain passages from Paul to show that women's subordination is divinely ordained. And—the concluding error—that the behaviour of an itinerant teacher is compared with laws and sayings devised in academic backgrounds. Jesus acted and reacted from his direct contact with real women.

These views are not limited to Catholic feminists. The Reverend Dr Diane Tennis, an American Presbyterian, summarizes the position in this way: 'Jesus is the one utterly reliable man in the lives of many women. While his maleness is not the primary word, it is a positive word. It delivers a judgement on patriarchy through the model of self-giving for men, and transcends patriarchy by legitimizing experimental authority for women.'

Jesus makes only one reference to himself in a feminine context. Addressing Jerusalem, just after having made the rather business-like statement that it is unthinkable for a prophet to meet his death anywhere but in Jerusalem, he says: 'How often have I longed to gather your children, as a hen gathers her brood under her wings; but you would not let me.' The idea of a masculine Jesus is not necessarily daunting to the feminists. If his intention was to install a new concept of leadership based on service and not on power, then only a man could mark the change because only men had power. And so the maleness of Jesus becomes a vital element and not an obstacle.

A further feminist argument is that Jesus evidently had an easy relationship with women and placed great importance on their company. There is nothing strange or suspect about this. It is a part, they argue, of his intention of favouring a genuinely balanced society, a balance which male predominance soon obliterated. The ecclesiastical handling of the issue is seen to imply embarrassment, particularly in the extraordinary extension of the role of the Mother of Jesus and the limitations imposed on that of Mary Magdalen. The latter is seen to have been closer during the period of Jesus's ministry, yet has somehow managed to gather the legend of having been a prostitute; an interpretation that is singularly lacking in scriptural proof and which suggests a desire to limit her importance in the story. She was the first to have the news of the Resurrection and thus became the original source of the historic uniqueness of the Christian religion, the belief that distinguishes it from all others. Jesus talks theologically with women, including the Samarian woman by the well, and only his women friends remain faithful to him throughout his crucifixion and burial. His mother, as well as Mary Magdalen, is given by John as being near the cross, but the main point of this passage appears to be to draw attention to 'the disciple whom he loved' rather than to his mother. Women share the experience of Pentecost. There is nothing in the Gospels to suggest that Jesus regarded women as secondary to men and so necessarily under male control.

The fact that Jesus did not include a woman among his apostles is seen by Catholic feminists to be, in part, counter-balanced by the special position accorded Mary, but this is quite different from apostleship. And one Catholic feminist pointed out to me that she preferred Mary Magdalen to Mary because she felt that the position of women became more subordinate wherever more veneration was given to the Madonna. Some quite strong-minded feminists nevertheless find attraction in the apparent change in Mary's view of her son. It is difficult to know what she thought of his ministry, though the evidence suggests that, for whatever reasons, her attitude changed from objection to participation. That is something which a modern-minded feminist can find sympathetic. The faith of few thinking people can always follow the same straight line. Another feminist argument is that it is no coincidence that the Christian churches that do not have a strong Marian cult allow a much larger place for women in their activities, including in some of them an equal part in the ministry. In the Catholic Church there are examples of nuns who almost become parish priests: but only because they almost run a parish—they cannot celebrate Mass, a priest still has to come to do that.

The severity and remoteness of the risen Christ in early Christian art is put forward as one of the reasons for Mary's prominence. The need for softer qualities was felt. There are plenty of other reasons, including the transfer to her of what was earlier directed towards some ancient mother-goddess (in fact this is said to be exactly what happened in the small Italian town in which I live, where veneration of the Madonna came early and easily because it replaced attachment to a lake-goddess already deep in public devotion). This element grew when the Mediterranean masses entered the Church after Constantine's promotion of Christianity. Some look to the subliminal promotion of a celibate clergy and others to the need for a symbol that did not leave God with only masculine attributes. Whatever weight one wishes to place on these, or other reasons, is now little more than a debating point. The real matter, as I have encountered it in talking with Catholics of varying views and with non-Catholics, is that the notable increase among ordinary Catholics in practical Marian devotion, of which pilgrimages to famous sanctuaries is the most evident, is accompanied by a growing interest among non-Catholics in the subject. This interest counts partly for the apparent lack of shock among other churches at the extremely pronounced Marian attitudes of the papacy in the last few years. I am sure there is an increasing awareness that the Catholic heritage includes some highly developed thinking and teaching about Mary as well as much devotion, even among many people who could not but regard themselves as belonging to the élite. The resurgence has come as much less of a shock to the ecumenical cause than would have been the case a decade ago.

It is arguable that too much can be made of the fact that there was not a woman among the twelve (or even the thirteen if one adds the choice by lot of Matthias, to replace Judas). A reading of the Gospels leaves the impression that Jesus felt more drawn to women than to Gentiles. Yet Paul was the first apostle added to the original group—according to Paul's own version of events—by Jesus himself, after the Crucifixion; and Paul was *par excellence* the apostle to the Gentiles.

Feminists look favourably on the efforts made to exonerate Paul from charges of actively disliking women. The famous statement ascribed to him: ' . . . the women should keep silence in the Churches. For they are not permitted to speak, but should be subordinate, as even the law says . . . .' is now, in the view of some scholars, to be seen as a later interpolation. This is not the real point. It is that the example of Paul shows that the Church was able, so shortly after the death of Jesus, to give a primary position—the primary position—to an aspect of its mission that Jesus had not excluded but also had not insisted on, namely the mission to the Gentiles that was to lead, among other things, to the shift of its centre from Jerusalem to Rome.

The turning point in too many ways for the Church is seen to be

Constantine's decision to tolerate all sects and favour Christianity in particular. Later in the same century, Theodosius completed the change by making Christianity the established religion of the Empire. The Christian priests, whatever may have been their situation at the time, were accorded the status of a caste—as well as the male monopoly—similar to that enjoyed by the pagan priests of the dying Empire, along with exclusion from property taxes and military services. If this reading is true, as far as the idea of the priesthood is concerned, Jesus might never have lived. A normal, decent, itinerant preacher of the type extremely common in Palestine would have served Constantine equally well. He sent his mother to collect relics in Palestine where the unpleasant Pilate had summarily condemned Jesus after a superficial hearing. Having killed Jesus, the Romans took the inheritance, and the heirs of the Jewish high priests had to prepare themselves for nearly 2,000 years of vicious persecution from the Christians.

Among the apostles only Paul had the temerity to give judgement on the question of relations between the sexes, calling for bachelorhood as the ideal, and marriage as the weak way out: 'It is better to marry than to burn.' Ordination of women and sexual questions can be seen as two different issues, but in practice they are close. The early idea, cultivated by the monks, of the blameless Mary, was of a spotless virgin seen in a anti-sexual way. She was not supposed to have sexual appeal, otherwise the whole house of cards would come toppling down. Yet, the medieval Mary contains something of the great lady of the master's court; the object of that strange, platonic love of the knights who exchanged gloves, vows of eternal devotion, but worshipped virginity. She was deserving of devotion because she could, due to her social position in celestial society, effectively intercede with the heavy-handed lord of the afterlife, who was to become the relentless judge of the Sistine Chapel, throwing the unworthy into hell and preserving a better fate for the saints. The devisers of these concepts belonged to the celibate male caste, and they have always concerned themselves with conflicts involving sexual practices. Conflict, not harmony; so who is to know what a normal, satisfied, reasonably good, early Christian couple ever felt about the relationship between men and women? All that remains is what priests—celibate priests belonging to a caste—quarrelled about.

This is a composite picture of the views of women, mainly Americans, who see the ordination of women on an equal basis to that of men as a proper and desirable aim. Some of the strength of the movement came from the profound change in the outlook of many nuns in the United States after the Vatican Council. This in itself should have caused a certain amount of male foreboding because it was the first time that the women's religious orders had lent weighty support to new ideas in the Church. These ideas came both from the contemplative nuns and from the sisters engaged in active apostolic work, such as teaching, nursing and the social services. The upheaval after the Vatican Council was great. Many nuns and sisters left their orders: 50,000 in a decade in the United States alone; 15,000 in Italy, even. Those who remained had a sizeable body among them seeking acknowledgement 'of the complete personhood of women and their eligibility for full participation in the Church's ministries'.

The words are those of Sister Nadine Foley who co-ordinated organization of the 1975 conference called: 'Women in Future Priesthood Now—A Call to Action'. She feels that the nuns and sisters have a long history almost coextensive with that of the Church itself, but it is not recorded in the mainstream of the Church's annals and the enigma of the lives of these women and the place they have in the Church has only become clearer in the current of contemporary life since the Council. She sees this Council as reversing the views on the Church of the sixteenth-century Council of Trent. Neither Council gave much time to women's religious orders but after Trent, in 1566, Pope Pius V issued a special Bull aimed at dealing with some of the tensions within women's communities of the time. His approach was to re-establish the concept of a strictly cloistered life for women who had taken vows of poverty, chastity and obedience. There were widespread instances of breaking of the rules by nuns who had been made over to the cloister by their families or were not satisfied with an enclosed life devoted to prayer and wanted to enter the field of charitable work. She commented in the Spring 1978 number of the inter-religious bulletin *Face to Face* of the B'nai Brith anti-defamation league:

> That this latter development was viewed as unseemly for women is evidence of the Church's basic view of them as delicate, impressionable creatures incapable of dealing successfully with the rigours of an exposed life in contact with the realities of the world. Understood to have a special propensity toward evil and sin, women needed protection even from themselves. For women who did not have the male protectorate of a family life, the legalized insulation of a cloistered life was the alternative.

Pious women did not share this view of themselves and there was a gradual growth of foundations for women who wanted active apostolic work. Many of the women who inspired these various movements are unknown. Yet, they must have been strong-minded and effective in gaining the support of bishops and local communities to enable them to operate. It was not until 1900 that they were recognized in canon law, by which time their numbers were high and their influence strong in, among other places, the expanding frontiers of North American life. They nevertheless continued to function within a regimented daily life based on the medieval cloister, despite the highly professional nature of much of the work they were doing and the increasing level of education among the nuns themselves.

The preparation for the Vatican Council brought more reflection on the position of the women in orders within the structure of the Church but also on the Church itself and what a renewed Church would expect of them. The Council issued a document on the renewal of religious life and Paul VI followed this in 1966 with a document specifying the rules for both men and women religious. Sister Foley summarizes it:

> They were directed to insure co-operation of all their members in organizing the task of renewal. Those in authority were to insure ample and free consultation of all the members through establishing study commissions, gathering data by means of questionnaires and other means, considering together the changes, adaptations and experiments that would make it possible for the religious communities to update themselves. The results were extraordinary. They went far beyond anything that could have been anticipated either by those who authorized renewal or those engaged in it.

The most striking innovation as far as the public was concerned was that many nuns gave up wearing the traditional habit. In addition, the school system suffered a blow because this principal occupation of many of the sisters was abandoned by a number of them who wanted to try other careers.

Some of the new ground brought them into closer contact with priests. Nuns joined priests and lay people in team ministries. They went into the parishes, hospitals, secular universities, high-rise housing projects, nursing homes, prisons, homes for unmarried mothers, residences for the elderly. They took an interest in politics and such specialized fields as dealing with alcoholism, legal aid for the poor, efforts at social justice, preaching retreat work. It was natural that they should begin to question, with so much unaccustomed activity and freedom, the limitations imposed on them as women which prevented them from becoming fully-fledged sacramental ministers. The lay world was rich in its own feminists and this too had its effect. Some of them began to discuss the official attitude of the Church towards celibacy. Here they found common ground with a number of priests as well as Catholic lay people.

At the same time, the cloistered nuns began a dialogue within their own world about their experiences. They left their cloisters to meet other nuns at regular sessions which gradually became concentrated on the issue of why the contemplative vocation had to be carried out within a physically closed background. Such regulations were not imposed on the contemplative orders for men. The contemplative life changed. Some of the convents became centres where people from outside could stay to study contemplation and share the life of the nuns. Some contemplative nuns went out to direct retreats. Their new attitudes bring tension between what they see as possible for them and what the official Church regards as impossible on the grounds that they are women. Sister Foley sees this as a creative tension:

> In many ways, the sisters, along with laywomen, as well as laymen and priests, are developing new models of collaborative ministry. To that extent they are leading the Church along paths newly discovered. Somewhere along the route lies a life-giving awakening of the Church to the fullness of human personhood wherein men and women together mirror the image of God and express that reality in the structures of the ministry.

The sights are high. That is clear. These ladies want a very different Church in which they will be able to take what they feel is their rightful place in the sanctuary. The curious point is that, in what is supposed to be a period of resurgence of the conservative attitude in Catholicism, support appears to be growing for a women's priesthood, despite all that it implies for change. Probably, the average Catholic who supports the idea of women priests does so more out of a feeling for fair-play than for theological truths about the intentions of Jesus towards the patriarchal society into which he was born. Nevertheless, statistics show that the support grows. It grew unusually fast in the wake of publication of the Vatican's document in 1977 against women in the ministry, which appeared in the year following the American Episcopal Church's regularization of women priests.

The pope strongly reconfirmed the traditional attitude during his visit to the United States in the autumn of 1979, but the issue cost him a dramatic public challenge of a kind he had hitherto never had to experience during his tumultuously successful travels. It took a woman to give him a moment of uncertainty, and the odd confrontation took place on 7 October 1979 at the Shrine of the Immaculate Conception in Washington. Quite unexpectedly a nun called Sister Theresa Kane, who as president of the Leadership Conference of Women Religious was presented to the pope, read a brief appeal to him in a trembling voice. Referring to the intense suffering and pain which was part of the lives 'of many women in these United States', she called for compassion and said that the Church 'must respond by providing the possibility of all persons being included in all ministries of our Church'. She was in ordinary clothes, not a nun's habit. The pope did nothing of what she asked. And the only satisfaction the nun received was a touch of the papal hand on her grey head in what looked reasonably like a gesture of compassion. John Paul II does this well: I remember a prelate attending the 1980 Synod who told me of his shock at the harshness of the pope's closing remarks but added that all was said 'in a tone of real compassion'.

The pope encountered a similar feminine challenge in Munich in November 1980 when a Catholic youth leader, Barbara Engl, said in an address to the pope during Mass that young people accused the Church of 'clinging fearfully to tradition'; and it too often answered their questions on friendship, sex and partnership with prohibitions. The pope did not reply. He had already been criticized by German feminists for solemnly visiting the tomb of St Albert the Great in Cologne, on the grounds that the saint had slandered both Jesus and women.

In Washington, the pope told his audience of nuns in his set speech that they were called to a generous and loving adherence to the teaching authority of the Church. He recalled to them their vows of poverty, chastity and obedience. He also reminded them not to abandon their traditional religious dress: 'It is not unimportant that your consecration to God should be manifested in the permanent exterior sign of a simple and suitable religious garb.' He was anxious that his attitude should not be seen as clashing with another of his policies. Speaking to priests in Philadelphia he said that the traditional decision to call only men to the priesthood 'is not a statement about human rights, nor an exclusion of women from holiness and mission in the Church. Rather, this

decision expresses the conviction of the Church about this particular dimension of the gift of priesthood by which God has chosen
to shepherd his flock.' So much for religious feminism.

The pope was equally traditionalist in his attitude towards
working women as a whole. Speaking of motherhood at the close
of the 1980 Synod on the family, he criticized the need for women
to engage in 'external work' and defined right-living families as
those in which 'the mother might devote herself fully to the
family'. He appeared to be taking into no account the increasing
opinion behind movements for women's emancipation, including
women in the Church.

From 1974 until 1979, those in the United States who agreed
strongly with the ordination of women rose from 11 per cent to 16
per cent. Those who agreed somewhat went from 18 to 24 per
cent; while those in strong disagreement dropped from 47 to 36
per cent, and those who disagreed somewhat dropped from 18 to
17 per cent. According to the Quixote Center in Mt Rainier,
Maryland, one of the organizers of the poll, the supporters of
women priests to a greater or lesser degree will outnumber
opponents within three years in the United States if present trends
continue. Within five years, convinced support should reach fifty
per cent. Within fifteen years, support for women priests will be a
consensus position. Opposition comes most sharply, they argue,
from the poor, less educated, older Catholics and those not in the
labour force. They also maintain that the pope's public objections
stimulated debate and caused Catholics to be increasingly ready
for women in orders. Polls cannot tell everything and interpretation is a sensitive matter. Yet, the general impression is that in the
United States at least—less in Canada—acceptance of the idea is
set to grow more widespread.

The answers to pollsters' questions are bound to be brief. I
sought a more relaxed treatment of the question of whether
women should be priests from Genevieve Garzero, who presides
over the World Union of Catholic Women's Organizations. She
has a softly spoken, non-insistent style, but leaves no doubt where
she supposes the future to lie.

'That is always people's immediate reaction when you speak of
feminists and Catholics—Oh! They want to be ordained priests.
That isn't the whole story: it is not the immediate story. The
immediate story is that there is such a lack of representation of
women and of the woman's viewpoint in the functioning of the
Church's structures. That would be one of the first things, while

the ordination of women is the last thing that should happen. There's more to it. The thing is there's so much of it going on because there is such a shortage of priests. And it is the women who are doing much of the pastoral service where it is needed.

'I can give you a background story. This World Union of Catholic Women's Organizations has its general assembly every four years and the last one was last February and I was in Bangalore in India, and in preparation for it there was a question of whether this matter should be put on the agenda. The more conservative said "No, we mustn't" and, well, of course, they prevailed, but what actually happened is that there was no discussion, there wasn't a round table, there wasn't a workshop where it did not come in somehow, some way . . . .

'There was one wonderful kind of informal affair entitled "How to Get On in the Church without Really Trying" and it was led by this Norwegian woman, outside. She was sitting under a tree and when we came by for just ten minutes she told her story. And it was that she had been not a Catholic but drawn to the priesthood, and so things went a little strangely for her. Finally, she worked her way into the Church and then said to the priest: "But what do I do? I am drawn to a life of service in the Church, but not to be a nun. What do I do?" He was a dear old man, she said, and he replied: "Well, I'll tell you what to do. You go in by the kitchen door and before you know it you'll be in the parlour." And, she said, it sounds corny but that's exactly what happened. Of course, it is an unusual situation in Norway where there's such a small percentage of Catholics, but in that particular parish the dear old man died, and the young man who was put into service there was overwhelmed by the job. And she said to him: "I see you have trouble keeping books. I'll do it for you." And before she knew it she was doing more than that: and before she knew it other people had a parish council set up, and they were participating more instead of letting Father do it all . . . .'

Genevieve Garzero does not see a clash between the two ideals of a woman who wants her share of participation and of the submissiveness of the Madonna as the Church portrays her: 'The idea of Mary as submissive and saying "yes", that's beautiful. I think Mary was living in her time. And as the pope said, she wasn't at Holy Thursday, she wasn't at the institution of the Eucharist . . . . In those days women didn't go out in the evening. She was there at Pentecost and the first people who got the message that Christ had risen were women. Go, tell the news. So there isn't any reason to suppose it is a clash. It's just a matter of everybody catching up with how we are evolving . . . .'

Italy has its feminists too. Some resent the fact that women account for 5 per cent of the people who work in the Roman Curia. As far back as 1974 the International Synod of Bishops received a report on women in society and the Church, which included the recommendation that the participation of women should be increased 'in posts of effective and recognized responsibility'. It is a dead letter. Emma Cavallaro, who directs the publications of the Catholic Action movement, comments: 'If this is grave and unjust for women, it is much more so for the whole Church which renounces living an experience of real communion and denies itself help and collaboration of which it does not even know either the possibilities or potentialities.' She sees the Christian vocation as 'deriving from the Spirit, not sex'. And there are also followers of the classic feminist view that the Church needs change, and part of that change must be a priesthood so different from today that the woman's place can be accepted naturally.

In Latin America, the feminists are, like so much of Catholicism, working nearer to the bone of repression, political repression that is, and not just their exclusion from so much of the life of the Church. Inevitably they have been affected by the North American experience, but theirs is a more bitter feminism. It is not just a claim for the rights of women. It is a demand to look at the horrendous realities of the social and political situation. Reality there is frequently far away from the pious attitude towards the family. The woman, of course, is the family. She is invariably shown in the Church's official outlook as the lynch-pin of Christianity's fundamental unit, which is supposed to recall the Holy Family and which remains the one sure element of life in a world needing stability. The Puebla Conference had fine things to say about the Latin American family: An 'Image of God', a 'Covenant of Persons in whose centre there is the dead and risen Christ' and, 'Conjugal love is communion and participation, not domination. The couple, sanctified by the sacrament of matrimony, is a Gospel of the paschal presence of the Lord.'

That is what the official documents of the conference said. And the Puebla Conference was supposed to have defined the Church of the future, the Church which soon will have within its ranks a half of the world's Catholics, a Church reborn from its renewed conscience after half a millennium in the sub-continent. But another truth was put forward at Puebla. A group of women

Catholics did so, outside the official conference, of course, and addressing themselves to anyone who would listen. They said:

> In recent times, the family has been looked upon as a basic, natural unit consisting of father, mother and children; where one grows up, is educated, satisfies basic human necessities and fulfils oneself.
>
> Facing this almost ideal image, we are confronted with the reality of the Latin American family. One-third of all families in our countries are headed by women: because of polygamy, abandonment on the part of the husband, death of the husband, and other reasons. It is also evident that the family has come to be, with growing frequency, a focus of intense and continuous violence.
>
> In Mexico, for example, it is estimated that 80 per cent of women who live with their husbands or companions suffer physical violence directly from the hands of the men they live with. Thus, we have to conclude that the family we know today, fragmented through internal violence and disregarded by diverse forces, is not necessarily the ideal nucleus of society.

It follows that the woman's place may not necessarily be in the home; or on picture postcards. Or talking to the Devil, or for that matter as a future priest. But the conclusion is very clear. The whole field of Christian life which includes the place of the woman, will be stony, full of tares, and infertile, if much deeper thought is not given it in good time.

I heard the most touching homage to Catholic woman in a parish in Africa. It was said with the greatest sincerity yet it is the saddest homage I have heard. Catholic women in America are now ready to stand up for themselves and put forward their claims in a way that eventually may prove irrestistible. African women must in many cases wear their Catholicism heavily because of its inflexible marriage laws. What is presumptuously called a Christian marriage can bring great pain when it is lived in an atmosphere where polygamy has ancient roots and where there are a lot of gods about who all have their little jealousies. This particular parish has a priest who knows the situation well. He is European. He has spent many years in Africa, perhaps too many years without a proper break, because he still sees the Catholicism he learned as a boy, long before the changes brought by John and the Vatican Council, as more suitable for the task of converting Africans and helping them maintain their faith. African culture, he says, is legalistic with belief in punishment and much less in individual

233

willpower. And so, the old Church was more suitable. It is pointless to leave a cake on the table and tell them not to eat it, which is the more personalized, more élite style of post-Council Catholicism. No, if they are not allowed to eat it, it must be locked away. And the ideas of intense personal prayer and participation at services, they already have that by nature. They have no need to be told it.

A traditionalist then, but a man whose life's work gives him the right to be heard with every respect. He has studied his people deeply; their habits, their weaknesses, beliefs. He hunts with them for his food. He has the bent shoulders and the masculinity of Wojtyla and the same ideas of the priestly caste. Most of what he serves at his table he has grown or shot himself. He knows the right amount of mineral water to add to a glass of the local wine to make it palatable. After saying an interminable grace, he surveys the medicine bottles around his plate. His doctor, who hunts with him, says that he is in excellent physical condition but that he needs this array of coloured bottles to justify a profound hypochondria. He talks about the idea of the family among his parishioners: 'If children are not born of legitimate monogamous marriages, they cannot be baptized. It is impossible to baptize them because they might follow the example of the parents. Our bishops want Christianity to depend on a Christian family background. In an agricultural society, more than one wife is a status symbol and an economic help. A person who does not have descendants remains a child. The generation continues not with the sons but with the grandchildren.

'Men see themselves in their grandchildren. A man who lives faithfully with one wife is a hero. He is apart from a whole tradition. The first wife is paid for by the family and so does not represent an effort on his part. The next are paid for by the husband only. The husband can be poisoned by his wives if he does not keep a proper balance between them. Witchcraft is as common as "you eat peanuts." The decision of the bishops to baptize only progeny of Christian families was a big and courageous decision. It could be especially hard for old men baptized late in life. The children of their sons would remain pagan.'

Then comes the great expression of homage. Given that Christianity is young and that paganism has thousands of years behind it, those who manage best are the women. What higher praise can be given? They have little preparation for Christian marriage. According to pagan precepts, they need not necessarily remain faithful as they must if they are to be able to provide the essential of a Christian marriage.

Others of their rules are nearer the Catholic view. If an unmarried girl becomes pregnant and the father is not known, the expenses must be met by her mother, who is regarded as partly to blame as her education was not sufficient to keep her daughter out of trouble. The local women regard abortion theoretically as homicide, but circumstances are admitted when it is seen as an acceptable means of escape. Married women abort when a child they are expecting may not be by their husband. A woman will abort if she becomes pregnant again only a few months after a child's birth. She does not want to be referred to by the phrase '*afudiche*' which means a woman who has one child after another. The practical fear behind this word is that the newly conceived child will take away nourishment from the child already born. The ideal spacing is seen to be a child every three years. The woman who miscarries tells her mother, who secretly buries the foetus. A strange relationship is maintained between the pregnant woman and her husband. He will not normally go hunting because his aim would be bad. If a man misses his prey several times, the other men will let him know that they think his wife is pregnant, and he will quietly go away.

I admire the best of the feminists and am convinced that, given the respect they deserve, they could substantially reinforce the Church by the changes they want to bring with them. I am sorry for African women who become almost the cult-objects of European priests because they succeed in their Christianity despite the unhappiness and unnaturalness their choice forces on them. They too deserve more respect. And my admiration is boundless for those women who have no problems of the sex of the divinity, of sexist language in the Scriptures and the liturgy, of ancestor-worship and rival wives, of the concept of what is pretentiously called a Christian marriage.

Such women exist. I know a few in several countries. There is still a reasonably young generation which contains in its ranks an occasional outstanding product of an education with the nuns. Most of what is heard about such an education is the sense of repression of natural instincts that it brings. Such consequences must now be more difficult in the Western world. The convents are not as closed as they were and the nuns themselves are nearer to the realities of modern living. There would be something to lament if the nuns totally lose their touch and there was no more evidence of the greatest virtue of their old system—the inculcation of a sense of dedication. This is the element which I find most distinctive among those fortunate women who not only survived a convent education but emerged stronger as a result of it.

The highest level of this dedicated performance can, reasonably enough, be found among the nuns themselves. While travelling I have several times encountered (usually theoretically rather than in practice), the nuns belonging to the order based on the teachings of Charles de Foucauld, the Little Sisters of Jesus. I say more in theory than in practice because these nuns genuinely seek concealment. They do not want to make themselves talked about. They do not want the covers of the news magazines. They feel that publicity would harm their activities. The nearest I came to seeing a group of them in the atmosphere of dramatic serenity in which they live was near the Uganda border. But the encounter never took place because the war which was to bring down Amin forestalled it and the plan had to be abandoned. I have since spoken to some of them elsewhere.

Their aim is the imitation of Jesus. They have no difficulty in imitating a man; no feminist urge to create difficulties about the question of whether a male Redeemer can equally well redeem women. They speak with total sincerity when they talk of love as being a quality which implies no discrimination or distinction between the sexes. They do not seek to express this love in what are commonly called good works. They do not have schools or hospitals or model farms. They live in groups of three or four among the people whom they feel might profit from an example of how they believe Jesus meant us to live. They live like the people around them: on a junk in Hong Kong harbour, in a mud hut in Africa, a hut in the Rome slums, in wool tents if they join the desert nomads. I shall never forget the rueful smile of one of these Little Sisters of Jesus who said that after spending some weeks in the southern Algerian desert—this desert interlude is obligatory—she had settled, as she put it, to following the life of nomads in Eritrea, living exactly the lives of these poor tribesmen. There was nothing special about the nomads, she said. They had no picturesque ways or the fascination of strange and intricate customs. Physically they were unremarkable too. They were totally ordinary. Then the war came. They were scattered. 'The conditions were no longer there for our work and so I came back to do some more studying.'

There are groups of the nuns among the textile workers in Montreal where one of their great aims is to bring some unity—this is one of their favourite words—to the extraordinary number of different nationalities now in the Canadian labour force. They are among the prostitutes of Turin, the shanty-towns of Casablanca, the hill villages of Calabria. And their object is pure example. They have no other way of teaching. They do humble work. They will speak, and their eyes become suddenly shining and distant, about the thirty years which Jesus spent working humbly in Nazareth. 'That must have had great importance for his mission,' they say. He did not want to be remarkable. He wanted to live as an ordinary man, in an ordinary family. There was unity there with the rest of his neighbours. They talk of this ordinariness and then they move, seemingly soundless but with long, quick, sandalled steps towards their simple wooden chapel. They give the plain blue habit a particular elegance: ironically, it is more or less the colour of blue jeans and yet so far apart from the world which the thought of jeans conjures up that the similarity sounds ridiculous. As they enter the chapel, these would-be 'ordinary' women first cross themselves, then they kneel and then they silently prostrate themselves, a seemingly shapeless blue being expressing total devotion, unrecognizable in any individual way and totally absorbed in this gesture of subjection which at the same time is one of emulation. Their eyes are to the ground but the symbol of their devotion is the little door, open above the almost undecorated altar: the open door reveals the host. A priest will come to celebrate Mass, a fact which they find neither unnatural nor irritating. I have never tried to talk about politics with them: it would be like talking blasphemy. They do not talk about the structures of the Church, though their feeling for the visible Church is deep.

Their inspirer, Charles de Foucauld, was a French cavalry officer who became first a priest then a monk, and came to his decision about the need for an exemplary spirituality during his periods as a hermit in the North African desert. He was murdered by accident. Their mother-house (they could not accept such Jesuitical terms as a headquarters because, unlike the Jesuits, they have nothing in common with any military order, indeed, they are the opposite of such a concept) is in Rome because they want to be at the heart of the Church. They have no worries about the changes which must come as the basis of the Church moves from Europe to other continents. They themselves (there are about 1,200 of them) come from all the continents. They welcome the idea that people young in their Christianity will bring a contribution to it. They accept that whatever happens to the Church happens because of the action of the Holy Spirit. They prefer to work among non-Christians, but if they are with nominally Christian people they accept the normal structures, going to church like exemplary parishioners. The one distinction they make is to wear their habits. They want it to be clear that they are Christian sisters, even if they are evicted from their homes by the police like the black neighbours among whom they have been living in a South African city, or are out of work like the other women when a factory closes.

They are treated with a certain awe by other missionaries. They are not even missionaries in any classical sense of the term because they do not preach as such. They show people what being Christian should be. They are totally different from the Sisters trained by Mother Teresa whose life is simple and in many ways exemplary but also depends on the work they undertake, the relief of the sick and the dying, teaching, even publicity on a massive scale—tasks which the Little Sisters do not regard as fostering their own style of mission.

They are not interested in numbers. They have a simple system of government which is based on an elected Superior and a Council. There would be more of them if they accepted every young woman who asks to be considered. Their principal house is very close to the place where Paul was supposed to have been martyred. I did not have the heart to ask any of them what they consider Paul would have thought of them. One wonders. Did he ever give any thought to those obscure years when Jesus was quietly working in Nazareth and, totally unpredictably, preparing a revolution, which all admit was the world's biggest religious event and which only a few try to follow in the simplicity of its origins?

11

THE FAILURE WITH SEX

THE QUESTION OF women, the question of divorce, the question of polygamy, even the question of the priesthood, contain a powerful element of sex and if there is one issue which it is fair to say that Christianity as a whole, and Catholicism in particular, has failed to handle successfully, it is sex. There is no further excuse unless there really exists a kind of urge to be gloriously wrong at any cost, like the handling of the Light Brigade. Lay people in the Western churches have lately made quite clear to the ecclesiastical authorities that they will accept a great deal of the official teaching on the fundamental religious beliefs but they do not, and will not, follow the disciplines on sexual teaching. Many bishops gathered the courage to try and force changes in the traditional teaching on birth-control at the 1980 Synod on the family. It is shameful that such a determination should require courage at all, but there is real fear among the farther-flung hierarchies of the consequences they may suffer if they publicly question the Vatican's attitude on sex. I know quite well a cardinal from a developing country, who might indeed have been pope now if the choice had gone to the Third instead of to the Second World, who feels seriously inadequate in his diocese which is over-populated and likely to become increasingly so. He nevertheless kept such views to himself during the Synod. He knows, as so many know, that the essential reason why the Vatican will not, unless forced, give way, is that the teachings on sex are a confusion which does no credit to the Church. But you cannot, of course, admit that.

The question of sex and other problems, such as ecumenism, suffer when the Catholic leadership is strong and popular, because

239

solutions will be sought with a wary eye on the consequences. There is the very real fear among profoundly worried Catholics that they should not criticize the Church in public, especially now that authority is being heavily reinstalled. Küng, the Dutch bishops, the extreme reluctance to release unwilling priests from their status, the outcome of the 1980 Synod with the pope's insistence on traditional thinking, all point in the direction of a strictly disciplinary outlook. I know a cardinal of the greatest authority, another among the possible popes, who is understood, privately, to be against the Church's teaching on birth-control, but who has said, also privately, that he has no intention of standing up in public and declaring his opposition, because of the consequences. When I say that one of the finest of Catholic defects seems to me to be excessive loyalty, I should add that there is this much less admirable side—which has its effect more on the hierarchy than on the ordinary Catholic—of fear of what might happen to a public critic of the Church's teachings.

And yet, the Church has greater responsibilities than maintaining its own style of authority. I do not mean maintaining its authority: that is something which it obviously has to do if it is to count at all, but the style of authority does not have to remain the same. Even worse, persistence with what much of the Catholic Church itself does not accept and what, certainly, the non-Catholic world looks on with grief, can have a menacing meaning; in the words of another Catholic priest concerned with global dangers surrounding the second millennium, the meaning is that 'the Church will make herself despised.' If you like, it means that Catholicism is entering what may be a decisive campaign to preserve the best in the human heritage with one hand tied behind its back.

What went wrong? The Gospels treat the subject of sex in a balanced and undramatic manner. It is impossible now to know how the early Christian communities looked upon sex. What has survived has been largely the outcome of controversies on particular aspects of the problem. Controversies are unreliable indications of the general practice of the times, because they overlook the reasonably well-regulated majority (as one can fairly suppose it was). An early element of confusion was the concept of original sin. This concept was not devised by Jesus himself but, largely, by Paul and Augustine. Whatever may be the truth or virtue of this teaching, it has had the effect of encouraging the attitude that the less thought given to sex the better, because it is somehow a contaminated subject. This attitude was not so damaging in the past as it has now become. Population and resources, the hedonism enhanced by the consumer society, the crisis of the family, the difficulties in convincing potential converts in the future bases of Catholicism in Africa and Asia of the superiority of Christian marriage, abortion, the tendency to align the Church's handling of the birth-control issues with its readiness to face other modern problems, are all powerful as well as profound matters that need clarity in their treatment and not prejudice or fear. There is the crucial point that Catholics in the unlikeliest of places are now claiming a new idea of loyalty. They listen to doctrinal teaching with respect, but insist that ordinary people have minds of their own. They no longer accept blindly, especially where the teaching is on weak ground—and the weakest is where sex is involved.

The Vatican itself has no illusions about the importance of sex. The dismal document issued in 1975, 'On certain questions concerning sexual ethics', opened with the admission:

> According to contemporary scientific research, the human person is so profoundly affected by sexuality that it must be considered as one of the factors which give to each individual's life the principal traits that distinguish it.

It then went on to condemn in harsh terms such aspects of sexuality as intercourse outside marriage ('every genital act must be within the framework of marriage'), and homosexuality (which is 'intrinsically disordered and can in no case be approved of'). The document quotes St Paul (surely an extremely unreliable witness on matters of sex), who describes homosexuals as abandoned by God. It also condemns masturbation while calling for a high esteem from everyone 'for the virtue of chastity, its beauty and its power of attraction'.

Whatever view one may take of the document's conclusions, its style is unfortunately stark and bureaucratic. St Paul was better when talking about the importance of charity than about sex or women. The eulogy of chastity with which the document ends is used explicitly in the context of human dignity:

> This virtue increases the human person's dignity and enables him to love truly, disinterestedly, unselfishly and with respect for others.

That is a very doubtful statement, especially the last part of it, as St Paul's behaviour showed, and the whole document expresses the escapist sentiment that if sex could be put out of sight, and chastity adopted as the normal habit, life would be easier and better.

The Vatican's statement on sexual matters is also dismaying because of the extreme claims made for the Church to have understood the whole problem once and for all:

> It will especially be necessary to bring the faithful to understand that the Church holds these principles not as old and inviolable superstitions, nor out of some Manichaean prejudice, as is often alleged, but rather because she knows with certainty that they are in complete harmony with the divine order of creation and with the spirit of Christ, and therefore also with human dignity.

This rigid, all-embracing view is under attack from many sides but shows no sign of ceding. Take, for instance, the problem of polygamy which has already been shown to bring great problems to African women. Here is a case involving instead a man, which was contained in the simply produced magazine for Catholic students at the University of Dar-es-Salaam in its first number for 1979. It is written as a dialogue between a Catholic priest and a Masai elder in his early fifties with three wives and fifteen children, who took intensive instruction in the Catholic faith and then had his request for baptism denied unless he agreed to put away two of his wives and the children he had had by them. The priest produces several pages of arguments against allowing a person living polygamously to become a Christian, ending with these words:

> 'Yes, but what about the pastoral inconvenience which will surely result? In other words, don't you see the problem of two entirely different matrimonial systems operating in the same diocese? And this might seem to undermine the priority given to monogamy. We should not overlook the fact that your admission to baptism will disturb the good order of the Christian community in the whole diocese.'

The Masai replies:

> 'Well, I see your point; nevertheless, I fail to understand a "so-called" Christian community which is not sympathetic and compassionate to those who are caught up in strong cultural traditions. Those who without fault of theirs, simply happen to be born into that particular "unfortunate" social system . . . . I wanted and wished with a good conscience to become a member of the visible church. Nevertheless, I think it is too high a price to pay for what seem to me to be unchristian and individualistic arguments against

my request. Hence, I had better remain as I am as long as I am sure and fully convinced that this is what God demands and expects of me.'

The student's own conclusion is clear: 'Personally, I think the official, traditional Catholic discipline too general and too legalistic to be practical.' He was then studying theology at the Kipalapal Seminary in Tabora. It echoed an anguished statement made years before by the novelist Morris L. West, a devout Catholic who lived in Rome for a time:

> There is something wrong with the quality of human relationships within the Church. There is the predominance of the system over the person. There is a concern for authority at the expense of truth . . . . the Church will lose many souls because men in authority want to save their face, and sometimes to save the face of dead men.

West was particularly shocked by the reference Paul VI made to the impending introduction of divorce in Italy, when he talked of the 'corruption and degeneracy' of those countries where divorce was legal. Morris West commented:

> The statement was so harsh and sweeping that many Catholics reacted from it. Those who had lived in Italy, who were aware of the large-scale concubinage, of the fact that the human rights of women and children were less protected here than they are in many western countries that have a divorce law, felt that this was a piece of special pleading that ill became their spiritual leader.

West said this in 1967 but the same could still be said now and, by all the indications, for the future as well, with perhaps even more justification. John Paul II, for all his *bonhomie*, was even harsher than Paul VI on these questions.

This sort of advertisement is common in newspapers in the United States:

> Meeting of divorced, separated and widowed Catholics of North Virginia, Panel on Annulment, 4 p.m. Sunday, at Marymount College Student Lounge, 2807 N. Glebe Road, Arlington

These are the people who, according to the courteous reply from Rome to the Congo bishops, are in the same category as the African polygamists. A divorced Catholic who remarried without obtaining an annulment would be in very much the same situation as a Masai tribesman with a wife too many. Indeed, the Holy

Office itself, in a reply to a request for guidance from the Congo bishops about polygamous marriages, drew the comparison. American Catholics have now reached the national average, where one half of all marriages end in divorce. They cannot legally remarry unless the Church annuls the first marriage or, better, they cannot regard themselves as full members of their Church communities, or take Communion, without having first completed divorce by annulment. The problem in pastoral terms is already huge however simple the legalities may make it sound; or, for that matter, papal reiteration of the Church's teaching on marriage. I asked Father Vincent O'Keefe, who is second only to the General at the Jesuit headquarters near St Peter's, what he thought and his answer on John Paul II's approach was:

> 'What I feel is that he's really gone after a clarity in the teaching. He's surprisingly clear and simple, I mean simple in the good sense, but he does leave the problem of the pastoral approach. Giving a clear line of what the Church's teaching is with regard to divorce doesn't solve the problem of all those people out there. And we know that there are an awful lot of them out there. Nor does it solve necessarily the problems of those people who do not agree with his teaching on birth-control. So there's a need, I think, even more so today, for a tremendous pastoral approach. How do you deal with these people? What approach do you take?'

The Church before John Paul II's accession had attempted to speed the work of the diocesan tribunals which grant annulments. It used to be essential to have two distinct hearings of every case, and agreement at the end of both hearings on whether or not the marriage should be declared annulled. Now the second set of hearings is waived. Instead, as far as the Church in the United States is concerned, the proceedings of the first hearing are sent to Washington, DC, where, occasionally, a spot-check is carried out and the proceedings reviewed.

These meetings of divorced and separated Catholics in student lounges or other places are friendly. The panel consists of three people who have had their marriages annulled and who talk about their experiences. They talk easily, almost as if they are wanting to share a therapeutic experience:

'I was reared in a Catholic family. I had twelve years of Catholic education. There was no serious relationship with a woman until I met the woman I married. We had a large church wedding. She was a Latin, but not a typical Latin. She was a lukewarm agnostic at the time and adopted affiliation as a Catholic probably to please me. We were married for twelve years. There are three children. The marriage was marked by turmoil. It ended in a Mexican divorce initiated by her. She remarried and that marriage lasted five years and she then divorced again.' The speaker was a man still physically young who was about to face middle age; small, fair and precise, unlike the woman panellist of Latin origin who preceded him and who had been rather emotional. He described how he moved out of his home and visited on Sundays when he took the children to church. His pastor had suggested that he might want to pursue an annulment. At first he did not seriously consider it. Some time later he attended a conference on separation and decided to look into it. He found out more about the annulment process and the changing attitude of the Church towards divorce. His pastor agreed to forward papers to the Annulment Tribunal and he was given a fifty-question questionnaire to complete with biographical details. The first reply was that he did not seem to have a particularly strong case but legal advice might make it more viable. He was heard by the Tribunal in March 1978.

The hearing was about what he expected. Most of it was a dialogue between himself and the president of the tribunal. The proceedings were taped. He felt no more nervous than at a normal job application. Within a week or so letters went out asking witnesses to testify, mainly his brothers and sisters. The former wife was informed of the proceedings and came and spoke for over an hour to his lawyer and was very helpful. She was in the midst of her second divorce. All requests for testimony were returned by the summer. He felt quite confident, estimating an 80 per cent chance of success. He had heard nothing by the autumn so at the end of October wrote a letter to ask what the situation was. Two days after, a letter arrived, which was not in reply to his, saying that the declaration of annulment had been agreed and was now in Washington, DC, for approval. He then received the final document containing canonical citations. The financial arrangement was unusually sympathetic and amounted to a request for a contribution towards expenses of 125 dollars. He felt all was reasonable and efficient and thorough: 'And that's the way it ended up.'

A well-dressed blonde, with a crucifix in evidence, explained that she was a convert and had been left by her husband with no way of paying the mortgage or buying food. The pastor at her church did not help her. She went 'church-shopping' to see if she could find something better but eventually returned to her parish church which by then had a new priest and a new assistant. She told the assistant she felt she had never been married. They talked and prayed and as they talked and prayed, the priest took notes. She applied for an annulment in February 1977 and was called before the tribunal in October. There were only two judges present as the third was ill. Things started well but then got worrying. The notary had to repeat what she said onto tape. She thus had to formulate answers to the judges' questions while checking the summary of her previous answer being taped by the notary. When she left the hearing, she could not say that she felt good. She did not feel that she had had a fair chance. She prayed with the priest and left everything in the hands of God.

In the summer of 1978 the priest telephoned to tell her that her ex-husband was co-operating. At the end of August she was told to telephone the tribunal. She heard that she could expect something in two weeks. Some weeks later she was told the same; and again in October. The papers finally arrived. She was elated: 'I was starting a new life for real. I was able to have joy again.'

In both these cases the defender of the bond was Father William Martin. Solid, energetic, intelligent, he was present at the Arlington debate: 'very defensive', too, as he put his own position after hearing the critical testimony of the panel. 'But tribunal people,' he said, 'despite all the horrors that have been described, do their best.' Moreover (and here he had a powerful card), he had worked earlier in his career at the Brooklyn Tribunal so that he could be of more help to the Arlington Tribunal. Brooklyn in matters of annulments is Eton, the Rolls-Royce of the situation; fast and reliable and, if not cheap, it is recognized as the best. Father Martin had worked there in 1974. He began with a clarification to the rest of us. 'Going to a divorce court simply ends, as far as we are concerned, a civil contract. Our tribunal [there was a lot of emphasis on that 'our'; sometimes the togetherness of Catholics leaves the impression that there can only be a few hundred of them instead of 18 per cent of the world's population] is not interested in ending anything. Its job is to see whether there ever was anything. The fact that most of the exchanges are with the chairman of the tribunal is because he is the only member who can put direct questions. He shows a particular respect for the defender of the bond, but the defender's job is not to defend at all costs. His real duty is to see that justice is done. The tape-recording of evidence could be troublesome but it is quicker than the old method by which the notary wrote a summary by hand.

'In Brooklyn,' he explained, 'the only grounds considered were psychological. Elsewhere other reasons could be put forward. Things went quicker in Brooklyn because they have five court-rooms going at once. There are fourteen priests always in attendance and ten others ready to deal with interrogations, with thirty-five on the secretarial staff. Other dioceses had far fewer people. The fees in Brooklyn are 500 dollars for persons inside the diocese and 850 dollars for people from outside. The sum due has to be paid before the hearings. In Arlington, petitioners are asked for 125 dollars as a contribution towards expenses, some pay more, others less.

'In Arlington the likely period in which you can expect a decision is officially a year but in practice it is between six and eight months. In Brooklyn a petitioner is told to bring witnesses. At Arlington, witnesses are named by the petitioner and approached separately by the tribunal. The main problems in the Arlington diocese are lack of personnel and lack of funds. The grounds we consider are impediments, that is, that a person is already married, or grounds such as impotency, an intention against children, or an intention against indissolubility of the marriage. Psychological immaturity has been added, with the development of psychological and sociological studies.

'In the Arlington diocese the priests are very helpful. The more that can be done at the first sessions with the parish priest the better. The tribunal sits twice a week. The other party is informed a week before the hearing of the petitioner. The other party can have his or her day in court but not at the same time as the petitioner. All petitioners to the ecclesiastical court must already have had a civil divorce, otherwise they cannot be considered. The proceedings are not contradictory. The object is the search for truth. People are married publicly and, when it comes to an annulment, the proceedings are often therapeutic for them. Often it is painful for them but it is better to lance it. One psychologist told me that people came forward with more truth about them-selves than they would at ten or twelve professional sessions.'

As I drove back with Father Martin to Washington, I mentioned that I had been told not to confuse American canon lawyers with Roman ones. In America the Association of Canon Lawyers had the reputation for being progressive, unlike the reputation of canon lawyers in Rome. Was this true? His reply as a Professor of Canon Law and member of the Association was that they did not regard themselves as particularly progressive but as very active. They wanted to do their jobs well and swiftly.

These tribunals give a strange impression, as Father Martin suggested, because they are quite different from divorce hearings or, for that matter, any form of legal proceeding familiar to Anglo-Saxons. They are a sifting of evidence gathered from a variety of sources and there is no clash between two parties. This is why psychiatrists are often deeply impressed with the tranquillity of annulment proceedings compared with the malevolence and emotional damage that easily follow a bitterly contested divorce case. A strong argument can be made for the assertion that divorces, as a general rule, have a damaging effect, while annulments can be beneficial. In both, a sense of failure is involved but in the process of annulment the human issues are not lost from sight. A remarkable tribute to the work of the Catholic Annulment Tribunals came from a non-Catholic consultant to these tribunals: Leon Salzman, Professor of Psychiatry at Georgetown University Medical School. Writing in the Jesuit periodical *America* in May 1979, he said:

> To liberate couples whose marriages, in spite of years of cohabitation and the presence of children, were founded on seriously inadequate or incompetent abilities to love, relate and collaborate in a life of mutual concern and regard, is an act of mercy, compassion and simple recognition of human dignity.

His whole impression is one of a greatly improved and useful institution:

> All in all, the notion that tribunals are serving as substitute divorce courts is an unworthy and malicious *canard*. The activity of marriage tribunals, which now process many more cases than they did in the past, only attests to the growing humanity of tribunal personnel and the desire to deal more understandingly with the lives of Catholics whose marriages are totally destructive.

This enthusiasm is in part justified. Improvement did not, however, come about just for humanitarian reasons. Lay people in the United States took full advantage of the new respect accorded them by the Vatican Council. Their relationship with the ecclesiastical authorities became a much more demanding one, and that demand has had to be met. At the same time, canon lawyers showed themselves to be remarkably open-minded to the need for change.

There remains the question of how to deal with the problem of Catholics who have not annulled, or not been able to annul, their marriages, and so find themselves in a situation of no longer being full members of the Catholic community. This is a problem in Anglo-Saxon countries, where it is almost considered a right, as well as in the Latin world, where the lay voice is still weak and clerical presumption strong. The Italian bishops issued a statement in April 1979 on 'non-regular matrimonial situations', in which they attempted to explain why the Church has to adopt what might seem an unmaternal attitude to these issues:

> In reality, the Church is Mother to Christians only if and to the extent that she remains the virgin bride of Christ, and faithful to His word and commandment: the love of the Church towards souls cannot be conceived if not as fruit and sign of her own love for Christ, her bridegroom and Lord.

Again the idea of total justification appears:

> The non-admittance of remarried divorced persons to the sacraments does not signify a punishment but only a love which wishes to remain authentic because it is inseparably tied to the truth.

And a lofty as well as high-handed attitude is taken in granting exceptions to the rule:

> When their situation does not offer a concrete reversibility because of the advanced age or the illness of one of them or both, the presence of children needing help and education, or for similar reasons, the Church admits them to sacramental absolution and to the Eucharistic Communion if, sincerely penitent, they undertake to interrupt their reciprocal sexual life and transform their tie into one of friendship, respect and mutual help. In this case, they can receive sacramental absolution and take Communion, in a church where they are not known, in order to avoid scandal.

The one conclusion to be drawn is that people can expect their dignity to be respected according to their own ability to demand respect. This may be all that can be said about the whole question of human rights. If so, the conclusion is a sad one.

> Men have fashioned you in many forms,
> But you were fashioned best in stone, God.

Those bitter lines are by an Indian poet, educated at a Catholic mission school.

Eloquent speeches were made at the 1980 Synod on the family about these divorced Catholics who saw no reason why they should be denied full membership of their church. It was known that seven out of the eleven language-groups into which the Synod broke up to prepare its proposals favoured a review of the problem. A second marriage could well be, in the honest view of some, the right and indissoluble one. But the eloquence went for nothing. In his speech closing the Synod, Pope John Paul II issued the harshest note possible about their fate: he told them that they could go to Communion only if they gave up all sexual relations with their married partners. In a somewhat convoluted passage, though nevertheless clear in its final meaning, he said, appropriately enough beneath Michelangelo's *Last Judgement* in the Sistine Chapel:

> Although it must not be denied that such persons can be received to the Sacrament of Penance, eventually and finally to Eucharistic Communion, when they open themselves with a sincere heart to live in a manner which is not opposed to the indissolubility of marriage: namely, when a man and a woman in this situation, who cannot fulfil the obligation to separate, take on themselves the duty to live in complete continence, that is, by abstinence from acts in which only married couples can engage, and when they avoid giving scandal, nevertheless the deprivation of sacramental reconciliation with God should not prevent them from persevering in prayer, penance and works of charity that they might find the grace of conversion and salvation. It is fitting that the Church present herself as a merciful mother by pouring forth prayers for these persons and by strengthening them in faith and hope.

In everyday language, he was saying to divorced and remarried Catholics who did not have annulments that they had to choose between going to Communion and having normal sexual relations with the person they had married. He was equally decided against birth-control.

This attitude of total certainty, which is at its strongest in John Paul II, is surely at its least justified when applied to the intimate, human, miniature maelstrom which sex presents. Other religions have not made the same mistake of confused inflexibility in dealing with such a mercurial subject. They could be put to one side as fake religions, but fewer Catholics would think in that way now. The idea that other religions are worthy of respect is not simply based on the recent Catholic acceptance of the principle of religious liberty. There is a growing impression, especially among

Catholics who live near such religions, that they possess in their own right powerful aspects of the truth.

Not that religions with a certain amount of sexual practices involved in their rites need, or should, be taken as examples, because they are normally as much out of focus as the Catholic teachings. They are more likely to be aimed at the sexual element in its purely reproductive guise, as a lauding of fertility which in no way solves the intimate problems of sex or of the status of the woman. While free of the traditional Catholic sense of shame, none of the subtleties are allowed: it is chamber music transposed for one brass instrument. Until the sense of shame attached to sex is removed, the problem itself cannot be properly examined. Typically, for those who know him, and surprisingly, for those who too early wrote off the reign of John Paul II as an aberration, the pope has sought to deal with this idea of guilt.

He did so by means of a series of talks during his Wednesday audiences, which he devoted to commentaries on the Book of Genesis. An attractive side of John Paul II is a certain poetic vision he has of man's dignity. He is at his best when he is talking about human dignity, the source from which he derives his teachings on human rights, which is where he is at his most convincing. He reached a happy moment at the audience on 17 January 1980, in which he dealt with the love between men and women; in this case the primordial man and primordial woman, Adam and Eve, who were, he pointed out, 'naked and experienced no shame'. He went on in a lyrical manner quite out of keeping with the usual formalities of papal utterances: 'The human body with its sex and its masculinity and its femininity is not only directed towards fruitfulness and procreation, but towards the capacity to express love, that love in which the man-person becomes a gift and, by means of this gift, actuates the very sense of his being and his existence.' He interprets this as meaning that they 'were free to give each other to each other and love each other mutually in full mastery of themselves'.

This talk split opinion in Rome: had he or had he not said something new? The dispute was interesting because the pope's words came shortly after the Sacred Congregation for the Doctrine of the Faith had issued a highly critical comment on the book *Human Sexuality*, published by a group of experts for the Catholic Theological Society of America. The book was published in 1979 and had been received as a contribution of weight by those who saw in it the basis for building a fresh sexual ethic, as well as by those who were highly suspicious of it, including many bishops. The pope's own views looked near to those of the censured American team: 'The creation accounts in Genesis', the team commented, 'show no trace of contempt for the human sexual nature, as if it pertained somehow to a lower order of nature, inferior to the spiritual or intellectual. Sex is but one aspect of human life, neither despised nor dominant, because never viewed in isolation.' But there is a formidable difference between the two approaches. The object of the American effort was clearly to provide a point of departure which inevitably would lead to changes in official Catholic teaching on the subject of sex. The Americans had behind them the extent of the damage which had been done to the Church in the United States by teachings on sex.

The highly intelligent sociologist Father Andrew Greeley maintains that the Church's reiteration of its ban on artificial birth-control caused more damage than any other single issue to American Catholicism. John Paul II either did not believe that, or did not feel it to be adequate reason to reconsider the Church's position. On 5 October 1979, during his American tour, he had reiterated the traditional teaching and had, in fact, been criticized on the grounds that his confirmation of the ban on birth-control conflicted with his stand on human rights, especially his concern for the hundreds of millions of the poor in the developing countries and, even more especially, for the children, whose plight had been shown more clearly than ever during the International Year of the Child. I remember a priest who strongly favours change in the Church's doctrine telling me of his anguish when looking at children in a slum in Haiti. He first felt guilt because the little children were beautiful and smiling and he asked himself if he could possibly justify his own attitude, which was to prevent such children from being born at all. Then he noticed that he saw very few above the age of eight or nine and practically none above the age of twelve. Once they reach that age, it was explained to him, they have to be put out of the house to fend for themselves in order to make room for the babies arriving or surely yet to come. Usually they manage to find somewhere to live because a system has grown up over the years by which they can have a space to sleep in a dormitory for ten dollars a month, but they have to find ways of earning the ten dollars, as well as what it costs to stay alive. The chances are few (practically non-existent) of being able to do so honestly, or decently. Then the period of anguish about the justice of his own work passed from the mind of the priest.

This was even more the case when he was told that the slums he had seen near Port-au-Prince were small in comparison with the rural slums of the interior. He knows, nevertheless, that one of the principal reasons why change is difficult is that the Church's doctrines have been built up over many centuries and are the consequence not only of teaching on the subject aimed at interpreting the Scriptures, but also of reactions to what has happened to the Church. Almost certainly these are the types of consideration which would weigh heavily with John Paul II. Presumably the Polish bishops knew as much as anyone what he would like to hear on the subject, and their statement issued on the last day of 1979 was an explicit and harsh reiteration of the traditional teaching.

Ironically, the earliest-known Christian written reference to contraception was in the form of an attack on a pope for allegedly having favoured it, albeit indirectly. The victim of the attack was St Calixtus, who was Bishop of Rome from 202 to 218. His critic was the writer of the *Elenchos*, or *Refutation of All the Heresies*, dated between 220 and 230, who was probably St Hippolytus, Calixtus's rival for the Roman see. He accuses Calixtus not only of having usurped the throne of Peter, but of having made himself responsible for 'concubinage' between Christian free women and their slaves. Probably what Calixtus did was to permit marriage between a free woman and her slave, which was not allowed by Roman civil law. These women were frequently rich or of socially well-placed families and, according to Calixtus's critic, 'want no children from slaves or low-born commoners, and use sterility-producing drugs or bind themselves tightly in order to expel a foetus which has already been engendered'. The women are accused of adultery; contraception and abortion are both condemned as murder.

The Church's teaching on birth-control did not arise, fully-grown and fully-armed, from the early days. The Old Testament is favourable to the patriarchal family, and the New Testament shows respect for virginity. The Old Testament texts taken to oppose birth-control are: God's condemnation of Onan, that unfortunate man whose name is for ever tied to birth-control—in his case *coitus interruptus*—for refusing to raise children by his deceased brother's wife; and God's command to men to 'increase and multiply; fill the earth and subdue it.' These quotations can be interpreted in various ways. Onan's offence may have been disobedience rather than avoiding the chances of conception. But certainly the Old Testament praises fertility as a blessing and is full

253

of warnings about the sexual attractions of women. David suffered from these, as did Samson and, the primary case, that of Adam himself. There is a distinct difference, which was maintained by the Christians, between sexuality and the aim of producing children. The New Testament's outlook on sexual morality is more rigorous than that of the Old. Jesus taught that even lustful thoughts amounted to adultery committed in the heart. But the Gospels do not insist on procreation as the purpose of marriage.

Pope John Paul II put his own gloss on the question of adultery in the heart in a statement which will follow him to the grave. While the Synod on the family was taking place, he continued his Wednesday audiences on the subject of sexuality. On 8 October, he came out with the assertion that adultery in the heart could be committed by a man who looked at his own wife with desire. For anyone inclined to follow the byways of theology on the point, St Thomas Aquinas talks of excessive demands on a wife as amounting to adultery, a view which he had taken from Jerome, who in turn had it from the pagan Sextus the Pythagorean. But the statement looked so bizarre, even if its true meaning of not abusing the marriage relationship was obvious, that the pope ran the risk of joining the ranks of those, such as Marie Antoinette on eating cake, who will be remembered by remarks that they themselves would not have regarded as of vital importance.

Throughout its history, Christianity has had to face a challenge on sexual ethics from its opponents, which helped drive it towards adopting stern positions. The Gnostics, in the period up to the early third century, followed by the Manicheans in the fourth century, both viewed procreation with repugnance and kept it apart from consideration of sexuality. In both cases, these opponents were regarded as dangerous and so required a firm answer. Mainly because of Paul's teaching, the New Testament offers a bias in favour of celibacy. Hence, a high purpose had to be found for marriage. In the intellectual background to the New Testament was the Stoic theory that only procreation divided sexual activity from lust. Much the same attitude was adopted by the Christians, who gradually saw procreation as the purpose of marriage and eventually refused to admit, until the second half of the twentieth century, that the two could be separated.

The great Albigensian heresy in the twelfth century brought another challenge to the Church's view of sexuality. The Albigensians were cruelly suppressed and totally annihilated, partly because of the views ascribed to them that pregnancy was the Devil's work while sexual activity outside marriage was acceptable. Their appearance and bloody end in ecclesiastical history had two effects. They were associated in the public mind with the Manicheans and so stimulated a new interest in Augustine's condemnation of the earlier heresy (which nevertheless in his younger years he had himself followed). The second consequence was to stimulate still more popular Marian devotion. In the twelfth century the *Ave Maria* with its salute to Mary as both maiden and mother summed up the Church's reverence for dedicated virginity and dedicated parenthood. It became the most popular prayer in Catholic Europe. In 1254, at a Council held at Albi, the town that gave its name to the heresy, the *Ave Maria* was chosen to be taught to every child above the age of seven, with the Creed and the Lord's Prayer.

Looking back at the Church's skirmishes with problems of birth-control, one is tempted to think that its unyielding doctrine became so as a reaction to many promptings and pressures. It would be unfair to forget that the dignity of women was probably enhanced by the Church's insistence on the indissolubility of marriage and the responsibilities of parenthood. These teachings have lasted into an age more at home with another view of sexual adventure, put forward at much the same time as the Albigensian heresy, that of the troubadors of Provence, whose verses summed up, for sophisticated audiences, a romantic form of love that had no connection whatever with procreation. Yet they, too, rose from a Catholic civilization.

To Rome, nevertheless, the function constantly fell (and still does), of having to draw the consequences from confusion. Sixtus V, the fiercest of the papal moralists, who drew inspiration from the atmosphere of the Counter-Reformation, issued a Bull in 1588 interpreting contraception as homicide. He decreed that, in canon law and in the penal law as applied to the papal states, the punishment for the use of 'these cursed medicines' was the same as for murder. The Bull was too extreme and remained in effect for only two and a half years.

The last—so far—of the great challenges came from the application of science to contraception with, behind it, a rational series of arguments aimed at justifying the practice. This was something quite different from the use by individuals of substances and potions known from antiquity. In 1798, Malthus provided a basis for a totally non-religious attitude to birth-control because he foresaw the threat of over-population. Bentham and James Mill examined the problem without reference to Christian thinking. By the middle of the nineteenth century, industrial methods were applied to produce cheap and simple contraceptives at high profit to manufacturers.

The Church was slow to answer. It lacked intellectual authority in the field, and also the situation itself was becoming still more complicated. The reiteration of traditional doctrine came first as a result of falling birthrates in Germany and France. The First World War, with its years of human slaughter, enabled the bishops to mix patriotism with morality. In 1913 the Germans condemned contraception as a 'serious sin', adding that the aim of Christian marriage was 'to secure the continuation of the Church and the State'. The French followed with a statement that the theories and practice of birth-control were 'as disastrous as they are criminal. The war has forcibly impressed on us the danger to which we expose our country.' Supporters of birth-control had much the same answer ready then that they use now: over-population is itself a cause of war. It did the Church's cause no good to have it fully backed by Hitler and Mussolini, both of whom opposed birth-control by legislation.

Rome once more laid down its authentic teaching. On 31 December 1930, Pius XI promulgated his encyclical *Casti Connubii*. This was the most weighty statement since Sixtus V's Bull of 1588. The immediate cause was the statement by the Lambeth Conference in August 1930 which had moved the Anglican Communion away from complete condemnation of birth-control. 'Certain persons', the pope wrote, 'have openly withdrawn from the Christian doctrine as it has been transmitted from the beginning and always faithfully kept.' He went on:

> The Catholic Church, to which God himself has committed the integrity and decency of morals, now standing in this ruin of morals, raises her voice aloud through Our mouth, in sign of her divine mission, in order to keep the chastity of the nuptial bond from this foul lapse, and again promulgates:
>
> Any use whatever of marriage, in the exercise of which the act by human effort is deprived of its natural power of procreating life, violates the law of God and nature, and those who do such a thing are stained by a grave and mortal fault

The cement looked to be set hard. In fact, the papal edifice against birth-control was less formidable than it seemed. The most important move towards change came from the papacy itself, once again from the unpredictable Pius XII. In October 1951, during an audience to Italian midwives, he gave his approval to the use of the rhythm method by all Catholic couples with serious motives for avoiding procreation. At the same time, he called for further research into the rhythm method and its possibilities. Whatever may be said about the reliability, or non-reliability, of the method itself, Pius XII broke with the idea that procreation could be the only object of marriage. His endorsement of the idea of responsible parenthood was to become more important than it appeared to be at the time. It was one of the bases for the demands for change put forward at the Vatican Council. The Council adopted both the concept of responsible parenthood and the dual purpose of marriage, accepting that human love should take its place with procreation. At the same time, references in its final documents were made to existing doctrine. A final decision on whether change should officially be made was left to the pope himself.

Time is a great natural changer. Just as a tide slowly transforms a seascape, so time can make dry land look like an ocean. The earth is now said to be threatened by submergence under the weight of its population. Only six and a half decades ago, birth-control was being attacked on grounds not only of morality but of a falling birthrate. Pius XI's solemn condemnation came before invention of the progesterone pill and he can hardly be credited with having the power to condemn what he did not know about. Nor need an encyclical be regarded as totally binding on future generations. Pius XI produced his encyclical only sixty years after proclamation of papal infallibility but theologians argue that his statement was not an infallible one. Other condemnations by the Church in the past have been quietly forgotten. The teaching against usury is a clear instance. If the Church had remained bound to its teachings on usury as it has to those on birth-control, it could not have accepted the capitalist system.

There are also precedents for leaving a subject in doubt when the right decision is difficult to perceive. The Commission that Paul VI set up to advise him on birth-control could not agree. A majority was in favour of changing the teaching. He would have been wise to leave matters in doubt but he overrode the majority and, in July 1968, published his famous encyclical *Humanae Vitae*. This newly condemned all forms of contraception except the rhythm method. It is fair to say that Paul VI never again looked as elated and carefree as he did at his public audience held at the summer residence of Castelgandolfo the day after the encyclical was published. It was the most unpopular act of his reign. It ran full tilt into the generally favourable impression left by the Council. It shocked a new generation of Catholics, particularly in the United States and the United Kingdom, where enthusiasm had grown throughout the heartening reign of John XXIII and the stimulatingly open debates of the Council. All this combined with higher educational standards among Catholics and with the feeling too that their church was being judged by the attitude it took to this one issue. It carried little weight with them that Paul VI strongly felt the need to defend papal authority when he saw it was likely to be undermined if he allowed change. The authority of Rome is not a vital component of an ordinary person's everyday life: sex is. Paul VI failed to read this obvious sign. He let the chance go by in the name of authority, instead of making use of it in the name of humanity. Or, had he simply left the matter in doubt he would have contributed to the idea that a quieter, less prominent style of papacy, with fewer pretensions and less concern for its own authority, would be in keeping with the needs of the second half of the century.

How far has this policy, reiterated by John Paul II, damaged the Church's ability to make a contribution to the problem of population? And, in doing so, of course, by its own definition, to the cause of human rights? On the issue of population as much as that of the rights of individual Catholics to a less stressful sex-life, Paul VI mistimed his move. The Church in the late fifties and early sixties could still convince itself that the world's growing population could be met by better exploitation of world resources. The Church called for redistribution of wealth, the creation of new wealth by means of advanced technology, and the opening up of still unused riches of the world. By the second half of the decade it was clear that optimism of this kind was misleading. Human rights, as the Church envisages them, would be increasingly distant unless there could be a reduction in population-growth rates. This does not mean that a reduction in the growth of population would bring about the desired economic and social progress; progress was simply seen to be impossible without it.

Humanae Vitae did not entirely cut off the Church from the population question. Dedicated Catholic demographers salvaged what they could and persisted with their attempts to prevent the Church from seeming impervious to this great issue. The phenomenon of increasing populations in countries with many millions already well below the poverty line, meant that a situation had arisen very different from any before in history. Christian principles honestly applied in the second half of the twentieth century were seen to lead to attitudes the reverse of those held in previous centuries. The era calling for large families was passing. There was no longer room for the patriarchal family, however attractive it might seem in a world full of uncertainties. This development meant reaching down to parish levels with the Church's teaching which had emerged from the concept of responsible parenthood and the right of the woman, or the couple, to decide how many children they want and the spacing of them. Catholics were expected to use the rhythm method as far as this was possible, but it was also argued, from more general Catholic moral principles, that where this was not possible and the need for responsible parenthood was a serious one, other contraceptive methods could be used.

This is not yet enough. It is something; but it also contains, at this half-way stage, an unexpected danger. This type of thinking is very sophisticated. Its expounders themselves maintain that its essentials have yet to reach the parish level. In practice, this means that educated Catholics able to think for themselves are in a totally different situation from the poor and the poverty-stricken, who are unlikely in the course of their unhappy lives to meet a priest able and willing to explain what the Vatican Council decided on responsible parenthood. So the Duessa image returns: the two-faced attitude—one for the bright and prosperous, and one for the ignorant poor who are supposed nowadays to be the main beneficiaries of the Church's action.

The main problem was put to me this way by a Catholic demographer: the methods allowed by the Church are not workable for large numbers of people in the developing countries, however beautiful they may be, and however much they may be pursued by Catholics with zeal and devotion. John Paul II himself, as did his predecessors, has urged further research to make these methods more effective, implying already that at present (and ever since the publication of the encyclical in 1968) they have not been effective enough in practice and attractive enough in their methodology for many people to want to use them. He estimates that only one Catholic in one thousand in the developing world has access to these approved methods. The alternative is complete abstinence or a lot of children. Abstinence, he feels (except in rare cases), goes against the teaching of Christ about 'two in one flesh' and even against the advice of Paul who advised temporary continence for a time for spiritual motives but insisted that it be a short period, in order to avoid temptation.

Interpretation of the encyclical varied. Some Episcopal Conferences were flexible. Others decided for a hard line and gave the impression that artificial contraception was intrinsically evil and, therefore, could not be used in any circumstances. This attitude was widespread in the Curia, and its advocates there put pressure on bishops to be inflexible. Some bishops found that the fairest way of facing the problem was to be loyal in public to the official teachings but encourage their priests to be understanding with people who found themselves in difficulties. And so another dichotomy arose between what the bishops said in public and what they recommended in private.

Yet another dichotomy, another form of Duessa, appears in the gap between acceptance by many Catholics of their Church's teaching on religious matters but not on private morality. Monsignor John Quinn, Archbishop of San Francisco, spoke on behalf of the National Conference of American Bishops at the 1980 Synod and pointed out that a study at Princeton University concluded that 76.5 per cent of American Catholic women (as compared with 79.9 per cent of all US women) were using some form of birth-regulation, and that 94 per cent of these Catholic women were using methods condemned by the encyclical. For answer, he was told by Cardinal Felici that statistics did not matter but doctrine did. Archbishop Quinn added that only 29 per cent of American priests were reported to believe that artificial contraception was intrinsically immoral and only 26 per cent would deny absolution to those who practised it. He saw contraception as posing 'a profound theological and pastoral problem for the Church'.

Almost three-quarters of English Catholics, according to a survey made before the 1980 National Pastoral Congress at Liverpool, saw nothing wrong in the use of artificial contraception. Some 63 per cent thought that Catholics should be allowed to divorce. More than two-thirds saw nothing wrong in marriages in which one of the parties is divorced. These strong divergences on personal morality are accompanied by a broad acceptance of religious doctrine. The only teaching which ran into difficulty concerns hell. Only 58 per cent thought that bad people would spend eternity there. At the same time, over 80 per cent said they thought there was such a place as hell, suggesting that, to the English Catholic mind, hell has no population problems. But what about the familiar problem of papal infallibility? The definition that 'under certain conditions, when he speaks on matters of faith and morals, the pope is infallible' was rejected by nearly a third of English Catholics as false. In its first number for 1979 the glossy French Catholic weekly *La Vie* published the results of a poll dealing with the 90 per cent of France's 53 million people who have a Catholic background and the 15 per cent who are active church members. Most of the active Catholics believed that the Church could take positions on questions of personal morality, such as birth-control. In the general population there was much less acceptance and over one half of the whole poll thought that fifty years from now the practice of confession, the ban on birth-control and priestly celibacy will all have gone. Rome ought to be spending sleepless nights when reading such results. It is not only the Dutch who are difficult, or American women. And not every divergence can be settled by the high-handed methods used against both.

English Catholics, moreover, are not a particularly contentious lot. They are exemplary in opposing violence and in supporting aid for developing countries, and take their religion more seriously—to judge by church attendance—than any other religious group in Britain. An overwhelming majority sees Christian unity as important. Yet 54 per cent (though only one-third of regular weekly Mass-goers) would accept married priests; and a quarter, women priests; and two-fifths, married ex-priests as part-time priests. Whatever the Church tells them, they do not divorce less frequently than the rest of the population. Diocesan reports prepared for the Pastoral Congress showed that the request was general for a reconsideration of *Humanae Vitae*, particularly in the situation which allows that although in principle contraception is forbidden, the 'informed conscience' could find a way out for it. Many Catholics found this dishonest. Almost every report made an urgent plea for a re-examination of teaching on admission to the sacraments of divorced persons. Rigidity was not understood on this point. The Church was seen to forgive anything, even murder, but not remarriage. The feeling among leading Catholics during the period of preparation for this congress was that its members should avoid being over ambitious and recognize 'what they were up against'. That advice might also be addressed to Rome. Like the women's movement in America, these human

261

demands in England are unlikely to lose steam as time goes by: rather, to gain it.

This pressure from the base had the desired effect of forcing the bishops into action. Without allowing personal considerations to enter into one's judgement, I believe it is fair to say that the outstanding speech delivered at the 1980 Synod came from Cardinal Hume, the Archbishop of Westminster. He had already made an appeal for a fresh approach to the pastoral problems presented by *Humanae Vitae*. He then made a second speech which ranged more broadly and placed the encyclical in the framework of what sort of a Church the Synod was seeking. It is brief but deserves reporting in full. The cardinal described a dream which had come to him at a moment in which he had fallen asleep during the Synod's deliberations:

> I heard a voice speaking, and it spoke of the Church, and I saw in my dream a vision. It was a vision of the Church. I saw a fortress, strong and upstanding. Every stranger approaching seemed to those who defended it to be an enemy to be repelled; from that fortress the voices of those outside could not be heard. The soldiers within showed unquestioning obedience—and that was much to be admired: 'Theirs is not to reason why, theirs is but to do and die.' It seemed thus in my dream, and then I remembered, upon awakening—it was only just to do so—that dreams distort reality. They exaggerate.
>
> Then I had another vision. It was of a pilgrim, a pilgrim through history and through life. That pilgrim was the Church. The pilgrim was hastening towards the vision, towards all Truth. But it had not yet reached it. It limped along the road. But meanwhile there were sign-posts to show the way, or rather they told you that this or that road was not the right one. The pilgrim is always in search, I reflected, and that can be painful. The leaders, too, of the pilgrimage are often themselves not always clear. They must sometimes co-agonize with the other pilgrims. Co-responsibility will always involve co-agonizing.
>
> The fortress was a temple, but the pilgrims lived in a tent. It is sometimes better to know the uncertainties of Abraham's tent, than to sit secure in Solomon's temple.
>
> Then I had another vision: I saw with great clarity that the insight of Paul VI in the encyclical *Humanae Vitae*, confirming the traditional teaching of the Church, was surely right. But alas we did not know how best to speak to the people.
>
> The road-signs point the way, but sign-posts become weather-beaten, and new paint is needed. It takes time to get the work done.

> My dream became a nightmare, for I saw the wrong paint being put upon the sign-post, and the last state was worse than the first.
>
> We must never fail to listen to the other pilgrims. And they need encouraging. We must speak gently, compassionately, co-agonize with them, lead them gradually and speak a language which enables them to say: 'Yes, that is right; it is now clear, we accept the teaching.' I saw the pilgrims happy because they had been led nearer to Him who is all Truth, and they sang their joy in praise and thanksgiving. I awoke, and I said, '*Vidi, gratias.*'

That speech, like several other brave, individual efforts to replace a repressive doctrinaire attitude by a more flexible and pastoral one, failed. The 1980 Synod was certainly the worst of the whole series in the sense of frustration it left at the end, when the more genuine and frankly better spirits within the Church had to admit that their efforts had been in vain. The best that could be said of it was that a few speeches were made which will not be forgotten, even if the Vatican machinery manages to keep references to a call for change out of the official results of the Synod. Archbishop Quinn had produced his figures on the state of contraception in the United States. But he also went on to describe a possible way around Paul VI's encyclical while avoiding the dangers inherent in criticizing a papal document. He said that there was no doubt that the teaching of *Humanae Vitae* on contraception was authentic teaching. Furthermore, the theological and philosophical reasoning underlying that teaching had great weight and could not be dismissed lightly. He went on:

> Yet the Church has always recognized the principle and fact of doctrinal development. We have frequently witnessed development in this century in the area of Scripture studies, in canonical jurisprudence and most notably in the Second Vatican Council in the areas of divine revelation, ecclesiology and religious liberty, to mention only a few. And so, whatever may be the answer, it would seem necessary in the area of contraception at least to raise the question: are there nuances and clarifications, further considerations and greater pastoral insights still to be elaborated? How will this Synod contribute to the removal of the impasse on this moral teaching, an impasse which is so harmful for the Church?

The short answer was, of course, nothing at all. The Synod was not permitted to contribute towards a search for an answer to the impasse. There were several propositions drafted to put to the pope which showed a warm and compassionate approach to dealing with the problems of sex. They were disregarded. In a sense, the Synod was memorable in providing the platform for a conservative group to assert that compassion was not an element in the moral teachings of Jesus and the prophets. It depends which Jesus you mean. And it also depends on how one judges the real weight of the various aspects of birth-control: the human problems it raises, the pastoral problems for priests, and the demographic threat looming over the whole planet.

Figures produced in the United States by the House Select Committee on Population show that 20 per cent of teenagers have sexual intercourse before they are fifteen. Fewer than a third of them use contraception and so a million unmarried teenagers become pregnant each year. Some 370,000 of these pregnancies end in abortion and make up one-third of the national total of abortions. About 235,000 end in illegitimate births and 100,000 are legalized by quick marriages. There is no sign in such statistics as these of a falling-off of the problem.

According to the United Nations Fund for Population Activities, there are now two abortions for every five births. In most developing countries, half the married women aged fifteen to forty-nine did not want any more children. But only half of them were using any modern contraceptive method. In Latin America, illegal abortion takes most victims of all among women between the ages of fifteen and thirty-nine. There can be no doubt, however, that, as the 1980 Synod showed, there is a widespread feeling against birth-control in parts of the developing world because it is seen to be a part of the West's price for aid. In the Philippines, for instance, I found people pointing out that the country already had the largest American Embassy in the world, which was following events throughout South-East Asia, and the largest military bases outside the United States, and surely the government's birth-control programmes were all a part of this massive imposition.

These assertions are denied, of course, and to a large extent I believe they are untrue. I can only describe my own experiences. There is little point in talking about the slums of Manila. I have seen them and they are part of the international picture of where the developing world is going: that is towards huge urban concentrations. I was struck more by what I saw in the remoter islands, which appear to be hardly touched by man. Yet soon the incursions are clear. I saw a great sea-eagle return to its nest at sunset and, with a strange look between anger and consternation, discover that its nest was empty of eggs. Swimming in the coral reefs is still a fascinating experience, but now you are likely to come across great gashes in the coral where someone has exploded a charge of dynamite so as to have pieces of coral for sale and stunned fish to collect for the market. Baby turtles are taken from the sea and sold by children in jars. All this, because the number of people trying to live from coral islands is increasing daily.

The idea of birth-control is not a fad of the West. The Indian bishops made the strongest statement by any bench of bishops in favour of a review of the question in their preparatory document for the 1980 Synod. The Indians wanted a pastoral statement from the Synod because of their great concern for 'the plight of those couples, many of them sincere and responsible Christians, who feel they have a genuine reason for practising birth regulation and find that natural methods are not workable in their cases for the time being'. They described contraception as 'one of the most serious and critical' problems confronting the modern Indian family. The bishops fully endorsed the teaching of the Church but assert that a couple's judgement on the number of children they should have 'should involve a consideration of their own good, and the good of their children already born or yet to come, an ability to read the signs of the times and of their own situation on the material and spiritual level and finally, an estimation of the good of the family, society and the Church'. They were practically asking that Catholics could behave on the issue like anybody else.

For years in his reports as head of the World Bank Robert McNamara issued a series of blunt warnings with this message:

> What we must comprehend is this: the population problem will be solved one way or another. Our only fundamental option is whether it is to be solved rationally and humanely—or irrationally and inhumanely. Are we to solve it by famines? Are we to solve it by riot, by insurrection, by the violence that desperately starving men can be driven to? Are we to solve it by wars of expansion and aggression? Or are we to solve it rationally, humanely—in accord with man's dignity?

This surely is the great question. There is another one, more personal and more intimate, but still concerning human dignity. In the years before publication of *Humanae Vitae* many lay people and some thoughtful priests had conscientiously found their own solutions to the problem of birth-control. They did not do so lightly. Yet they saw their efforts reduced to nothing by the encyclical. Lay people could be disappointed, surprised, angry, whatever reaction came their way, but it must surely have been the priests who suffered most. They presumably felt that they had a right and duty to interpret the Church's teaching as best served their faithful. This relationship was destroyed and the idea of service in moral leadership was also damaged.

Young priests, in particular, have probably suffered most in the period following the Vatican Council. These men have had more difficulty than any in understanding their role in society. They were brought up during the Vatican Council's debates with the promise of new ideas about the Church and society. Older priests are better off. Many of them do not like the Council's reforms and even if they must accept the new liturgy and other strictly ecclesiastical innovations, they can grumble that things are not what they were. The younger men have to try to establish a different form of priestly identity. The world around them has as much difficulty as they in understanding their role. They must make these difficult efforts against a background of a reinforcement of discipline along the traditionalist lines of the priestly caste. If they do not accept this, they cannot, in many cases, even hope to leave. The order from Rome to close ranks is not necessarily an effective defence or, for that matter, a posture for advance. The priesthood, John Paul II has confirmed, is for ever: celibacy is a 'sign of freedom that exists for the sake of service'; and the priesthood is not for women.

One of the decisions made by John Paul II at the beginning of his reign which caused profound anxiety was the halt in dealing with cases of priests who wished to leave priestly orders. In fact, this decision was less a ban on laicization than a move to allow the pope time to deal with the question in his own way. It is said on good authority that he was pressed into producing legislation by the Brazilian bishops who told him that unless a start were made with laicization he would risk running into demonstrations during his tour of Brazil from men wanting to leave the priesthood— which would look worse on the television screens than Sister Kane's exploit in Washington. The new arrangements were made known in the autumn of 1980. They laid down three conditions under which a man could apply to leave the priesthood. The first was that a long period had passed since he had lived as a priest and he was now in a situation which he could not leave. This means presumably that he had a wife and family. The second was that of a man who had not enjoyed full liberty in choosing the priesthood, and the third was mistakes made by a priest's superiors who had not noticed early enough that he was not suited to the celibate life. The process was not intended to be easy, however, and it was judged to be more rigorous than the regulations followed by Paul VI. Petitions had to be addressed to Rome and not, as formerly, to the local bishops. And it was made very clear that laicization would be granted, if at all, as a great favour and in no way as the petitioner's right.

I asked a young priest who comes from the borders between southern and central Europe how he saw the priesthood in modern life. He said: 'The priest today is a man alone. Probably he has never been so alone as today in the whole of the Church's history. Celibacy is just the tip of the iceberg. In a society like ours, people living in the same building do not know each other, or speak to each other. For the priest, solitude can be terrible. I want the Church, the archbishops and the bishops, all of them at a collegial level, to re-examine from the bottom the whole question of the priest's emotional preparation. It must be done without fear because a church that feels fear is not a church with faith in the workings of the Spirit.

'The administrative and bureaucratic aspects of parish life can quite well be done by lay people. The priest must share such functions with the laity because they cost him much time, especially such matters as the preparation of documents for marriages in a busy city parish. The present idea of the return of the laity means that they can deal with visiting the sick and with the liturgy; though celebration of the Eucharist must remain the privilege of someone specially consecrated to this. Holy Orders are this consecration. One can ask if other people can be consecrated for the task who are not permitted to do it now, such as married men, or women if you like. But whoever does it must have a specific mandate from the Church which carries out the consecration for this purpose. The important fact is that the Church, the People of God, the Faithful, give this mandate not to create a priestly caste but to provide the means by which a particular service is provided. The scarcity of priests means that lay people will have to do more and more. Thank God there is much talk of a permanent diaconate. We must think of very small parishes. Take villages in the hills with a hundred and fifty people, or two hundred or three hundred who already have no priest. There it is essential that lay people keep alive the idea of the Church wherever there is a chapel, a baptistery or a bell-tower.

'My personal opinion on why so many priests have defected is that they could not stand the lack of affection. Usually, the crisis of faith enters after the crisis of affection. There is a whole transformation in the priest's relationship with society. He used to be everything: lawyer, teacher, adviser, and so had no crisis of identity, or of satisfaction in his work and his personal relationships. Now, suddenly, he has the chance of being just a priest and at the same time society has become secularized and does not allow him to exist just as a priest. That is why there is a shortage of young men willing to enter the priesthood. The idea of the priesthood is too stark. They are alone. There is no gratification to be had. The priest must pay personally the difficulties facing the priesthood as such. Then youth nowadays is fragile. They are without great ideals. They lack confidence and fear compromising themselves for ever, just as in marriage. Young people believe in the indissolubility of marriage and for this reason fear they cannot take it on. The quantity of young men going into the priesthood has fallen but the quality is high.

'Young people are confused. They will join a group which will call for abortion, which means killing life, while at the same time the same group calls for the protection of children or of the countryside. There are symptoms that they want to leave the towns, to go off and contemplate, but so far they are only symptoms. They want a father-figure. In 1968 the attack on institutions was intended as an attack on everything a father stood for. Then they felt orphans. Some tried Communism but this new father disappointed them. They must be helped because they could now fall back into some form of pagan mythology. I hope that the hierarchy understands that applause is not necessarily a sign of a recuperation of the faith. It can also be just a sign of fanaticism for a protagonist.

'The priest should live radically in his own life the experiences of Jesus Christ. He should not allow himself to be suffocated by lay people who are now reappropriating their share in the life of the parish. At the same time the parish itself should be changed because the idea comes too easily, and now it is the custom that priests have a kind of managerial monopoly. He must be given the space in which to live the experience of Jesus. The idea of joint management with lay people is so far too theoretical. The priest must look for inspiration to the Council and to the first years of Christianity, in order to understand his own vocation and that of his lay people. What matters is the substance, not the system. The priest must be balanced; a man who lives and anticipates his times. Unfortunately, his training is usually wrong. There needs to be an end to all myths. Some of the experiments in training have gone too far. Training should provide him with a robust spirituality. It must not be too formal. His emotional needs must be studied. There is so much talk of respect for life, the gift of love, respect towards other churches with a married priesthood, while nothing at all happens inside our own Catholic Church. I raise no question of whether priests should or should not be married. Discussion should allow the individual to make up his own mind in a mature way, as to satisfying his need for affection. The ancient Church did well to propose religious orders as a celibate alternative to the priesthood. Affection is not only marriage. There must be more study of anthropology and not just philosophy and theology which have had too much attention. In the priesthood too there must be respect for man in his physical, biological dimension; the social and psychological dimension. There is too much talk about human rights when, in fact, they are trodden underfoot in our own household.

'My great fear, I must tell you, is that we shall see the end of open challenges to the present situation. Many priests, many religious are tired of disappointments. What many of them are doing now is listening, watching and then, without drawing attention to themselves at all, making up their own minds as they think fit. It is a form of silent challenge and it is very dangerous.'

I wonder what Rome would like less: a silent challenge or a noisy one. It may have to face both. Sexuality and the priestly caste are two of Catholicism's most delicate yet weighty problems, and they have some points in common. There can be no doubt that Catholic orthodoxy sees that the answers to both are in the Scriptures, and the Church can do nothing else but try and apply what is written there. But modern biblical scholarship and a generally more critical attitude make this a more difficult and insufficient approach. The voice, like that of an ageing soprano, is no longer what it was. In one of the world's great short stories, a wonderful singer adored by the crowds loses her voice. The shock to the public was profound. 'They felt that as long as Pellegrina was singing to them, on the stage, the earth had not been abandoned by the angels.' Sometimes now that sense of being abandoned is there.

The treatment of sex has given this impression. What seems to have escaped consideration is that, in the near future, an inadequate approach to sex will be increasingly serious, not only for the world at large, because of the problems of population, but also within the Catholic Church itself. Opinion is changing. Intelligent lay people are willing to go on record as disagreeing with the teaching of the popes on birth-control. At the same time, other intelligent lay people (or even the same ones) are organizing a different type of church, less formal, less hierarchical: the church of prayer-groups which meets in individual homes instead of in ecclesiastical buildings, a church of spontaneous prayer, of the charismatics; a more everyday, more personal church. For this type of church, the family situation must at least be clear, the individual relationships at least acceptable among the members of the groups. The atmosphere around the family must be rational: it cannot depend on the juridical anathemas of a whole host of little Sistine Chapel Christs. That would simply be another example of the institution killing spontaneity. The priestly caste, the old-fashioned idea of the parish, will both be victims. But what will come in their place will not function unless the intimacy of worship is founded on an intelligent outlook on physical intimacy. This is not an age of hypocrisy about sexual matters. I was told in the Philippines that perhaps a half of the priests have a lasting relationship with a woman, and the communities they serve accept this fact without difficulty. The only condition is that they look after their woman well and it is better, I was told, if they do not follow the habit among Filipino men of having two families. What point is there in pretending that such things do not happen? The pretence is not there where such things are common.

12

BECKETS AND COMMUNISTS

I
T WAS SNOWING very hard in Esztergom, which is what
traditionally happens at Christmas in Eastern Europe, but
the snow was the only thing I met there which followed the
pattern of what one is supposed to expect. The day was in fact
four days after Christmas. It was Becket's feast day and that was
enough, or should have been, to bring a sense of excitement to the
huge nineteenth-century cathedral, with its cupola copied from St
Peter's, where vespers were about to be sung for the most
dramatic (if not the most sympathetic) of English saints who
brought the spiritual power into conflict with the state. Becket
was revered in Hungary from the time of his death, and Esztergom, the seat of the Hungarian Catholic primate, has a hill named
after him with a chapel on it in his honour. This was due to
historical accident. The wife of the Hungarian King Bela III had
previously been betrothed to the son of Henry II, and Becket had
not only arranged it but had brought the Capet princess from
France to England for the ceremony and won her admiration. And
so his death was deeply felt in Hungary, which at that time was a
country certainly as important as England and culturally at a
brilliant level.

In fact, quite apart from the hill named after him, Becket makes
three appearances in the cathedral library. In one of them, the
codex writer Pál Váci, who was a Dominican provincial, made the
reading of Aquinas's *Summa Theologica* easier by underlinings in
red. He finished his work on 29 December 1480—as he pointed
out, the feast of St Thomas of Canterbury. The other two are
initial portraits of the saint: in the first letter of the text of Becket's
Mass in the Esztergom missal of 1512 and in the text for the office

of his feast in the Esztergom breviary of 1558. Now, with the Communists in power, the feast of the English saint would surely be the moment for the Church to exert whatever independence was still allowed it.

I have already said that John Paul II had been compared by a high-ranking member of the Roman Curia to T. S. Eliot's Becket. The complete absorption in his role, the actor's talents for making his points against the monarch, the sense of security he gave to the faithful of Canterbury, who gathered under the cathedral wall for comfort, all these gifts were seen to underline the similarity between two dogged and rather flamboyant representatives of the Roman Church's claims against the State. Esztergom, for those with fairly long memories, is associated with the enmity between the Communist regime and Cardinal Mindszenty, whose show-trial shocked the West in the immediate post-war years and who went on to be a less heroic but never negligible figure after his release from prison during the 1956 rebellion and his subsequent refuge in the American Legation. He was in the Becket mould except that he avoided martyrdom at the hands of the supporters of the state. Given the chance of the 1956 uprising, he fled from them to sanctuary with the Americans. He is now a 'saint' of the Catholic Right, but people of any leaning or conviction would regard him as an outstanding personality in the early frontal assault of the Communist world on the Catholic hierarchies.

At Esztergom there is a stone plaque on the wall of the cathedral recalling that in 1936 the Catholic Church's International Eucharistic Congress was held there under the chairmanship of a papal legate, Cardinal Pacelli, later to be Pope Pius XII. He wore vestments, still kept in the cathedral treasury, which were embroidered by the daughters of Maria Theresa. The only time that Eliot's play was performed in Hungary was during that conference. I have no way of knowing whether Mindszenty went to see it but it is nice to suppose that he did. And Wyzsinski too, the Polish primate, because he is much in the same mould: men intent on filling their roles to the utmost so that, through their aspirations, the share of the Catholic Church in the nation's life cannot be overlooked or treated with anything but respect—if necessary, the respect inherent in physical violence against it.

The snow was too heavy and the wind too strong to go and look at the remains of the old royal castle near the cathedral, and perhaps that was symbolically just. There is no heroic struggle in Hungary between Church and State. Before arriving at Esztergom, I had been given signs that some Catholics thought there should be. I was at the Christmas Eve Mass in the rebuilt Gothic coronation church of St Matthias in Budapest, which is huge but far too small for the streams of people pressing to get in through the main doors, like powerful tributaries breaking into the mainstream of the Danube itself. A bearded student in the white robes of an acolyte said to me that he wanted more resilience in the Church's dealings with the Communist authorities. He saw this as inevitable now that a pope of determined character from Eastern Europe was on the throne. The Italians before him had been, the young man said, splendid and cultivated gentlemen but without a real understanding of Communism when it was in power. Now a pope was in office who understood what that meant and the need to be strong in opposing it. I had heard the same from a nun in Egger, up near the Czech border, who was of an age which made it difficult for her to accept as a thing of the past the confiscation of practically all the Church's property in Hungary and the reduction of the priestly caste to figures of fun. Only a saint, she said, could set out to be a priest nowadays because he not only would be called up for military service as soon as he asked to enter a seminary, and so run the risk of losing his vocation, but would be mocked for his choice of the priesthood: mocked! She wanted more heroism in reply.

The vespers for Becket were not heroic. He seemed almost a familiar figure. The homily preached by the primate, Cardinal Lékai, was emphatic: he made clear the strength of Becket's readiness to die for the Church and for Christ. He is a small man and physically rather frail, but his voice and preaching are steady and determined; so is his outlook on the place of heroism in the contemporary church. He does not see the need for it. His choice as the cardinal-primate followed the wishes, it is said, of the Hungarian authorities.

He told me that this was not a time for the Beckets of the world. He arranged this annual service on Becket's day as an ecumenical more than a political occasion, and an Anglican chaplain was present to take part in the service. The cardinal said that he believed the Church must help in the search for harmony. He remains deeply distressed by the effects of war and remembers as though it were yesterday how the retreating Germans destroyed all the bridges across the Danube. There must be no more war, he insisted. He had just seen something else of the war's effects, from the other side, while in Berlin a matter of weeks earlier for the funeral of Cardinal Bengsch. There was still a lot of damage to be seen, he said. Harmony meant stopping war and it began in relationships between human beings, between institutions; where co-operation was possible it should be sought in good faith. Enmity spread into larger acts of violence. I asked him if he thought that János Kádar's regime was one with which such honest business could be done. He said he was convinced that it was, and that he believed John Paul II thought as he did.

The young acolyte and the nun would not agree. It may be that the frail-looking Cardinal Lékai is building on a stronger idea than that of showing ecclesiastical teeth in the direction of the regime, especially as Hungarian Catholicism is different from Polish Catholicism. It is less total to begin with. Only a little more than half of the country is Catholic, and being less total means that it is less totalitarian in outlook. Hungarian Catholicism is not a part of the history of the nation in the way Polish Catholicism is: only to the extent that Catholics like other Hungarians experienced the bitterness of the 1956 uprising which taught them that they could not oppose brute force. In Poland, religion cannot be separated from the heroic idea of the nation. This is not only a question of temperament and psychology. Constitutionally the Polish primate has had the role of being virtual ruler of the country between the election of one king and another. There is a strong element of the prince in the way Polish bishops think. John Paul II is an outstanding example of this outlook. Not surprisingly he is said to have little time for Cardinal Lékai. It is also said that throughout the conclave which preceded his election, Wojtyla never once addressed a word to Cardinal Lékai.

In Hungary, Catholicism was reimposed by the Austrians when they drove the Turks out of the kingdom. Protestantism was more natural. Catholicism had not served as a national rallying point during the bitter century and a half of Turkish domination. It is not that now. And so being Hungarian is very different from being Polish. It is no less distinctive; perhaps more so because Poles are more directly involved with Western thinking, in part because of their close Roman allegiance. The Hungarians have contributed to that thinking but from a more original stance. There is almost a narcissism among Hungarians, who seem to find the mere fact of being Hungarian an absorbing pursuit. Go to the theatre to watch them overjoyed at seeing Hungarian virtues extolled in *Hàry Janos*, or follow the joy with which they will explain the historical background to the particular dish they are serving. Go to the national museum in Budapest and one of the world's most moving sights is the way ordinary Hungarians walk, in silence, to the sound of incessant solemn music, around the coronation regalia of the Hungarian kings, with, as centre-piece, the crown of St Stephen, known popularly as 'the holy crown'. It had been taken to America at the end of the Second World War and the Americans, in a moment certainly of wisdom, returned it to Kádar. It is a charming object: the pendant jewels and the unvertical crucifix surmounting it give it a wayward dignity of its own. There the people go, standing in orderly queues to look at this embodiment of the nation, which the authorities suggest is not really Stephen's crown at all. But the people want to see it as that: they want to see in it the country's history and destiny and they do so with a certain quiet intimacy usually foreign to emotions of this kind.

They do not have the same need that the Poles have to feel that they live as much outside their own frontiers as within them, which helps explain how strongly the Poles feel about belonging so intimately to the Church and why there was such magnificent emotion in Poland when John Paul II went home on his historic journey after his election. The photographs put up by the strikers in the Gdansk shipyards during the early turmoils of 1980 showed how the Poles felt that having a pope in Rome meant that they could feel strong in putting their demands at home because Rome was no longer simply the centre of their religious loyalty but belonged to one of them. They could never have felt so confident —or over-confident—had John Paul II not been on the papal throne and shown a continued interest in his country. For all the danger, the link had its good moments; one of the finest was during that summer when tension was growing in Poland and the world wished the strikers well: Wojtyla, after a brief homily in St Peter's Square, made his first reference to Poland's problems by asking the crowds, very quietly, 'Pray for my country!' It was clearly not to be the last time.

So what, in terms of the Communist connection, did the election of Wojtyla mean? I confess quite readily that after seeing quite a few popes come and go, I did not think that the cardinals would turn to a Communist country for the first non-Italian pontiff in 500 years. When I look back to October 1978, when he was elected, I recall with ample self-criticism that there were two moments before the opening of the crucial conclave when I should have understood that his chances were very good indeed. One was the very friendly effort by a powerful cardinal—who went on to play a crucial part in the election—to explain to me why I should put Wojtyla high on my list. Another was an indirect word from a priest who had spoken to a cardinal, then in semi-disgrace, who was close to Wojtyla and thought his chances to be excellent. That cardinal is now back in high favour. I rejected both on the grounds of pure reason. The political consequences would be too complicated. The Church would never make life more difficult for itself when it did not have to. Whatever doubts Wojtyla had about accepting the papacy apparently concerned the possible troubles his election would bring to the Church's political relations with the East. Certainly this consideration was strong. To most people's eyes, the Catholic Church remained one of the leading expressions (and expressers for that matter) of Western culture. There was no widespread feeling yet that the Third World was about to make the running. And so the choice of an East European was much like saying that Eastern Europe was a part of the whole European heritage and not a series of satellites of the Soviet Union, which was there in the one role of occupying power. The election could have been interpreted as meaning that the Russians had no right to be there.

The nun and the acolyte in Hungary would have seen the situation in this way. They would not have resented the fact that the new man from the East on the papal throne was a Pole and not a Hungarian. Both said that Poland was one of the very few countries with which the Hungarians had never been at war. Some cardinals who voted for Wojtyla were no doubt limited enough in mentality to suppose that they were striking a body-blow against Communism. If that were the case, in a phrase dear to Wojtyla himself, there was a sign of contradiction in what they did. Something had evidently happened to Polish Catholicism under Communism for it to be given the huge prize of the papacy, which had never come its way in a thousand years of extreme devotion to Rome. The election showed that, whatever one might think of Communism, it had helped Poland produce a pope. It may have done a lot more.

The attitude of the nun and the acolyte misses something which is essential to the Polish papacy. It was put to me by an active Catholic university professor from Barcelona, Joaquin Navarro-Valls, whose field is psychology. Of the pope's Polish background he said: 'It is very important that he comes from a Communist country but not for the reasons that are usually heard. From 1946 when he became a priest he has carried out all his pastoral work in a country in which the official structures are unjust. He could have no help from the authorities, from the politicians, from the press or television, which were denied him. And so he devised a form of pastoral work which was highly personalized. His appeal had to be from his own person to other persons. He concentrated on men, not on structures, which is something new for the West where there is a great deal of talk about structures, and how, and whether, they should be changed. He sees good and bad as in the heart of man which is his chosen battlefield. His first encyclical, *Redeemer of Man*, expresses this singularity. He is talking of a single Christ and a single Man. He is constantly underlining at his general audiences that he is speaking to "all of you". We in the West talk of sinful societies but that is not possible. Sins of society come from personal sins even if it is a Hitler or a Stalin who put them into practice. Everyone must be responsible. That is why Wojtyla is hard with his priests and his bishops and much more understanding of people further away from the Church. The key in his thinking is not to send away the "impure" or show to them a Christ who is too demanding, while he will not let the "pure" fall into the ways of the bourgeois because Christ is presented to them in too charitable a way.'

He added: 'Of course Wojtyla's talents as an actor have been a great help to him in this appeal directly to the individual in the crowd. There is nothing to object to in this. I once did a study of the psychology of actors. A fine actor, take Olivier for example, is not hypocritical when acting a role. He fully believes in it.'

On the question of Communism, Wojtyla's presence should help clarify Catholicism's hitherto ambivalent attitude towards it, comparable to the Church's attitude to women in the mixture of reactions and irrational fears it invokes in many an ecclesiastic's thinking. Just as with the status of women, the question is not whether to be for or against Communism, it is something much deeper, and even Wojtyla himself is by no means free of confusion. He talks with awe about the way Christianity emerges despite all efforts at repression. He tells the story of a Russian conscript whom he met in Cracow in 1945, who asked to enter the seminary. At that time Wojtyla was himself studying for the priesthood and had had to do so secretly during the German occupation. Poland was the one country where the Nazis tried to destroy the Catholic Church, precisely because it was so much a part of the nation. Briefly at least, the arrival of the Russians was a liberation for the future pope. The Russian who wanted to enter the seminary (without apparently quite knowing what it was) had constantly heard people around him assert that God did not exist. Yet he still believed in God's existence. The effect on Wojtyla of that meeting was, he said, to teach him 'one great truth: how wonderfully God succeeds in penetrating the human mind, even in the extremely unfavourable conditions of systematic denial of Him'. At the same time, he accords to Marxism the distinction of having provided the deadliest temptation yet since the creation. He is fascinated by the first three chapters of Genesis. In the third chapter the Devil speaks—to the woman of course—of the effect of eating the forbidden fruit: 'Your eyes would open and you would become like God.' For the first time, that supreme temptation has found its right historical context with the Marxist teaching that sets man above God.

Surely the Church cannot have it both ways. Either God will penetrate the human mind, however powerful the measures taken to prevent this, or the Marxist form of atheism is the deadliest temptation since man has been on earth. There is the limpid example of Poland itself, that a government professing atheism is a stimulant to religion. It would be interesting to know exactly which pressure has had more effect on the Polish Church: the Vatican Council or the atheist government. One might suppose that it is the latter, just as in the United States the Council was easily beaten as a political influence by the effects of Kennedy's election. The failure to keep Marxism properly in focus is a tiresome element in Catholicism because it does not arise from doubt but from too many certitudes, some of them contradictory.

There is a facile view that Catholicism and Communism are similar. This leads to two conclusions, both probably wrong. The first is that, being so similar, the two organizations are bound to a condition of constant conflict: 'The Word' as the professionals put it, 'and the anti-Word'. The second is that, being so similar, they understand each other's problems and so their relationship is marked by mutual, if unspoken, respect leading inevitably to agreement. Both views are superficial. The Church, whatever one's prejudices may be, deals specifically with matters of a spiritual nature, whereas Communism specifically does not. The conclusion is not that a Communist cannot have ideas about spiritual matters; he does not necessarily exclude himself from them, but, with some rare exceptions, they are not the reasons why he is a practising Communist—while they are the reasons why a person is a practising Catholic.

The issue reached a dramatic height in Italy when, in the June 1976 election, a group of leading Catholics stood as independents in the Communist lists. The Italian hierarchy and Paul VI were horrified. The unusally open-minded Bishop of Ivrea, Monsignor Luigi Bettazzi, a veteran of peace marches and supporter of conscientious objection, wrote a letter to Enrico Berlinguer, the Communist leader, in which he said:

> Among you there have always been some Christians by origin, maintaining a certain religious practice. But never have there been such sensational cases involving well-known Christians, publicly committed to remaining so. The reaction of the Catholic hierarchy is understandable, given its concern to avoid not only ideological confusion but, above all, upset in the 'Catholic world' in the face of such a new development, raising so many new problems. But this in no way detracts from your decision which, even if it had been prompted by tactical political reasons, remains courageous and open to important consequences.

The bishop himself was criticized by many of his colleagues, and at the Vatican, for writing his controversial letter without consulting other members of the hierarchy.

As for the view that alleged similarity is a force of attraction, the Church does not show this at all in its relations with Communism. From the beginning there has been a feeling of uncertainty and unfamiliarity. What to do for the best has eluded it fairly regularly. If it does so in the future, the consequences will be more serious because this is a field where a genuine neutrality by the Church could be of great help: this was a conviction of John XXIII, who was forced to try to pull the whole caravan back on the neutral road from the watering-place of virulent anti-Communism where his predecessor had left it, strident and stationary.

The Vatican did not immediately declare its hostility to the Russian Revolution in 1917. Thirteen years went by before it did so. Indeed, prompt reaction would have been against Rome's customary conduct of affairs. There had been no great affection in Rome for the Tsar, who was much more concerned about the Russian Orthodox Church than the far fewer Catholics, and who lived in a religious background that saw Moscow as a direct rival to Rome. A negotiation with Kerensky's provisional government was going reasonably well before the Bolsheviks took power, and the Vatican was quick to grasp the opportunity of filling three bishoprics, one being the See of Mogilev, the principal Catholic diocese spreading from St Petersburg as far as Siberia. The arrival of the Bolsheviks made few immediate changes, though they cancelled a provision in the agreement concerning official financial help for religious institutions. Again, the centre of religious attention in Moscow was the Orthodox, not the Catholic, Church, and White Russian exiles detected in the Vatican's dealings an underhand attempt at improving the situation of Catholics in Russia at the expense of the Orthodox. A statement in Paris referred to the 'crooked paths of the base politics of our time' and was taken to refer to the pope.

Confusion in Russia was inevitable after the upheaval. In January 1918, all ecclesiastical property was confiscated. Catholics, like other denominations, were still permitted the use of their churches which had been declared the property of the state. At the end of that year, the archbishop was imprisoned, but was released after twelve months. Three bishops were expelled from their sees, yet, amidst all this uncertainty, the Vatican was still able to make appointments. In December 1921, a vicariate apostolic was established in Siberia while, as late as February 1923, a new diocese was set up at Vladivostok, though this was soon abolished. In September the following year, the Vatican closed its relief mission to Russia. In March 1926, Monsignor Eugenio Pacelli (later Pius XII) consecrated a Jesuit bishop in Berlin, Father Michel d'Herbigny, whose task it was to go into the USSR to consecrate several bishops secretly, and to inform them officially of their appointments as apostolic administrators. With the consolidation of Stalin's power, harsher steps were taken against religion.

The period of mutual denunciations had begun. In June 1930, Stalin told the Sixteenth Party Congress of the 'clerical crusade led by the pope against the Soviet Union'. Less than a year later, Molotov described Roman Catholic priests as 'spies, serving on the anti-Soviet General Staff' and accused the Vatican of having 'in the past few years [tried] to intervene actively in international affairs—to intervene, of course, in defence of capitalists and landlords, the imperialists, the incendiaries of war'.

Popes had denounced Communism before, along with a number of other ideologies, some of which were later seen to be innocuous. The time was coming for a full-scale condemnation. It came in Pius XI's encyclical *Divini Redemptoris*, which spelt out the papacy's views on the subject: 'Communism is intrinsically wrong and no one who would save Christian civilization may collaborate with it in any field whatsoever.'

There could hardly have been a more downright, unconditional verdict. It was elaborated on by the next pope. In 1949 Pius XII decreed excommunication for those who supported Communism; and he also did something no other pope had done—he issued three encyclicals in three days, condemning the Russian suppression of the Hungarian revolt in 1956. At the end of that year he used his Christmas message to speak of the dangers of coexistence and dealings with Communism: 'Out of respect for the name of Christian, compliance with such tactics must cease, for, as the Apostle warns, it is inconsistent to wish to sit at the table of God and at that of his enemies.'

There are some fine examples of this style of thinking in the Curia. One of the most famous was a sermon preached in January 1960 in the Basilica of St Mary Major (near the miraculous Madonna of Perpetual Succour) by Cardinal Ottaviani, an inflexible traditionalist and, at that time, Head of the Holy Office. From the pulpit he condemned the forthcoming visit to the USSR of the Italian president, deploring that a Christian could shake the hand of Nikita Krushchev, 'leader of all those who every day turn back to killing and crucifying Christ'.

Pius XII was scarcely dead before different music on Communism sounded, though not yet very loudly: John XXIII had arrived to resume the search for what he described as the Church's 'perfect neutrality' and he knew that he had only a short time to change the style and much of the music too. Was the change so complete a transformation as it seems? To be fair to the Vatican, the charge of duplicity would be out of place. Jesus chastised his disciples for thinking as men think instead of as God thinks. The Vatican, in a humbler but not more modest way, says something similar. The Church has standards of its own which ordinary people are not expected to be able to grasp. Paul VI came out with this very clearly in his audience to foreign correspondents at the Vatican in early 1973:

> If the Church must have a good knowledge of the world she must care for, and if she must arouse broad co-operation from her children, her decisions are based upon the Gospel and her own

living tradition, not on the world's spirit nor on public opinion, which often fails to grasp the complexity of the theological or pastoral problems at stake.

An institution dealing with souls must have its own mysteries, even in pastoral questions: the impalpable must be institutionalized too. In fact, the Church's standards would not suffer half as much as the prelates fear, if they were clearly explained.

Duplicity would not be accepted as a charge because in seeking to handle the Russian Revolution the aims remained the same, even if the methods were reversed. The Vatican would have had no quarrel with the revolution if instead of being persecuted the Church had been left free to conduct its own activities. Traditionally, preference for one regime or another was not given on political grounds; it depended on the regime's attitude to the activities of the Church, and, in the past, on the papacy's sympathy, as an absolute monarchy, for other absolute monarchies. A doctrinaire socialist rule, as in Tanzania, is regarded benevolently because of its respect for the Church. Inevitably benevolence will change when the regime, equally inevitably, takes a more severe stand on the activities of a church that is fundamentally conservative. This has been the traditional role of the Church: deal with anyone as long as the Church's position is enhanced as a result. The classic statement of that attitude came in May 1929 with Pius XI's assertion: 'Where there is a question of saving souls, or preventing greater harm to souls, We feel the courage to treat with the Devil in person.' In the past the Devil has taken different political forms for the Catholic Church: liberalism, democracy, socialism, Communism; but the Devil of the day has been dealt with as long as advantage for the Church's interests can be gained.

The second reason why the change from spurning to dealing with Communism was not as complete as it seemed, is that Pius XII has not yet found his historical niche. He brought Catholicism perilously near a crusade against Communism and a kind of lodgement with the Western allies as protectors of the Vatican—a similar role to that of the medieval emperors. He was the first pope to bring the Church near acceptance of democratic principles. Yet he is remembered as authoritarian, allegedly too gentle with the Nazis, and largely concerned with condemning Communism; his democratic propensities were few—telephones at the Vatican had long leads in his day, so that a prelate telephoned by

Pius XII could comfortably answer the call on his knees. Pius's carefully respectful public attitude to democracy may have been stimulated by his anti-Communism and the predominantly Western company that he kept. Yet he was proud in denying papal blessing on the German invasion of the USSR, despite the persecution of the Church there. He went out of his way to say that he could not be reproached with 'wishing to harden the opposing fronts'. However difficult it may be to agree with him, he did not appear to think that his own anti-Communism was excessive.

Would this supposedly arch-conservative, in today's different atmosphere, be treating with the Devil? The answer in the highest reaches of the Vatican now is that he would. He, too, accepted the Church's traditional diplomatic methods and would have been ready to use them to seek breathing space for the Church's work. This view was put to me without hesitation by Cardinal Casaroli, John Paul II's Secretary of State. After Pius XII's death, John XXIII needed several months to assert himself over the Curia. This is the reason usually given to explain why his reign saw a tightening of the Vatican's anti-Communism. The first sign of change came shortly before the opening of the Vatican Council on 11 October 1962. From the previous 27 September to 2 October, Monsignor Jan Willebrands, head of the Vatican's Secretariat for Christian Unity, and later Cardinal-Archbishop of Utrecht, was in Moscow. The outcome of his talks was that the Russian Orthodox Church sent observers to the Council. Willebrands probably gave assurances that the Council would not be used for expressions of anti-Communist feelings. This outlook would be in line with John's own, which was not inclined to condemnations. On 10 February 1963, John was able to express his satisfaction at the liberation by the Russians of Monsignor, later Cardinal, Slipji, primate of the Ukrainian Catholics, who had spent eighteen years in a Soviet labour camp, his Church having been practically destroyed as a corporate body. This bitter fact, rather than his own sufferings, no doubt explained why Slipji spent his exile in Rome in constant opposition to negotiation with the Communists. Less than a month later, the pope received Alexei Adzubei, son-in-law of Krushchev. They talked privately for eighteen minutes in the pope's library, as part of what John's able secretary, Monsignor Loris Capovilla, called 'the pope's holy diplomacy'. On 10 April, John published his encyclical *Pacem in Terris*, in which he defined his approach to Communism. His point was to make a distinction between false philosophies and the practice based on them. He said:

> Again it is perfectly legitimate to make a clear distinction between a false philosophy of the nature, origin, and purpose of men and the world; and an economic, social, cultural and political programme, even when such a programme draws its origin and inspiration from that philosophy. True, the philosophic formula does not change, once it has been set down in precise terms, but the programme clearly cannot avoid being influenced to a certain extent by the changing conditions in which it has to operate. Besides, who can deny the possible existence of good and commendable elements in these programmes, elements which indeed conform to the dictates of right reason and are expressions of man's lawful aspirations?

John wept privately for people's failure to understand what he was doing. He was also blamed for contributing towards Communist advances in Italy. His conclusions did not remain untouchable even within the Vatican itself. Giovanni Benelli was still Substitute at the Secretariat of State under Paul VI, before leaving for the Archbishopric of Florence, when he gave an address to the Austrian Foreign Policy Society in Vienna which included this question: 'Given that every *practice* is the expression of an idea, by admitting a collaboration on the practical plane, does one not admit implicitly, does one not implicitly accept the ideology from which such practice is derived?' But John was no longer alive to give the answer. His outlook has nevertheless survived as the Vatican's official approach to the question of practical dealings with the Communists. Even the allegation that he helped the Italian Communists no longer arouses much interest.

Even before the election of a non-Italian pope, there was a feeling that Italian affairs exercised much more than their proper weight in the formulation of papal policy. This was true. Pius XII was deeply involved in Italian affairs; so was Paul VI, though with John's example to follow, he was discreet. Before his election, John Paul II had little experience of Italian affairs. He had spent a lot of time in Rome, both as a student and as an archbishop, but he kept very much to the Vatican side of the river, his spare time being spent in physical exercise and friendship with fellow Poles. In the summer of 1979 he received a remarkable compliment, of a kind. Enrico Berlinguer, the Communist leader, told his Central Committee about concerted anti-Communist moves which had caused the Party to lose votes, but he exonerated the Vatican from having taken any part, and actually expressed his appreciation for its behaviour. Obviously, no pope would have wanted Italy to be ruled by the Communists, even though Berlinguer is far from being a potential revolutionary tyrant and is married to a practising Catholic, who has brought up their children under Jesuit guidance. It took the popes a long time to understand that much of their past blatant anti-Communism must have helped, more than it damaged, the Communist cause, and, in terms of the Vatican's international position, the damage far exceeded whatever gains were made in Italy. It is often argued that Communism itself is a religion. Nyerere, the Catholic President of Tanzania, argues in this way: Communism, he said, goes so far as to satisfy the religious needs of its members because, by rejecting religion, it has created a completely new belief, a new religion. Communists have their saints, he says, and now they have a theology appropriate to their system: they have socialist discussions that are completely theological. He makes the old mistake of visualizing relations with Communism as contact between two churches.

What does the Vatican really think? That is not a question which can be answered directly because there are several different opinions within the sacred walls of the Curia and even more outside of them. That is a part of the problem. It has not helped, to put it mildly, that the prelates conducting policy towards Communist states have had to suffer continual criticism, a constant breathing down the back of the neck, from the over-wary or the thoughtlessly anti-Communist while they have been trying to carry out these necessarily delicate negotiations, which may not be immediately productive. I asked the man who master-minded the policy established by John XXIII and promoted, if with a worried caution, by Paul VI.

Casaroli explained his position in these terms: 'I believe that only very rarely have the Church and the Holy See had to face so complicated, difficult and delicate a question. I would say that after the first persecutions of the Church the great problems have been the schism between Eastern and Western Christianity, the rivalry between emperors and the popes, the Reformation and the French Revolution. These are the great crises which the Church and the Holy See have had to face. Relations between the Church and Communism enter into this gallery of really huge questions, some say the biggest of all. The schism raised questions of faith and so did Protestantism but they both left faith in Christ intact. The French Revolution did not deny the existence of a Supreme Being. In its deism it retained the idea of the transcendent. Even in its most crude period, under Robespierre, the Revolution retained belief in the Supreme Being. In social terms, moreover, certain traditional values were allowed to continue.

'But Communism, in practice and in its doctrine, expresses a radical atheism. It allows nothing above man. Moreover, on more general questions it wants change, such as the abolition of private property. From the Church's point of view, the clearest aspect of Communism is that it is atheist. The Church is also touched by limitations on its liberty. This is not only grave in itself but is grave because of its extent. It is both lasting and huge, and so Communism is a direct menace to every church and every religion. This places on us the responsibility to listen to all criticisms because the problem is so big. Once having listened we must come to some conclusions. The Holy See must have its policy. What we ask is that when the pope and the Holy See arrive at a decision, we must be in a position to ask the Catholic world, if not others, to accept it. There is no dogma involved but if we wish to succeed we must remain united.

'Of course Communism was a much easier problem for the Holy See when there was no dialogue. It was simple for the Church to condemn and protest. The problem emerges only now that there are some elements of dialogue and negotiation. The Church is following its traditional policy of not giving way on essential principles but remaining ready to look at possibilities of practical agreements. It is in no way possible to accuse the Holy See of having abandoned any questions of doctrine.

'I can understand people who say that all this is useless and only struggle remains; but personally, although I am no prophet, I refuse to take as a principle that there is nothing to be done. I have the impression that the younger generation in Communist countries is different: it is not like the first generation but it is not exactly clear yet how they are different. Then there is the criticism that the Communist world is in difficulties, and needs the Church, but why help them? I believe we must from a sense of responsibility. We are all involved in questions of peace. Our action for peace is closely followed in the world. I remember how at the United Nations Special Session on Disarmament where I spoke, people wanted to hear the pope's views. Our policy must be to avoid war and to insert some little seeds, to help to allow some seeds of liberty to grow, because where there is liberty, the Church has no need of anything else. There will be setbacks; there have been some. It is important not to be discouraged and to remember that time is on the side of liberty.'

There are plenty of prelates who disagree with him: the West Germans are probably the set of bishops most uniformly suspicious of negotiations with the Communists. They prefer struggle. 'They talk of Czechoslovakia and Hungary,' says a Vatican official, 'but they are looking at East Germany.'

I cannot personally give any first-hand indication of the situation of Catholics in the Soviet Union. It is worth an interpolation to explain this because, I suppose, it tells something about Soviet thinking on the subject. I went to the Soviet Embassy in Rome to ask for help in looking at their treatment of religion, especially their Catholics, and was told to apply in detail in writing. I did so, pointing out that I would be visiting many parts of the world and was particularly anxious to see something of the Russian Orthodox Church and its relations with the Catholic churches in the Soviet Union. The reply was to ask me to obtain a letter from the chairman of the publishing house which had commissioned the book, supporting my own application. This was duly written and delivered. In the ensuing year I called in person and by telephone several times and was generally assured that everything was in hand though there were usually some additional difficulties. Would I, for example, be prepared to visit other religious denominations, such as Muslims or Buddhists? Yes, of course I would. Then the embassy counsellor said that he would be going to Moscow and would take up the matter personally. When he came back, he explained that the reason why my case had not been dealt with in Moscow was because, being British, the application should be made in London. As a meeting of leading churchmen, including the Cardinal-Archbishop of Westminster, was due to take place (it was later postponed because of the Afghanistan crisis) at Tallin in Estonia in January 1980, I asked *The Times* to make an application for a visa to the Soviet Embassy in London. They received the reply that, as I normally lived in Rome, the proper place to make the request was Rome. The Foreign Manager of *The Times* then wrote to the Soviet Embassy in Rome asking that the visa already applied for more than a year earlier should be granted so that I could go to Moscow and on to Tallin. The answer was a curt letter saying that I had made no application for a visa. At this point there was nothing else to do but depend on second-hand sources.

The Soviet Union is clearly the prime example of the one great power that is Communist and has a long tradition of Christianity (and other religions) among its inhabitants. The authorities publish no statistics on membership of religious groups because their importance is minimized, and their freedom of action curtailed. It is thought in the West that about thirty million Soviet citizens, out of a total population of 260 million, belong to the Russian Orthodox Church, which is the country's biggest religious institution. There are still about four million Roman Catholics, and three million people who belong to other denominations; there are about forty-five million Muslims and two million Jews.

Constitutionally, only atheists have the right to propagate their thinking. The 1977 Constitution puts the matter explicitly enough:

> Citizens of the USSR are guaranteed freedom of conscience, that is the right to profess any religion or none, to celebrate religious rights or to conduct atheistic propaganda. Incitement or hostility in connection with religious beliefs is prohibited. In the USSR the Church is separated from the State and the school from the Church.

Churches and religious groups are at an obvious disadvantage. The state has the schools and the media at its disposal for promoting atheism. The churches have to rely to a great extent on the liturgy alone. The situation was put starkly by Vladimir Kuroyevdov, Chairman of the USSR Council for Religious Affairs, in an article published by *Izvestia*, the government newspaper, in January 1978. He said that while freedom of conscience was guaranteed, the Soviet Constitution emphasizes that the most important duty of all Soviet citizens, including believers, is the observance of Soviet laws.

> . . . It is forbidden to break Soviet legal provisions relating to religious cults; to use gatherings of believers for inciting them to shirk their civil duties and opt out of socio-political activities; to perform religious rituals which are harmful to the health of citizens, and so on.

A network of restrictions, some of them unpublished, have kept the churches strictly tied ever since the requisitioning of all church property by the state in 1918. Tens of thousands of churches have been destroyed or converted into warehouses, cinemas, clubs, or put to other secular purposes. There are few buildings available for prayer, and new congregations wishing to register sometimes have to build a church of their own. If they do, they still have to follow regulations that lay down strict limitations. A building for prayer must be a long way from schools, children's homes, kindergartens and youth clubs, so as not to demoralize young people. It must be remote from crowded places, party or trade-union buildings or barracks of the armed forces, so that the church could not be regarded as equal in importance to such bodies. Citizens must not be bothered by the behaviour of these cults, for instance by the noise of singing. It is normal for there to be protests at the proposed opening of a church, protest prompted by the local Party as a rule, requesting the use of the building for more urgent purposes. Churches are not recognized in law as 'public organizations' as are unions and approved sporting and cultural bodies. They are legally denied the status of 'juridical persons' and so their right of complaint and redress is very limited. Churches and religious groups are supervised through the USSR Council for Religious Affairs. Its statutes are secret but some of its functions have been made public. It 'keeps a register of religious associations, prayer houses and buildings, and establishes the procedure for the presentation of related data on religious societies or groups of believers, on their executive and auditing agencies and on the ministers of the cult'. According to Western sources, the Council is controlled and staffed largely by the KGB.

There are detailed reports on the non-legal, non-constitutional methods with which the authorities try to combat religious influence. Teachers in schools are said to exert pressure on children to renounce the Christian faith of their parents. Those who refuse are frequently rebuked and held up to ridicule before their classmates—a traumatic experience for sensitive young people. Again, the weapon is used by denying higher education to Christians who refuse, on grounds of conscience, to join the atheistic Komsomol, or Young Communist League. Religious conversion during higher education can result in expulsion from college. Likewise, finding a job is difficult. Factory directors are inclined to discriminate against believers, especially those who take an active part in the work of their church; they refuse to employ them or else give them work with little responsibility and few prospects. It is said that believers who attain professional qualifications are sometimes prevented from exercising them.

Christian leaders have had to face the most unpleasant official sanctions of periods in psychiatric hospitals, or criminal trials which lead to prison, labour camps or internal exile.

Due to this fundamentally hostile attitude to any form of religious expression, many Christian leaders have come to accept official interference and supervision as the necessary price for the survival of their church or group. Those who give way are used for propaganda purposes and encouraged to be active in Communist-controlled front organizations, such as the Christian Peace Conference based in Prague, and the World Peace Council. They are able to blunt criticism of Soviet infringements of human rights at the World Council of Churches, to which the main churches in the Soviet Union belong (and to which the Roman Catholics send only observers). This is by no means the whole picture. The pope received a letter in October 1978 from three members of an unofficial Christian Committee for the Defence of Believers' Rights, in which they criticized the late Metropolitan Nikodim's approach to relations between Church and State and suggested that his accommodating attitude towards the government did not ease the situation of believers but simply gave assurances to the authorities that leading churchmen could be relied on not to create difficulties. This created divisions between the hierarchy on the one hand and on the other between the laity and ordinary priests.

The largest of the officially recognized Christian churches in the Soviet Union is the Russian Orthodox Church. Because of the part it has played in Russia's history, it is, in general, viewed more favourably by the authorities, as is the case in Romania and Bulgaria, than are the Catholics who look abroad for spiritual guidance. The activities of Orthodox congregations are strictly limited to celebrations of the liturgy. The priests are in effect salaried liturgists. That is why services in the USSR have this combination of a popular strength combined with a museum effect. There is an acute shortage of priests. There are three surviving seminaries out of the fifty-seven that existed before the revolution and places are strictly limited. Georgia's autonomous Orthodox Church has about forty functioning churches compared with the pre-revolutionary 2,000 parishes. The ancient Armenian Church has about three million followers and maintains its strength because of the close relationship between the nation and religion in Armenia.

About 80 per cent of Catholics live in Lithuania and the remainder mostly in the Ukraine and Latvia. Lithuanian Catholicism has nationalist overtones, and religious feeling has been associated with outbursts of opposition to Soviet rule. There have been riots and cases of self-immolation. There are about 800 to 900 priests in the Lithuanian Church and one seminary (with another for Latvia). There are about 630 congregations in Vilnyus, the capital, alone. According to the clandestine *Chronicle of the Catholic Church in Lithuania*, the KGB tries to recruit those who choose to study religion for the priesthood, by threatening to prevent them from being chosen for courses unless they agree to work for the security services. It is also said that the KGB is active inside the seminaries, creating conditions of fear and insecurity among the aspirants to the priesthood.

In a sense, the most tragic of the Catholic churches in the Soviet Union is the Ukrainian Church. It used to belong to the group of Uniate churches in Eastern Europe and the Middle East which followed the rites of the Eastern Orthodox Church but maintained loyalty to the pope. They were still, and remain, in communion with Rome. The immediate post-war period saw virtually the end of this church in its home territories and, as a consequence, the Vatican's growing feeling for a need to condemn Communism. The Ukrainian Catholics were forcibly integrated into the Russian Orthodox Church in 1946, while two years later those in Romania were similarly forced into the Romanian Orthodox Church. There were accusations at the time that the Ukrainian Catholics were involved with the Germans in an effort at gaining their national autonomy. Some people at the Vatican who have closely followed this subject believe that the accusations were not without some foundation.

Officially the Ukrainian Catholic Church exists only outside the Soviet Union. At the Ukrainian Synod, which John Paul II called in March 1980, some twenty-one bishops came, though none from the Ukraine itself. It is thought that there may still be four or five bishops working secretly in the Ukraine. In 1945, when the Ukrainian Church was officially dissolved, the Soviet authorities arrested eleven bishops and confiscated all church property. Some of these bishops are known to have died in prison; Slipji himself, the leader of the community as Major Archbishop of Lvov, spent eighteen years in a labour camp before John's intervention with Krushchev brought about his release. The Ukrainian Catholics in exile, led by Slipji himself, have been among the strongest critics of the Vatican's policy of negotiating with Communist governments. The emigrant Ukrainians also believe that one of the reasons why their church has been so harshly treated is because of its connection with the re-emergence of Ukrainian nationalism, another case in which Catholicism has become identified with national aspirations. Slipji moreover, in his declining years, was increasingly involved in a controversy with the Vatican, because of his demands that he should be accorded the rank of patriarch and his scattered church given the additional autonomy which goes with a patriarchate. Paul VI opposed this claim. John Paul II went further and by taking into his own hands the calling of a Synod at which he himself presided, set out to make clear where authority lay.

The procession of Communist dignitaries visiting the popes has been fairly complete: Podgorny, Gromyko, Kádar, Gierek, Ceausescu. Relations are reasonable with Hungary. Paul VI was able to say to János Kádar, who visited him in June 1977, that the call marked 'almost the point of arrival of a slow but uninterrupted process which, in the course of the last fourteen years, has gradually brought closer the Holy See and the Popular Republic of Hungary after the long period of a remote relationship and of tensions the echo of which is still not entirely spent'.

Poland is now a case apart. There were some typically East European similarities between Cardinal Mindszenty and Wyszynsky, the Polish primate. Both saw their offices as part of the nation's temporal history. Mindszenty, before his arrest, had a Bluebeard-like habit of opening the window, rather than the door, of his residence at Esztergom to show the great expanse of lands that once belonged to his archbishopric, trailing away to infinity. Wyszynsky unashamedly embarrassed guests by drinking toasts to a Greater Poland that he saw as including the Baltic republics. But the Polish Church was much stronger and well able to make use of its strength. Wyszynsky was not happy about Casaroli's activities, feeling that relations with the Polish state were the natural prerogative of the Polish hierarchy, which he had kept so remarkably under control (including Wojtyla, until he became pope). With a typical combination of Roman and Balkan thinking, Cardinal Seper, the Yugoslav head of the Sacred Congregation for the Doctrine of the Faith, told Wyszynsky not to agree to Casaroli's desire for the establishment of diplomatic relations between Poland and the Vatican as this would mean the arrival of a nuncio in Warsaw.

Yugoslavia had been the first East European country to have normal relations with the papacy. Czechoslovakia was much the hardest case, and remains so. Devout Czechoslovaks weep in a moving way at Mass in Rome as if for decades they had been denied a proper outlet for the public religious emotions, which is so. No church in Czechoslovakia had the strength to speak as a part of the nation and so all were comparatively easy prey to repression. Not only in religious terms is the country split; history has left it with two main national groups and no common language. The western part which is Czech was traditionally Protestant and industrialized. There now seems to be widespread indifference towards religion on a greater scale than elsewhere in Eastern Europe. The Catholics are stronger in the rural areas of Slovakia. Both formed part of the Austro-Hungarian empire from the seventeenth century and, in general terms, the Protestants were inclined to foster nationalist movements while the Catholics were known for their intolerance. Freedom came in 1918 and went again as the prelude to the Second World War. All churches are now controlled by the government and the Catholics have experienced more repression.

That is why, in late 1978, it was estimated that 1,600 parishes out of 4,600 were vacant, while 500 priests were subjected to menial work, for having spoken out too freely. Christian families have to make the tragic decision whether to allow their children to be brought up openly in their faith, which will almost certainly mean their exclusion from higher education. Since 1971, religious orders—who have anyway had their property confiscated—cannot accept novices. Existing members of religious orders cannot take higher education or vocational training or read theology and nuns cannot train as nurses. It is the bleakest picture of all in Eastern Europe—with one exception.

The exception is Albania, the country from which it is said that all aspects of God have been exiled. Whether religion appeared in the form of Islam, Eastern Orthodox or Catholicism, it has been savaged by the regime to the point that some of the horrors still seem almost incomprehensible if one did not accept the increasingly obvious truth that brutality is very much nearer to humanity's normal condition than it is pleasant to think. Religion has been a victim of history. When it was a Roman province with the attractive name of Illyria, Albania was probably visited by Paul. Even now it looks inviting and beautiful across the narrow strait from Corfu. You feel you could almost walk to it when the sea is calm because the pull of curiosity is so strong. Have they really established the first godless state there, a new Jerusalem in reverse, a place where the transcendental has no place, except the prison-yard?

The great schism between Eastern and Western Christianity damaged the Church in Albania. There was a brief moment in the fifteenth century when the country acted under Gjergy Castrioti as a bastion of Christendom against the Turks. But it fell like the rest of the Balkans and was for five centuries a Turkish province. About 70 per cent of the people accepted the imposition of the Muslim faith, most of them becoming Bektahsis, a tolerant sect regarded as heretical but tolerated none the less. About 18 per cent remained Eastern Orthodox Christians, particularly in the south near Greece, and 11 per cent remained Catholic, while pockets of pre-Christian paganism made up the remainder. Independence was won from the Turks in 1912, lost again during the First World War, and in 1928 independent Albania established a monarchy and had a brief period of relative felicity before the Italian invasion of 1939. In this period, the Catholic Church was active beyond what its statistical following might suggest, somehow managing to identify itself more closely than the Muslims or the Eastern Orthodox with the nation's aspirations. Work was undertaken to break down the 80 per cent illiteracy, open hospitals and orphanages, help women's emancipation, end the vicious blood feuds for which the country was famous, and eradicate paganism. Enver Hoxha, who had ruled the country since the war, was himself a former Muslim schoolteacher. Under him the country became a junior partner to its larger neighbour, Yugoslavia, which annexed its province of Kosava, an area with a million very poor inhabitants. It still gives an impression, with its strongly Turkish flavour, of what Albania must have been like before Hoxha had fully applied his revolution. When Yugoslavia was expelled from the Comintern in 1948, Albania became immediately subject to the Soviet Union but escaped from this limitation by agreeing to become a Chinese presence in the West. The country is easily manageable: mountainous but compact, never exceeding 200 miles in length or 100 miles in breadth. When the Chinese Red Guard movement attacked religion in 1966 and 1967 as part of the Cultural Revolution, Hoxha had already broken the Church, but he did the same as the Chinese, laying down that 'the religion of Albanians is Albania'. In theory, he had a point, in that the three main religions had in fact been a dividing not a fusing factor in the national consciousness, because Eastern Orthodoxy looked to Greece, Islam to the Arab world and Catholicism to Rome. The death of Mao and the development of a more pragmatic regime in China brought fresh change. In 1978 Albania and China severed relations. The future is uncertain. Albania cannot remain totally isolated, despite the phrase of its joint ruler Mehmet Shehu: 'We shall eat grass rather than betray our principles.' Does the future mean any possibility of the return of some degree of religious tolerance?

Albanian exiles maintain that for certain the authorities have murdered six bishops, sixty secular priests, thirty Franciscans, fifteen Jesuits, ten seminarians and eight nuns, all of whom are said to be known by name. Certainly Catholics suffered most because they were the most articulate and active among the three faiths. At the time of the advent of Communism there were 300,000 Catholics with ninety Albanian priests and thirty Franciscans in 123 parishes. They were strongest in the north around Shkodrë and in the hills. There were two archbishops, one at Shkodrë and the other at Durrës, and both refused Hoxha's proposal to establish a national church. One died in a labour camp in 1946, and the other two years later in prison where he was serving a sentence of twenty years. The Jesuits were banned in 1946 and the Franciscans in 1947 after the police planted arms in a church as an excuse for their dissolution. In 1946 alone some twenty priests were known to have been killed and forty imprisoned. Some sixty non-Albanian priests and nuns were expelled after being held for six months in a labour camp. It is said that Shehu personally beat the remaining bishop in office, a man aged seventy-four. In 1967, following the Chinese example, all places of worship were closed and belief in God forbidden. The 327 Catholic churches were converted to other uses such as sports centres, flats for workers and, in one case, a seat for the secret police. There has recently been a move to restore some mosques and churches to provide museums for tourists. Tourists can also visit a museum at Shkodrë dedicated to anti-religion. A representation of the Trinity shows the Father as Imperialism, the Son as Revisionism and the Spirit as the Vatican. There are signs that religion still exists. The government periodically issues warnings against 'religious proclaimers' and secret groups of Christians. Crucifixes and icons are said to be secretly venerated in homes, but all this information is sketchy in the extreme.

A fact which is remarkable is that two people of Albanian

descent, though born outside Albania, have strongly influenced contemporary Christianity. One is the late Ecumenical Patriarch of Constantinople, Athenagoras, a huge man physically with great warmth of personality, whose meetings with Paul VI—especially their embrace in Jerusalem—opened the road to greater understanding between the two main groups of Christians. The other is Mother Teresa.

As for China, the challenge is immense, and so is the stimulus provided by the fact that the Vatican made one of its historical errors by coming down on the wrong side in the controversy concerning the 'Chinese Rites'. In a sense, but a less subtle sense, the same problem is there now, because during the break in 1949 which isolated Chinese Catholics from the rest of the Catholic world, the government set up an organization called the National Association of Patriotic Catholics. This association has elected its own bishops without the approval of Rome. In 1958, Pius XII condemned it, among other reasons because bishops and priests imprisoned or exiled for their Catholic faith regarded it as a creature of the regime. It is still active. In July 1979, the election of another bishop was announced, that of Michael Fu Tieshan, to the See of Peking. Without the Vatican's approval, these elections are illicit but not invalid: there is a continuity of ordination by validly ordained bishops but they lack the seal of Rome's consent. Despite this insistence by the more open Chinese authorities on continuing to regard the Association as the Church in China, John Paul II in August publicly expressed appreciation of the new respect for religion being shown in China. He said he hoped that the opportunities for direct contacts with Chinese Catholics would increase. A delicate problem was clearly taking shape.

Father Michael Choo went back in 1979 after thirty years. He was allowed great freedom to move about and meet people. This was the report on the Choo visit given to me by one of his superiors in Rome: 'We, the Society of Jesus, have somewhere in the number of 120 Chinese Jesuits in mainland China. At present we have information on only a few of them; we don't know whether they are alive or dead or where they are. Father Choo was able to make contact with about ten of them and these would be ten who have been released from either prison or work camps. Now they are earning their living like almost anybody else but they are still not free to exercise their function as priests, or any kind of public apostolate. Hopefully this will come later; the openings he found were not so much religious as educational, technical and scientific ones. The Chinese are interested in medical schools, for obvious reasons, I think. They are interested in engineering schools, in people who can teach these things, or would be interested to set up these faculties, and languages too. They are tremendously interested in languages and English is very high on the list. The other side of it is that the Chinese are sending out students so that they can go to different countries and take degrees. These are not the typical young students we might be familiar with: these are people in their late thirties or forties anxious to bridge the gap that happened during the so-called Cultural Revolution, when for ten years or so education went to the dogs. People were not prepared: no research was going on. Now they are desperately trying to recoup in that area. They have a financial problem on how to finance these activities but they are trying to get some sort of programme going with friendly nations.

'For us, the interest is in religion. We would be very interested in doing what we can to help, but there is no question of forcing our way in. Here we are. It's more going in as educators, as people who can help in the development area . . . .'

In March 1980, Cardinal König, the Archbishop of Vienna, spent ten days in China with a very free mandate from the pope to see what could be done. He admitted that the invitation was as Cardinal-Archbishop of Vienna rather than as head of the Curia's Secretariat for dealing with non-believers. The distinction was made in order to suggest that there was no official nature to his journey, though it was clear that the pope would be extremely interested in what he brought back. He was unable to meet Catholics who did not belong to the Patriotic Association and he said himself that he could see no way of reconciling the members of the Association institutionally with the Vatican. He had the impression that Catholics had to keep their distance from Rome in return for being allowed some sort of distinctive life in their Association.

Arguably—and this is the point of great delicacy—the Catholic Church has changed substantially since 1949 and since the period of Pius XII's last years, which brought the condemnation of the Patriotic Association. The Vatican is now in a position to give more to China and ask less in return. It is a question of how far the lesson is clear to both sides. It would be a pity from the Catholic point of view if the great prize of China were to be lost once again for a lack of flexibility in Rome.

There is little sense in reviving the accusations of repression against the Catholic Church in the past. They cannot, however, be made to disappear conveniently, just because a new approach is found more efficacious in modern circumstances. The mistakes of the past remain too readily available for use by the opponents of Christianity as a whole. Some of the wisest words on this subject were said by the late Cardinal Beran who, as Archbishop of Prague, had been imprisoned both by the Nazis and the Communists. He was released to attend the Vatican Council but was not allowed to return to Czechoslovakia, and he died in Rome. His brief address to the Council has never been given the weight it deserved, probably because it challenged too many prejudices and interests. His subject was persecution. He not only denied the right of the Church to persecute, or the right of others to persecute religion, but he issued a reminder, more valuable probably now than then, against the belief that a persecuted church necessarily prospers. He said:

> From the very moment in which freedom of conscience was radically restricted in my country, I witnessed the grave temptations which, under such conditions, confront so many. In my whole flock, even among the priests, I have seen not only grave dangers to faith but also grave temptations to lying, hypocrisy and other moral vices, which easily corrupt people who lack true freedom of conscience.

Here he was placing himself firmly against the view which is now so fashionable, that a finely burnished new Christianity will emerge from Communist persecution. (It is worth noting in passing that much less is said about a new Christianity that might emerge from the right-wing persecution frequently conducted by tyrannies in the name of Catholicism.)

He continued:

> If this repression of conscience is knowingly directed against true religion, the gravity of such a scandal is evident to every Christian. However, experience shows us, too, that such procedures against liberty of conscience are pernicious, morally speaking, even if through them the good of the true faith is intended or pretended.
>
> Everywhere, and always, the violation of liberty of conscience gives birth to hypocrisy in many people. And, perhaps, one can say that hypocrisy in the profession of the faith is more harmful to the Church than the hypocrisy of hiding the faith which, anyway, is more common in our times.

The imposition of Catholicism by force, as happened above all in Latin America, is something well in the past. Beran saw, however, how that tradition continues to cause harm.

> So, in my country, the Catholic Church at this time seems to be suffering expiation for defects and sins committed in times gone by in her name against religious liberty, such as in the fifteenth century the burning of the priest John Huss and during the seventeenth century the forced re-conversion of a great part of the Czech people to the Catholic faith . . . .
>
> By such acts, the secular arm, wishing or pretending to serve the Catholic Church, in reality left a hidden wound in the hearts of the people. This trauma was an obstacle to religious progress and offered, and offers still, facile material for agitation to the enemies of the Church.

So much is enough to keep the past on record while not permitting it to distort one's expectations for the present. The Catholic Church is no longer oppressive in the way it seeks conversions. It is also respectful towards other Christian bodies and other religions. The Vatican Council accepted the principle of pluralism without surrendering Catholic insistence on possessing the whole of the one true faith. John Paul II's ultra-Catholicism has not cancelled a decade and a half of progress.

Ironically, it was to Czechoslovakia that Casaroli made his first East European journey, in May 1963, and ten years later he managed to reach agreement on the nomination of some bishops. Bearing in mind the repressive nature of the Czechoslovak regime, he was able to say that the agreement, whereby the Vatican chose a new bishop from four names proposed by the government, represented a matter of importance for both sides: 'important but negative for them; important but positive for us.' Nevertheless, in 1980 there were more bishoprics empty than filled.

The fundamental criticism of Casaroli that goes beyond his handling of relations with the East (which was never his only concern, even before he became Cardinal-Secretary) is that he has spent his life in Rome. Apart from diplomatic missions, he has known no other life than the Curia. This may not be as limiting as it sounds. After all, if God penetrates the mind of a Russian conscript, there can be little limit on what can make its way through to the Curia, if the person concerned is receptive. However, what may happen is that the atmosphere of Rome makes the Communist problem look different from what it really is.

Rome looks a cynical city, surrounded by an air of having already seen more than everything, but it also adds an artificial sense of drama to events and causes. Rome, moreover, has been the object of sometimes ill-advised campaigns to keep it out of Communist hands. One personally involved Pope Pius XII, who tried to impose an extreme right-wing alliance on the Christian Democrats as a means of assuring a defeat of the Communists. This is a heady atmosphere and the fact that in 1976 Rome had a Communist mayor for the first time—though the Vatican walls did not come tumbling down—has not removed the sense of tension. Rome is also the capital of Italy and there have been times, notably in 1948 and 1976, when fears were purposely aroused, certainly exaggerated, about the danger of a left-wing majority.

This particular flavour of political incense may have helped overload the Communist issue. Clearly it is an issue of great importance to the Church, as it is to the world in general, but to neither can it be regarded as the supreme question. There are more similarities apparent now in the problems of the Communist and the Western worlds than there are differences. The correction of the Church's course by John was not just a matter of leadership affecting only the Church's government. It began a more profound work of correction in encouraging the Church in the West to take a more critical look at itself, to shake off the easy supposition that all that was wrong with the world came from Communism. It is now much more difficult for a bishop to see Communism as totally overshadowing the problems of the consumer society and the aftermath of industrialization. Even where the danger of Communist expansion is most acute, which is in the Third World, Catholicism's present position runs much less of a risk of simply trying to impose European liberal values as its only alternative to Marxism. That would be to repeat the eighteenth-century mistake of opposing social unrest and eventually revolution by supporting the absolute monarchies of the time as the bulwarks of Christian civilization.

13

VIOLENCE AND LIBERATORS

OR THE FIRST AND Second Worlds, the days of the Beckets may be over, but not for the Third World. It was 29 December, Becket's feast day, when the Hungarian primate talked of the need now for harmony rather than conflict, of the search for unity rather than division, at all levels, in order to stop violence and war. It was just before Easter, on the evening of 24 March 1980, that Monsignor Oscar Arnulfo Romero y Galdamez, Archbishop of San Salvador, lifted the chalice during Mass at the chapel of the Hospital of the Divine Providence, which he had founded for the treatment of terminal cancer. He said: 'In this chalice'—raising it high—'the wine becomes blood which was the sacrifice for the salvation of this people. May this sacrifice give us the courage to offer our own bodies for justice and peace', and at that point the killer struck, putting a .22-calibre bullet in his heart which then lodged in his left lung, sending blood pouring from his mouth as he lay on his back by the altar with just sufficient breath to forgive his assassin.

More than anything, Romero was a martyr to the cause of Catholicism's new political role. It is fashionable nowadays to argue that Christianity has no political part to play and that when it does so it can only be making a mistake. The idea is overwhelmingly attractive that all Christians should be little brothers and little sisters of Charles de Foucauld, exemplary, sweet, humble, prayerful, retiring, but innocent of the world of affairs and making political faction look like blasphemy by comparison with their holy conduct. The Catholic Church, as such, has seldom refused a political role. It may well try to put most emphasis on the spiritual content of what it is doing, or the spiritual inspiration

301

of its political action, but often the effort shows. It now is in theory freer from political engagement than at any other time. The pope is not the ruler of substantial territories, required to take part in the normal activities of the political head of a size-able principality. Yet, it is symptomatic of the Church's present role that its representatives signed the Nuclear non-Proliferation Treaty and returned to international negotiation on its grandest scale by being present at the Helsinki conference while keeping its largest representation abroad in New York at the United Nations, where the office of its observer was called by Paul VI 'a super nunciature'. It is the only diplomatic office of the Vatican with a telex, apart from Washington. Political tasks have never been so engrossing for the Church, and, to do the Vatican justice, politics have been as much pressed on it as originating from any will in Rome for greater involvement.

I first met Archbishop Romero at Puebla where he played a rather insignificant part in the work of the Conference of Latin American Bishops, held in early 1979. In fact, he himself gave an impression rather of insignificance. He was short with an olive complexion and heavy glasses. He seemed timid in manner and looked out of his element. On the basis of this first conversation I was left perplexed that he had an immense reputation as a hero. The second time I saw him was at a press conference where he was brighter but the whole atmosphere was impressively tedious: much of the Latin American press treated him as a great star, giving him a long, standing ovation both at the beginning and at the end of the conference. The room was hung for the occasion with photographs and statistics about repression in the Republic of El Salvador. The country is named after Jesus and its particular religious feast is in honour of the transfigured Christ. I had not at that time been there but I was beginning to feel the need to do so. The accounts of the cruelties seemed to me to be exaggerated. I asked one of the priests on the staff of the Jesuit General why Romero appeared rather uninterested in the conference and was given two explanations. Apart from Romero, the chairman of El Salvador's Episcopal Conference was present and was an extreme reactionary, his views totally the reverse from those of San Salvador's archbishop. Indeed, Romero was in a minority of two to four in his National Conference and the Jesuit said that he may have been happy with the way the chairman was damaging the cause of reaction by speaking at Puebla in an absurdly conservative manner. The other reason the Jesuit gave was that Romero was not at his best with fellow-bishops unless they were his friends. 'You should see him', he added, 'among his own people. Then you will really see what he is like.' I half decided to do so. I briefly saw Romero again. He was standing in the corner of the entrance hall of the seminary building in which the conference was being held. It was the last day: he did not say much except: 'Why not come to see for yourself?' I then went to Mexico City to stay with friends and my host removed all doubts: 'Go and hear Romero preach in the cathedral, he is there every Sunday, and you will understand the problem of Latin America.'

I arrived in San Salvador in the late evening. The first sign I saw said: 'Welcome to the world of Panam.' I made a mental note to forget that quickly if I really wanted to enter the world of the Latin American poor, though, as left-wing priests in this continent would say, 'The world of the multinationals is indeed the world of the poor.' I should add that I had not been given a particularly brilliant impression of Romero in some of the highest echelons of the Vatican where he was obviously not in favour: the feeling was that he was causing too much trouble and was over-influenced by some leftward-leaning advisers. It was soon clear that his relations with the nuncio in San Salvador were poor, which was not very indicative because the nuncio was himself scantly respected. The archbishop thought, or at least so he said, and I have the impression that there was a certain amount of willing self-deceit here, that he had the support of John Paul II. 'He shares my views,' he said, but not with much conviction. The Cardinal-Primate of Hungary had said the same. I remembered an Irish bishop said to me, 'We feel we have a lot in common with the pope's country: we share a lot of the way the Poles feel.' Everybody in the Catholic world wants to feel that the pope is beside them, encouraging them, understanding them, agreeing with them; that is another form that Catholic loyalty takes: they are all doing what the pope wants.

Romero is an excellent example of a Catholic prelate originally without political pretensions who was inevitably drawn into the centre of the political struggle in his country to become the one point of resistance to the republic's rulers. He was born in Ciudad Barrios, near San Miguel in the south, son of a telegraphist. He left a poor family background to study for the priesthood and was ordained in 1943. In 1970 he was appointed auxiliary of San Salvador and then Bishop of Santiago de Maria four years later. In January 1977 he became Archbishop of San Salvador in succession to Monsignor Chavez y Gonzales who had reached retiring age and was felt by the government to be too liberal in his views. Romero was regarded as tranquil by comparison, conservative and attracted to the dogmatically severe and traditionalist 'Opus Dei' movement. The government backed his candidature, as in the case of Lékai. A group of progressive and politically minded Jesuits, mainly Basques, teaching at the Catholic university in San Salvador, told me that they prayed together that this man who later became a hero to them would not be appointed and that someone more socially conscious and energetic should be given the post. Romero was nevertheless chosen and within a matter of weeks—twenty-five days to be exact—the government's forces had massacred a still unknown number of demonstrators in the next square to San Salvador's ugly and unfinished cathedral. The new archbishop could scarcely do less than condemn the murders from his pulpit. The square where the massacre took place is dedicated, ironically, to *Libertad* and had been chosen for a protest on 8 February 1977 against the fraudulent election that brought General Carlos Humberto Romero to the presidency (he was deposed about a year before Romero's murder and was no relation to the archbishop; his main skill was apparently in horse-riding). The police cleared the square by firing into the crowd and cleaning away the blood with fire-hoses. Some say nineteen were killed, others say fifty and still others talk of a hundred or more. Probably no one knows any more, as life is an easily perishable commodity in a vicious tyranny of this kind. Into this void of human feeling and human consideration, a response from a genuine Christian cannot help but include political elements, and the government will see to it that such protest is immediately attacked as politically inspired from the Left.

Less than two weeks later, the archbishop lost a close friend and one of his best priests, in the murder of Father Rutilio Grande, the parish priest of Aguilares, who was killed with two members of his congregation. This priest had an interesting history. He was a scholarly Jesuit and had attempted parish work only to find satisfaction outside the academic world. He had been hurt by the unfavourable reaction to a sermon he had preached while teaching at the San Salvador seminary. In it he had recalled the origins of El Salvador's name and looked forward to a transfiguration of the republic in a Christian sense. He was regarded as too outspoken for those times, some eight years before his murder.

Father Grande sought to achieve something of this aim of

transfiguration in the parish of Aguilares, a poor town about an hour's drive through the fields of sugar cane (and several police checks) outside San Salvador on the road to the Honduras frontier. He went well prepared. He studied new liturgical and pastoral methods for six months in Belgium and Ecuador, in the latter with another remarkable Latin American prelate, Monsignor Leonidas Proaño Villalba, Bishop of Riobamba. He brought with him to his 37,000 parishioners of Aguilares a complete break with the idea many had previously accepted, that God made some people rich and some poor and there was nothing to be done until Christ the Judge apportioned praise and blame, rewards and punishment. They were taught to value their own dignity, poor though they were; to find a sense of solidarity; an idea of the grace of living. The effects were soon seen. Exploitation of the sugar-cane workers was more vigorously opposed. Solidarity was encouraged by the formation of small groups meeting in semi-clandestine conditions to measure everyday life against the standards of the Gospel. They were taught how to live a human life despite inhuman surroundings. That could mean only conflict with landowners, with police, with the political system.

On 12 March 1971, Father Grande was killed. He had probably been threatened with death: he talked several times about dying, asking the three priests who worked with him not to give him an elaborate funeral but to make sure that there were plenty of flowers.

One of the three drove me to Aguilares. According to his official papers he was a civil engineer. There was no way of knowing he was a priest and he said that the police would make trouble for us if they knew that he was. He was a Basque; about two-fifths of El Salvador's priests come from outside the country, mainly from Europe. The fact that the Basque presence among priests is strong is because Franco would not allow them to work in Spain. I had lunched that day at the Jesuit House where the professors at the Jesuit university in San Salvador live. It is a pleasant, simple villa in a residential area on the outskirts of the city. Sobrino, whose writing on Christology in relation to the Latin American background has been highly influential, said: 'Pity you were not here a few weeks ago. The place was surrounded by two hundred police. They had marksmen on the roof opposite to shoot us if we tried to leave. They searched every room for subversive material but of course they found none. Then they went away.'

In the church at Aguilares there is a huge portrait of the murdered Father Grande to the right of the altar. It is the second to be placed there by the parishioners since his death—the first, I was told, was destroyed by the police. While we sat under the palm trees in the garden of the church, there was a constant, low-toned but almost obsessive sound of singing. They did this before the Mass for an hour or more, a nun told me. It is intended to remind the faithful to prepare themselves for Mass and also to remind the authorities that the church is there and functioning among them. The parish priest is from El Salvador; so are the nuns but they had trained and worked in the United States. One said that she had been happy working in New York but was bored there with doing nothing but devotional exercises and washing plates. She needed more than that.

The wounded have been treated in that garden. The church itself was taken over by the police for a month in April 1977 and used as a headquarters during a period of occupation of the land by peasants. The atmosphere is almost conspiratorial. The parish has now about 50,000 inhabitants with one parish priest and four nuns. The country area is divided into six zones, each of which has an average of four small Christian communities. These communities meet secretly and each member takes a turn as sentry to give warning of the arrival of the police. Many of them sleep in the fields at night for fear of arrest. They come and go to their meetings one by one so as not to attract attention. The leaders of the communities try to get to Mass on Friday night and take the Blessed Sacrament back with them to distribute among the group, but not at the main church of Aguilares because it is regarded as dangerous. The object of the teaching and discussion is to measure the reality of life against New Testament requirements: 'to put', in one parish priest's phrase, 'feet on the Gospel.' This is an excitement that a priest will no longer find in Western Europe or the USA. Arguably, this should not be an issue; priests should be happy doing whatever they are called to do, but if priests still have importance, they must be made to feel it. The priest's identity is one of institutional religion's greatest problems. To see young priests and nuns with a sparkle and conviction is not so frequent a sight to allow it to go unnoticed. They talk with fervour of how their vocations came to mean something to them once they became involved in the struggles of the Church in Latin America. I remembered that Archbishop Romero told me that young people seeking to be priests wanted 'to be part of a Church that identifies itself with the poor'. Their enthusiasm recalls, in contrast, the remark of a disappointed priest in the southern USA: 'My advice to most seminarists is: leave!'

It is not that religion is there to make priests and nuns happy with a more active life. It may well be that where the priests are happiest religion thrives, though that need not necessarily be the case. The real point is that when they are working in these conditions the possibility of remaining apart from politics is non-existent. That they are pleased about this is another matter altogether, though not a negligible one given the amount of dissatisfaction among priests and nuns, particularly in the Western world.

The archbishop made clear to me that these young priests feel they have no alternative. He said that he always tried to follow the teachings of the Church. The mere fact of preaching the Gospel brought him into conflict, he said, with the authorities, who then denounced the Church as subversive and influenced by Marxists. I asked him if there was not a real danger from Marxism. He replied: 'Yes, there is indeed some danger from Marxism but it is not clear how much because the Left works clandestinely and not openly. In any case, the main danger is in the reaction it provokes from those attempting to hold back all social change in the name of anti-Communism.'

He gave me a copy of a pastoral letter which he had published in August 1978 under his own signature and that of the Bishop of Santiago de Maria, the only one who thought as he did on social questions. It says a great deal about violence but its most effective statement comes with a passage about the scene on Mount Tabor when Jesus was transfigured. The five people with Jesus—Moses, Elijah, Peter, James and John—were all, it said, men of violent disposition. Jesus, through his work for the building of justice and peace in the world, managed to contain the aggressiveness of these rich temperaments. This is one way in which this unhappy country can be seen in the light of its distant, mysterious, enigmatic saviour-patron, but a lot of faith is needed to suppose that one day the violence will be contained by spiritual authority. To what extent was there violence and how far could a distinction be made between violence imposed by personal cruelty and that which is a natural product of the system? The question is important because El Salvador can in many ways be regarded as a microcosm of Latin America's ills, and the concept of 'institutionalized sin' is one which is fashionable and was held by

Archbishop Romero. It is a concept very distant from John Paul II's insistence on the personal element in behaviour, whether good or bad.

Romero accepted the reading of the situation as one of institutionalized violence; he used this argument in replying to critics who accused him of supporting violence. He explained his view in this way: 'The Church has not incited brother against brother but has recalled two fundamental considerations. The first regards institutionalized violence: when there is a situation of permanent and organized injustice, then the situation itself is violence. The second is that the Church knows that in such a situation any word, even if really inspired by love, will sound as if it is violent but it cannot fail to say this word.'

He had organized a group of young lawyers to give free legal aid to the families of the victims of injustice. They had their offices in a church school in a San Salvador suburb. The reason they were there, one of the permanent staff of three students told me, was because there are about 2,000 lawyers in San Salvador and about a dozen of them were willing to help the poor, particularly if political questions were involved, and so the Church had to intervene (they repeated that it had to intervene) in what amounted to a political field. The young men who had these two rooms in the main courtyard of the school were very clear about what they were doing: their main efforts were directed at applying Habeas Corpus which was enshrined in the constitution but not respected. The day I saw them was the day after the government had repealed the public-security law which had been widely criticized as repressive. That law gave the government special powers for dealing with alleged sedition and violence, laying down procedures for the treatment of suspects. The young men were not happy about the repeal of the law. The repeal had satisfied the superficial idea that a law of this kind was tyrannical, but, they said, although they could not stand the law, its existence had at least meant that people could not disappear so easily without anyone knowing where they had gone. In effect, it had reduced the number of people vanishing without trace. They said that they had succeeded in about 80 per cent of the cases which they had initiated under the terms of the law. Their problem after the repeal was to find the legal basis for their actions.

One of the young men went on: 'The government has closed all democratic channels for the people's needs and desires, and if Communism exists, this is because it is the only way ordinary people can express their objections. If there is anything here against the democratic order it is the government's insistence on preventing any expression of opposition. In the last two or three general elections there was an evident situation of fraud, hence people do not believe in the democratic method.

'All the people we have helped here in this office were accused of subversion because in this country any protest, for better wages and a better standard of living, is seen by the government as subversion. Strikes are also broken under public-security legislation. Since 1940 only two strikes have been recognized as legal. The grounds on which the government usually opposes strikes are that the proper procedures have not been followed. Workers are supposed to advise management of their intentions a fortnight before they go on strike. Once the workers declare a coming strike their leaders are arrested.

'A few days ago workers in a branch of public transport set a strike and informed the authorities. The government by law had four days to decide whether or not the strike was acceptable. On the next day police arrested forty people: one of them died in prison and most of them were tortured. There were many witnesses to this. We estimate that 85 per cent of people arrested under the public-security legislation were tortured. There is, however, no system of torture. It is just left to the guards to do what they feel like. Once a person is arrested here they are supposed to appear before a tribunal within three days. We happen now to be handling a case of a person who has been held without trial for twenty-five days and many people have witnessed the tortures he has suffered. We assume that he is in so bad a physical state that the authorities have to hold him longer before showing him to his family. This is a common situation. It is not the exception. Certainly it is illegal detention. We believe that political repression is not an isolated fact: it is connected with economic and political problems which are getting worse, and so repression will get worse because people will be protesting more. If you take the official figures, one-half of the working population takes one-tenth of the national income. Between 5 and 7 per cent take 40 per cent. Since these figures were issued, the situation has got worse. If the Church here were not supported by international public opinion, this office could not function. International pressure is very useful and in some ways the only effective help to the Church which is the only institution defending human rights. The government does not interfere in our work but when legal proceedings are initiated, obstacles are put in our way. People working here are told they must watch out. The people here look on the Church's task as the protector of human rights more than preaching the Gospel. We cannot deal with all the cases brought to us.'

The bulletin of Archbishop Romero's office published three months before his murder carried a notice asking for news about the exact fate of a family of fourteen people 'exterminated' because they had been educated by their father, Pablo Mendoza, to respect the human person and love the poor. The people said to have been killed consisted of five children, five nephews, two brothers-in-law, a cousin and a son-in-law of Mendoza. The same issue of the bulletin gave statistics about violence. From 1966 to December 1979, 205 persons had disappeared for political reasons. In 1978 and 1979, some 1,501 persons had been imprisoned for political reasons. The national security forces in the course of the same two years had killed 896 persons. Apart from the six priests killed, eleven were in prison and twenty had been expelled from the country. From 22 to 31 January 1980, there had been 167 deaths and more than 200 injured. The worst single day was 22 January when twenty-one demonstrators were killed and 120 injured. The archbishop strongly denounced the killings in his sermon of 27 January in which he told the armed forces that their duty was that of serving the people and not the privileged few.

On the office wall there was a framed newspaper report of the request of 118 British Members of Parliament to give Archbishop Romero the Nobel Peace Prize. I asked the young lawyers what they thought of the hierarchy. The answer was: 'Most bishops want to maintain a position allowing them lines of contact with the government. They are not much in contact with human suffering and so see our problems in the abstract and do not want to become personally involved. Some may also be afraid of Communist infiltration of the Church but this is not the main reason for their attitude. Before Romero's appointment we were disappointed with the bishops but he listens to the people: he is in touch with them. He is deeply impressed with the suffering of the people. This is probably the main reason why he acts as he does. He has been criticized for the way he talks. Many people who hold economic and political power accuse the Church, and in particular the archbishop, of Marxist leanings. They have never been able to bring any proof. One of the reasons for the cruelty is that the soldiers who rule here come from poor families and are then accorded big privileges. Many higher-ranking soldiers are trained in Panama or the United States where they are taught anti-Communism. The archbishop is from a humble family of *campesinos* from near the border with Honduras.'

El Salvador has one of the highest birthrates in the world and one of the lowest standards of nutrition. One-third of its labour force is unemployed and another third underemployed. Justice no longer has meaning. Apart from the arbitrary arrests, torture and official killings that are widely reported, the ordinary visitor is quite likely to see scenes such as the stopping of a motor-coach by the police and the arrest of all its passengers, all young people. 'What will happen to them next', said a priest who witnessed the scene with me, 'is that they will have their hands roped together by the thumbs and the rope put under a tap so that the water shrinks it and makes it very painful. The reason is that they like inflicting pain and they are short of handcuffs.' The youthful prisoners looked serious and harmless. The police exuded evil and fanatical stupidity.

Romero's martyrdom did not put a stop to violence: not even to allow the hero a decent funeral. This is the account of that shocking event which Father James L. Connor, President of the Jesuit Conference in Washington, published in *America* magazine.

All went peacefully through a succession of prayers, readings, hymns until the moment in his homily when Cardinal Ernesto Corripio Ahumada of Mexico, the personal delegate of Pope John Paul II, began to praise Archbishop Romero as a man of peace and a foe of violence. Suddenly a bomb exploded at the far edge of the plaza, seemingly in front of the National Palace, a government building. Next, gun shots, sharp and clear, echoed off the walls surrounding the plaza. At first the cardinal's plea for all to remain calm seemed to have a steadying impact. But as another explosion reverberated, panic took hold and the crowd broke ranks and ran. Some headed for the side streets, but thousands more rushed up the stairs and fought their way into the cathedral.

As one of the concelebrating priests, I had been inside the cathedral from the start. Now I watched the terrified mob push through the doors until every inch of space was filled. Looking about me, I suddenly realized that, aside from the nuns, priests and bishops, the mourners were the poor and the powerless of El Salvador. Absent were government representatives of the nation or of other countries. The ceremony had begun at 11 a.m. and it was now after noon. For the next hour and a half or two, we found ourselves tightly packed into the cathedral, some huddled under the pews, others clutching one another in fright, still others praying silently or aloud.

The bomb explosions grew closer and more frequent until the cathedral began to shudder. Would the whole edifice collapse? Or would a machinegunner appear in a doorway to strafe the crowd? A little peasant girl of about 12 named Reina, dressed up in her brown-and-white-checked Sunday dress clung to me in desperation and cried, 'Padre, téngame.' We lived through that horror of bombs, bullets and panic—now dead bodies were being carried into the cathedral from outside—for nearly two hours. At certain moments one could not help wondering if we would all be killed.

I only saw the obvious stated in one place. That was a letter from a judge in Macerata who wrote to the *Corriere della Sera* asking why a travelling pope had not immediately set off for San Salvador to pick up the chalice which had dropped from Romero's hands and continue the Mass which the murdered archbishop had begun. Why indeed? I would place that failure on the same level as the Küng affair: both events show aspects of the Vatican which the outsider will never understand. I was told by a priest in Rome that he had had the same feelings and had expressed them. He was highly connected and was taken to the Vatican where he was privately shown a large file on Archbishop Romero, in which other bishops, from Latin America and elsewhere, expressed privately to the Vatican their opposition to the line he followed. This was taken to be good reason for allowing the murder to pass almost uncommented. What happened to Rome's Becket who offered the protection of the cathedral to the fearful women of Canterbury?

Father Connor again:

> As I sat huddled in the El Salvador Cathedral with thousands of terrified peasants, I found myself viewing the Salvadoran social situation with the poor and from their perspective of weakness, terror and oppression. I was given a vivid experience of the power of evil that can permeate the institutions and behaviour of those who fight to uphold an unjust system.

He might have added that terrorism only takes place when its perpetrators know that there will be no strong protest against what they do. They knew to what extent the archbishop was alone, because the development which had happened inside him was intimate, was a nuisance to his superiors and the subject, probably, of inaccurate reporting to Rome. It is true that Romero had been summoned back several times to give an account of himself, but these were not the conditions in which he showed to advantage. He would have been happy to know, however, that his principal mourners were the poor.

The awakening of the Catholic Church was endorsed in 1968 at the Medellin Conference of the Latin American hierarchy. In 1979, at the time of the Puebla Conference, it was estimated that in the whole of Latin America in the preceding decade about 1,500 priests and Catholic militants had been killed, imprisoned, or exiled. There was a bishop among those killed, the Argentinian Angelelli, as well as thirty-six priests. Amnesty International estimated that there were 17,000 political prisoners in Latin America, and over 30,000 people had vanished. The example of El Salvador was not so much out of step. Most governments in the sub-continent are dictatorial. Many of them claim that they are inspired by Catholicism and are protecting their countries' heritage from the threat of Marxism. This outlook is summed up in the philosophy of the national security state. The whole drive of this political theory is anti-Communist and conservative of the existing social pattern. The dictators who subscribe to this ideology can claim some sort of historical backing. Catholicism has been entrenched in the sub-continent since the Spaniards and Portuguese brought it under papal auspices in the sixteenth century. The Church has had to attempt an impression of renewal from a very difficult start. This process of shaking off its past political behaviour has not come from a troubled conscience so much as a realistic approach to a situation that shows clearly that the Church can no longer expect to be heard unless it dissociates itself from tyranny and injustice and, by implication, from much of its past.

D. H. Lawrence is suddenly likely to strike an instinctive vein that reveals a great deal in a few lines. He found this sort of vein with a remark applicable to religion in Mexico which went far beyond one country, in his novel *The Plumed Serpent*:

> For Jesus is no Saviour to the Mexicans. He is a dead God in their tomb. As a miner who is entombed underground by the collapsing of the earth in the gangways, so do whole nations become entombed under the slow subsidence of their past. Unless there comes some Saviour, some Redeemer to drive a new way out, to the sun.

Throughout Central America, Jesus is represented as a dead god, usually suffering the effects of torture and whipping, and frequently dressed in black robes or a robe of rust red, the colour of congealed blood. Even this depiction of hopeless suffering can be regarded as a form of protest against reality. It is only as a child that Jesus is represented as living and full of feelings unconnected with suffering or death.

Around the time of the Feast of Christ the King, the village streets fill with Christ-dolls and thrones to go with them, made in the traditional form of ecclesiastical chairs. There is an intense chatter around these impassive, elderly childish faces as the women try to decide which one they want to dominate the home; which child with a crown and a far-away look. Once installed, the child will be talked to, will hear intimate requests and be made to feel part of the complicated set of emotions that together amount to family life in a simple civilization. He will be treated with respect for what he is: the boy born to be king; and for what he will become: the flogged, wounded, pale man with a beard made straggly with sweat.

The reality is dreadful. Most of the sub-continent is under authoritarian rule. Much of the economy is dominated by multi-nationals who take out basic raw materials in return for impossible wages. Repression is of the crudest kind. The huge American influence has proved incapable of forcing military regimes to abide by some of the fundamental rules of fair government. Injustice, death, imprisonment, disappearances, violence, torture, are a part of the life of the sub-continent, and violent reaction to them is equally commonplace—at its most acute in Brazil, Paraguay and El Salvador.

The Catholic Church's role in this tragic story is of vital importance for a number of threatening reasons. About one-half of Catholicism is already to be found in Latin America, and the population is increasing very quickly. Politically, Latin America gives a deeply worrying indication of what the rest of the world would be like if it were to lose its ballast of political wisdom and moderation, which, it is well not to forget, does not look that remote a possibility for the West. The Western world will probably be much more like Latin America in the year 2000 than it is now. Latin America will be more and more with us as the second millennium approaches. A third reason why this region is so vital is that the Catholic Church there has made a remarkable attempt at renewing itself, including the rare step of publicly apologizing for its past mistakes.

Simplification is never easy in the field of institutional religion and its relationship with politics, and this is especially true where the temptation is to generalize, yet situations vary. There are strong differences between the hierarchies as well as divisions within individual Episcopal Conferences. There is still a strong conservative element in the Latin American Church. Argentina, for instance, has more reactionary prelates than has Brazil. More than anywhere else, Latin American raises the issue of the Church's relationship with violence, even more strongly than in Ireland, or Italy or the Basque country.

At the same time, Latin America has laid the foundations of a new and more realistic outlook on the contemporary situation, which has already been extremely influential. It is an attempt at bringing Catholicism back to the realities of life. The aim is to replace something which has always suffered from having been imposed by something devised from the basic facts of life. This is no easy subject because it has produced excesses and excessive reactions. The fundamental point is very simple. Latin American thinkers have evolved a new way of defining the responsibilities of Catholics. They study the situation in which the people, meaning the poor, live, and compare it with the Gospel accounts of the words and the actions of the historical Jesus. At the same time, they give much prominence to the exodus stories of the Old Testament as examples of the liberating presence of God in the biblical tradition. The methods of analysis of the situation are sometimes borrowed from Marxism, and the whole outlook is the opposite of the view that the purpose of the Church is to formulate doctrinal truths and pray. There is a fresh sense of the need for Christians to apply the principles of their religion to the societies in which they live, most of which in Latin America are dictatorships. The label given to these efforts is that of 'liberation theology' which is a pity because this is the sort of phrase which frightens people. Liberation to many minds is something which is almost sure to be dangerous and at its best will be embarrassing, like some de-complexed individual who rises from the psych-iatrist's couch and immediately begins to act badly.

I asked the extremely balanced Mexican theologian Father Carlos Soltero, how he saw developments in Latin America in his field and he replied: 'Theology cannot be a sort of abstract disquisition but has to be very much in contact with reality. Since reality in the world, and especially in Latin America, is a reality of poverty and lack of justice, the theological thinking of Latin Americans has gone along these lines. God's message and God's good news of salvation have also to mean an impulse to liberation, liberation from the really bad things that are afflicting our people, our poverty, our injustice.'

He was quite clear that such an attitude necessarily brought the Church into the political sphere: ' I do not think it can be avoided. No, an announcement of the Gospel along these lines has very many political consequences, but I think there is a fairly neat distinction between a Gospel message that has political consequences and a real political intervention on the part of the Church. The Church does not want, I think, to intervene in political affairs but feels her function is to announce the Gospel and this has a very large set of political implications and consequences.'

On the question of Marxist tendencies among liberation theologians, he said: 'Well, there is the danger of simplification when you speak about the theology of liberation because there are as many tendencies as there are theologians. I personally think that some of them have perhaps gone too far in their admiration of, and their recourse to, Marxism. That is my point of view, and I would not say that it is a feature of liberation theology itself. I do not think so. Of course these theologians see that, in order to construct an incarnated theology, theology has to take into account the real situation of the country and its people. In order to understand the situation, they have found the Marxist analysis of reality a help. I think that that can have some dangers but I also think that their efforts to understand reality have been honest and sincere. They have tried at the same time to adhere firmly to the Gospel and to the Christian faith. I think we have to be patient with these efforts and wait and see and not condemn them in advance.'

He added a comment on the views of these theologians on Jesus himself, which had not been well received by John Paul II: 'The aspect of the figure of Jesus which liberation theologians insist on is his engagement with the poor; that he came very especially to be with the poor and to be a poor man himself and to bring the good news to the poor . . . .'

The Church as a whole in Latin America should be given credit for taking a new course. It is not easy, to say the least, for Catholic bishops to admit their mistakes. At the Conference of the Latin American Church, with representatives from all the hierarchies, held at Puebla, they managed to do so with grace. They also managed to agree on an admirable analysis of the Latin American situation. The conference was overshadowed by the fact that

Pope John Paul II opened it as part of his highly publicized first journey outside Italy, and made a rather heavy-handed speech in which he set out his own ideas on Christology. Some of the satisfaction of the conference's work was diminished later by the election of a highly conservative chairman of the permanent organization of the Latin American bishops, but it would be absurd to underestimate the achievement of a Church which for centuries was regarded as the sleeping partner of colonial authority, in attempting now to seek a genuine relationship between its message and its knowledge of the Latin American reality. Several months after the end of the Puebla conference I was looking across the lake at Geneva, towards the old centre that Calvin knew, listening to a theologian prominent in the World Council of Churches, and his first comment was that the Catholics were at last on the move in Latin America.

This is neither the whole question nor the whole answer and the best of the liberation thinkers would concede as much. They are quite aware that they are a minority in the Latin American Church as a whole. A summary of what they feel was expressed with precision by the Peruvian priest Gustavo Gutierrez: 'The deep human impact and the social transformation that the Gospel entails, is permanent and essential because it transcends the narrow limits of specific historical situations and goes to the very root of human existence: the relationship with God in solidarity with other men. The Gospel does not get its full political dimension from one or another political option, but from the very nucleus of its message. If this message is subversive it is because it takes on Israel's hope: the Kingdom as "the end of domination of man over man; it is a Kingdom of contradiction to the established powers and on behalf of man." And the Gospel gives Israel's hope its deepest meaning: indeed, it calls for a "new creation". The life and preaching of Jesus postulate the unceasing search for a new kind of man in a qualitatively different society. Although the Kingdom must not be confused with the establishment of a just society, this does not mean that it is indifferent to this just society. Nor does it mean that this just society constitutes a "necessary condition" for the arrival of the Kingdom, nor that they are closely linked nor that they converge . . . .'

This is an intellectual argument, and it so happened that, for me, the most practical description of liberation theology came not from America but from a priest actively engaged in its application

317

to reality in Thailand. Liberation theology is no longer a Latin American affair. It has had its effect throughout the Catholic Church where problems of injustice and poverty are rampant.

I was in the Huaykwang suburb of Bangkok, half an hour's drive from the centre, at the Catholic Council for Development. Its executive chairman, Father Luan Nakphansa, was about to leave the job when I went to see him, and this factor, presumably, meant that he was more than usually anxious to explain his outlook. Thailand is not El Salvador but it is a conservative country ruled by a conservative administration with the help of the army.

Father Nakphansa quickly explained the Council's background. The Thai bishops decided to set it up after the Vatican Council, and gave the responsibility to Bishop Mansap (a vital and extremely engaging prelate), who appointed the chairman. The object was to make known the Church's teaching on human development, largely through seminars. The seminars dealt mainly with justice in society, with the task of making people aware of the need for justice. Twice a year the Council organized courses in rural leadership, community organization and development. Their aim was 'to do away with the dominant power, economic, social and cultural, because under domination people cannot develop. We must do away with what oppresses people. I am following liberation theology and you will find our scriptural basis in the fourth chapter of Luke. The mission of Christ is there and that is our theme and our answer.'

His first biblical reference was this quotation by Jesus of Isaiah at the beginning of his ministry:

> So he came to Nazareth, where he had been brought up, and went to the synagogue on the Sabbath day as he regularly did. He stood up to read the lesson and was handed the scroll of the prophet Isaiah. He opened the scroll and found the passage which says,
>> 'The spirit of the Lord is upon me because he has anointed me; he has sent me to announce good news to the poor, to proclaim release for prisoners and recovery of sight for the blind; to let the broken victims go free, to proclaim the year of the Lord's favour.'
> He rolled up the scroll, gave it back to the attendant, and sat down; and all eyes in the synagogue were fixed on him.

Father Nakphansa referred as well to an earlier passage in Luke which describes the teaching of John the Baptist about the need for honesty, not to be corrupt, not to use the power of the state to oppress the people.

The man with two shirts must share with him who has none, and anyone who has food must do the same. Among those who came to be baptised were taxgatherers, and they said to him: 'Master, what are we to do?' He told them: 'Exact no more than the assessment.' Soldiers on service also asked him, 'And what of us?' To them he said, 'No bullying; no blackmail; make do with your pay!'

The Magnificat also came into his theme, and this was one of the rare occasions on which I heard the name of Mary associated with social justice. In particular he liked the verses:

The deeds his own right arm has done disclose his might:
the arrogant of heart and mind he has put to rout,
he has brought down monarchs from their thrones,
but the humble have been lifted high.
The hungry he has satisfied with good things,
the rich sent empty away.

The Church recites this every day, he said, with some anger, but never touches the real point, because it would conflict with the political power. While trying to follow liberation theology, 'we cannot simply apply what is done in Latin America because we cannot use violence. Only in special cases you may listen to your conscience and decide that violence can be used. In Ireland for instance they judge that violence is necessary. We cannot impose our views on them but, according to Jesus Christ, there can be no violence.'

He did not align the Thai bishops with his own thinking. The majority shared the capitalist ideology, he said; with one, perhaps two, who were socialist. He regarded himself as a socialist. He did not blame the bishops for their attitude. If they were too socialist they would give a bad impression. 'Our weight is felt through the schools which are accepted by the dominant class. Our schools are full of an élite. Before, they had no schools of their own. Now the government has its own schools which are probably better than ours.

'The Mass is still very Roman. If we try to experiment, we are told we are going astray. Experiment is not accepted here. We must follow diocesan instructions. There are some progressive priests who experiment but most are Western priests, Redemptorists, Salesians, Jesuits, but the bishops and the ordinary people do not like it. We here have a seventh group just finishing a twice-yearly course. There are six girls out of twenty-four. Some of the participants are Buddhists. We make no distinction. We try to get

Muslims but that is very hard. There is no difficulty in our relations with Buddhists. What we want as a rule is to be witnesses to Christ. We try to show them what a Christian should do and we leave it at that. If they want to join us they can, just as if someone comes here for help with a project it does not matter if they are Catholic or not. We teach them to co-operate and to organize. We do not do relief projects except in bad cases. Our projects deal with water resources, buffalo and rice banks. We give a female buffalo to a group which becomes the property of the group and they arrange for it to breed. Rice is lent to people who are too hungry to work the fields. In December, when they harvest the rice, they give back the amount they borrowed with an additional two or three per cent.

'The seminaries are full with 150 students. Empty seminaries are one of the signs of the decline of the West. Soon Europe will be a mission territory. European birthrates are falling and nothing is done about immigration. Within a century or so all the real Europeans will have disappeared. We opened our own major seminary seven years ago and the first priests have emerged from it. Before, the élite had to go to Rome to study. I went to Penang.'

I found this account a fascinating mixture of conservatism and advanced social thinking. Its differences from its Latin American inspiration are imposed by the fact that Thai Catholics make up less than 0.5 per cent of the population.

An overwhelming Catholic majority does not necessarily cancel all feelings of humility as these two passages from the message to the people of Latin America sent from Puebla show. The first is the acceptance of fault:

> Christianity, which is the bearer of the originality of love, has never been practised in its integrity by us Christians. It is true that there has been much hidden heroism, much silent sanctity, and many marvellous gestures of sacrifice. Nevertheless we recognize that we are still a long way from living everything we preach. For all our failures and limitations we ask pardon, we the pastors, also of our brothers in the faith and the rest of humanity.

Dostoevsky could hardly have produced better sentiments.

The second passage touches on the relationship of religion with reality.

> Because we believe that the re-examination of the religious and moral behaviour of men and women ought to be reflected in the political and economic processes of our countries, we invite all,

without distinction of class, to accept and take up the cause of the poor, as if they were accepting and taking up their own cause, the very cause of Jesus Christ.

When it was fashionable in some bright circles to give God up for dead, one of the replies on an equal level of seriousness was that he was alive and well and living in Argentina. This is altogether too specific; what can be said is that the Christian conscience is genuinely moving in Latin America and because of the critical way it is moving, it either cannot or should not avoid a political role. That is the remaining area of choice and so it will remain until the political and social systems become reasonably respectful of basic human requirements.

The pope needs his 'little corner of earth' where he can feel free; the Vatican's policies are traditionally directed at winning a space for action by the Church within countries with Catholics in their population. Latin America is now a massive reminder that an ordinary human being, just to be and remain nothing more than ordinary, needs a minimum of mental and physical wellbeing to allow him to function. This is true of men anywhere. The distinction in the case of Latin America is that it is a huge zone of oppression and traditional injustice, exploited economically, despised politically, feared for the dreadful object-lessons it provides of what happens to the human race when the social structure is unjust, breeding terrorism and huge inhuman cities and, as well as all this, it is almost entirely Catholic. Many of the persecutors were no doubt brought up as Catholics at Catholic schools, of good Catholic families, like many of the fighters for liberation against oppression, whether Catholic or Marxist.

Social developments themselves are a harshening influence. The Brazilian Cardinal Arns maintains that in his archbishopric of Sâo Paolo the primary problem is that of the immigrants. Every year, he states, 300,000 poor people come to the city to look for work without any preparation at all for life there. The problem he sees is how to receive them, how to stop them becoming lost in the life of the city, losing both their religious feelings and their human qualities . . . .

When conditions are harshening to the point of dulling human qualities and the need to force change is urgent enough, the simplest form of political intervention emerges with the work of the terrorists. Their activities in the Catholic world are found in parts of Latin America, in Ireland, in Spain and in Italy. In all these manifestations the element is sought of what might be called a Catholic contribution. Does Catholicism have to share some of the blame for this typical phenomenon of the second Christian millennium? To be soft on Communism used to be the damaging allegation of the fifties: something similar is now alleged about the Catholic mentality and its relationship with terrorism.

There are some obvious connections: it is a well-worn truth by now that several of Italy's leading terrorists, or people suspected of supporting the terrorists, had strict Catholic educations. I spoke to a prominent investigator into Italian terrorism who said that in the course of his investigations he had spoken to leading church-men for two reasons: one was to try and understand better the mentality of the terrorists; the second was to know more about the priests who were on his lists of persons believed to be ready to offer sanctuary willingly to the terrorists of the Left. He added that, in the recent past, meetings of extremist groups, some of which had future terrorists among them, had taken place in halls put at their disposal by priests. One in particular which he mentioned was held in Florence in 1971 with representatives present of the Black Workers' Congress, two groups of Black Panthers, the IRA, a group from the Dominican Republic and others from Switzerland, West Germany and France. The hall was put at their disposal by a Jesuit.

The same phrase was used by two different people about the clergy in the Basque country of Spain and in Ireland: a writer on terrorism who does not insist much on the theory that Catholic-ism has a lot to answer for said that priests that he had met in Ireland seemed to feel more Irish than priests. I was given a similar judgement on the Basques. The first commentator, though agree-ing that Catholicism's contribution should not be pressed too hard, added: 'Of course, there is a part of the Catholic mentality which will never admit to being wrong and so they will believe implicitly that what they are doing is right.' The view of a traditionalist Catholic intellectual was that Catholicism could indeed become dangerously revolutionary and cruel if cut off from its anchorage in the transcendental. It is then of course no longer Catholic, but takes on a character of desperation because the religious foundations and disciplines have gone. There is another point, applicable both to Italy and to Ireland, that terrorism has now lasted so long that any philosophical roots which it once might have had have probably now been replaced by sheer professionalism. The attraction of violence in Ireland is said to be failing. According to Monsignor Edward Daly, the Bishop of Derry, young people are beginning to understand that violence achieves nothing. There was still plenty of it in the air of Derry: when I asked directions in the centre of the city for the Catholic cathedral, people showed me the long and circuitous route I was advised to take rather than risk attack by walking through a neighbourhood known to be violent.

There are wide differences in the views of Irish clerics about violence and its origins. Monsignor Daly maintains that the Ulster issue is not primarily a religious problem at all but a post-colonial situation, which he compared to Rhodesia. 'The Provos seem able to strike at will. There is much less backing for them now though in the Catholic community, but it fluctuates. If the British troops do something stupid for instance, people are shocked and the Provos can whip up passion behind them. What we have here is not so much Roman Catholics against Protestants but Roman Catholics against anti-clericalism. Ecumenical meetings are picketed by Paisley's men. Any Protestant churchman or politician who shows any sense of *rapprochement* or willingness to come closer or work closer with members of the Catholic Church will usually find that it is the prelude to the end of their careers. Protestants find they are losing their supporters to Paisley and so are getting more hard-line. You see that for the European elections the Catholics voted for a moderate—John Hume—while the Protestants voted for the extremist Paisley. Here, historical memories are still long. Protestants fear that if there is a change in the situation they will suffer the same sort of things that the Catholics have had to suffer. Remember that Derry, which is 70 per cent Catholic, did not have its first Catholic mayor until 1974.

'In Derry there has been a close relationship between people and priests. Usually the priests backed civil rights movements but were frequently under attack for not protesting enough. When the Church took a stand against violence many young people felt let down by the Church and stopped practising. But in the last three years there has been a big increase in church-going. About 90 per cent of our Catholics go to Sunday Mass. We also help organize ecumenical committees to deal with such problems as alcoholism and wife-bashing. I would say that a living, caring church is emerging.

'Many worry about the effect of the violence on children. It seems to me that only those directly involved in violence suffer. In general, the children have been very resilient. Many young people have known only violence from the age of about six, hence their revulsion against it because they see that it goes on for years but achieves nothing. I myself have given the last rites to thirty-four people including some British soldiers. I would say that 90 per cent of the population is against violence.

'Paisley's appeal is based entirely on anti-Rome sentiments. He frightens people by telling them what will happen when the Vatican gets it hands on the North; he plays on fear that Catholics are simply marionettes manipulated by Rome. The mere fact that an idea was put forward by the Catholic bishops would result in its rejection, however good it was, on the grounds it was a Roman plot. That is why we are loath to promote ideas publicly.

'Our policy as bishops is the following: Britain must stop regarding the Irish problem as a domestic issue and bring it into the international arena. The European Community might provide this arena. Another move must be made similar to the Sunning- dale experiment by which both sides would be represented right up to cabinet level. The British government should declare that the unity of the Irish people is desirable and the Irish Republic must react by reviewing the legislative situation. They should arrive at some form of federation, and ultimately, a long, long time in the future, the time would be ripe for a united Ireland.'

All this is said in the full knowledge that it is unacceptable politically to Ulster's Protestants. However much the attempt is made to find some other label for the Northern Ireland tragedy, it is clear that religion has a great weight. The cost has been dreadful and much too easily forgotten: since the intervention of the British troops in August 1969, over 2,000 people have died and 20,000 have been injured. What is worse is the indifference and the bleak acceptance of what should be regarded as an intolerable situation. I went to Ulster for the first time in 1979 and although I live in a country where the terrorists are active enough, I had not foreseen how shocking the impression is that Northern Ireland makes. Some bright commentators maintain that the terrorists intend installing a Marxist state which would make the whole island a European Cuba. That, by comparison with the atmosphere now, could scarcely be much worse. It might even be preferable to the slow process of calcification of human qualities which is happen- ing now.

A Redemptorist monk on the Falls Road talked about the vandalism and the violence within the Catholic community. They threaten each other with the IRA; they cruelly beat up people whom they feel are out of line, and not on matters concerning the Protestant and Catholic abyss—just if you are out of line. A recent victim was a mentally retarded boy who had not shown the proper respect for the dominant gang in the area. Police are not accepted in the Falls Road area, and so these people know that only a gun brings results. They are convinced, the monk went on, that the only way the Great Powers will take notice is if they are made to suffer violence. It is regarded as the only lesson they will understand. And if, of course, you cross the line laid down by religious prejudice, there is trouble. Some nuns and priests took part in a peace march in a Protestant area and they were spontaneously embraced by Protestant women. When the same nuns and priests took part in a peace march in the Falls Road they were stoned: 'Peace without change is a sell-out here.'

The monk regularly visited the 'blanket-men' in the Maze prison. These are inmates who were demanding special status as political prisoners. They refused to be regarded as common criminals. The British government changed its attitude three times on these IRA demands for special recognition. They were granted this 'special category' status in 1972 and the minister then responsible, William Whitelaw, has since said that he made a mistake. The idea of political status was in practice withdrawn in March 1976. Many men convicted after that date, who could have expected that status had it not been withdrawn, began a long and revolting form of protest. They refused to wear prison clothes and so wore none at all. They would not work and so lost all privileges except basic ones laid down by statute. They later took to fouling their cells and so reduced their own living quarters to disgusting and foul-smelling conditions. In October 1980 the British government decided to abolish prison uniform throughout Ulster. This, in effect, gave the IRA prisoners the substance of what they wanted without granting them the principle. The decision was taken on the eve of a hunger-strike, at a time when the Irish primate, Cardinal O Fiaich, was known to be pressing for a move to end the self-imposed horrors of prison life for the IRA. It was immediately denounced as a surrender by the Reverand Ian Paisley, leader of the extremist wing of Ulster Protestantism.

This is the description the monk gave of life for the protesting prisoners: 'They put on their trousers to go to Mass. Provos traditionally have a gun in one hand and their beads in another. Some of them have been denied all physical and intellectual stimulus for two years. The state should be above such things. The average age of the blanket-men is between eighteen and twenty-two. I have my doubts that they can survive what they are doing to themselves psychologically. Some of them are reading the Bible for the first time. We also found that they were tearing out the pages of their Bibles to smear their faeces on the wall of their cells. I find when I go there that the smell makes me ill—it is overpowering. They are doing this as a protest against having their special status taken from them and being treated as ordinary prisoners. That is why they refused to wear prison clothes.'

This Redemptorist was a generously built southern Irishman. He had a lot that was interesting to say about the Church in Ireland but on the question of politics and violence he was as perplexed and as saddened as any of the good people on either side of this vicious quarrel. He hoped there would be a statement of intent on future unity from the British government so that there would no longer be a political issue about which to quarrel, and then the religious aspects might be less highly charged. 'You know that in the mid-seventeenth century the pope officially told his representative in Ireland, the name was Rimuccini, to keep out of politics. The reply that went back to Rome was that there was no way. I would say that the Protestants are not fighting primarily against religion though they feel that home rule means Rome rule.' Moreover, as time passes, the power of religion itself is, he said, being whittled away. By the time we reach the year 2000, attendance at Mass will have dropped to 40 per cent, which is less than half the figure revealed by the 1974 survey. 'We are conscious of a dreadful falling-off of the faith, especially in these urban areas. Certainly the political incentive is less strong. Years ago before independence, to be anti-English meant being Irish and Catholic. There is less of that now. Even so, those who used to pack the churches did so for the wrong reasons: three out of five did so out of fear or habit.'

There is still plenty of old-fashioned religion in the Falls Road. That particular morning was a special one: first, it was Father's Day. The famous Catholic ghetto had a lot to celebrate. A line of small children at Mass take turns to stand in front of the microphone to read little poems or messages to their fathers who smile broadly but with a touch of embarrassment at a jolt from the wife. The priest calls for prayers to thank father for all that he has done to help the family. Every seat is taken and the back of the huge, nineteenth-century church is packed with people standing, many with children in their arms. In the hall across the square, young people are practising traditional dancing. Catholics, a priest points out, are much more concerned than Protestants with maintaining popular culture. The Protestants, he said, seem to have none, or prefer to forget it.

It was not just Father's Day that was packing the church that morning. There was also a novena in honour of a painting of the Madonna that happens to be in Rome but is much revered in Falls Road, because of the Redemptorist connection. The painting is known as the Madonna of Perpetual Help. Girls outside the church sold little orange booklets telling the story of this image. It is said to be Eastern in origin and was brought from Crete to Rome at the close of the fifteenth century. After its arrival in Rome, strange events took place. One was that the Virgin appeared to a little girl and told this favoured child that she wished to have her picture exposed for veneration between the two Roman basilicas of St Mary Major and St John Lateran. The picture was enshrined over the high altar in the Augustinian Church of St Matthew that indeed lay between these two basilicas. The image was honoured there for three centuries (1499–1798) and was called 'The Mother of Perpetual Succour', because the Virgin, when giving her message to the child, introduced herself as 'Holy Mary of Perpetual Succour'. In 1798 St Matthew's was destroyed by a French army and the Augustinian fathers took the picture to a neighbouring monastery. Later they placed it in their own oratory at St Maria in Posterula where it remained hidden until 1866.

In the meantime, a new church was built by the Redemptorists almost on the site of the old St Matthew's. The miraculous picture was rediscovered at Posterula and Pope Pius IX, having heard its story, ordered that it be restored to its former place of honour and entrusted its guardianship to the Redemptorist Congregation. He commissioned them to spread everywhere devotion to the picture: 'Make the Mother of Perpetual Succour known', he said, 'throughout the world.' That is how she came to Falls Road in Belfast. One of the petitions in the order of service of the novena devotions is that 'All our people may be usefully employed and have decent houses to live in . . .' That perfectly reasonable request is, alas, in the Northern Ireland of today, dependent on a political decision and an end to violence. Meanwhile, the missing sense of security is being provided by Valium. In 1979 the one and half million people in Northern Ireland took thirty-five million tranquillizers.

Is religion what really makes the Irish problem intractable? Is the miserable state of Ulster simply the last, anachronistic, war of religion in Europe? And if so, how is it that Catholics and Protestants have settled comfortably into the prevailing political system in all the other countries of Europe as well as in the United States? The answer seems to be that elsewhere Catholics and Protestants, even when in a minority, have managed to find issues on which to vote which do not directly concern their religion. Most Catholics in England vote for the Labour Party, but that party's attempts at favouring specific Catholic interests are not notable. Almost everyone in Italy is nominally Catholic but that has not prevented a Protestant from becoming prime minister, and there the real issue is less whether Catholic interests should be cultivated than whether Catholics should any more be expected to vote unitedly for their own political party, the Christian Democrats. The Christian Democrats in West Germany like to give the impression that they have Evangelical support as well as Catholic votes. That intermixture might have continued in Ireland had it not been broken by the issue of self-government for Ireland which dominated the political scene from 1886. The break in the North between Conservatives (who were Protestant) on the one hand and the interdenominational Liberal Party ceased to be the dividing line, because the Liberal alliance broke on the national issue, and the new line saw Protestants on one side and Catholics on the other. No political issue has been found which will allow the people of Ulster to part religion from politics. This is the distinguishing feature of the Irish tragedy, which has made of it a fertile stage for terrorism and degradation. Religion's healing power is only likely to be able to operate when politics alone become the dividing issue.

My conversations in Ireland took place before John Paul II visited the country on the way to the United States, and before Cardinal O Fiaich, the Irish primate, made his appeal in London in March 1980 for British Roman Catholics to speak up on the issue of Ulster:

> Perhaps at times it is the Catholic Church alone which can get across the message to the people of Great Britain that only a tiny minority of Irish people can be called terrorists, and that the desire of so many Irish men and women to see their country united is a

natural and legitimate thing, no less worthy of support than the desire of other Irish men and women in Northern Ireland to remain within the United Kingdom.

Almost to the day that the cardinal spoke of that tiny minority of terrorists in Ireland I had the chance to read letters dealing with the Vatican's reaction to the kidnapping in Rome in March 1978 of Aldo Moro, the best known of Italy's Catholic politicians and, with Mountbatten, who died at the hands of the IRA, the most illustrious victim so far of any terrorist group. The letters were written by Moro himself from captivity at the hands of the Red Brigades. One was to Pope Paul VI and another to his wife in which he complained bitterly of the refusal of the Vatican to bargain with the terrorists for his release. One is typewritten and was presumably a copy taken by his captors for their files. The handwriting of the second is awkward and clearly that of a man under great tension, though lucid for all that. Moro always had a rather ponderous hand. Its sprawl had increased as a result of the tension of seizure and captivity. He was trying to find a way to save his own life, and the letter to the pope was intended to do two things: first, to complain about an article which had appeared in the Vatican's newspaper, *L'Osservatore Romano*, stating that the Church could have no part in any action amounting to surrender to pressure from the terrorists. The second aim was to persuade the pope to use his influence with the Italian government to accept an exchange of political prisoners which would, Moro thought, have brought about his release. 'Having seen', he told the pope, 'here in my prison, a severe article of the *Osservatore*, I am extremely worried by it because what other voice, if not that of the Church, can break the crystallization which has taken shape, or what humanism is there higher than Christian humanism? And so my prayers, my hopes, those of my unfortunate family which Your Holiness was so kind to receive a few years ago, are addressed to Your Holiness, the only person who can bend the Italian government to an act of wisdom.' In the letter to his wife, Moro refers to the Vatican's attitude of no negotiation as 'ignoble and unworthy of the Holy See'.

These letters are moving testimony to the last efforts of a politician, who was himself a born negotiator, to fend off what was probably his inevitable end. They are fascinating because he clearly thought that the papacy would have been willing to make contact with his captors. It may simply have been a desperate tactic, or he may have thought that his long personal friendship with Paul VI would somehow have brought the Vatican into a negotiation. He placed his hopes in the papacy but Paul VI would go no further than an appeal, a very beautiful one, but nothing more; while later, long after Moro met his fate, John Paul II was to prove implacable in his condemnation of terrorism. A matter of days after writing these letters, Moro was executed by his captors. Instead of the one bullet which ended Archbishop Romero's life, a whole burst encircled his heart.

As the anniversaries pass of the day on which Moro was kidnapped, the background is once more gone over in leading articles, at conferences, at discussions, and one of the subjects inevitably raised is whether Catholicism should be blamed for shaping the minds of some of the country's terrorists. The pope's lead helped muster the Church's forces to increased condemnation of the phenomenon but the idea of guilt is unpopular. I remember one of the most indignant and unpleasant-sounding reactions to a political speech that I have heard came during the Christian Democrat National Congress in Rome in early 1980 when one of the delegates spoke of terrorism and commented, 'There are also some sons of ours among them.' Howls of dismay greeted the observation. (In fact, the allegedly terrorist son of a leading Christian Democrat was later involved in a celebrated political scandal.)

I find it difficult to suppose that terrorism is just a passing phenomenon. Equally difficult is the idea that there will be more social justice in the future world, more consideration for the poor and fewer suffering oppression. It is in this sense that Archbishop Romero was a more important figure than many people supposed. Many of his fellow-bishops in Latin America opposed his behaviour, and their views were taken into full consideration at the Vatican. Another reason why the Vatican underestimated him was the same limitation from which I suffered myself: it was impossible to understand his significance, just as it was impossible to grasp the horrors of El Salvador's regime, without going there. Moreover, the Vatican's political reporting from the capital was of no high quality. The cause of Romero's martyrdom was very simple—he fell a victim to the idea that the Church must accept a political role if that is the inevitable consequence of its denunciation of injustice and its defence of the poor. El Salvador was the terrorist system raised to a form of government. His challenge to it was not at all on the lines of Becket—almost the opposite. He was reluctantly forced into asserting the claims of the unprivileged and the poor and the suffering. He was not putting forward the claims of one authority against another. His approach was also the opposite of terrorism. This is not to imply that Becket had anything in common with terrorism, but to suggest that his day is done, for the moment at any rate.

14

RACE AND RIGHTS

I WAS TOLD IN Washington that American Catholics accept capitalism because they feel that America has shown that it can work. In Milwaukee I was told that Catholics in Communist countries were much more critical of injustices in their system than Catholics are about the shortcomings of the Western world. In Dar-es-Salaam I heard argued with considerable conviction that the priest of the future would have to learn to live as part of a socialist society, and uncomfortably at that. Somewhere in the middle of this apparent confusion were the accounts I had in Toronto, Montreal and Quebec of the Canadian Church's challenge to the ethics of the business world and the consequent allegations that the Church had fallen into the hands of the Left.

What this means in effect is that the Catholic political presence is not limited to situations of high drama. This presence does not have to involve intrigue and murder and resistance to oppression. It can be quite ordinary but not, for that reason, unimportant. Relations with the political world in societies which are not oppressive can be as fundamental in effect as a clash with a tyrant There are two classic cases as far as the relations with capitalist societies go: there is the French-Canadian experience of a church which, at great cost, has freed itself from its traditional position as part of the political system, and there is the example of the Church in the United States which has reached the position due to it at the heart of national affairs from humble beginnings as a church largely made up of poor immigrants.

I was having tea with Cardinal Carter in Montreal and he told me that attendance at Mass in Quebec province had dropped in a matter of a few years from about 80 per cent of Catholics to about 10, 'and in some places they don't even make that.' He is Archbishop of Toronto but was staying with his sister in Montreal for St Patrick's Day. I had supposed that the Catholic Church would still be strong in Quebec. Traditionally it represented an integral part of French-Canadian culture and ethnic identity. If the Catholic Church had failed to defend the position of the French in Canada, the British would not have been forced to respect this huge enclave of old-fashioned European culture in the midst of the New World. It has a strong separatist movement which has known its moments of violence and could be seen as in some degree similar to the Irish question. It seemed to have everything to maintain its appeal. I had taken for granted that French-Canadian Catholicism would still follow its old-fashioned ways. Quebec, after all, represented a large survival, outside France, of French provincial life untouched by the French Revolution, and many priests at the beginning of the nineteenth century who were used to the partnership between Church and State which marked the *ancien régime* fled to Canada after the revolution and brought their extreme conservatism with them. I would have looked to the English-speaking rather than the French-speaking Catholics to provide a sense of initiative and modern ways, though without the French weight of Catholic fervour.

But the cardinal said that his traditionally English-speaking archdioces raised more money for the Church than the whole Quebec province. The French-speakers are nowadays much less conservative than English-speaking Catholics and their society is more secularized. The situation was different from that of the United States and sometimes the opposite: the Church in the United States was much more clerical. He said: 'Here, especially in Quebec, there is now a lot of anti-clericalism. The Church in Canada respects private property. We do not mind a little profit but profit in itself is not regarded as enough. In the United States the Catholics had to build their own system of schools and that is why they have such an exaggerated view of money.' Suspicion crept in at this point and I remembered the warning of a priest about the cardinal: 'Emmett Carter may try to con you.' Then I remembered something else which confirmed what the archbishop was saying: the sign on the till in a Louisiana bar which read, 'Trust him: he paid in full for our sins.' What better reason could there be for worship?

Three cardinals' hats hang like so many dusty anachronisms in the apse of Quebec's basilica, a warning of the mummified condition in which the Catholic Church can find itself when it becomes an integral part of the system. That was what the Catholic Church did in French-speaking Canada, and those dusty hats are a symbol of the price that had to be paid, eloquently expressed that bitterly cold morning by the few people at Mass and the high average age as well as middle-class origins of those left to contemplate the vestiges of what used to be a great army. The drama of Quebec's Catholicism is one of the outstanding cautionary tales of the century and, perhaps for that very reason, often overlooked.

In Quebec, the Catholic Church controlled the hospitals, social services, schools and universities; it inspired legislation on morals; and it was politically in open alliance with the defenders of this strange enclave of French culture in the North American continent. The British were generous to the Quebec Church, legitimizing its position in 1774 and granting it special powers, including the possibility of raising taxes because they feared Quebec might look south towards the thirteen rebellious colonies. The idea of the immigrants that a new mode of the *ancien régime* could survive in Quebec was correct. Its end did not come until about twenty years ago.

Before the Second World War there were signs of challenge to the system. Young Catholics heard about political liberalism apart from the context of anathema with which the Church surrounded it, and about the trade-union movement too, which the Church also condemned. Change was due to begin but was artificially suppressed. There came the war and then the sixteen years of rigidly conservative rule by the vigorous and inflexible Maurice Duplessis that ended only with his death in 1959. He sat on Quebec, in the cardinal's words, and impeded development. His departure allowed room for what was called 'The Quiet Revolution', a misleading name because it has been compared in strength of feeling with the civil-rights movement in the United States. Cardinal Carter sees it more as an example of 'violent evolution'. 'They simply blew the lid off a pot which had been kept boiling too long.' The Church was banished from its place in institutionalized society and, at times, must have looked near to extinction. For instance, the 1971 national census showed that twelve times as many inhabitants of Quebec said they did not believe in God, compared with the 1961 census. Practically everyone went to church in Duplessis's time. The basilica still gives this feeling of being accustomed to crowds. Why else would the few people gathered under the cardinals' hats seem so painfully insufficient?

The relationship is a strange one between the Catholic Church and Quebec's urge for its own identity. The French-Canadians felt—they still feel—oppressed by the English-speaking minority. 'English is power' is one of their bitter phrases to express how much they resent the fact that a person must have English to back his ambitions. The English-speaking Catholics used to be shown profound disdain by being described as 'Protestants without knowing it'. But the French-Canadians turned on their own church when the revolution came, casting it aside as one of their oppressors and so the Church lost its hold over society. Some of its priests probably sympathize with the separatist movement which seeks to make Quebec province independent from the rest of Canada, but their contribution is not important. For the Church, now, to show some relevance it has to be seen to be involved in the cause of genuine justice. The effect has gone far beyond the French-speaking areas. Canada has about ten million Catholics, which is half the population, and more than two-thirds of them are in Quebec province. What happens there has its effect throughout Canadian Catholicism. The Quebec revolution is one of the reasons why Canadian Catholicism is now nearer in social commitment to the Latin American Church and to Europe than it is to the Church in the United States.

In 1979, Montreal saw the biggest of the 155 St Patrick's Day processions in its history. For hours the centre of the city was blocked with top-hatted Irish, the effigy of the green-clad saint himself riding in an open car. 'It is', said a member of the crowd, 'almost a sacred affair.' There were representatives from 185 parishes, clubs, unions, even a local fire-brigade, from all over the province, and visiting contingents from across the border in the United States. Green balloons, top-hats hung with shamrock and clover, buttons labelled 'Kiss me—I'm Irish' set the atmosphere. For the first time the parade was televised by the Canadian Broadcasting Corporation, and the sun shone from a cloudless sky to give the final seal of triumph to an impressive occasion. The procession was a mile in length. There were 300,000 people to watch it. The message was clear: with separatism in the air, a substantial section of the English-speaking Catholics wanted to point out that they were very numerous and that they, too, had been in the province for a long time but separatism was not for them. There was no need for the organizers to refuse permission for supporters of the reunion of Ulster with Ireland to take part in the parade with their banners, for the obvious to be perfectly clear: the Irish Catholics preferred a situation of English-speaking minority predominance to separatism on the lines of French Catholic ambitions.

The head of the Jesuits in Toronto, Father William Ryan, happened to have lived in Washington immediately before moving north. He was in a good position to compare the Catholic Church in the two countries. The United States, he said, had a much more authoritarian tradition. Bishops would seldom act on their own initiative. In Canada the tradition is that when there is trouble, send a bishop. In the States, the bishops boycotted conferences of women's movements; but not here, though the feminists are less strong in Canada. When the priests were organizing after the Vatican Council they invited a bishop to sit in on their meetings. 'This must mean', he said, 'that some of the bishops feel more self-possessed: they will act on their own. They must trust the people, I guess.

'Moreover, Canadians are always looking for a way of avoiding confrontation. This is probably due to our English roots and to our conscious efforts in the past not to provoke a clash between the French and the English-speakers. This is not by tradition a Church of confrontation.

'At the height of its power in Quebec, it was the most pervasive Church anywhere in the world. It penetrated every facet of life but wherever there was a clash between nationalism and a bishop, nationalism won. In 1890 a bill was put to the Quebec legislature against the use of trains for Sunday excursions. The measure was introduced by the Protestants and backed by the Catholic bishops. The measure failed. During the period of disengagement when the Church turned over welfare work and schools to the state, there were never violent attacks on the Church nor resistance from the Church to disengagement. We are now facing the first generation of highly educated French-Canadians. Despite the drop in attendance at Mass, the bishops did not panic. Women are becoming active in French-Canadian parish life. Two are chancellors of diocesan courts. There is much more criticism of capitalism than in the States and social views are much more advanced. There is a good deal of Marxism in Quebec: it seems more at home there than anywhere else in North America. There is close co-operation with the Anglicans, the Presbyterians and the United Church in the social field. Legislation on medical care came into being because the churches and the unions were together on the issue. There is nothing comparable in the States to this ongoing dialogue which takes the form of a real and effective coalition. On the Alaska pipeline for instance, the Church took up the Indian cause, and got the route changed. At the 1971 Synod in Rome, Monsignor Alexander Carter, brother of the cardinal and Bishop of Sault Sainte Marie, was cut off while speaking against the multinationals.

'It is a mistake to look just at Quebec: other provinces want sovereign powers for different reasons, such as Alberta, or British Columbia. This attitude is difficult to combine with strong international stances. This loosening process makes government from the centre almost impossible. Under Lester Pearson Canada had a leadership role which it no longer has. The Church feels this also: the National Episcopal Conference is one of the best in the world and until about 1970 was effective, but partly due to the Quebec question this has changed. The change is also due to the feeling that the regional base should be strengthened. Quebec and Ontario, in particular, now have strong regional conferences but the National Conference is weakened. There is tension on this. Some blame the French-Canadians for splitting the Church; others say that it is the best thing that could have happened. There is no unanimity among the bishops on separatism. They say they will "go with the people". They are not officially supporting unity or separatism though they insist on the rights of minorities.'

Catholicism in the United States will probably in the end have to come round to something resembling the critical posture towards society of the Canadian Church, especially the attacks on the multinationals and what used to be called, in a Europe rather less to the right than it now is, the unacceptable face of capitalism. But the situation in the United States is much more complicated, both racially and ideologically. In fact, in many ways it could be the church of the future *par excellence*, if it eventually finds its balanced orientation. In the meantime, it can certainly boast the pure example of a political event which meant much more to American Catholicism than any religious event. It was Archbishop Rembert Weakland, of Milwaukee, former head of the Benedictine order, who put the issue succinctly: 'The election of Kennedy had far more importance for American Catholicism than the

Vatican Council.' New vistas were opened of a kind that the African bishop summed up with his comment on the election of a Polish pope that, at last, anyone could be elected. So, with Kennedy's election, the fearing of never fully belonging to American society was exorcized. Curiously, the Vatican at the time was not particularly happy about the election of Kennedy. There was obvious satisfaction that the greatest country of the Western world had its first Catholic president, but there were subcurrents of feeling that Kennedy personally was not the ideal person to break into the magic circle—too superficial, too rich, too unpredictable. As his reputation has fared since, that was not so misplaced a view.

For American Catholics, there was relief that they no longer had to applaud the spectacle of a tubby little Archbishop of New York, Cardinal Spellman, who rushed to Vietnam with vulgar flag-flying and belligerent encouragement of the troops, in the hope of proving that American Catholics were just as American as anybody and every bit as patriotic, with no less propensity than other prominent citizens—as the late Cardinal Cushing showed when photographers were about—to put on funny hats and kiss children. Weakland himself is probably the model, modern American Catholic prelate: highly intelligent, with international experience as head of his religious order, sophisticated, self-assured and less perturbed about the heavy-handedness of Rome than at the quality of his fellow-bishops, which generally, in America, is regarded as still too low to lead this Church at such a crucial moment, both in its own life and in its growing international awareness. Even the Kennedy election solved only part of the problem. Before that event, Catholics felt themselves to be a second-class minority in a Protestant society. After the election, they no longer had to prove anything. They began to take their place in society and, in Weakland's words, 'probably were not ready for it'.

This in itself is not very remarkable considering the speed with which Catholicism has grown. In 1776, there were about 30,000 baptized Catholics in the newly born United States, and they represented the same percentage of the population as Catholics in Asia today—around 1 per cent. There are now well over sixty million—approaching a third of the population—and they are the biggest single religious group. Of this sixty million a little under one million are Negroes; perhaps a third are Spanish-speakers, largely from Mexico and Puerto Rico, and the rest come from the earlier waves of immigrants, led by the Irish. The system of capitalism which has made America the greatest power in the world was formed on the backs of Catholic immigrants. Most of them were of humble origin: they came from countries in Europe that had no interest in them and were relieved to see this weight of hopeless humanity leave their shores. They were castaways thrown by the million onto an ocean which made of them the basic raw material of America's industrial power. Developing industrial might needs the cast-offs, and if they are not available they have to be created, as was the experience of the Industrial Revolution in Britain which transferred its labour from the land to improvised slums where life lost most of its humanity.

Many of the immigrant communities were led by their priests, and this explains why Catholicism in the United States was able to retain the loyalty of the working classes. Collaboration between Catholicism and the trade unions has been traditional. Andrew Greeley sees the unions as the other crucible, with the parishes, in which American Catholicism was formed. There is now apparently an undermining of this co-operation. Catholic leaders share public criticism of the unions on the grounds of alleged greed and corruption in the movement, and they attack the unions on the grounds of fostering racism. That is probably a part of the process of full Catholic integration into American society, as is the fact that Catholics have now reached the national average on divorce —Catholics and non-Catholics alike now see one in two of their marriages end in divorce. Almost surely, criticism of the unions cannot be taken to mean that American Catholicism is now on the side of big business. From the Kennedy election to the drawn-out intensification of the Vietnam war there may have been the feeling about capitalism expressed at the National Episcopal Conference that Catholics, like other Americans, 'feel we have made it work'. If they still feel this (and, as I say, I think many do not), they would be running against two formidable shapers of Catholic opinion.

The first is recent papal teaching. Paul VI was strongly critical of capitalism, mainly because of the blame he felt it must bear for the increasing injustice of rich and poor countries in the world. John Paul II has never lived under a capitalist (or for that matter a democratic) system, and, far from absence making the heart grow fonder, he is unrelenting in his attacks on what he clearly sees to be the worst of modern problems: the permissive consumer society. I asked a high-ranking prelate in the Vatican whether I was right in supposing that the pontiff abhorred the permissive society more than the Communist society to which he was accustomed, and I had an unequivocally positive reply. John Paul II is not at home with capitalism and I very much doubt that he would agree that America has shown that capitalism can work. One gathers the Dalai Lama would agree with him, despite his years of exile and the Chinese attempt to obliterate Buddhism from Tibet.

The Catholic position on capitalism and democracy is of fundamental importance for the future, because at least it seeks to question the usually unspoken but widely held belief that capitalism and democracy are the natural partners and that democracy cannot be made to work within the framework of any other economic system. That belief is what the National Episcopal Conference, reflecting the views of the American bishops, seems to be endorsing. Certainly the American example is the weightiest demonstration of the two acting together that the world has known. It must, however, bring difficulties for American Catholics: for a start, the Church itself is not a democratic body. Bishop Thomas C. Kelly, general secretary of the Conference, puts the Church's feelings about democracy in this way: 'We try to say this Church is not a democratic society but people here see democracy in everything. The Church influences democracy but democracy does not have an effect on the Church.' Even if one puts aside John Paul II's dislike of the West's economic system in practice and the Church's refusal to endorse democracy fully, there is a close resemblance between Catholicism's way of judging both economic and political systems. It does not endorse: it judges the merits and defects of any system by the extent to which the system allows scope for the Church's activities and aims. There is a degree of economic as well as political agnosticism in the Church's current appraisal of society.

This is how Bishop Kelly put the American Church's position in testimony to Democratic and Republican Platform Committees for the 1980 presidential election. He set off from the position which dominates much of Catholic thinking about public affairs: the promotion of human rights. These were the three moral principles which he saw to be at the heart of Catholic teaching on social and economic justice:

> 1. Human dignity is the criterion of a just economy and a human world. It is protected by a set of fundamental human rights. These include the right to the basic necessities without which full human development is impossible.

340

Pope John Paul II during his recent visit proclaimed this essential human dignity. In his address to the United Nations, for example, he said: 'Every analysis must start from the premise that . . . every human being is endowed with a dignity that must never be lessened, impaired or destroyed, but must instead be respected and safeguarded.' In enumerating basic rights essential to human dignity, Pope John Paul listed, among others, the rights to employment, food, housing, health care and education.

2. The primary responsibility of the state is to serve the common good. It has a responsibility to adopt economic policies to ensure that the essential needs of all its people are met. These needs include adequate income, employment, food, shelter, health care, education and access to the necessary social services. All persons have the right to these basic necessities; and the government as the provider of last resort has the responsibility to ensure that they be made available to all.

3. As Christian believers, we are knowingly and willingly biased in our approach to social and economic problems. We stand with the poor and attempt to analyse public policy with a special concern for them. When their fundamental rights are in danger, we protest: when programs are offered to improve their condition, we applaud.

Papal thinking as expressed by Paul VI and, much more aggressively, by John Paul II is harsh on capitalism, and this harshness coincided with blows to the system from other sources. Vietnam broke the image of irresistible and idealistic power based on the twin foundations of free enterprise in the economy and in politics. Oil was equally damaging. 'We suddenly found ourselves', in the words of a lofty American prelate, 'held to ransom by a bunch of Arabs.' This was part of the vision of 'much greater confusion and uncertainty' to which Monsignor George Higgins, the Conference's secretary for special concerns, referred in his commencement address at the Catholic University of America in May 1980. He went on: 'We are now better off as a nation because Americans and American Catholics in particular are now more willing than ever before to question, to criticize, to challenge and, if necessary, to oppose in a responsible manner . . . this or that policy of our own Government.'

The second great shaper of Catholic opinion, after the concerted blows from papal teaching to confidence in the economic system, is the experience Americans are receiving at first hand of what rampant capitalism can do. Latin America is close. The Church there has woken from its long tradition of acquiescence with the

political power which was part of the imperial inheritance. It has
taken the lead in the demand for recognition of social justice and
human rights, which is now a part of Catholic teaching given
much prominence. It is a reminder to North American Catholics
that not so long ago they were a church of the nation's poor. It
touches tender consciences. Latin American ideas on liberation
theology are thought unlikely to be particularly influential in the
North because of two defects: the method of some of these
thinkers is Marxist, and North American Catholics do not feel
themselves as living under a regime of repression.

They do, however, constantly hear from Latin American
Catholics struggling for basic rights that the teaching about the
national security state which effectively denies them these rights
comes from the United States military. I heard this assertion
frequently in Central America. It is also a favourite theme of Dom
Helder Camara, the celebrated Archbishop of Olinda-Recife in
Brazil. He is a man of just instinct. Smart intellectual opinion is
inclined to reject him because he has involved the Church in
politics without even knowing what his own politics are, changing from the Right to an advanced form of socialism. He will
outlast the smartness. He has the same fears as Cardinal Arns for
the new urban communities. He estimates that every week a new
slum district is created in the city. But what fundamentally
concerns him are two things, one that is bad and one that is good.
The bad is the notion of national security, which he believes
comes from the United States and sees anti-Communism as the
basic issue by comparison with which every other issue—including Jesus, whether transfigured or not—pales. He hates the
multinationals, and he sees their great backer in the trilateral
commission of the United States, Japan and Western Europe. He
saw Brzezinski, Carter's national security adviser, as its main
inspirer. ' . . . When people put national security above all other
values, as their ultimate concern, this is terrible, because if national
security takes precedence over all principles and rights, then
anything is possible under the pretext of serving national
security.'

I would be unhappy if I were an American listening to the
strictures of Dom Helder. But I have said that there is also a good
side. Dom Helder is not a pessimist and he sees as a great reality
the immense proliferation of 'grass-roots communities' in
Brazil—the famous *comidades de base*, which have no such neat
definition in English. He sees the future liberation as dependent on

the 'grass-roots communities in the underdeveloped countries and the small groups of people of goodwill in the privileged countries. This is a call to liberation, and God is involved.'

And so Latin America can be regarded as a great practical stimulant to North American Catholicism. Where will influential 'people of goodwill in the privileged countries' be found but in the United States? Moreover, and this is a vital element in American Catholicism, the Third World is already present in it, and probably in a matter of generations will predominate. Blacks and Spanish-speakers are already there to upset the uneasy calm which white Catholics appeared to have achieved. This is another of the North American Church's strengths, for the future. It is now an integral part of American life but it is also about to become the meeting point of a Western Catholicism, orientated towards Europe, with a Negro and a Spanish-speaking Catholicism, both of which are rooted in the Third World, not in the comforts of what Wojtyla finds unacceptable in American life. This is the impression I had from meetings with some of the most know-ledgeable prelates in the United States, and not necessarily American.

This is an authoritative non-American view of the American scene: 'The Catholic Church began here among poor, ill-educated immigrants. The only educated person (and then only half-educated) was the priest. The image remains of the priest as the one man who knows everything. Some bishops here still believe that they have the answers to everything and so are inclined to answer stupidly to a lot of questions. The biggest weakness of the bishops is their lack of doctrinal information. This is very serious. Theology here is well behind Europe. Bishops know little about the teachings of the Vatican Council and many priests are main-taining paternalism and masculine leadership. It is difficult to find the right bishops because so few priests have the proper training. It is essential to send some of them for further studies in Europe, to Louvain, or to Rome, which is improving, to Innsbruck or to Paris. Until ten years ago, the All Hallows seminary in Ireland was still sending priests to the United States. This is the sort of thing which has a bad effect on vocations.

'I would say that here, in the Church as a whole, there is a marked conservative trend. This is also reflected in the seminaries. This is the "me" generation. They are not socially-minded, they are anti-intellectual and going a little towards fundamentalism. They pray and they read scripture but they do not want exegesis.

They are tired of having had everything put in doubt. People want something that is not moving all the time.'

Yet, the situation is still moving and, once again, in a direction that means more rather than less political involvement for American Catholics. The same commentator pointed out that ethnic identity had proved important in keeping Catholic immigrants Catholic: Italians, Irish, Germans, Poles. Because of their religion, they were able to go into the melting-pot while retaining their own identity. He said that these ethnic considerations should be kept but now the problem is the materialistic view of life, the concern for an easy life, for comfort and pleasure, and this breaks down the differences. He sees the future as bringing three distinct Catholic Churches in the United States: a black Church, a white Church and a Spanish-speaking Church. The aim of the blacks (of whom only a mere 900,000 are Catholics out of a black population of fifteen million) is to end segregation but they are no longer interested in integration. The idea of integration is a thing of the past. Negro Catholics feel themselves doubly a minority: they therefore feel they must impose their black identity on the Catholic Church.

They do so effectively, to judge from a highly emotional Mass I heard sung in New Orleans. The priest was white but almost the entire congregation was black. They sang traditional hymns, some of them Baptist in origin, with a highly trained choir (the choir-master himself was a Baptist). The swaying and the brightness of the eyes revealed a genuine intensity of religious feeling. After the Mass many of the parishioners went to eat lunch and drink beer together. The tension was enhanced by the behaviour of the white priest: his methods were charismatic. He saw the Mass as 'a freeing of the spirit'. The mistake had been made, he said, of expecting all churches to follow a Roman liturgy. 'What we do is a Catholic Mass. For us the Eucharist is a diamond jewel in the midst of a beautiful background of singing.' A woman called Clare said that there were 400 families in the parish. They had a prayer-group and they organized days of renewal. She could remember a quarter of a century ago when blacks could only sit in the back few rows and only take Communion when all the whites, mostly Italian and German, had finished doing so. 'In the early sixties the whites started moving out of the district. Almost no one came to the church, just five or six whites and a few blacks on a Sunday for Mass. Then the parish frontiers were changed and part of an overcrowded parish was brought into this church. They did not want to come to it because it seemed dead. A priest called Father Putnam was appointed. He was strongly for social reform like housing and food and other changes. We had the "black panthers" here and Father Putnam organized a breakfast for them. A number of people here are still in social reform but I would say the spiritual side has gone up now. Father Putnam married his secretary. There were no hard feelings. We have since had two "Putnam Days" to keep in touch with him. After he left, he studied urban renewal and is now working with prisoners. We hope to integrate dance into the liturgy, and drama too: we have a form of cantata in mind.'

A double image, each aspect highly important, begins to emerge of the Church in the United States: its followers are increasingly becoming a mixture of races like that from which the United States itself was made and, secondly, there is an image and a confused evocation of the Church of the future in the world at large, which is becoming increasingly a Third World Church, a black Church, a Spanish-speaking Church with far less than before of the European about it. The blacks are for the moment few numerically, but it is worth remembering that Africa is the continent where Catholicism is growing fastest. The Hispanic speakers of Latin America are already dominant in world Catholicism in terms of numbers, and highly influential in ideas as the regional conferences at Medellin and Puebla showed. To this I would add another influence which is near in some ways to Latin America but important for itself. Catholic renewal in the Philippines is becoming a strong force. It is certainly not under American influence but it is a part of the world where, despite independence, Americans are still numerous, and many American Catholics are brought into contact with what is happening there. Both the American Embassy and their bases there have increased in importance as a result of the withdrawal from Vietnam. The Church in the Philippines is finding itself quickly, both in the way it is adapting worship to local cultures and in its opposition to the excesses of the Marcos dictatorship. Cardinal Sin is a shrewd leader who is aware of the dangers of violence and of armed rebellion (which has been taking place for years in parts of the country, involving far left-wing insurgents in the north and Muslim rebels in the south). Should the Americans one day see that the regime on which their presence depends has been swept away by popular insurrection, they will find that the attitude of the Catholic Church will be vital to their future relationship. This attitude is already helping to shape a national identity more effectively than Marcos's 'New Society'.

Catholics in the Philippines are comparable to the North Americans in the sense that they have several Catholic churches living side by side. There is still a strong conservative strain— there are more conservative than progressive bishops—and the balance between them is kept by the less committed centre. There is a rather fierce, socially conscious, newly awakened section of the Church which is the most formidable opponent to the political regime. And there is a third element, whether reached by passing first through the other two, I do not know, which is concentrating on no more nor less than practising a constant Christian witness, offering a presence of Christians who are trying to act as such. The lay movement is strong. So, too, is the organization of such useful methods of evolving a Christian viewpoint on events as the publication of news-bulletins containing genuine news. The major superiors of the religious orders in Manila, for instance, publish an excellent summary of the news in cyclostyled form which balances what can be read in the officially controlled press. A comparative detail, but it was a seminarist, who was among the survivors of a ferry-boat which sank after a collision off San José, who said that they were kept for two hours in soaking wet clothes so that the president's wife, Mrs Imelda Marcos, could get there to be televised giving new heart to the survivors. The seminarist told his friends, who passed on the news that her presence was not the prompt and sudden event it was officially made out to be. At an abbey, I was told that two of its members were absent: one was in touch still but in hiding after being sought by the authorities; the other was missing and was supposed to be a prisoner somewhere, or dead. The network of information, much of it semi-clandestine, is excellent. Catholic activists are taking the lead in seeking out victims of arbitrary arrest or reporting cases of gross cruelty. Conditions under martial law are forcing the Church to find a better way and its own way of being Filipino.

To return to the nature of Catholic society in the States; this is how the American Assistant-General of the Jesuits, Father O'Keefe, who comes from Jersey City, sees it: 'It is something like the United States itself where you have all these different cultures coming together, sometimes melting into a third substance, sometimes resisting and maintaining their own particular identity. That is what I think is interesting. Now another thing is that Catholics were considered to be about the lowest class in the country on the social, economic and political level but now they have reached a comfortable middle-class status, and even higher, and it is difficult in many spheres to distinguish a Catholic from a non-Catholic, whether they be male or female.

'Now the States is great for polls and we have had some very interesting polls. There was one done by Gallup for the Catholic Press Association which showed there was little perceptible difference in the reactions one had from Catholics and non-Catholics with regard to birth-control, with regard to divorce —things of that sort—and it also showed that "better" Catholics by and large were ones that had had a college or university education. I mean better in the sense of more frequent, more profound participation in the liturgical ceremonies of the Church, and those expressly saying that religion was an important dimension in their lives. By and large the college and university-educated Catholic has adjusted and accepted more easily the changes that were rung in by the Vatican Council, and they feel in a position to make up their minds and their own consciences. It is not that they reject any teaching that would come to them from the pope or the Vatican Congregations. But they feel they have enough general education and religious educational background to study these things and to say: "While I take into consideration what the Holy Father says in his official writings, whether of the force of encyclicals or documents of lesser importance, or the productions coming out of the different Roman Congregations, on such things as birth-control, or on divorce and sexual ethics, I am interested in them and will discuss them and bring them up with priests until I feel to be in a position to make up my own mind and conscience about these things." They would make an informed decision, informed in the sense that they will have studied the pertinent literature, discussed and asked about it and they then feel that in good conscience they can act one way or the other. This is now a very dominant thing in the culture of Catholics in the States. You have a much better informed body of people that is not passive or just receptive but does feel free enough and at ease enough and competent enough to question certain things. This is very different from our earlier Church which was mostly an immigrant Church where people were struggling to find their own place in life.'

He too is very much taken with the racial complexities in American Catholicism, which are placing a deeper mark on the Church as a whole: 'I also think that in the States we have in the episcopal body—we have over 300 bishops—something where we should see some changes. One obvious one for the very near future is that among the very large Spanish-speaking population there is a need, a felt need, for Spanish-speaking bishops who would be in sympathy with the feelings, the desires, the way of reacting and all the rest of it of these people of Spanish culture. There are at least twenty million of them and that number will only increase. It is a very difficult number to fix exactly because a good number of these people would be in the United States in one or other illegal way. And they are undoubtedly hesitant about giving out information, but I would say twenty million is a minimum. And of course this Spanish-speaking population is a highly concentrated one, mainly in the south and certain big cities. It is interesting to know, for instance, that in Chicago, which is not in the south, there is a very heavy Spanish population. Miami is another concentration: some people point to Miami as the city which will become one of the biggest Central Latin American cities, both because of its location and its inflow. We have a high school in Miami run by our Latin American Jesuits, many of whom are from Cuba and Santo Domingo. This school is the successor of a school we had in Havana which had many distinguished alumni including Fidel Castro. It started up in Miami and soon needed new buildings. It is not just a school, it is a centre for these Spanish-speaking people. It is where they meet, adults, families as well as children. A lot of people go to the liturgy because they know it will be in Spanish. And you have parts of the United States that are bilingual. Our Jesuits in the New York area, when they join they have to learn Spanish if they do not have it already. This is compulsory.'

He places the emancipation of women as high in American Catholicism's distinguishing features. In the States there are not only very intelligent women but very vocal and articulate women who have banded together and learned the political processes and how to use the media. He does not see this as a particularly religious phenomenon, but as part of a whole cultural development. The question of the demands of women within the Church is nevertheless regarded by many people as potentially capable of changing much of the nature of American Catholicism. I spoke to a bishop who is not at all unsympathetic towards the women's movements in the Church. In his diocese, for example, he had placed a woman in charge of ecumenical contacts. But he complained that there was no mechanism by which women's demands could be handled in public: 'Rome does not understand the intensity and emotional depth of this problem. There certainly is a lunatic fringe, but in the middle there are good women who suffer, and the bishops feel threatened by it. They do not know how to dialogue about it with Rome and it is not altogether clear what the women want. We have a group of *avant-garde* nuns up here and they talk of "a loving, caring, priesthood". I believe the basis of much of this is frustration rather than theology.'

The women are an important aspect, but only one aspect, of the series of upheavals that struck American Catholicism's apparently rock-like assurance of the pre-Vatican Council days, and from which it seems now to be emerging. The women have to be taken into account together with the Vatican Council itself, changes in the idea of the family, the sexual revolution, Kennedy, Watergate and Vietnam, all of which had a deep effect on Catholicism by changing either its attitude towards itself or attitudes in general towards institutions. The *New York Times* in January 1979 summed up the 'slow, painful recovery' in the following terms:

> A mood of uplift can be sensed among Catholic charismatics during prayer-meetings, among church-goers warmly exchanging the 'kiss of peace' during Mass, and among members of the laity volunteering to distribute communion wafers as 'extraordinary ministers of the Eucharist'. It is also visible in the church's initiatives on behalf of social justice and in tending to its newest immigrant members, the Hispanic people flooding into inner-city churches in such places as Los Angeles, San Antonio and New York.
>
> Undergirding these random expressions is a new sense of pride in being Catholic, as much a part of the individual who may attend Mass only at Christmas as it is of the person bowed daily in devotion. It is the attitude that Catholic culture, tradition and heritage, are celebrations of life despite continuing controversy over ritual and exactitude of belief.

It is clear that the election of John Paul II has fed this new pride. Many American Catholics may find his conservative views difficult to accept; impossible, for some of them. But he certainly fulfils the need for a leader, which goes beyond the semi-hysteria shown towards him by the Poles of Chicago and Milwaukee. I remember Andrew Greeley at a press conference in Rome after the death of Paul VI, when an Italian woman asked him what sort of a pope Americans wanted: 'We want', he said, with a certain raptness, 'a pope we can be proud of.' There was a lot there in that answer of the American need to be able to express the loyalty of ordinary Catholics for their church. Before the Council, this expression was an excessive clericalism and an excessive reverence for Rome. That had to go. The cost was high. Young men found the priesthood too binding a proposition as they faced doubts about the whole concept of institutional religion. The number of seminarists dropped in a decade from 40,000 in 1969 to 14,000 in 1979. Members of women's orders at last found that they were being exploited, in schools, hospitals and in their own nunneries. The total of 176,671 in 1969 dropped in ten years to 130,804. Even if the concept of Catholic schooling were not under re-examination throughout the Church, the American Church would be facing serious difficulties in finding staff who were not expensively drawn from the lay world.

A break with habits of the past has naturally brought controversy as to whether the amount of change is too little or too much, or even desirable at all by comparison with the inflexibilities of belief in the Catholic Church of the last generation. A passage in the same *New York Times* analysis defines the change in views on authority:

> The trend toward individualism and dissent worries many in the Church because it suggests a lack of common belief and a breakdown of tradition. Others are convinced that pluralism is not only inevitable but healthy, if not carried too far. Both sides agree, however, that fewer Catholics look to parish priest, bishop or Pope to decide matters of conscience.

This is obviously a harder church to live in than the old, unquestioned rock, with its base in the north-eastern industrial cities and the mid-west.

It is the question of race which keeps coming back; race and a newly emotional content to religion which is connected with race and runs parallel with a far higher educational level among Catholics. I believe this issue of race is something that goes deeper than the racial problems inherent in the American scene. The search for the individual identity, or a corporate one, nowadays has a racial element far beyond the boundaries of the United States, though it is particularly strong there because of the number of different races and traditions present. Among the Catholics, coming fresh to the realities of human rights and the need to avoid racial discrimination, the differences become immediately obvious because they are not limited to colour or to language or to the national characteristics of the country of origin. They are differences of mentality, which nowadays is politely but not always correctly referred to as a person's culture. Examples, even if they seem like mere details in religious practice itself, can show how wide these differences are.

Take the cases of baptism and confirmation. There are dioceses where Spanish-speaking Catholics have settled where the normal rule among Catholics who have been there longer is that a child is baptized so long as there is some assurance of a Catholic upbringing, and is then only confirmed so long as there is some certainty that they will live a Catholic life. For the Spanish-speakers, any attempt by the priest to try and impose conditions for baptism can be bitterly opposed. The old magic is there, rather than the new religion. The same type of problem is present in the seminaries. The Spanish-speakers cannot understand the Cadillac-type seminary with swimming-pool and parking for the cars of the seminarists.

The multi-lingualism is not easy. This is a bishop's account of how one particular church-building is put to use: 'A church in the centre of the city was once the church almost exclusively of German-speaking immigrants. Now the Germans have moved away to the suburbs but they come back to the church, especially the old ones, for an early morning Sunday Mass, and so, in the early morning there is a rather formal Mass to satisfy these elderly Germans. After this there is a Mass for Negroes who have come up from New Orleans but have been in the city for two or three generations and so are already rather traditionalist in their religion. Then there is a Spanish Mass done as if this were Mexico. At midday it is the turn of the young Negroes who want jazz and a modern liturgy. The same city has two Croatian parish churches; one is rather Americanized, the other still as if it were in Zagreb.'

The effect of discrimination in the past is still present in this multi-racial church. Father O'Keefe points out that many black Christians would be of a Baptist tendency, while inroads had been made by Islam. There were comparatively few Catholics among the black population but their number is increasing, which means there are relatively few black priests and even fewer bishops. Part of that he ascribes to discrimination.

'Even if you have equality before the law, it is a long time before this touches practical life. You remember the old slogan "equal but separate". This meant in the field of education the blacks had second-class facilities, schools, faculty members, and examinations into college were geared to the white mentality. Until the fifties and sixties there was separation between the two groups in Catholic schools, particularly in the south. The blacks consequently went off to a very hard start, they had to climb the mountain twice to get into a good position. What the Church must still do, I think, is recognize the great contribution which blacks can make and are making already to the Church in the United States. In the field of liturgy, in the field of family relations too. When it was a question of replacing Cardinal Baum as Archbishop of Washington, DC, a good number of people said that it would be good to put a black Catholic bishop in there. The population is far over 50 per cent black. You have a black mayor. For some reason, that did not happen, but we do need black people in prominent decision-making positions in the Church much as we have had blacks who made it up the scale in military life. You can see that what we need is a group of bishops who will reflect this bubbling life among the people. We need black and Hispanic bishops so that you would have a good mix right inside that body itself.'

He concluded with some remarks about the usefulness of this bubbling element which is outside the experience of the more traditionalist, white Catholicism. 'It is interesting that the charismatic movement has a great appeal among the blacks and the Spanish speakers. This is not the type of thing you could say was just an emotional binge. It is not that. It is just that the dry, Anglo-Saxon approach means little to these people. It is not what their culture is used to. I can remember teaching theology, and we had a good number of Filipino Jesuits. And part of the training was to practise giving a sermon. You could see that the way the Filipino would deliver it would strike an Anglo-Saxon as being over-emotional, but when you came to analyse you would see that it was not just a rational approach but a much more human thing, lots of descriptive phrases, an appeal to feelings, not being afraid to use emotive words. And the same is true of the blacks. They are used to this. You have to appeal to the whole person and not just to the rational side. I also think this takes place during the liturgy. One of the things which struck people after the Vatican Council was that part of the Mass where you have what was called the "kiss of peace", where you greet each other with a sign of peace which can be the taking of the hand, an embrace, a hug, or something like that. Well, you could see that some of our older Catholics were not at ease with this. Whereas blacks and Hispanics and some of our younger people were right at home with it. For it is something that comes to life. It is not like you were riding the subway, like a lot of lumps of wood in there. No, no, you are human beings who are supposed to be united in this highest act of worship and so why not deal with this other person as a person on a level where, in a sense, you can let your hair down . . . .'

With all this ferment, it was regrettable, if not worse, that the pope's visit to the United States in October 1979 was, as one of the most intelligent members of his entourage told him on the flight back, the most superficial of his journeys so far. He had a personal triumph and he reiterated doctrine with clarity and, given the circumstances, irrelevance, because doctrine is familiar to the increasingly educated American Catholic. His interventions on such matters as birth-control, divorce and the priesthood (with no real indication of the significance of the women's movement) were not in any case taken to heart. There was no way in which they could have been. That is why the centre-piece of that visit was not one of the many speeches made to Catholic audiences but his address at the United Nations on the subject of human rights. It was too long, but it gave world-wide prominence to a teaching typical of this pontificate, which it needs to be effective. It is difficult for a policy on human rights to be effective, but as an aspiration it is attractive.

It is a policy which John Paul II's warmly human style is able to express movingly. This is a part of what he said in New York:

Today, forty years after the outbreak of the Second World War, I wish to recall the whole of the experiences by individuals and nations that were sustained by a generation that is largely still alive. I had occasion not long ago to reflect again on some of those experiences, in one of the places that is most distressing and overflowing with contempt for man and his fundamental rights—the extermination camp of Oswiecim [Auschwitz] which I visited during my pilgrimage to Poland last June. This infamous place is unfortunately only one of the many scattered over the continent of Europe. But the memory of even one should be a warning sign on the path of humanity today, in order that every kind of concentration camp anywhere on earth may once and for all be done away with. And anything that recalls those horrible experiences should also disappear for ever from the lives of nations and states, everything that is a continuation of those experiences under different forms, namely, the various kinds of torture and oppression, either physical or moral, carried out under any system in any land: this phenomenon is all the more distressing if it occurs under the pretext of internal 'security' or the need to preserve an apparent peace.

It is good to hear a pope speak this way, just as his denunciation of violence during his stop in Ireland was good listening. The fact that his appeals go unheeded is probably for the moment inevitable. He is nevertheless expressing sentiments which can be shared by people far outside the Catholic world, who no doubt are encouraged to know that at least one person at this level of international importance still thinks in this way.

It was ironic that shortly after the American visit the Vatican took the controversial step of removing Father Robert F. Drinan, a priest publicly identified with campaigns in favour of human rights, from his seat in Congress. When the directive arrived, Father Drinan was seeking re-election for what would have been his sixth term as the Democratic representative for a Massachusetts district. The directive was all the more disagreeable because it came a matter of days before the deadline for the filing of candidacies. The Vatican sought to explain that no criticism was intended of Father Drinan but that the move had been taken in application of a traditional Church policy, given renewed emphasis by John Paul II, that ordained priests ordinarily should not run for elective office or be otherwise engaged in partisan politics. The affront was nevertheless felt, and the question immediately raised of how this policy would be implemented in other parts of the world where priests hold ministerial posts: in Nicaragua, for instance, the government which overthrew the Somoza dictatorship had a priest as foreign minister and another as minister for culture, the formidable poet Father Cardenal. Some of the troubling questions raised by the Vatican's move were reviewed editorially in *America*:

> The debate over priests in politics is complicated by the notoriously slippery terms involved. 'Politics' can mean many things to many people. Here in the United States, for example, the Catholic hierarchy quite rightly engages in active lobbying in pursuit of its own institutional interests and the larger goals of justice, equality and peace. In Italy, the hierarchy is much more involved in the affairs of one political party, the Christian Democrats, an entanglement that often seems to the outsider unfortunate for both Church and nation. In Poland, under the dominant leadership of the Cardinal Primate, the Catholic hierarchy is considered the only significant political rival to the Communist Government. Presum-

ably, Pope John Paul II does not wish to discourage any of these forms of political activity.

Unfortunately, there are countries where any attempt by priests to speak on behalf of justice and human rights is branded 'meddling in politics' by defenders of the status quo. Reactionary elements in these countries will undoubtedly exploit the Vatican directive to Father Drinan for their own purposes.

This was a clumsy act which cannot have helped throw light on the pope's thinking on the sacred and the profane, or the need to separate the priestly caste from the political arena. Yet Rome would undoubtedly have no criticism to make—indeed the promptings would surely be of encouragement—against other forms of direct political intervention by the Catholic Church on far more questionable issues.

The issue which I heard most frequently raised to prove this point in practice was the most delicate issue of all in the Catholic relationship with the political arena. Abortion is a tragic subject. It is becoming increasingly so because more and more it is being made to carry the heaviest weight in the Catholic armoury not just of weapons but also of the Church's efforts at facing modern problems such as violence and war. First, as a weapon: I was eating lunch in Washington with a group of priests who were, I suppose, about the best-informed group the capital could provide at one table and, in addition, several were old friends who had proved over the years that they were men of genuine and sensitive sentiments. We had not got very far with a conversation that broadened out to touch on most of the questions uppermost in American Catholicism when the first reference came to the use of the issue of abortion as a means of destroying political opponents. The technique was to demand a straight and totally unequivocal statement from a politician, a yes or a no, depending on which way the question was put, and if the response was insufficiently clear, to campaign for the candidate's defeat. The same method was used to keep the non-traditionalist Catholic out of the life of the Church. Bishops were pressurized to remove from Church programmes people who were on the 'hit-list' of the extreme anti-abortionists. Of course for politicians of all kinds, whether Catholic or not, a single, weighty weapon, so simple that it can be understood by all, as effective against the intellectually gifted as against stupid opponents—probably more so with the former—is a godsend. It recalls the famous phrase adapted from Gide by the Italian writer Leonardo Sciascia, who wrote to the Cardinal-

Archbishop of Palermo with a warning against the type of self-styled Catholic who 'uses the crucifix as a blunt instrument; a blunt instrument with which to knock a man unconscious before robbing him.' That was written during the Italian general election campaign in 1976 and, although he was referring to Catholic politicians in his own country, the parallel has been credibly drawn between the way the issue of abortion is treated in Italy and the United States. The bishop who made this comparison to me claimed that when he said this to his fellow-bishops many of them regarded him as a traitor.

He said: 'I am finding as a bishop great difficulty in keeping this issue straight. I can teach the doctrine, but to put a lot of money into campaigns to make state and federal laws meet these teachings is another question altogether and one in which I am not interested to take part. If we want to be consistent we should take the same radical stand on other issues. Our bishops' conference decided to give testimony to Congress in favour of the SALT negotiations on the grounds that they represented a small step towards the Church's goal of total disarmament. Why don't we demand on arms what we claim for abortion—total acceptance of what we believe? I was recently addressing an audience of high-school girls and their families. The girls understood what I was saying, but not the parents who rang me up all the afternoon with their complaints.'

Exploitation of the issue of abortion is all the more regrettable given that the Catholic Church everywhere is insisting more and more on this subject. In itself this need not be regrettable, even if many people would probably feel more in sympathy with the African pagan woman who dislikes the idea of abortion yet sees its usefulness in a number of well-defined situations. What looks more disturbing is that teaching against every form of abortion is being increasingly presented as the Catholic Church's principal contribution to the suppression of violence. This surely is an instance of dogmatic unreality which exceeds its own proper boundaries and becomes both rhetorical and heavy-handed. There are moments when a state of grace can still mean a state of doubt.

The Church has avoided the false respectability that would have come to it had it emerged as the established religion of the country instead of just the largest single religious group. Neither its origins nor its character nor the constitution would allow such a status, and the Kennedy election was the nearest it could come to a development of this kind. Most big airports in the United States give an idea to arriving passengers of the state's refusal to endorse a faith. At Chicago the notices say: 'The airport advises you that you may be approached by religious personnel seeking money donations. The courts uphold such liberties based on the constitutional rights of freedom of religion. The airport in no way [and this is written in capital letters] endorses these solicitations.'

I was indeed approached: a girl, with gold rimmed glasses, and a bony face set in a fixed smile, came up to me with a pink carnation in her thin and freckled hand, and I suppose this sign meant that she was a Moony. Had I not been in a hurry, and by temperament worried about meeting people I have just been warned against, I might have asked her for one or two explanations of details of this odd faith. What intrigues me about it is the view of the Moonies that Jesus was in fact thwarted in his mission (though the Moonies claim nevertheless to be Christians). They argue that, according to the prophecy of Malachi, Elijah would precede the true Messiah. This was the role for which John the Baptist was destined but he refused to be Elijah. By doing so, he alienated the mission of Jesus from the Jewish people. The split was final. Jesus now had to decide what to do about failure. The vision he had at the Transfiguration decided him that he had to become a suffering Messiah not a kingly one, and death would put an end to his mission while the world would await another Messianic age. I had also been impressed by reports of the vast ceremony in Seoul (the founder of the Moonies is Korean) in February 1976 when ninety-six buses brought identically dressed brides to the wedding of 1,800 couples, all chosen for each other by the wisdom of Moon.

There is a bizarre element to American religious life and it will probably come to trouble Catholicism increasingly as the racial balance changes. But there is something attractive, not bizarre, about that idea of Moon that the Transfiguration was a negotiation more than an effort at surrounding Jesus in supernatural glory. No doubt Elijah had something to say about the inexplicable refusal of the Baptist to play his proper historical role. It is as if Blücher had failed to arrive at Waterloo and Wellington had decided that his task was hopeless. I find the Transfiguration a recurring image, but never before as a moment for a whole divine strategy to be changed. I should have talked about it to that tense-faced girl selling flowers, constitutionally, at the airport. But timidly I just pushed by.

15

GROUPS AND BONDS

I N THE CENTRAL AFRICAN state of Zaire, the Church is proud
of its liturgical revival. And why is there a liturgical revival?
Because there is little else that the Church is allowed to do.
It has managed to keep intact its theological centre, which very
nearly fell victim to Mobutu's attempt to remove Christianity
from the country and did indeed see its ties cut with Louvain, but
it is the adaptation of the liturgy to local needs and culture that
gives Zaire its leading position in this field, especially in the way
traditional music is used in the Mass. The churches in Kinshasa
offer extremely advanced and popular liturgical experiments. The
bishops in Zaire are often frustrated at being able to do too little to
help advance the public life of their country, apart from occasional
condemnations of corruption and injustice, but the churches are
full and there is real emotion expressed within them.

The best brief statement of what was happening there remains
the contribution to the 1977 Synod in Rome of Monsignor Albert
Yungu, the Bishop of Tshumbe, in which he confidently expressed the view that the trials the Church had undergone under
Mobutu had been a real means of purification, of growth and of
grace:

> As a result of recent events, we are no longer able to rely on the
> traditional means of apostolate and catechism (schools, youth
> movements, press, radio, etc.). The Church in Zaire is now
> focusing its catechetical work on liturgical and semi-liturgical
> celebrations, on the one hand, and on programmes for Christian
> education outside the school system on the other hand. The former
> aims mainly at adults while the latter is more concerned with
> young people.

GROUPS AND BONDS

As a matter of fact, all this is simply the practical application of
the important options of our Episcopal Conference, namely: the
building of small Christian communities, the setting up of non-
ordained ministries and the gradual withdrawal of the institutional
church from the control and administration of temporal affairs.

The idea of the small Christian communities is now widespread
throughout the Catholic world and early official sanction to them
as the principal unit in Christian life was given them in Africa. In
December 1973, the Bishops of Kenya, Malawi, Tanzania,
Uganda and Zambia concluded that the way to an adult Christian
community was through the formation of these small groups.
Three years later the bishops decided to give these groups the first
pastoral priority, removing this distinction from the parish. The
bishops bluntly said that the parish was useful in Europe and the
United States, but not in the mission areas. This was their way
around the canon (216) which was taken to be the basis of the
parish system. It states:

> The territory of every diocese shall be divided into distinct
> territorial sections; and each portion shall have its own proper
> church to which the Catholic population of the district will be
> assigned. Such a church is presided over by a rector as the proper
> pastor for the necessary care of souls.

The African bishops disagree with the notion that the parish is the
implementation of this canon, arguing that the real explanation for
this reading was a limited concept of the Church, inadequate and
incomplete because it did not actively involve the whole Church
in Christian life. Active involvement was left to the priest and his
immediate helpers. The rest had a passive role.

Detailed descriptions of the nature of these communities was
given to the Synod by one of their strongest advocates, Monsignor Christopher Mwoleka, Bishop of Rulenge in northern Kenya,
near the border with Uganda. He said:

> That each community may be a 'community with a human face', it
> has to be small enough to enable a network of inter-personal
> relationships to develop and grow among its members. A sense of
> belonging must be fostered through services prompted by mutual
> concern. This community then is the Church in its most local
> form, present in a concrete and particular way, of which each
> Christian is happy to be a member. This is the necessary 'locus' for
> genuine ongoing religious formation.

He went on to describe the typical organization of a group. (It is difficult that no good English label has been devised for this phenomenon: 'base' or 'basic community' are both ugly. In the Philippines, where the groups are extremely important, they are referred to as 'BCCs', basic Christian communities. A lot is heard of them there. The extremely able Bishop Francisco Claver states that 'it is in the BCCs that real thinking and acting in a more or less massive way are taking place.') Bishop Mwoleka numbered the various facets of the organization of a group as follows:

1. A prayer-leader animates the members of the community with the spirit of prayer, leads the weekly Bible service and conducts Sunday services without a priest.
2. One in charge of religious formation aids the parents to fulfil their responsibilities towards their children and helps form adult catechumens.
3. A counsellor of marriages befriends and helps married couples before, during and after marriage.
4. A promoter of community-spirit promotes brotherhood and concern, and initiates projects for the common good.
5. A guide to sacraments fosters the sacramental life of the community in various ways.
6. A promoter of self-reliance makes the members of the community aware of the financial needs of the Church, and promotes projects for fund-raising.
7. A co-ordinator sees to it that each charge is performed and that all are carried out in harmony.

I was reading the records of the 1977 Synod in the library of a group of Italian missionary priests in Tanzania. Most of them had a long experience of the country and all of them had a good relationship with their charges. Several of them were very practical: one was leading an experiment in tobacco-growing with a group of subsistence farmers, another was a legendary hunter, another was a doctor and specialized in the improvisation of hospital equipment from the most unlikely cast-off materials, in an effort to get round the difficulty of importing what he needed. He was extraordinarily ingenious: 'a sort of Leonardo da Vinci', his colleagues said. Most of them accepted the reality of the basic groups. The bishops after all had ordered the system for Catholicism's future. But they did not hide the fact that they still believed more in the older idea of parishes and mission-stations. And to a priest whose life, as a missionary, is devoted entirely to his faithful, it must have seemed strange when reading Bishop

Mwoleka's account of the basic communities to see that he speaks only once of priests: in the passage where he states that the prayer-leader conducts services without one.

With or without a priest, the groups clearly have a vital part in regimes which are anti-clerical; just as they do in parts of Latin America. The groups in a country such as Mozambique, for instance, provide a foundation for passing on the faith to the children and offering mutual support to each other. In countries where Catholicism is under stress, they are presumably crucial.

A different set of difficulties faces Catholics in countries which are not antagonistic. Liturgical experiments of the kind which are so advanced in Zaire (and which brought an unfortunate statement of misgiving from John Paul II when he toured Africa in spring 1980) can be found elsewhere in Africa, but they are of a less adventurous kind. Imaginative missionaries in East Africa devise quite emotionally charged services, too, making use, for human effect, of traditional songs and instruments. The difference from Zaire is that such experiments as there are are usually to be found in the countryside rather than the towns and cities. In East Africa the cities are more conservative. They can afford to be because on the face of it the political regimes are not dictatorial—at least not in their dealings towards the Catholic Church, which they do not regard as an enemy or a rival. In Kenya and Tanzania, the Church itself is conservative. There is a lot of looking over the shoulder towards Rome. More than one person in Africa said to me that we shall have to wait for the second generation of African bishops to see whether the continent will provide genuinely African leadership. The first African to be ordained a priest, Willibald Mwapi, was still alive, aged eighty-seven, when I was there. The first African to be created cardinal was Dar-es-Salaam's archbishop, Cardinal Rugambwa. He is a tall, impressive, rather reserved man, of clearly aristocratic tribal origins, seeming long accustomed to power, approachable and charming on the surface but, beneath the appearance, a model of old-fashioned orthodoxy. He has a simple study overlooking his cathedral in the Tanzanian capital, and appears relaxed and affable. His relationship with the government is clearly easy. His views on ecumenical relations were put very explicitly for him by a member of the government who is also Catholic: 'over my dead body'.

Tanzania is an illuminating example of the Catholic dilemma when a church is faced by a political situation that does not give clear indications of what attitude the ecclesiastical authorities should take. This is not just an African problem: it happens to be clearer in Africa. Since independence, Tanzania has been ruled by one man, Julius Nyerere, who is a practising Catholic. His entire career has been based on his Catholicism.

Nyerere was his country's leading politician when independence was granted in 1961 and is rightly proud of having made the change without loss of blood. Tanzania is now a socialist country where practically all political power is in the hands of this product of the Catholic mission schools. That, in itself, is a stimulating combination. He was a schoolmaster before he gave himself entirely to politics and is still consciously trying to teach his people how to be socialists. They acknowledge this by calling him 'Mwalimu', which means teacher; they accept his constant exhortations to do better as well as his many didactic speeches and his many pamphlets charting progress in his and his country's search for what he calls 'the national ethic'. He sometimes sounds like a reversed version of Shaw's charming black girl in search of God. Nyerere settled his religious beliefs while still a young man and went on to experiment with socialism. Shaw's seeker did her best to understand missionaries, to deal with St Peter with a paper church on his back claiming to be a rock, and with Jesus himself whom she took to be a conjuror, before finally giving up her quest for God because marriage to a socialist took up all her time.

Yet Nyerere is strangely ambivalent about his Catholicism. In some senses he makes a parade of it. It is widely known that he attends early morning Mass at St Peter's church, a modern building near his home a few miles out of the centre of Oyster Bay. It is a Swahili Mass and almost the whole congregation is black. His supporters say that Nyerere goes to church as one black man among many others and behaves as an average member of the congregation. In fact he does avoid the first row but when the time comes to take Communion he walks slowly and alone up the aisle—a thin, fragile-looking figure with grey hair and square little moustache—kneels at the altar rail, stays for a minute or so in silent contemplation, and then slowly returns to his place, all eyes following him as he settles back once again among his staff.

In January 1979 the figures were published of a census conducted in Tanzania the previous August that gave the total population as 17,551,925, of whom just over seventeen million were on the mainland and the rest on Zanzibar. The total was about one million above the estimates. The local English-language newspaper, controlled by the government, carried an unsigned leading article, supposed to have been written by Nyerere. In Catholic style, it rejected the view 'that regards a large population as the root of all our problems. It is like putting the cart before the horse.' At the same time, the census ignored religious distinctions, which was ridiculous because of their importance in a country with many Muslims, especially on the coast, and Animists, as well as other Christians.

This was presumably Nyerere again with his own obsessive fear that religion might become too significant an issue. Muslims are particularly sensitive about figures suggesting that their numbers are diminishing, especially on the coastal plain which was, at the time, seeing an increase in immigrants from the countryside. When the population was still thought to be sixteen million, the Catholics estimated that they were about three million, the Muslims four million, the Protestants one million, while the remaining half of the population was pagan.

Nyerere's ambivalence is reflected in the Catholic Church's attitude towards him and his socialist government. Sometimes the priests talk as if they cannot believe their luck in having this devout little man at the head of the state with which they have to deal. He has undoubtedly been good to them. Whereas in Central America, a priest will have to hide his identity behind a visiting card, describing him as a civil engineer, and an open-necked shirt, in Tanzania it is normally useful to travel with a priest. They are well thought of, except by a few fanatical socialists in the party machine outside the capital.

The foundation of Nyerere's socialism is the gathering of farmers and their families together in villages of a size large enough to justify state aid in the form of schools and dispensaries, as well as efficient marketing arrangements for the community. The members of these village communities are supposed to leave behind them their simple ideas of subsistence farming on the best land they can find, and turn to working communal land for the good of the community as a whole under the supervision of the village manager. The whole system turns around the authority of the one party allowed to function, which was founded by Nyerere. The leading administrative officials in the country are the regional commissioners who are also the party's regional secretaries. Nyerere claims that the socialism he has devised for his country has it roots in African tradition: a closely knit community, based on the family, where people are ready to help each other in moments of difficulty. Co-operation within the family is extended to the clan and then the tribe; an attitude he says he is developing with the system of socialist cells. There were said to be about 8,000 collectivized villages by early 1979. Undoubtedly, heavy-handedness was common when peasants were forced from their homes into these new villages. In some cases the sites were badly chosen. Only about half of the villages had a properly trained manager.

Nyerere claimed that he was building on a base of African tradition. The main drift of the African, when left to his own devices nowadays, is, however, towards the towns. There they find little to do. The city makes for violence. On the waterfront at Dar-es-Salaam, overlooking the sweep of the palm-fringed port, a house dating from the last century was built for the harem of the Sultan of Zanzibar, who used to rule a strip of the coast as well as the island itself. It is now the house of the White Fathers, the biggest Catholic missionary order in Africa. They are tough and experienced, and walk their visitors out of the zone of violence to the newer part of the town rather than let them leave the house alone.

In most of Africa, the Church is a missionary church. This means that Christianity was brought by white men, is still dependent on white missionaries, suffers from the psychological connection of both having been a part of the process of colonialism and still behaving in a European way, intellectually and in practice. Almost all the countries of black Africa have abolished the political structures left them by the colonial powers.

Another element is common to most of the continent: the theoretical basis of these new states is a form of rural socialism. Just as Catholicism came later to Africa than to Latin America, and was not imposed with the help of massacres, so the style of political activity is less radical. These socialist regimes are authoritarian but there is not the chronic instability of Latin America, caused by reactionary repression that incites and releases a revolutionary Marxism as the alternative. Catholics in Latin America are between two fires: in Africa there is usually only one fire and the problem is how near the Church should want, or be allowed, to approach it.

Given that one of the Church's principal problems is to escape from its white face and its colonial past, an obvious solution would be to try to adapt itself to the rural socialism practised or preached in most of black Africa. Nyerere maintains that his socialism is based on brotherhood, mutual help, avoidance of exploitation—all ideas that could appeal to the active Christians present in his country. Catholicism as such (apart from whatever views individual Catholics may have) has no difficulty in accepting a concept which denies the need for a division between the majority and the minority. Such internal democracy as exists in the Catholic Church as an institution, aims at finding the widest measure of agreement and not a majority against a minority. The long debates in the Vatican Council, for instance, were frequently heated and as full of fire as exchanges should be when the speakers feel that they are debating the effects of history's central event. In the end the overwhelming majority usually found it could agree on the form of words the commissions prepared.

This is an ancient outlook, very close to the hearts of Mediterranean people, rather than Anglo-Saxons, who prefer the neat distinction and the alternative. Nyerere claims to have passed from one to the other as experience taught him. He says: 'My ideas of democracy are Western. I never questioned the two-party system until I was confronted with the problem in Tanganyika. Is it necessary for a democracy to have a two-party system? I said "No". It's no good standing on Mount Kilimanjaro and shouting our disagreement.' Again: 'It could have been a multi-party country but I see no necessity for that. We are rejecting this idea that only a two-party system can be a democracy.' He is arguing, like a Latin American theologian, from what he believes to be reality. This has brought him into the traditional Catholic line of thought on the question of majorities and minorities. In place of opposition, he devised a series of checks and balances intended to permit correction without any serious questioning of basic policy —and still less of who should carry it out.

The Church in Tanzania is very gentle with Nyerere: 'We do very well from him', was the phrase of a European missionary. There is still, nevertheless, this strange abyss between an institution that is old-fashioned in its structure, conservative in purely Catholic matters, and recognizably European even if all but two bishops are black, and, on the other side of the abyss, authoritarian black socialism that has failed so far to give an effective basis to the economy or an acceptable level of living to the farmers involved in their collectivized villages. The church, because of its privileges and uncertainties, does not provide the constant, objective criticism which would help correct the lack of opposition and draw attention to such abuses—from corruption to cases of denial of normal human rights—inevitable in a state fashioned and monopolized by one man. Nor has the Church made the alternative logical move of throwing its weight in favour of the state that treats it so well, by seeking to insert itself within African socialism.

To take a stronger attitude towards the state would bring the risks of tension. Nyerere is no longer young. His type of Catholicism is distinctly utilitarian. He presumably believes in it but he does not permit principles to come between him and any useful political objective. Many of the younger men around him have less diffidence and no personal attachment to Catholicism. Even now priests in the countryside are quite likely to come across officials whose socialism does not extend to a warm embrace of the Catholic Church. With Nyerere gone, these people are likely to be more vocal.

The creation of the villages set a nasty problem for the institutional, hierarchical Church. Would a priest be expected to share the lives of these villagers, in all their primitive simplicity and confusion? How could a priest remain apart, as is his traditional place in society, while attempting to minister to the needs of his people? How could the two ideas of caste and service be maintained in the haphazard conditions of socialist experiment? The answer is very simple. The total participation of the Church in this experiment would mean a different kind of priesthood and a different approach to the idea of hierarchy. The priest would, in effect, be that romantic being, surrounded by an aura of distrust by hierarchies in most parts of the Catholic world, the worker-priest. He would have to live the life of a villager at a standard few priests could know, or tolerate. Not only the Europeans would have great difficulty; African priests would feel that they were being sent to live in a way they had themselves chosen to leave, their whole training would have been directed to enhancing the attitude that they were different.

African images are strong. A young priest set off from north-eastern Italy to be a missionary. In his first year he fell sick with a bad case of malaria. He was out in the bush, alone except for an African boy. He made himself a rough bed and sent the youth to find some tea in the nearest village to act as a stimulant so that he could continue his journey. The boy came back in the evening with the news that there was no tea. The priest, who was feeling still worse, told him to look for coffee. The boy came back early the next morning to say that he could not find coffee. The priest realized that he would save himself only, literally, by himself and so set off very unsteadily, with his head swimming, in the direction he took to be correct. He kept going for some hours before collapsing completely and woke to find that he was in a native hut with villagers tending him. He survived but his physique was ruined; he is now in late middle-age and his most real experience probably remains this early coming to terms with Africa.

While telling this story, he stopped by the side of the road near a parked bus, miles from the nearest town, Morogoro. The bus driver asked if there was space to take some of the passengers back to the town. The bus had broken down. Someone had left for Dar-es-Salaam to find a spare part—that had been two days ago. The passengers were not sad; just looking rather more serious than usual, as women tended improvised fires for cooking and the rest squatted in the shade thrown by the ancient bus itself. Two days had gone by so far. Many more might well pass, by which time the passengers would have fully come to terms with their fate. A new community might have taken root: not planned but no less imposed for that.

The mere name Zanzibar is evocative of perverse romanticism. It was the last centre of the slave-trade. The old slave-market is now the site of an ugly, dilapidated Anglican cathedral. The mark is still on the island. Drive into the country, which is beautiful and luxuriant, with its palms and bananas, its bread trees, its occasional clove and cinnamon trees; swim from a beach that looks carved from coloured coral, and nearby you will find the caves where slaves were kept, out of sight of the British patrol boats, in the years between the closing of the public market and the international agreement to end the trade altogether From the scented island of Zanzibar, the slave-traders, the explorers and the missionaries crossed to the coast at Bagamoyo, which was the mainland coastal station for the slavers. The remains are still there of the first Christian church built in East Africa. There are some old chains too, used to fetter the slaves. Exploring, slaving and converting were activities very closely involved. The missionaries collected funds for ransoming slaves. A cash payment meant that some unhappy captive, dragged from his native village in the interior, would at least be spared the horrors of the slave auction in Zanzibar, the beating to show the prospective buyers how strong he was, and death by having his throat cut if no buyer could be found. They were simpler days in terms of what was right or wrong. Politics were a long way away and greatness was rewarded with affection and honour. The mission fathers have this account of the return there of a great explorer who was also a great missionary:

> On 24 February 1874, a party of weary African porters arrived at the Mission and—unlike other groups of Caravan personnel—entered in deep silence the compound. One of the burdens they carried was deposited at the door of the church. The canvas ground-sheet around it made one think of a camp-outfit; the way in which it was treated, however, suggested it was not. A story goes that all stood there in reverent silence until one of the Fathers showed up. Then one of the men came forward and said: '*Mwili wa daudi*': the body of David.
>
> They were the remains of the great Dr David Livingstone, carried by his faithful Africans from Lake Bangweolo to Bagamoyo—a distance of roughly 1,500 miles. After his death, on 1 May 1873, these faithful men had reduced the body of their great friend to the condition of a mummy and now, after a trip of almost nine months, they found themselves with their burden at the coast, where they were given a warm welcome by the Holy Ghost missionaries.
>
> Immediately these missionaries, to whom he was well known, sent messages by dhow to Zanzibar and meanwhile charged themselves with the task of preparing a provisional coffin. A few hours later the body was placed in the church of the mission at the feet of a great number of ransomed slaves—men, women and children, to whom this great man had devoted his life. The day after, the remains of the famous missionary and explorer were handed over to the British Consul, Captain Prideaux, who conveyed them to Zanzibar for shipment to England . . . .

Then there was a lying-in-state at 1 Savile Row, followed by burial in Westminster Abbey. Livingstone was not a Catholic, of course, but that is hardly relevant. There are still dhows drawn up on the sandy beach, and the coastal road becomes a sandy track before it reaches Bagamoyo, as if the planners preferred to forget the existence of the place with its shaming and sublime associations. Yet there it is, the place where the great Catholic missionary effort in East Africa began. The most generally accepted calculation of which continent will become, in Catholic terms, the continent of the future estimates that Africa will do so. Latin America is overwhelming in numbers but still suffers from the schizophrenia which is a consequence of having had Catholicism imposed by imperialist force as part of an alien culture. Asia has too few Catholics and the daunting presence of the worlds of Hinduism, Buddhism and Islam. More than the Africans, the

Asians are inclined to take what Melville, in *Billy Budd*, called 'the clerical discourse' in a way

> not wholly unlike the way in which the primer of Christianity, full of transcendent miracles, was received long ago on tropic isles by any superior *savage*, so called—a Tahitian, say, of Captain Cook's time or shortly after that time. Out of natural courtesy he received, but did not appropriate. It was like a gift placed in the palm of an outreached hand upon which the fingers do not close.

Perhaps there are more like that than one thinks. But to write a book about Catholicism entails a certain suspension of disbelief, in the sense that one has to suppose that a reasonable number of Catholics actually believe in their faith, closing their fingers on the gift placed in their palms. Yet the great bulk of human indifference cannot be overlooked and it is a weight which both institutional religion and the rising sense of religiosity are trying to pull to their sides. I know no way by which to estimate the relative strengths of such forces, and I doubt that anyone else does. I can say that tropical islanders of the superior *savage* type were happy to describe themselves as 'Romanos' but I have not the remotest idea what that means in terms of specific beliefs.

In a sense, it would be pleasant to suppose that the shift of Catholicism to the non-European, non-Anglo-Saxon parts of the world would bring a greater innocence and less dogma. The passage from Melville which follows his description of the way a Tahitian accepted Christianity from Captain Cook recounts the sentiments and strangely emotional action of the chaplain of the *Bellipotent* as he wisely decides not to try and instruct Billy Budd in the Christian faith as a prelude to his unjust hanging from the yard-arm:

> Since he felt that innocence was even a better thing than religion wherewith to go to judgement, he reluctantly withdrew; but in his emotion not without first performing an act strange enough in an Englishman, and under the circumstances yet more so in any regular priest. Stooping over, he kissed on the fair cheek his fellow man, a felon in martial law, one whom though on the confines of death he felt he could never convert to a dogma; nor for all that did he fear for his future.

But it will not be like that: less European does not necessarily carry the promise of more innocent. Nor even of greater freedom. There are irons at Bagamoyo taken from the legs of ransomed slaves, and, rightly, they are relegated to a modest museum, to be looked at, studied, touched, so that each can come to his or her conclusion about the wider significance of the freedom which accompanies faith. Intellectually the idea of bonds cannot be put aside, and John Paul II expressed this well in his address to the Pontifical Academy of Sciences at its meeting on 10 November 1979 to mark Einstein's centenary—the meeting at which the pope proposed the rehabilitation of Galileo as a good Catholic. John Paul said of Einstein:

> The Church, full of admiration for the genius of the great scientist which reveals the mark of the Creator Spirit, without entering in any way into a verdict, which is not her task to do, on the doctrine of the great systems of the universe, proposes nevertheless this same doctrine to the consideration of the theologians to discover the harmony existing between scientific truth and revealed truth.

I think that we should, modestly, be attempting something similar, whatever terminology we may wish to use: an attempt at estimating whether this vast religious institution can be seen as coinciding with the needs of a humanity threatened seriously from several sides. This harmony is not easy to establish for two reasons. The first is that the exact dilemma facing humanity is complex and not easily definable because it is not exactly understood; also, at the heart of Catholicism there is necessarily an area of a kind of spiritual anarchy. 'A person is realistic in my view,' said the Jesuit theologian Karl Rahner, 'only if that person believes in God and lets himself or herself fall into that tremendous, unfathomable abyss.' Or, as Father Rahner adds: 'The true system of thought really is the knowledge that humanity is finally directed precisely not toward what it can control in knowledge but toward the absolute mystery as such . . . .' This is the total opposite to the view that religion should be looked at only with complete indifference. My sights were set somewhere between the two.

INDEX

INDEX